Guide to the Macintosh® Family Hardware

Second Edition

For Macintosh Plus,
Macintosh SE,
Macintosh SE/30,
Macintosh Portable,
Macintosh II,
Macintosh IIx,
Macintosh IIcx,
Macintosh IIci,
and Macintosh IIfx

Addison-Wesley Publishing Company, Inc.

Reading, Massachusetts   Menlo Park, California   New York
Don Mills, Ontario   Wokingham, England   Amsterdam   Bonn
Sydney   Singapore   Tokyo   Madrid   San Juan

Simultaneously published in the United States and Canada.

ISBN 0-201-52405-8
ABCDEFGHJI-MU-9543210
First printing, May 1990

Contents

9 Floppy Disk Interfaces / 327

Figures and tables

2 Architecture of the Macintosh Computers / 47

3 Processors and General Logic / 87

4   Versatile Interface Adapter (VIA) ICs / 147

5 Memory / 189

6 Power Supplies / 239

7 Macintosh Plus Mouse and Keyboard / 273

13 Sound / 427

14 Expansion Interfaces / 443

A   Macintosh Family Hardware Specifications / 467

B   Hardware-Related Global Variables / 489

Preface **About This Book**

Welcome to the Apple® *Guide to the Macintosh Family Hardware,* second edition. This book provides overviews of the architectures of Macintosh® computers and descriptions of the hardware components that make up those computers.

This book provides background and reference information for developers: hardware engineers designing peripheral devices for Macintosh computers and system programmers who need an understanding of the hardware in order to optimize their code. See the sections "Additional Reading" and "About the Macintosh Technical Documentation," later in this preface, for other books you may need.

This book is not intended to be an introduction to the basic concepts of computer hardware—you should be familiar with the terminology used in the electronics industry and with the general principles of microcomputer design and operation. Working knowledge of the Macintosh system will also be helpful.

▲ **Warning**   This book is not intended to provide information or instructions for repairing or servicing your Macintosh computer. Attempting to service or repair the computer yourself could damage the computer and will invalidate the warranty. ▲

This preface describes the contents of this manual and the conventions used throughout the book. It also lists some other books that you might find useful, and tells you where to write or call for more information about Apple products.

What this book contains

The following is a brief outline of the contents of this manual. See the table of contents for a complete list of the subjects covered in each chapter; see the index to find a specific topic discussed in this book.

Organization

Guide to the Macintosh Family Hardware describes the nine Macintosh models available at the time the book was published. It also contains information about earlier Macintosh models: the Macintosh 128K, the Macintosh 512K, and the Macintosh 512K enhanced.

The nine current Macintosh models are

- Macintosh Plus
- Macintosh SE
- Macintosh SE/30
- Macintosh Portable
- Macintosh II
- Macintosh IIx
- Macintosh IIcx
- Macintosh IIci
- Macintosh IIfx

Instead of describing each model separately, this book describes each major feature for all models that have the feature. This approach has two benefits: first, it avoids unnecessary repetition of descriptions of features that are the same on different models; and second, it clarifies the differences between different models.

Each major feature in the Macintosh family is the subject of its own chapter. The major features are as follows:

- processors and control logic
- Versatile Interface Adapters (VIAs: interface ICs)
- memory organization and expansion
- power supplies and control
- keyboard and mouse on the Macintosh Plus and earlier models
- Apple Desktop Bus™ (on all models since the Macintosh Plus)

- floppy disk interfaces, two types: Apple 800 KB drive and Macintosh FDHD™ (SuperDrive™)
- serial I/O ports: similar on all models
- SCSI ports: similar on all models
- displays, three types: built-in video, expansion card video, and flat panel
- sound: two types of hardware for generating sampled sound
- expansion interfaces, two types: NuBus™ and processor direct

This book has two appendixes; Appendix A lists the specifications for each model and so serves as a quick reference for readers looking for information about a particular model. Appendix B lists hardware-related global variables.

This book also contains a glossary of technical terms used in the book and an index.

Approach

This book contains information of several different kinds, including

- specifications of internal hardware features
- explanations of important subsystems, such as the different expansion interfaces, the Apple Desktop Bus, and the different types of displays
- detailed information needed by third-party hardware developers
- guidelines for hardware and software developers

This book provides in-depth information for certain features that are not documented elsewhere. For example, the chapter about the Apple Desktop Bus (ADB) includes more detail and more guidelines than the other chapters because this material is not available elsewhere.

Some features are not fully described in this book. Of those features, some are described in detail in other books: for example, the NuBus expansion bus is more fully described in *Designing Cards and Drivers for the Macintosh Family,* second edition. Other features are not described in detail because developers never need to deal with them: for example, the Apple custom ICs used for controlling the disk I/O port.

Visual cues and conventions

The following visual cues are used throughout the manual to identify different types of information:

◆ *Note:* Notes like this contain interesting sidelights.

△ **Important**   Text set off like this contains important information that you should read before proceeding. △

△ **Developer tip**   Boxes like this contain hints and recommendations about the best way to use the hardware. △

▲ **Warning**   Warnings like this direct your attention to something that could cause injury to the user, damage either software or hardware, or result in loss of data. ▲

When new terms are defined, they appear in **boldface.** Those terms are also defined in the glossary.

Hexadecimal numbers are preceded by a dollar sign ($). For example, the hexadecimal equivalent of decimal number 16 is written as $10.

Address ranges are given as *lower address through higher address* or *lower address–higher address;* in either form the range is inclusive of the given endpoints. Names of signals on a bus, on the other hand, are given as *highest-numbered signal–lowest-numbered signal.*

A preceding slash (/) is used to indicate an active-low signal; for example, /ACK.

The following abbreviations are used:

Kbit   kilobit: 1,024 bits

KB   kilobyte: 1,024 bytes

Mbit   megabit: 1,024 kilobits, or 1,048,576 bits

MB   megabyte: 1,024 kilobytes, or 1,048,576 bytes

GB   gigabyte: 1024 megabytes, or 1,073,741,824 bytes

This book distinguishes between *boards* and *cards* as follows: a board is a permanent part of the computer (for example, the main logic board), whereas a card can be added or exchanged by the user to expand or reconfigure the system.

Assembly-language variable names

The addresses of various hardware components are listed in this book as assembly-language variable names. These names—and system global variables—are included as equate (EQU) statements in the Macintosh Programmer's Workshop (MPW™) Assembly Language files named HardwareEqu.a and SysEqu.a. Those files are located in a folder named AIncludes.

The MPW development system, which includes the MPW Assembler and the AIncludes folder, is available from the Apple Programmers and Developers Association (APDA™). The AIncludes folder is also available as a separate product from APDA. The address of APDA is given in the section "How to Get More Information," later in this preface.

Additional reading

For an introduction to the hardware and system software of the Macintosh family of computers, see the *Technical Introduction to the Macintosh Family*.

If you are interested in developing a card or a driver for any members of the Macintosh family of computers, refer to *Designing Cards and Drivers for the Macintosh Family*, second edition.

For a reference for the Macintosh System and Toolbox plus a discussion of user interface guidelines and some basic hardware information, see *Inside Macintosh*.

This book does not contain complete specifications for hardware components built by other manufacturers. You may need some or all of the manufacturers' technical specifications for the following integrated circuits:

- 6522 and 65C23 Versatile Interface Adapters; Rockwell or VTI

- MC68000, MC68020, and MC68030 microprocessors; Motorola

- MC68851 Memory Management Unit; Motorola

- MC68881 and MC68882 Floating-Point Coprocessors; Motorola

- 5380 SCSI Controller; NCR

- Z8530 Serial Communications Controller; Zilog

- Sony sound chip; Sony

About the Macintosh technical documentation

Apple Computer, Inc., provides a suite of technical books that explain the hardware and software of the Macintosh family of computers.

The original Macintosh documentation consisted of the first three volumes of *Inside Macintosh*. Shortly after the introduction of the Macintosh Plus (with the 128 KB ROM), Volume IV of *Inside Macintosh* was released as a delta guide. That is, Volume IV covered only those aspects of the Macintosh Plus that were different from earlier Macintosh computers. Later, a fifth volume was added, called *Inside Macintosh,* Volume V. It is also a delta guide, covering the new and different features of the Macintosh SE and the Macintosh II computers.

As the variety and the sophistication of Macintosh computers evolve, so does the documentation. In order to provide information that is comprehensive—and that provides answers to specific questions—Apple is now providing a whole family of books. Each of these books gives complete information about a single subject, and may include some information that also appears in *Inside Macintosh*. This book and *Designing Cards and Drivers for the Macintosh Family,* second edition, are two of the books in this suite.

For programmers and engineers who are new to the Macintosh world, Apple has created two introductory books: *Technical Introduction to the Macintosh Family* and *Programmer's Introduction to the Macintosh Family.*

In addition to the books about the Macintosh itself, there are books on related subjects. Examples are books about the user interface and Apple's floating-point numerics, and the reference books for the Macintosh Programmer's Workshop.

Table P-1 gives a brief description of each of the books in the Macintosh technical documentation.

■ **Table P-1** Macintosh technical documentation

Book	Description
Introductory books	
Technical Introduction to the Macintosh Family	Introduction to the Macintosh software and hardware for the classic Macintosh, Macintosh SE, and Macintosh II
Programmer's Introduction to the Macintosh Family	Introduction to programming the Macintosh computers
Inside Macintosh	
Inside Macintosh, Volumes I–V	Reference for the Macintosh System and Toolbox for the original Macintosh, Macintosh Plus, Macintosh SE, and Macintosh II
Single-subject books	
Guide to the Macintosh Family Hardware, second edition	This book: reference and developer's guide for the Macintosh Plus, Macintosh SE and SE/30; Macintosh II, IIx, IIcx, IIci, and IIfx; and Macintosh Portable
Designing Cards and Drivers for the Macintosh Family, second edition	Hardware and device-driver reference to the expansion capabilities of the Macintosh II family, Macintosh SE and SE/30, and Macintosh Portable
Related books	
Human Interface Guidelines: The Apple Desktop Interface	Detailed guidelines for developers implementing the Macintosh user interface
Apple Numerics Manual, second edition	Description of the Standard Apple Numerics Environment (SANE®), including SANE software for the MC68881 floating-point coprocessor
Macintosh Programmer's Workshop 3.0 Reference	Description of the Macintosh Programmer's Workshop (MPW), Apple's software development environment for all Macintosh computers

You may also find useful information in the following earlier books, now superseded:

Designing Cards and Drivers for Macintosh II and Macintosh SE	Earlier hardware and device-driver reference to the expansion capabilities of the Macintosh II and Macintosh SE
Macintosh Family Hardware Reference	Earlier reference to the Macintosh hardware for the classic Macintosh, Macintosh SE, and Macintosh II computers

How to get more information

There are several sources of technical support for Macintosh programmers and users. This section tells you how to contact APDA, Apple user groups, and Apple Developer Services.

APDA

APDA provides a wide range of technical products and documentation, from Apple and other suppliers, for programmers and developers who work on Apple equipment. For information about APDA, contact

APDA
Apple Computer, Inc.
20525 Mariani Avenue, Mailstop 49-A
Cupertino, CA 95014-6299

800-282-APDA (800-282-2732)
Fax: 408-562-3971
Telex: 171-576
AppleLink®: APDA

User groups

Apple user groups are associations of individuals who share information about Apple computers and related products. For information about Apple user groups in your area, call this toll-free number:

800-538-9696

Ask for extension 500.

Apple Developer Services

Apple's goal is to provide developers with the resources they need to create new Apple-compatible products. Apple offers two programs: the Partners Program, for developers who intend to resell Apple-compatible products, and the Associates Program, for developers who don't intend to resell products and for other people involved in the development of Apple-compatible products.

As an Apple Partner or Associate, you will receive monthly mailings including a newsletter, Apple II and Macintosh Technical Notes, pertinent Developer Program information, and all the latest news relating to Apple products. You will also receive Apple's Technical Guide Book and automatic membership in APDA. You'll have access to developer AppleLink and to Apple's Developer Hotline for general developer information.

As an Apple Partner, you'll be eligible for discounts on equipment and you'll receive technical assistance from the staff of Apple's Developer Technical Support department.

For more information about Apple's developer support programs, contact Apple Developer Programs at the following address.

Apple Developer Programs
Apple Computer, Inc.
20525 Mariani Avenue, Mailstop 51-W
Cupertino, CA 95014

Chapter 1 **Introduction to the Macintosh Hardware**

This chapter provides an introduction to the computers that make up the Apple® Macintosh® family. The chapter lists the features of each computer and briefly describes the similarities and differences among the computers. Chapter 2 introduces the individual hardware components of the Macintosh computers; the remaining chapters describe those components and other hardware features in detail.

Table 1-1 on the next two pages is a matrix showing the current Macintosh models and their main features. It summarizes the information presented in this chapter. Portions of the matrix also appear in later chapters, where individual features are described more fully.

■ **Table 1-1**   Summary of features of the Macintosh computers

	Configuration	CPU	Other processors	Memory mgt. ICs	General logic ICs	Control ICs	Memory expansion
Macintosh Plus	Compact	MC68000	(none)	PALs	PALs	1 VIA	RAM SIMM
Macintosh SE	Compact	MC68000	(none)	PALs	BBU	1 VIA	RAM SIMM
Macintosh SE/30	Compact	MC68030	MC68882	Part of MC68030	GLUE	2 VIAs	RAM SIMM, ROM SIMM
Macintosh Portable	Portable	MC68000	Power Mgr.	Part of MC68030	VDI, CPU GLU & Misc. GLU	1 VIA	RAM SIMM
Macintosh II	Open (6 slots)	MC68020	MC68881	AMU or PMMU	GLUE	2 VIAs	RAM SIMM
Macintosh IIx	Open (6 slots)	MC68030	MC68882	Part of MC68030	GLUE	2 VIAs	RAM SIMM, ROM SIMM
Macintosh IIcx	Open (3 slots)	MC68030	MC68882	Part of MC68030	GLUE	2 VIAs	RAM SIMM, ROM SIMM
Macintosh IIci	Open (3 slots)	MC68030	MC68882	Part of MC68030	MDU & RBV	1 VIA & RBV	RAM SIMM, ROM SIMM
Macintosh IIfx	Open (6 slots)	MC68030	MC68882 & 2 IOPs	Part of MC68030	OSS & FMC	1 VIA & OSS	RAM SIMM, ROM SIMM

Power	Mouse & keyboard	Floppy drive	Serial ports	SCSI ports	Display	Sound	Expansion method
Hdw. on/off switch	Macintosh	800 KB	SCC	SCSI	Built-in B&W video	PWM	(none)
Hdw. on/off switch	ADB	FDHD	SCC	SCSI	Built-in B&W or exp. card	PWM	68000 PDS
Hdw. on/off switch	ADB	FDHD	SCC	SCSI	Built-in B&W or exp. card	ASC	68030 PDS
No on/off sw. (sleep)	Special ADB, trackball	FDHD	SCC	SCSI	Flat panel or ext. video	ASC	68000 PDS
Kbd. on, softw. off	ADB	800 KB	SCC	SCSI	B&W or color on exp. card	ASC	NuBus (6 slots)
Kbd. on, softw. off	ADB	FDHD	SCC	SCSI	B&W or color on exp. card	ASC	NuBus (6 slots)
Kbd. on, softw. off	ADB	FDHD	SCC	SCSI	B&W or color on exp. card	ASC	NuBus (3 slots)
Kbd. on, softw. off	ADB	FDHD	SCC	SCSI	Built-in B&W or color, or exp. card	ASC	NuBus (3 slots)
Kbd. on, softw. off	ADB	FDHD	SCC	SCSI DMA	B&W or color on exp. card	ASC	NuBus (6 slots) & 68030 PDS

△ **Important** Memory sizes, addresses, and other data are specific to each type of Macintosh computer and are provided only for informational purposes. To maintain software compatibility across the Macintosh line, and to allow for future changes to the hardware, you are strongly advised to use the Macintosh Toolbox and Operating System routines wherever provided. In particular, never use absolute addresses to access hardware, because those addresses are different on different models. △

The following Macintosh computers are described in this book:

■ The Macintosh 128K computer, with an MC68000 microprocessor running at 8 MHz, 128 KB of RAM, 64 KB of ROM, and a 400 KB internal disk drive.

■ The Macintosh 512K computer, with an MC68000 microprocessor, 512 KB of RAM, 64 KB of ROM, and a 400 KB internal disk drive. Except for the additional memory, the Macintosh 512K is identical to the Macintosh 128K.

■ The Macintosh 512K enhanced computer, with an MC68000 microprocessor, 512 KB of RAM, 128 KB of ROM, and an 800 KB internal disk drive. The ROM and disk drive in the Macintosh 512K enhanced computer are the same as those used in the Macintosh Plus. In all other respects, the Macintosh 512K enhanced is identical to the Macintosh 512K.

■ The Macintosh Plus computer, with an MC68000 microprocessor running at 8 MHz, 1 MB of RAM (minimum), 128 KB of ROM, and an 800 KB internal disk drive. The RAM in the Macintosh Plus can be expanded to 4 MB. Other enhancements in the Macintosh Plus include a Small Computer System Interface (SCSI) port for high-speed communications with disk drives and other peripheral devices, new connectors for the serial ports, and a keyboard with built-in cursor keys and numeric keypad. The Macintosh Plus, Macintosh 512K enhanced, Macintosh 512K, and Macintosh 128K are sometimes referred to collectively as the *classic Macintosh computers*.

■ The Macintosh SE computer, which is similar to the Macintosh Plus except that the Macintosh SE has a faster processor clock (16 MHz) and provides for an expansion card. The expansion connector provides direct access to the processor bus including all the MC68000 address, data, and control lines on the logic board. Other features introduced in the Macintosh SE include provision for a second internal floppy disk drive or an internal hard disk drive, faster access to RAM and to a SCSI hard disk, and the Apple Desktop Bus™ (ADB) interface for communicating with input devices. The current Macintosh SE has 1.4 MB FDHD™ floppy disk drives (FDHD stands for *floppy disk, high density*). This higher-capacity drive is also called SuperDrive™. Macintosh SE computers manufactured prior to September 1989 have the same 800 KB floppy disk drive used in the Macintosh Plus.

- The Macintosh SE/30 computer, which combines the compact size and internal video display of the Macintosh SE with the greater speed and improved sound of the Macintosh II–family computers. Like the Macintosh IIx, the Macintosh SE/30 has an MC68030 microprocessor running at 16 MHz and an MC68882 mathematics coprocessor. The Macintosh SE/30 has the same Apple sound IC as the Macintosh IIx. Like the Macintosh SE, the Macintosh SE/30 has the new high-capacity floppy disk drive (FDHD) and an expansion connector that provides direct access to the processor bus. The video circuits in the Macintosh SE/30 emulate a NuBus™ video card, so that the same ROM and operating system can be used in the Macintosh SE/30 as in Macintosh II–family computers.

- The Macintosh Portable computer is based on the Macintosh SE. It differs from the Macintosh SE in that it uses special low-power-consumption components throughout, including an MC68HC000 microprocessor. The processor in the Macintosh Portable runs at 16 MHz, twice the speed of the processor in the Macintosh SE. The Macintosh Portable also has a built-in flat-panel display, a built-in trackball, a rechargeable battery, and special power-control circuitry to conserve power and retain the contents of RAM when the machine is not in use. The Macintosh Portable uses the high-capacity FDHD floppy disk drive and the custom sound IC used in the Macintosh SE/30.

- The Macintosh II computer, which differs from all earlier Macintosh computers in that it has a separate video monitor and allows users to insert and remove expansion cards. The expansion bus (called NuBus) provides access to the processor bus and all the devices on the logic board for up to six expansion cards. Other features of the Macintosh II include an MC68020 microprocessor running at 16 MHz, an MC68881 mathematics coprocessor (also called the *floating-point unit,* or *FPU),* memory expandable to 8 MB, provision for both a second 800 KB internal floppy disk drive and an internal hard disk drive, faster access to RAM and to a SCSI hard disk, and an Apple custom sound IC. Like the Macintosh SE, the Macintosh II uses the ADB interface for communicating with input devices. The Macintosh II has no external connector for floppy disk drives.

- The Macintosh IIx computer, which is similar to the Macintosh II except that it has a more advanced microprocessor (the MC68030, running at 16 MHz), the MC68882 mathematics coprocessor, a new floppy disk interface, and FDHD drives.

- The Macintosh IIcx computer, which is similar to the Macintosh IIx except that it provides three NuBus slots rather than six, has a smaller footprint, accommodates only one internal FDHD drive, and provides a connector for an external floppy disk drive.

- The Macintosh IIci computer, which is similar to the Macintosh IIcx except that it has built-in video circuits and a faster processor clock (25 MHz). The Macintosh IIci has an interal connector for an optional RAM cache card that provides even faster processing. A special-order model of the Macintosh IIci comes equipped with a custom parity IC and 9-bit RAM SIMMs that provide parity generation and detection.

- The Macintosh IIfx computer, which is similar to the Macintosh IIx except that it has a faster processor clock (40 MHz), built-in RAM cache, and intelligent I/O processors (IOPs) for improved performance. The IOPs relieve the main processor of routine tasks on the ports for the floppy-disk, ADB, and serial I/O. Similarly, the SCSI channel has true hardware DMA (direct-memory access) that provides faster data transfers and frees the main processor for other tasks.

△ **Developer tip** To learn how your program can determine on which Macintosh computer it is running, use the Environs procedure and the SysEnvirons function described in *Inside Macintosh*. Some additional information about which hardware components are connected is available in the global variable HWCfgFlags. The meanings of the bits stored in this variable are listed in the Macintosh Programmer's Workshop file HardwareEqu.a, which is in an MPW™ folder named AIncludes. △

Exterior features of the Macintosh computers

This section describes and illustrates the external appearance of the members of the Macintosh family.

Macintosh 128K, 512K, and 512K enhanced computers

The Macintosh 128K, 512K, and 512K enhanced computers are identical in appearance, with built-in video and sound, a separate keyboard, and a mouse. They include an internal floppy disk drive and external connectors for peripheral devices such as disk drives, digitizing pads, modems, and printers.

Figure 1-1 shows a front view of the Macintosh 128K, 512K, and 512K enhanced computers. Notice the video screen, disk drive access opening, keyboard, keyboard connector, and mouse.

■ **Figure 1-1** Front view of the Macintosh 128K, 512K, and 512K enhanced computers

Figure 1-2 shows a back view of the Macintosh 128K, Macintosh 512K, and Macintosh 512K enhanced computers. Notice the connectors for the two serial ports, the floppy disk drive port, the connector for the mouse, and the sound jack.

■ **Figure 1-2** Back view of the Macintosh 128K, 512K, and 512K enhanced computers

Macintosh Plus computer

The Macintosh Plus computer has the same exterior appearance as the earlier Macintosh computers, but has different external connectors. The front view of the Macintosh Plus is identical to that of the Macintosh computers that preceded it. Figure 1-3 shows a back view of the Macintosh Plus. Notice that a connector for the SCSI (parallel) port has been added and that the connectors for the two serial ports have been changed from DB-9 connectors to mini 8-pin connectors.

■ **Figure 1-3** Back view of the Macintosh Plus computer

Macintosh SE and Macintosh SE/30 computers

The Macintosh SE and Macintosh SE/30 computers are compact machines, with built-in video and sound, a separate keyboard, and a mouse. Each includes an internal floppy disk drive (FDHD). The Macintosh SE can have either a second internal floppy disk drive or an internal hard disk drive. The Macintosh SE/30 has an internal hard disk drive; a second internal floppy disk drive is not available as an option in the Macintosh SE/30. External connectors are provided for peripheral devices such as disk drives, graphics tablets, modems, and printers. The Macintosh SE and Macintosh SE/30 have a similar case and have the same external connectors.

◆ *Note:* The original Macintosh SE used the same 800 KB floppy disk drive as the Macintosh Plus. The current Macintosh SE, manufactured September 1989 and later, uses the FDHD drive; it is identified by the letters *FDHD* on the front.

Figure 1-4 shows a front view of the Macintosh SE computer. Notice the video screen, disk drive access openings, keyboard, and mouse.

■ **Figure 1-4** Front view of the Macintosh SE computer

Figure 1-5 shows a front view of the Macintosh SE/30 computer. Notice the video screen, disk drive access opening, keyboard, and mouse.

■ **Figure 1-5** Front view of the Macintosh SE/30 computer

Figure 1-6 shows a back view of the Macintosh SE computer. Except for the label, the back of the Macintosh SE/30 is identical to that of the Macintosh SE. The connectors are identical to those used by the Macintosh Plus, except that the mouse connector has been replaced by two connectors for the Apple Desktop Bus and the sound jack has been moved. Notice also the location of the punch-out panel for a connector to an optional expansion card.

■ **Figure 1-6** Back view of the Macintosh SE computer; the Macintosh SE/30 looks the same

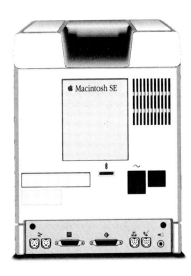

Macintosh Portable computer

The Macintosh Portable computer is similar to the Macintosh SE. The Macintosh Portable has several built-in features that enhance its portability: battery power, flat-panel display, built-in keyboard, and trackball pointing device. Each Macintosh Portable includes an internal FDHD drive and either a second internal floppy disk drive or an internal hard disk drive. The Macintosh Portable has the same set of external connectors as the Macintosh SE with two exceptions: it has only one external ADB connector, and a telephone jack has been added for use with an internal modem.

▲ **Warning**　　The Macintosh Portable computer cannot provide the power required by most ADB devices; only low-power-consumption devices should be connected to the ADB connector on the Macintosh Portable. Connecting any other ADB device to the ADB connector can result in improper operation of the Macintosh Portable computer. ▲

Figure 1-7 shows a front view of the Macintosh Portable computer. Notice the flat-panel display, the keyboard, and the trackball. The access openings for the floppy disk drives are on the right side of the unit.

■ **Figure 1-7**　Front view of the Macintosh Portable computer

Figure 1-8 shows a back view of the Macintosh Portable computer. Notice the telephone jack for use with an internal modem, the video connector for an external monitor, and the power input connector for DC power from an external battery charger.

■ **Figure 1-8** Back view of the Macintosh Portable computer

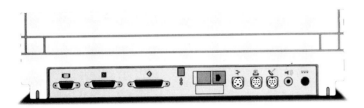

Macintosh II–family computers

The design of the Macintosh II–family computers is modular: each Macintosh II–family computer is made up of several units, including

- main system unit containing the main logic board, the power supply, and the expansion slots
- external video monitor
- video display adapter card, installed in one of the expansion slots
- Apple Standard Keyboard or Apple Extended Keyboard
- Apple Standard Mouse

The main system unit of the Macintosh II, Macintosh IIx, and Macintosh IIfx computers can contain either one or two internal floppy disk drives and can contain a 5.25-inch or 3.5-inch hard disk drive. The main system unit of the Macintosh IIcx and Macintosh IIci has one floppy disk drive and can contain a 3.5-inch hard disk drive. External connectors are provided for peripheral devices such as hard disk drives, digitizing pads, modems, and printers. The Macintosh IIcx and Macintosh IIci computers have an external connector for a floppy disk drive.

◆ *Note:* The Macintosh II, Macintosh IIx, and Macintosh IIfx computers do not have external connectors for floppy disk drives. Although you can connect a Hard Disk 20 to the external floppy disk drive of the Macintosh IIcx and Macintosh IIci, the Macintosh IIcx does not have a driver for the Hard Disk 20 in ROM.

Figure 1-9 shows a front view of the Macintosh II, Macintosh IIx, and Macintosh IIfx computers. Notice the video display monitor, disk drive access openings, keyboard, and mouse.

■ **Figure 1-9** Front view of the Macintosh II, Macintosh IIx, and Macintosh IIfx computers

Figure 1-10 shows a back view of the Macintosh II, Macintosh IIx, and Macintosh IIfx computers. Notice the connectors for the two serial ports, the SCSI port, the external sound jack, and the two connectors for the Apple Desktop Bus. Notice also the locations of the punch-out panels for connectors to optional expansion cards.

■ **Figure 1-10**   Back view of the Macintosh II, Macintosh IIx, and Macintosh IIfx computers

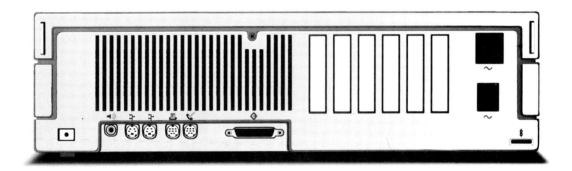

Figure 1-11 shows a front view of the Macintosh IIcx and Macintosh IIci computers. Notice the reduced size compared to the Macintosh II and Macintosh IIx.

■ **Figure 1-11**   Front view of the Macintosh IIcx and Macintosh IIci computers

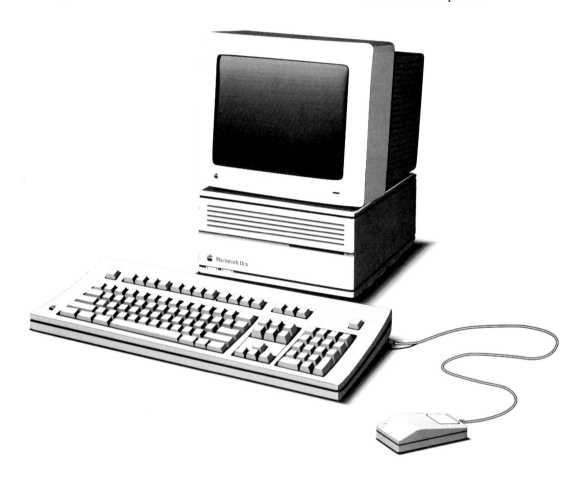

Figure 1-12 shows a back view of the Macintosh IIcx computer. Notice the addition of a connector for an external floppy disk drive and the new power switch.

■ **Figure 1-12**   Back view of the Macintosh IIcx computer

Figure 1-13 shows a back view of the Macintosh IIci computer. Notice the addition of a connector for a video monitor.

■ **Figure 1-13**   Back view of the Macintosh IIci computer

Inside the Macintosh computers

This section lists and briefly describes the internal components of each member of the Macintosh family. These components are described in more detail in the following chapters.

Classic Macintosh computers

Figure 1-14 shows the interior of the Macintosh Plus computer. The microprocessor, RAM, ROM, and the various input/output ICs are located on the main logic board (also called the *digital board*). The vertical analog board contains the power supply and video circuitry for the built-in monitor. The interiors of other classic Macintosh computers are similar in appearance to the interior of the Macintosh Plus.

■ **Figure 1-14**   Interior view of the Macintosh Plus computer

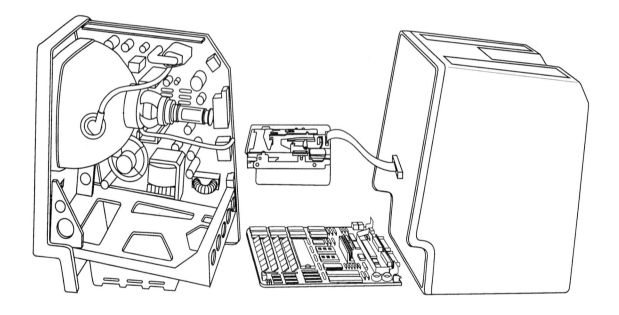

Each of the Macintosh 128K, 512K, and 512K enhanced computers contains the following components:

- A Motorola MC68000 microprocessor, running at a system clock frequency of 7.8336 megahertz.

- Several programmable logic arrays, referred to as *PALs,* that provide address decoding and control signals.

- Random-access memory (RAM), permanently soldered onto the main logic board. The Macintosh 128K has 128 KB of RAM, and the 512K and 512K enhanced Macintosh computers each have 512 KB of RAM.

- Read-only memory (ROM). The ROM contains Macintosh Toolbox and Operating System routines.

- The video monitor.

- A sound system consisting of a Sony analog sound IC, built-in speaker, and external sound port.

- A 6522 Versatile Interface Adapter (VIA) IC, used to communicate with the keyboard, the mouse, and the real-time clock (RTC).

- An 8530 Serial Communications Controller (SCC) IC, providing two independent ports for serial communication.

- The IWM (Integrated Woz Machine), an Apple custom IC used to control the floppy disk interface.

- A floppy disk drive. The Macintosh 128K and 512K computers each have a single-sided 400 KB disk drive; the Macintosh 512K enhanced and Macintosh Plus computers each have a double-sided 800 KB disk drive.

In addition to the components of the Macintosh 128K, 512K, and 512K enhanced computers, the Macintosh Plus computer contains the following:

- A 5380 Small Computer System Interface (SCSI) IC, for high-speed parallel communication with devices such as hard disks.

- Connectors for RAM expansion on the main logic board.

- Up to 4 MB of random-access memory (RAM), provided on two or four small, plug-in printed circuit cards called *SIMMs* (Single In-line Memory Modules).

Macintosh SE and Macintosh SE/30 computers

The Macintosh SE and Macintosh SE/30 computers are compact models with advanced features, notably a single internal expansion slot, the FDHD drive (also called the *SuperDrive*), and provision for a built-in hard disk.

Macintosh SE computer

Figure 1-15 shows the interior of the Macintosh SE computer. The microprocessor, RAM, ROM, and the various input/output ICs are located on the main logic board. The vertical analog board contains video circuitry for the built-in monitor and a cooling fan. The power supply is enclosed in a metal box and mounted on the analog board; a cable from the power supply plugs into the analog board. An optional expansion card attaches to a connector on the main logic board.

■ **Figure 1-15**   Interior view of the Macintosh SE computer

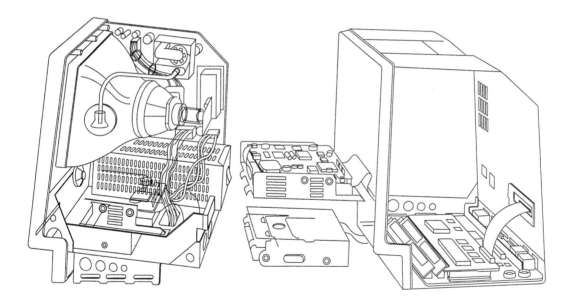

Each Macintosh SE computer contains the following components:

- A Motorola MC68000 microprocessor, running at a system clock frequency of 7.8336 megahertz.

- An Apple custom integrated circuit, the BBU (Bob Bailey Unit), which provides address decoding and control signals.

- A programmable logic array, the GLU (General Logic Unit), which supplements the BBU with some additional control logic.

- Up to 4 MB of random-access memory (RAM), provided on two or four SIMMs.

- Read-only memory (ROM). The ROM contains Macintosh Toolbox and Operating System routines.

- The Apple Desktop Bus (ADB) used to communicate with the keyboard, the mouse, and other input devices.

- A 96-pin expansion connector, providing internal expansion capability plus access to the MC68000 bus. In this book, this connector is referred to as the *Macintosh SE 68000 processor-direct slot (PDS)*; in earlier books, this connector was referred to as the *SE Bus connector.*

- The video monitor.

- A sound system consisting of a Sony analog sound IC, built-in speaker, and external sound port.

- An Apple custom version of the Versatile Interface Adapter (VIA) IC, to support the ADB and the real-time clock (RTC).

- An 8530 Serial Communications Controller (SCC) IC, providing two independent ports for serial communication.

- The SWIM (Super Woz Integrated Machine), an Apple custom IC used to control the interface to the FDHD drive. The SWIM is an enhanced version of the IWM.

- One FDHD drive (double-sided 1.4 MB floppy disk drive) and provision for a hard disk. The FDHD drive can read, write, and format single-sided 400 KB disks, double-sided 800 KB disks, and high-density 1.4 MB disks.

- A 5380 Small Computer System Interface (SCSI) IC, for high-speed parallel communication with devices such as hard disks.

◆ *Note:* Macintosh SE computers manufactured before September 1989 used the IWM custom IC to control the floppy disk interface. Those machines came with one double-sided 800 KB floppy disk drive and provision for either a second 800 KB floppy disk drive or a hard disk.

Macintosh SE/30 computer

The interior of the Macintosh SE/30 computer is similar in appearance to that of the Macintosh SE, although the components on the logic board in the Macintosh SE/30 are more closely related to those in a Macintosh IIx. Figure 1-16 shows the interior of the Macintosh SE/30.

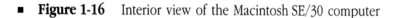

■ **Figure 1-16**   Interior view of the Macintosh SE/30 computer

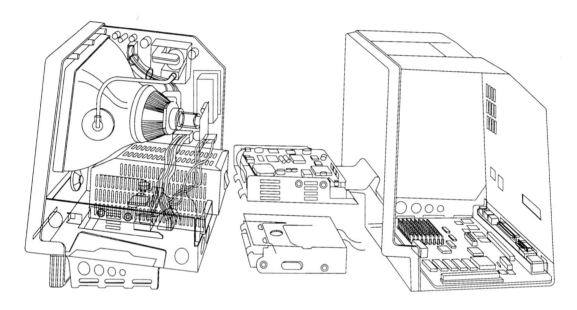

Each Macintosh SE/30 computer contains the following components:

■ A Motorola MC68030 microprocessor, running at a system clock frequency of 15.6672 megahertz. In addition to a higher clock rate than the MC68000, the MC68030 provides 32-bit data and address buses, data and instruction caches, a built-in memory management unit, and other enhancements.

■ A Motorola MC68882 mathematics coprocessor (also called the *floating-point unit,* or *FPU*).

■ An Apple custom integrated circuit, the GLUE, that provides address decoding and control signals. (The name *GLUE* is a play on words, based on the acronym *GLU* for *general logic unit* and the fact that the GLUE IC "glues together" the other ICs by providing handshaking between the I/O devices and the processor.)

- Up to 128 MB of random-access memory (RAM), provided in four or eight SIMMs.

- Read-only memory (ROM), provided in one SIMM. The ROM contains Macintosh Toolbox and Operating System routines.

- Video RAM, provided in two 256 Kbit RAM ICs, for a total of 64 KB of RAM.

- Video logic, implemented by several PALs. The Macintosh SE/30 video logic emulates a NuBus video card installed in NuBus slot $E.

- Video ROM, provided in one 8 KB ROM IC.

- The Apple Desktop Bus (ADB), used to communicate with the keyboard, the mouse, and other input devices.

- A 120-pin expansion connector called the *Macintosh SE/30 68030 processor-direct slot (PDS).*

- A sound system consisting of an Apple custom digital sound-synthesizer IC, the Apple Sound Chip (ASC); two Sony analog sound IC; a built-in speaker; and an external stereo sound jack.

- Two Apple custom Versatile Interface Adapter (VIA) ICs, to support the ADB and other I/O devices.

- An 8530 Serial Communications Controller (SCC) IC, providing two independent ports for serial communication.

- The SWIM (Super Woz Integrated Machine), an Apple custom IC used to control the interface to the FDHD drive. The SWIM is an enhanced version of the IWM.

- One FDHD drive (double-sided 1.4 MB floppy disk drive), and provision for a hard disk. The FDHD drive can read, write, and format single-sided 400 KB disks, double-sided 800 KB disks, and high-density 1.4 MB disks.

- A 5380 Small Computer System Interface (SCSI) IC, for high-speed parallel communication with devices such as hard disks.

Macintosh Portable computer

Figure 1-17 shows the interior of the Macintosh Portable computer. The Macintosh Portable is unique in the Macintosh family in that it contains a battery large enough to power the entire unit. The interior space is divided among the battery, the power supply, and the main logic board. In addition to the RAM, ROM, microprocessor, and I/O ICs, the main logic board includes circuitry and logic to conserve power and monitor the battery, plus control circuits for the flat-panel video display.

■ **Figure 1-17** Interior view of the Macintosh Portable computer

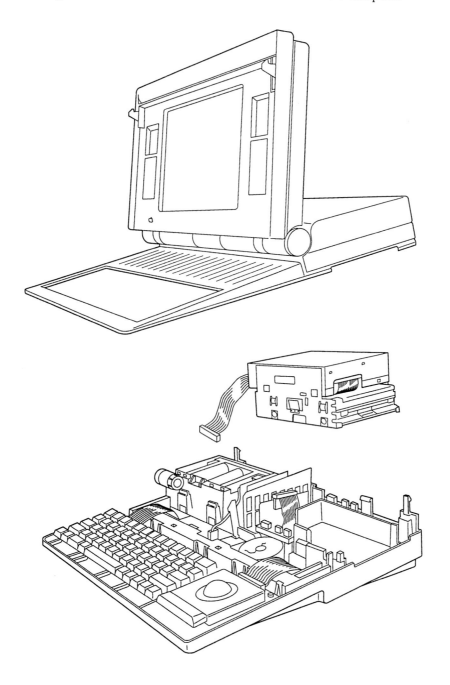

Each Macintosh Portable computer contains the following components:

- A Motorola MC68HC000 microprocessor, running at a system clock frequency of 15.6672 megahertz.

- Two Apple custom integrated circuits that provide control signals and address decoding.

- An Apple custom integrated circuit that provides data and control signals for the flat-panel display.

- Random-access memory (RAM), permanently soldered on the main logic board. The Macintosh Portable has 1 MB of permanent RAM.

- A 50-pin internal RAM expansion connector.

- Read-only memory (ROM), permanently soldered on the main logic board. The Macintosh Portable has 256 KB of permanent ROM, containing Macintosh Toolbox and Operating System routines.

- A 50-pin internal ROM expansion connector.

- A 32 KB video RAM.

- An active-matrix flat-panel display.

- A keyboard microprocessor that interprets keyswitch transitions and functions as the ADB transceiver for the keyboard.

- Two identical 34-pin connectors, on either side of the machine, that can be used for the keyboard, trackball, or optional numeric keypad.

- A sound system consisting of an Apple Sound Chip (ASC), two Sony analog sound ICs, a built-in speaker, and an external stereo sound jack.

- The Power Manager IC, a Mitsubishi 50753 single-chip microprocessor. The Power Manager IC directs the power control circuits and serves as the real-time clock (RTC) and ADB transceiver in the Macintosh Portable.

- An Apple custom Versatile Interface Adapter (VIA) IC, to support the Power Manager IC.

- A CMOS version of the 8530 Serial Communications Controller (SCC) IC, providing two independent ports for serial communication.

- An 18-pin internal connector for an optional modem card that can communicate with the processor through one of the SCC IC's serial ports.

- The SWIM (Super Woz Integrated Machine), an Apple custom IC used to control the interface to the FDHD drive. The SWIM is an enhanced version of the IWM.

- One FDHD drive (double-sided, 1.4 MB floppy disk drive), and provision for either a second floppy disk drive or a hard disk. The FDHD drive can read, write, and format single-sided 400 KB disks, double-sided 800 KB disks, and high-density 1.4 MB disks.

- A 53C80 Small Computer System Interface (SCSI) IC, for high-speed parallel communication with devices such as hard disks.

- A sealed lead-acid battery. The battery can be recharged with the separate battery charger provided with the computer.

- A 96-pin expansion connector. In this book, that connector is referred to as the *Macintosh Portable 68000 processor-direct slot (PDS)*.

Macintosh II–family computers

All the computers in the Macintosh II family share the same modular design with multiple expansion slots and external video monitors. The Macintosh II, Macintosh IIx, and Macintosh IIfx computers have six expansion slots and are similar in appearance, with main units 18.66 inches wide. The Macintosh IIcx and Macintosh IIci computers have three expansion slots and main units that are 11.9 inches wide.

Macintosh II and Macintosh IIx computers

Figure 1-18 shows the interior of the main system unit in the Macintosh II computer. The interior of the Macintosh IIx computer is nearly identical in appearance to that of the Macintosh II. The microprocessor, RAM, ROM, and the various input/output ICs are located on the computer's main logic board (also called the *motherboard*). The main system unit also contains the power supply and a cooling fan. You can install optional expansion cards by plugging them into NuBus expansion slots; note the presence of a video expansion card for the external video monitor.

The Macintosh II computer contains the following components:

- A Motorola MC68020 microprocessor, running at a system clock frequency of 15.6672 megahertz.

- A Motorola MC68881 mathematics coprocessor (also called the *floating-point unit,* or *FPU*).

- An Apple custom integrated circuit, the GLUE, that provides address decoding and control signals.

■ **Figure 1-18** Interior view of the Macintosh II computer

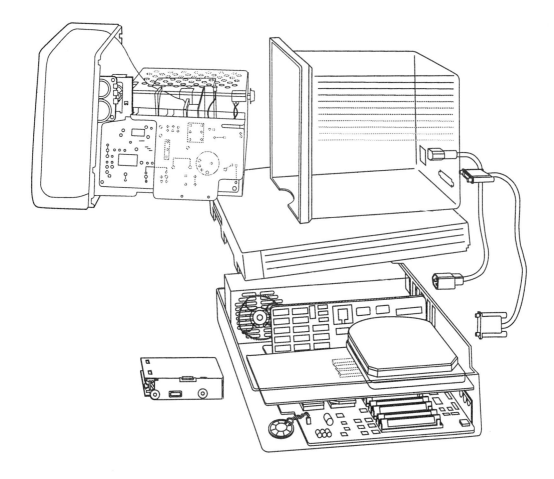

■ A memory management unit (MMU) IC, which translates between the logical addresses used by software and the physical addresses of the hardware devices on the Macintosh II main logic board. The standard configuration for the Macintosh II uses the Apple proprietary Address Management Unit (AMU, also known as the *Hochsprung Memory Management Unit,* or *HMMU*). If you want to run a virtual memory operating system such as A/UX® (Apple's implementation of the AT&T UNIX® operating system), or use virtual memory with system software version 7.0, you must replace the AMU with a Motorola MC68851 Paged Memory Management Unit (PMMU). (You can also continue to run earlier versions of the Macintosh Operating System after the PMMU is installed.)

■ Up to 128 MB of random-access memory (RAM), provided in four or eight SIMMs.

- Read-only memory (ROM), provided in four 512 Kbit ROM ICs. The ROM contains Macintosh Toolbox and Operating System routines.

- The Apple Desktop Bus (ADB), used to communicate with the keyboard, the mouse, and other input devices.

- Apple's implementation of the NuBus, providing six internal expansion slots. An Apple custom IC, the NuChip, controls the bus interface.

- A sound system consisting of an Apple custom digital-sound synthesizer IC, the Apple Sound Chip (ASC); two Sony analog sound ICs; a built-in speaker; and an external stereo sound jack.

- Two Apple custom Versatile Interface Adapter (VIA) ICs, to support the ADB and other I/O devices.

- An 8530 Serial Communications Controller (SCC) IC, providing two independent ports for serial communication.

- The IWM (Integrated Woz Machine), an Apple custom IC used to control the floppy disk interface.

- A double-sided 800 KB floppy disk drive, and provision for both a second 800 KB floppy disk drive and a hard disk.

- A 5380 Small Computer System Interface (SCSI) IC, for high-speed parallel communication with devices such as hard disks.

The Macintosh IIx computer contains components identical to those in the Macintosh II except for the following differences:

- The Macintosh IIx computer contains a Motorola MC68030 microprocessor, rather than the MC68020 used in the Macintosh II. The MC68030 offers a data cache in addition to the instruction cache present in the MC68020, and provides a built-in memory management unit. Because the MC68030 has its own memory management capability, the Macintosh IIx does not have the separate MMU IC present in the Macintosh II.

- The Macintosh IIx has the SWIM (Super Woz Integrated Machine), an Apple custom IC used to control the interface to the FDHD drive. The SWIM is an enhanced version of the IWM.

- The Macintosh IIx has one FDHD drive, and provision for both an internal hard disk and either a second FDHD drive or an 800 KB floppy disk drive. The FDHD drive can read, write, and format single-sided 400 KB disks, double-sided 800 KB disks, and high-density 1.4 MB disks.

- The Macintosh IIx has an MC68882 FPU rather than the MC68881 used in the Macintosh II.

- All ROM in the Macintosh IIx computer is provided on a ROM SIMM.

Macintosh IIcx and Macintosh IIci computers

The Macintosh IIcx and Macintosh IIci computers are smaller versions of the modular design of the Macintosh II family. Both machines have only three NuBus slots and room for a single internal floppy disk drive. Figure 1-19 shows the interior of the Macintosh IIcx computer; note the presence of an expansion video card for the video monitor. Figure 1-20 shows the interior of the Macintosh IIci computer; it can drive a video monitor without an expansion card.

The Macintosh IIcx computer contains many of the same components as the Macintosh IIx, as shown in the following list.

■ A Motorola MC68030 microprocessor, with data and instruction caches and a built-in memory management unit. Because the MC68030 has its own memory management capability, the Macintosh IIcx does not have the separate MMU IC present in the Macintosh II.

■ A Motorola MC68882 mathematics coprocessor (also called the *floating-point unit,* or *FPU).*

■ An Apple custom integrated circuit, the GLUE, that provides address decoding and control signals.

■ Up to 128 MB of random-access memory (RAM), provided in four or eight SIMMs.

■ The ROM is provided in four 512 Kbit ROM ICs. The ROM contains Macintosh Toolbox and Operating System routines. A connector for a ROM SIMM is also provided.

■ The Apple Desktop Bus (ADB), used to communicate with the keyboard, the mouse, and other input devices.

■ Three internal expansion slots using Apple's implementation of the NuBus. An Apple custom IC, the NuChip30, controls the bus interface.

■ A sound system consisting of an Apple custom digital-sound synthesizer IC, the Apple Sound Chip (ASC); two Sony analog sound ICs; a built-in speaker; and an external stereo sound jack.

■ Two Apple custom Versatile Interface Adapter (VIA) ICs, to support the ADB and other I/O devices.

■ An 8530 Serial Communications Controller (SCC) IC, providing two independent ports for serial communication.

■ The SWIM (Super Woz Integrated Machine), an Apple custom IC used to control the interface to the FDHD drive. The SWIM is an enhanced version of the IWM.

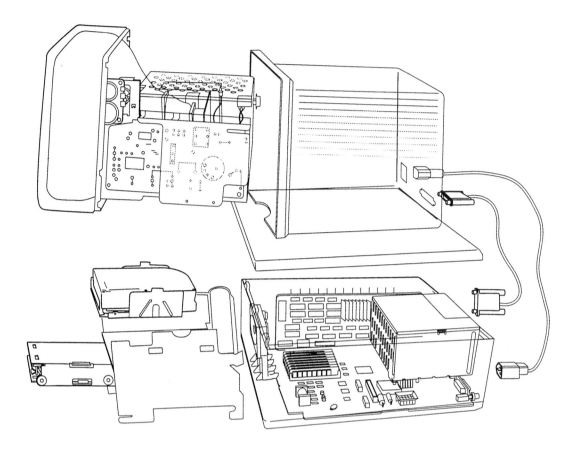

■ The Macintosh IIcx has one internal FDHD drive and provision for a built-in hard disk. The Macintosh IIcx also has a connector for attaching an external floppy-disk drive. The FDHD drive can read, write, and format single-sided 400 KB disks, double-sided 800 KB disks, and high-density 1.4 MB disks.

■ A 5380 Small Computer System Interface (SCSI) IC, for high-speed parallel communication with devices such as hard disks.

■ **Figure 1-20**   Interior view of the Macintosh IIci computer

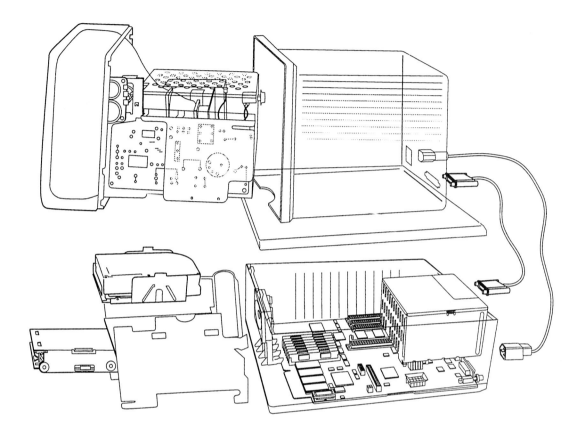

The Macintosh IIci computer contains components identical to those in the
Macintosh IIcx except for the following differences:

■ The Macintosh IIci computer has built-in video circuitry and an external connector for
  a video monitor. (You can also use a video card in a NuBus slot, as on other
  Macintosh II models.)

■ The Macintosh IIci has two Apple custom integrated circuits, the MDU (Memory
  Decode Unit) and RBV (RAM-Based Video controller), that control memory addressing
  and provide the special memory features for the built-in video circuits.

■ The Macintosh IIci has an additional connector on the main logic board for a fast RAM
  cache card.

■ A special-order model of the Macintosh IIci comes equipped with a custom parity IC
  and 9-bit RAM SIMMs that provide parity generation and detection.

The Macintosh IIfx computer

Figure 1-21 shows the interior of the main system unit in the Macintosh IIfx computer. The interior of the Macintosh IIfx is similar in appearance to that of the Macintosh II.

■ **Figure 1-21**   Interior view of the Macintosh IIfx computer

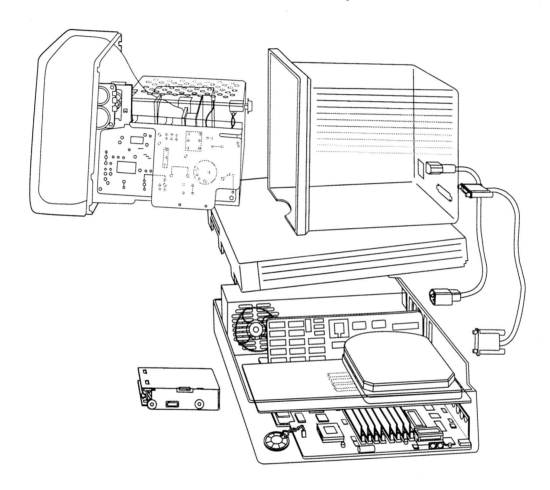

The Macintosh IIfx computer combines many of the features of the Macintosh IIx with advanced features of its own, as shown in the following list.

■ A Motorola MC68030 microprocessor, running at a system clock frequency of 40 megahertz. The MC68030 has data and instruction caches and provides a built-in memory management unit.

- A Motorola MC68882 mathematics coprocessor (also called the *floating-point unit,* or *FPU*).

- An Apple custom integrated circuit, the Fast Memory Controller (FMC), that controls main RAM as well as 32 KB of high-speed cache RAM on the main logic board.

- A special-order model of the Macintosh IIfx comes equipped with a custom PLD (programmable logic device) IC and 9-bit RAM SIMMs that provide parity generation and detection.

- Up to 128 MB of random-access memory (RAM), provided in four or eight SIMMs.

- Read-only memory (ROM), provided on a ROM SIMM. The ROM contains Macintosh Toolbox and Operating System routines.

- An Apple custom integrated circuit, the Operating System Support (OSS) IC, that provides address decoding and control signals.

- Six internal expansion slots using Apple's implementation of the NuBus. Three new Apple custom integrated circuits, the BIU30, BIU2, and CGTO, provide the interface between the NuBus and the main processor bus.

- A 120-pin expansion connector called the *Macintosh IIfx 68030 processor-direct slot (PDS).*

- A sound system consisting of an Apple custom digital-sound synthesizer IC, the Apple Sound Chip (ASC); two Sony analog sound ICs; a built-in speaker; and an external stereo sound jack.

- One Apple custom Versatile Interface Adapter (VIA) IC to support I/O devices.

- Two Apple custom integrated circuits with built-in processors, the I/O Processors (IOPs). One IOP controls serial I/O and AppleTalk® I/O through the 8530 SCC. The other IOP controls the SWIM and contains the ADB interface that communicates with the keyboard, the mouse, and other input devices.

- An 8530 Serial Communications Controller (SCC) IC, providing two independent ports for serial communication.

- The SWIM (Super Woz Integrated Machine), an Apple custom IC used to control the interface to the FDHD drive. The SWIM is an enhanced version of the IWM.

- One internal FDHD drive, and provision for both an internal hard disk and either a second FDHD drive or an 800 KB floppy disk drive. The FDHD drive can read, write, and format single-sided 400 KB disks, double-sided 800 KB disks, and high-density 1.4 MB disks.

- An Apple custom integrated circuit, the SCSI DMA, that provides true direct-memory access capability for high-speed parallel devices such as hard disks.

Memory-mapped device selection

The MC68000 processor's 24-bit address bus provides 2^{24} (16,777,216) unique addresses. If all of these addresses were dedicated to memory, the processor could address 16 MB of RAM and ROM. Similarly, the MC68020 and MC68030 processors' 32-bit address buses can each address 4 GB of memory. However, all Macintosh computers use certain address ranges to select devices in addition to memory. Besides the address ranges used for RAM and ROM, other address ranges are used for the VIAs, the SCSI IC, the IWM or SWIM, the SCC, expansion cards, and so forth. Because this device-selection scheme uses the memory-address lines, it is referred to as **memory-mapped device selection.**

Each time the processor reads or writes to a device, it places an address on the address bus and asserts the address strobe. In the Macintosh computers with MC68020 or MC68030 processors, a memory management unit (MMU) translates the logical address from the processor into a physical address to be used on the main logic board. The MC68030 processor—which is used in the Macintosh SE/30, Macintosh IIx, Macintosh IIcx, Macintosh IIci, and Macintosh IIfx computers—has a built-in MMU. In the Macintosh II, which uses the MC68020, the MMU is a separate IC (the AMU or the PMMU). A special-purpose logic circuit in the computer (such as a PAL, the BBU, or the GLUE) decodes the address to determine which device is being selected, and asserts the device-select signal. The area of address space used for selecting devices is called **device address space.**

Within the address range of a given device, different addresses may have different effects. In the Macintosh SE, for example, $58\ 0000$ selects a SCSI read, whereas $58\ 0001$ selects a SCSI write. If the BBU receives an address in the range $40\ 0000$ through $4F\ FFFF$, it selects the ROM; address bits 1 through 17 select specific locations in the ROM. If it receives an address in the range $00\ 0000$ through $3F\ FFFF$, the BBU selects the RAM, and the RAM multiplexers (MUXs) present the address to the RAM ICs to select specific locations in memory.

The MC68000 does not actually have an external address line A0; instead, it uses two data strobes to provide the low address bit. When data strobe /LDS (Lower Data Strobe) is asserted, A0 is considered to be true (1), indicating that data lines D7 through D0 have valid data; and when data strobe /UDS (Upper Data Strobe) is asserted, A0 is considered to be false (0), indicating that data lines D15 through D8 have valid data. When both /LDS and /UDS are asserted, the operation is word-wide and data lines D15 through D0 all have valid data.

Address maps for 24-bit addresses

Figure 1-22 shows in a general way how the address space is allocated in the Macintosh 128K, 512K, and 512K enhanced computers. Figure 1-23 shows how the address space is allocated in the Macintosh Plus. A more detailed address map is given in the section "Address Map for the Classic Macintosh Computers" in Chapter 3.

Figure 1-24 shows how the address space is allocated in the Macintosh SE computer. A more detailed address map is given in the section "Address Map for the Macintosh SE Computer" in Chapter 3.

Figure 1-25 shows how the address space is allocated in the Macintosh Portable computer. A more detailed address map is given in the section "Address Map for the Macintosh Portable Computer" in Chapter 3.

◆ *Address maps:* The address maps in this chapter include dark shading, light shading, and unshaded areas. Dark-shaded areas indicate addresses that are assigned to devices in the basic configuration of that computer. Light-shaded areas indicate addresses that are decoded but might not be used, such as expansion RAM space; some of those areas (as noted) are reserved for use by Apple Computer, Inc. Unshaded areas are not decoded.

Note that the address maps are not to scale; you must look at the actual addresses to determine the relative sizes of address ranges in the address maps.

■ **Figure 1-22** Simplified address map for the Macintosh 128K, 512K, and 512K enhanced computers

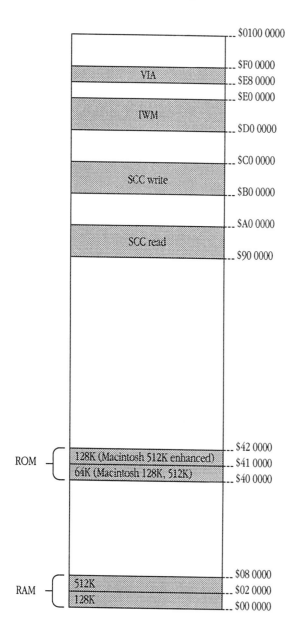

■ **Figure 1-23**   Simplified address map for the Macintosh Plus computer

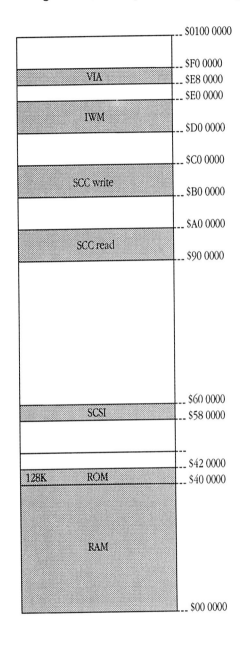

■ **Figure 1-24**   Simplified address map for the Macintosh SE computer

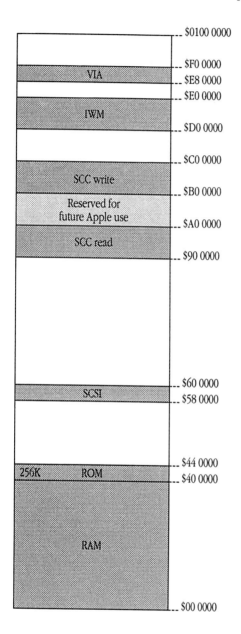

■ **Figure 1-25**   Simplified address map for the Macintosh Portable computer

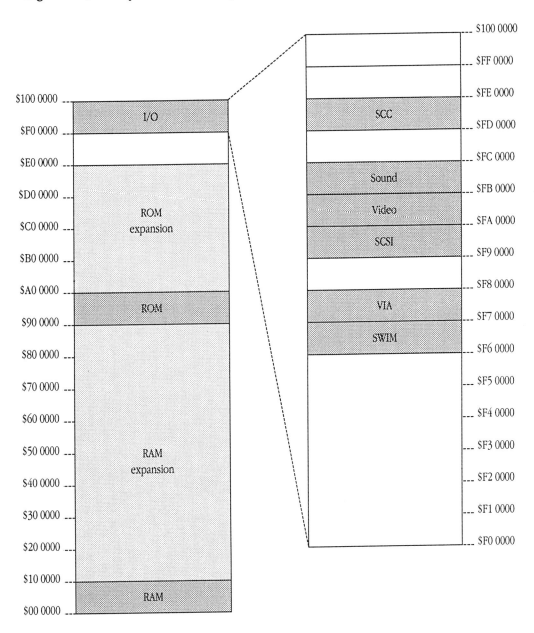

Using 32-bit addresses

Because the classic Macintosh, Macintosh SE, and Macintosh Portable computers use an MC68000 processor, which has a 24-bit address bus, versions of the Macintosh Operating System prior to system software version 7.0 normally use only bits 23 through 0 for addresses. The AMU (or PMMU) IC in the Macintosh II and the built-in MMU in the MC68030 microprocessor make it possible for these versions of the Macintosh Operating System to work with the 32-bit Macintosh computers. To allow the operating system to operate in 24-bit mode on a 32-bit computer, these MMUs take the lower 24 bits of the address coming from the processor and translate them into a 32-bit address.

When the Macintosh II computer is operating in 24-bit mode and the processor addresses memory or another device on the main processor bus, the MMU translates bits LA23 through LA20 from the MC68020 into bits A31 through A20. These signal lines are shown in the block diagram of the Macintosh II in Chapter 2 (Figure 2-6). The MMU ignores the top 8 bits (LA31 through 24) in performing the translation. In the Macintosh models that have an MC68030, this address translation is performed within the MC68030. Address translation is described in more detail in the section "Address Maps," in Chapter 3.

Address maps for 32-bit addresses

The next four pages show memory address maps for the Macintosh models that have 32-bit addressing. More detailed versions of the address maps are shown in Chapter 3.

Figure 1-26 shows how address space is allocated in the Macintosh SE/30 computer. Figure 1-27 shows how address space is allocated in the Macintosh II, Macintosh IIx, and Macintosh IIcx computers.

Figure 1-28 shows how the 32-bit address space is allocated in the Macintosh IIci computer. Figure 1-29 shows how the 32-bit address space is allocated in the Macintosh IIfx computer. More detailed address maps are given in the section "Address Maps" in Chapter 3.

■ **Figure 1-26** Simplified address map for the Macintosh SE/30 computer

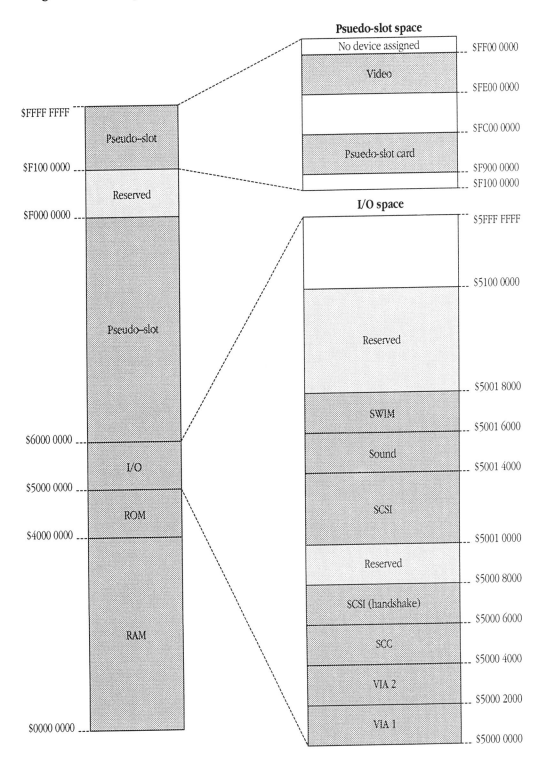

Psuedo-slot space

No device assigned	$FF00 0000
Video	$FE00 0000
	$FC00 0000
Psuedo-slot card	$F900 0000
	$F100 0000

I/O space

	$5FFF FFFF
	$5100 0000
Reserved	
	$5001 8000
SWIM	$5001 6000
Sound	$5001 4000
SCSI	
	$5001 0000
Reserved	
	$5000 8000
SCSI (handshake)	$5000 6000
SCC	
	$5000 4000
VIA 2	$5000 2000
VIA 1	$5000 0000

Main map (left column):

- $FFFF FFFF — Pseudo-slot
- $F100 0000 — Reserved
- $F000 0000 — Pseudo-slot
- $6000 0000 — I/O
- $5000 0000 — ROM
- $4000 0000 — RAM
- $0000 0000

Figure 1-27 Simplified address map for the Macintosh II, Macintosh IIx, and Macintosh IIcx computers

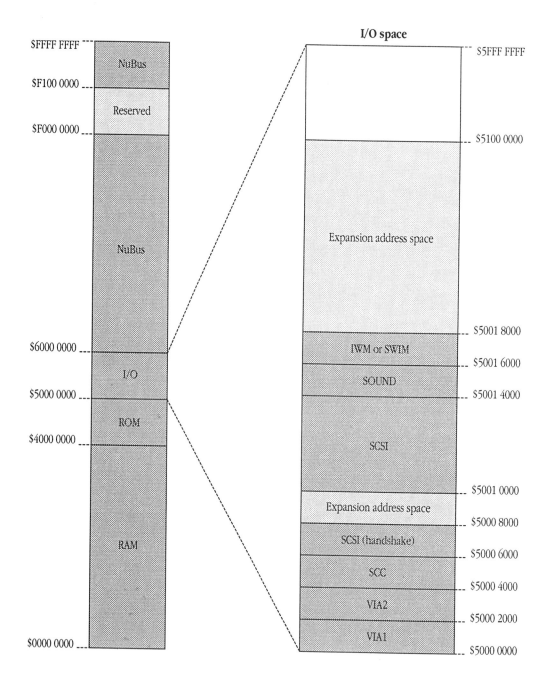

■ **Figure 1-28** Simplified address map for the Macintosh IIci computer

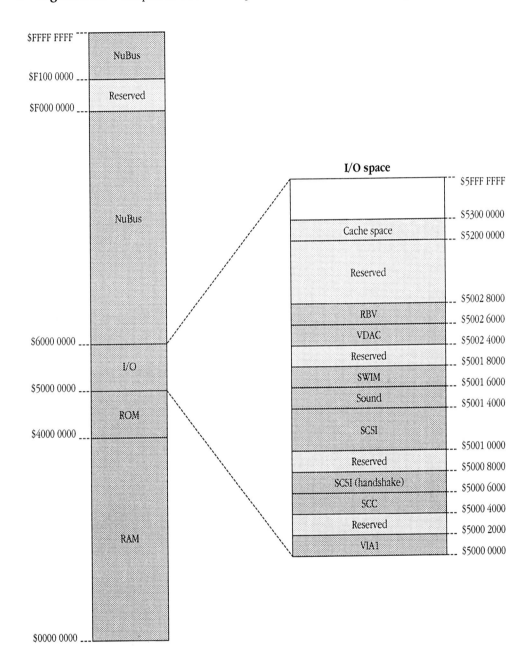

■ **Figure 1-29** Simplified address map for the Macintosh IIfx computer

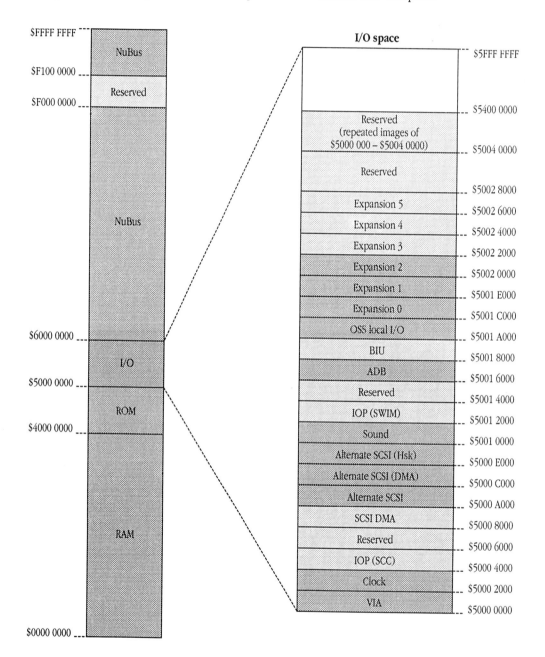

Translating 24-bit addresses to 32-bit addresses

Figure 1-30 illustrates the 24-to-32 bit address translation used by the Macintosh SE/30 computer and by the Macintosh II–family computers. Notice that, whereas there are only 8 MB of address space available for RAM in the 24-bit address map, that is only a small portion of the 1 GB of address space available for RAM in the 32-bit address map. The ROM, I/O devices, and NuBus slots also have proportionately more address space assigned to them in the 32-bit address map. A more detailed address-translation map is given in the section "Address Map for the Macintosh SE Computer" in Chapter 3.

When your application is running the Macintosh Operating System in 24-bit mode, it can use a special system call to switch the MMU to 32-bit mode. When your application is running under an earlier version of the Macintosh Operating System than version 7.0, the only reason to switch to 32-bit mode would be to address a NuBus card that needs more than 1 MB of address space. Some operating systems, such as A/UX, operate in 32-bit mode at all times. See the chapter on the operating system utilities in *Inside Macintosh* for information about switching between 24-bit and 32-bit modes.

■ **Figure 1-30**   24-bit to 32-bit address translation

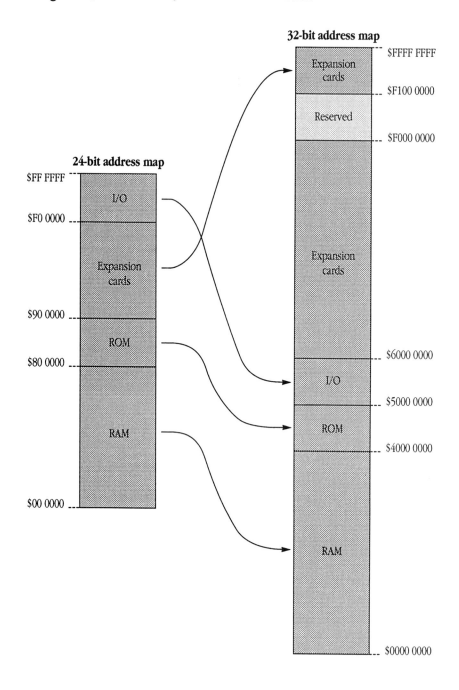

Chapter 2 **Architecture of the Macintosh Computers**

This chapter provides an overview of the architecture of the Macintosh computers and gives brief descriptions of the hardware components of each computer. These components are described in greater detail in later chapters.

	Configuration	CPU	Other processors	Memory mgt. ICs	General logic ICs	Control ICs
Macintosh Plus	Compact	MC68000	(none)	PALs	PALs	1 VIA
Macintosh SE	Compact	MC68000	(none)	PALs	BBU	1 VIA
Macintosh SE/30	Compact	MC68030	MC68882	Part of MC68030	GLUE	2 VIAs
Macintosh Portable	Portable	MC68000	Power Mgr.	Part of MC68030	VDI, CPU GLU & Misc. GLU	1 VIA
Macintosh II	Open (6 slots)	MC68020	MC68881	AMU or PMMU	GLUE	2 VIAs
Macintosh IIx	Open (6 slots)	MC68030	MC68882	Part of MC68030	GLUE	2 VIAs
Macintosh IIcx	Open (3 slots)	MC68030	MC68882	Part of MC68030	GLUE	2 VIAs
Macintosh IIci	Open (3 slots)	MC68030	MC68882	Part of MC68030	MDU & RBV	1 VIA & RBV
Macintosh IIfx	Open (6 slots)	MC68030	MC68882 & 2 IOPs	Part of MC68030	OSS & FMC	1 VIA & OSS

Block diagrams

This section contains block diagrams for all the Macintosh computers. The functions of the parts shown in the diagrams are described in the remaining sections of the chapter.

Compact and portable Macintosh models

The next five pages show block diagrams of the compact Macintosh models and of the Macintosh Portable computer.

The Macintosh 128K, 512K, and 512K enhanced computers are designed around a Motorola MC68000 processor, which has internal 32-bit data and address registers, an external 24-bit address bus, and an external 16-bit data bus. The major components plus the data and address buses of these computers are shown in Figure 2-1.

The Macintosh Plus and Macintosh SE computers also use an MC68000 processor. The major components plus the data and address buses of the Macintosh Plus computer are shown in Figure 2-2. Notice the addition of the SCSI controller and the SCSI connector to the components of the earlier Macintosh computers.

The major components of the Macintosh SE computer plus the data and address buses are shown in Figure 2-3. Notice the addition of the Apple Desktop Bus (ADB), the expansion connector, and an interrupt-request line for the SCSI controller. Notice also that the BBU handles many functions—such as direct memory access for video and sound—handled by discrete logic components in earlier Macintosh computers.

The Macintosh SE/30, like the Macintosh II–family computers, uses a Motorola MC68030 processor. The MC68030, like the MC68020, has 32-bit registers and buses. Because the 68030 has a built-in memory management unit, the Macintosh computers that use that processor do not have a separate AMU/PMMU device.

The Macintosh SE/30 computer combines many of the features of the Macintosh II–family computers with the compact size and processor-direct expansion slot of the Macintosh SE. The major components plus the data and address buses of the Macintosh SE/30 are shown in Figure 2-4.

The Macintosh Portable computer uses the MC68HC000, a low-power-consumption, high-speed version of the MC68000 processor used in the Macintosh SE. The architecture of the Macintosh Portable is similar to that of the Macintosh SE, with the addition of an Apple Sound Chip plus circuitry to support the flat-panel display and the battery. The major components plus the data and address buses of the Macintosh Portable are shown in Figure 2-5.

■ **Figure 2-1** Block diagram of the Macintosh 128K, 512K, and 512K enhanced computers

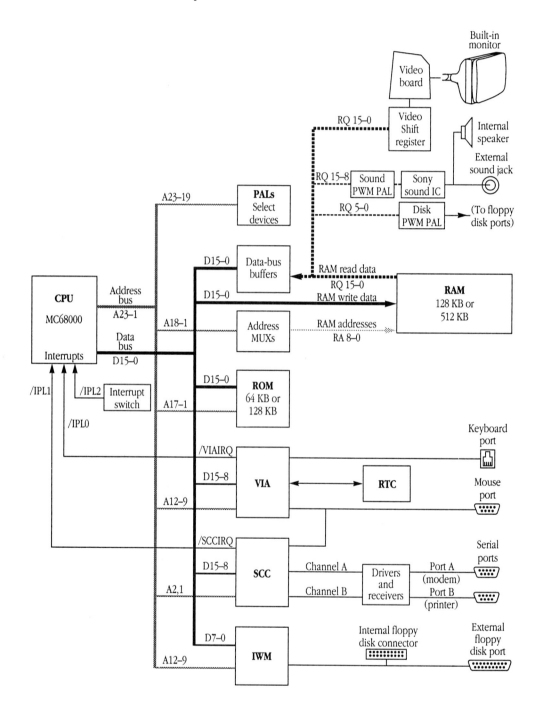

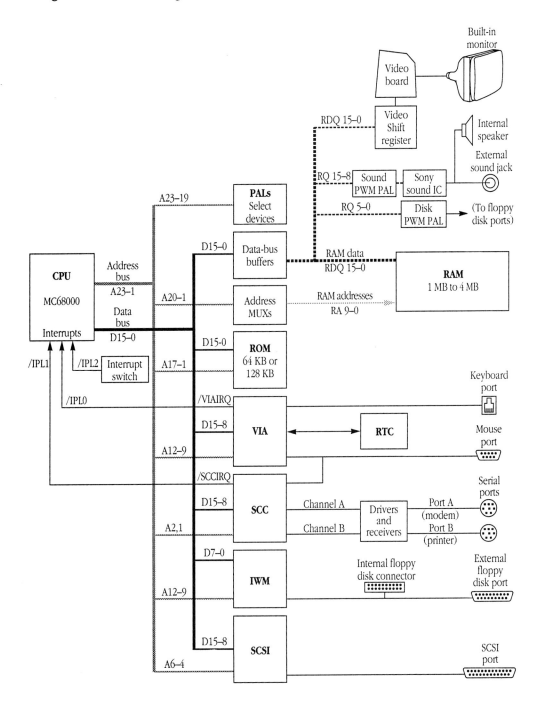

■ **Figure 2-3** Block diagram of the Macintosh SE computer

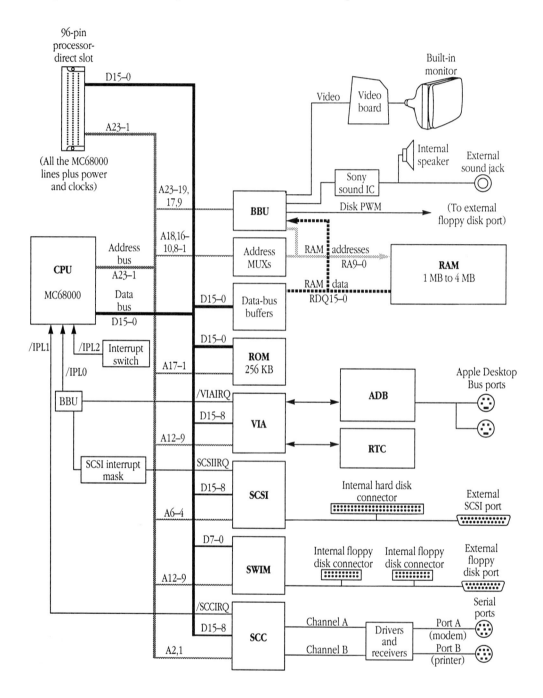

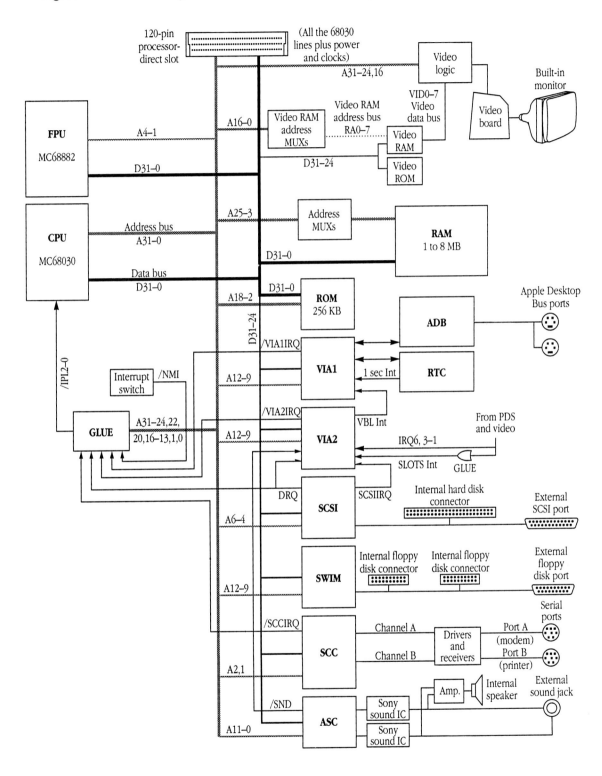

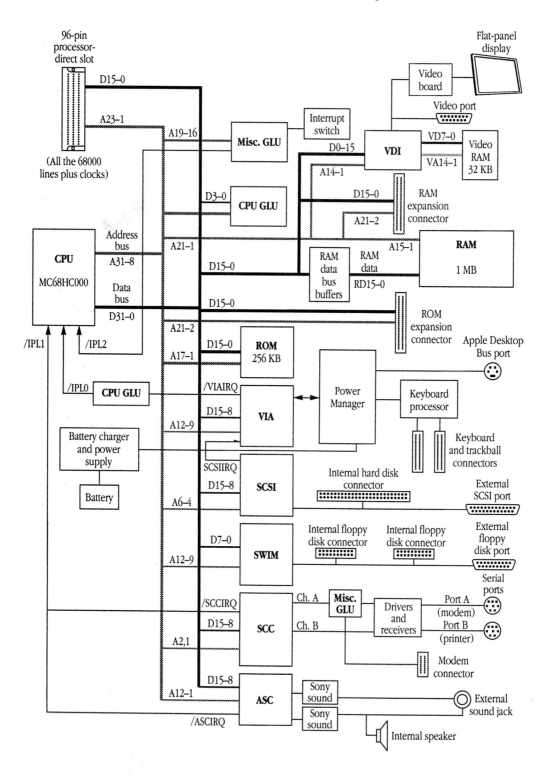

Macintosh II family

The next four pages show block diagrams of modular machines in the Macintosh II family: the Macintosh II, Macintosh IIx, Macintosh IIcx, Macintosh IIci, and Macintosh IIfx.

The Macintosh II computer is designed around a Motorola MC68020 processor, which has internal 32-bit data and address registers, an external 32-bit address bus, and an external 32-bit data bus. The major components of the computer plus the data and address buses are shown in Figure 2-6. Notice the addition of the NuBus interface, the MC68881 mathematics coprocessor (the floating-point unit, or FPU), the memory management unit (the AMU or PMMU), a second VIA, and the Apple Sound Chip. Notice also that all interrupt requests go to the GLUE IC; only the GLUE IC can assert the interrupt signals to the MC68020.

The Macintosh IIx computer is very similar in design to the Macintosh II, with the major exception that the Macintosh IIx has an MC68030 processor, and therefore does not have a separate AMU/PMMU device.

The architecture of the Macintosh IIcx is identical to that of the Macintosh IIx, with the exception that the Macintosh IIcx has only three NuBus expansion slots, has only one internal floppy disk connector, and has an external floppy disk connector. The major components plus the data and address buses of the Macintosh IIx and Macintosh IIcx computers are shown in Figure 2-7.

The Macintosh IIci computer, while it has many of the same features as the Macintosh IIcx, has a different internal design. In the Macintosh IIci, a pair of Apple custom integrated circuits, the MDU (Memory Decode Unit) and RBV (RAM-Based Video controller), provide memory addressing along with special memory features needed for the built-in video circuits. The Macintosh IIci also has a connector for an optional RAM cache card for improved performance. The PGC (Parity Generator and Checker) is an optional custom IC that works with 9-bit RAM SIMMs to provide parity generation and detection. The major components plus the data and address buses of the Macintosh IIci computer are shown in Figure 2-8.

The Macintosh IIfx computer, which resembles the Macintosh II and Macintosh IIx in appearance, has its own complement of Apple custom integrated circuits, including two custom IOPs (I/O processors), FMC (Fast Memory Controller), and SCSI DMA, a custom SCSI controller with direct-memory-access capability. The Macintosh IIfx also has 32 KB of high-speed cache RAM on the main logic board. The major components plus the data and address buses of the Macintosh IIfx are shown in Figure 2-9.

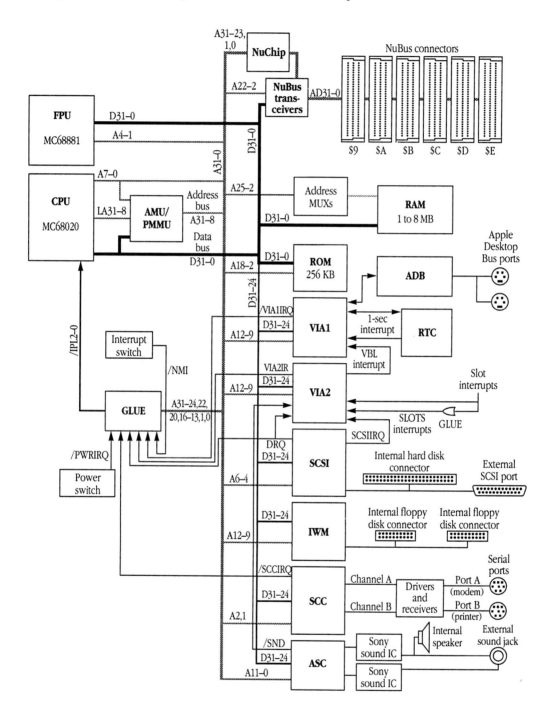

■ **Figure 2-7**   Block diagram of the Macintosh IIx and Macintosh IIcx computers

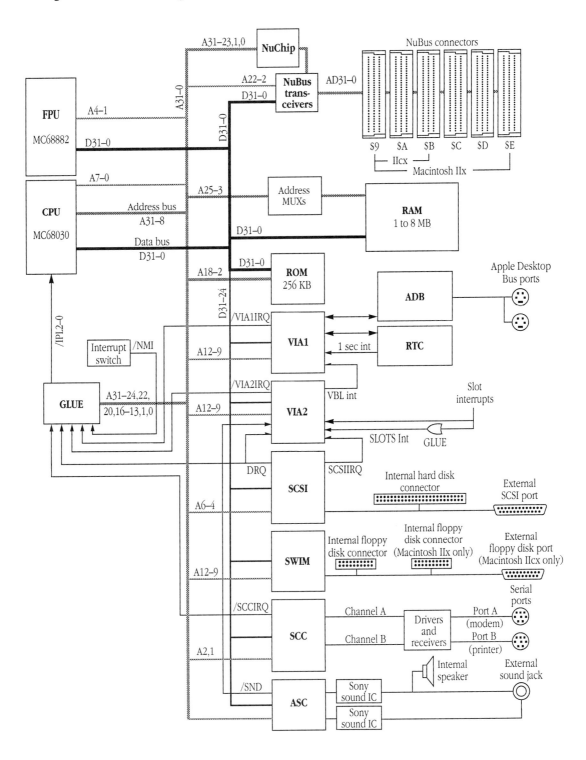

■ **Figure 2-8**   Block diagram of the Macintosh IIci computer

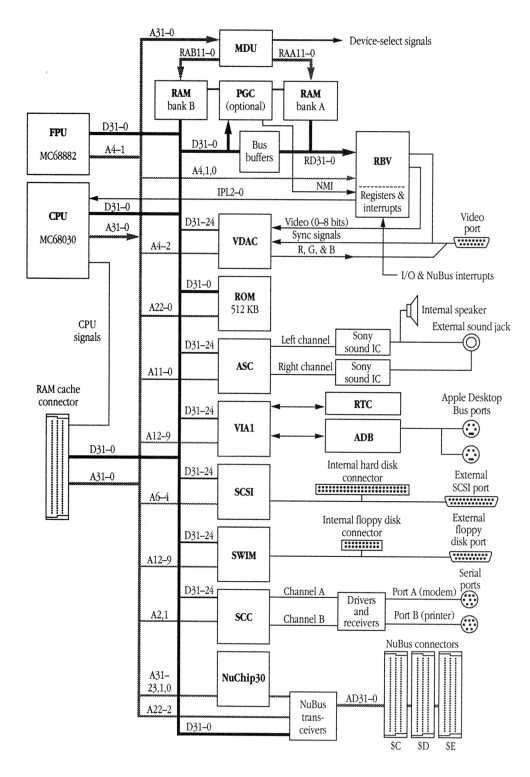

■ **Figure 2-9** Block diagram of the Macintosh IIfx computer

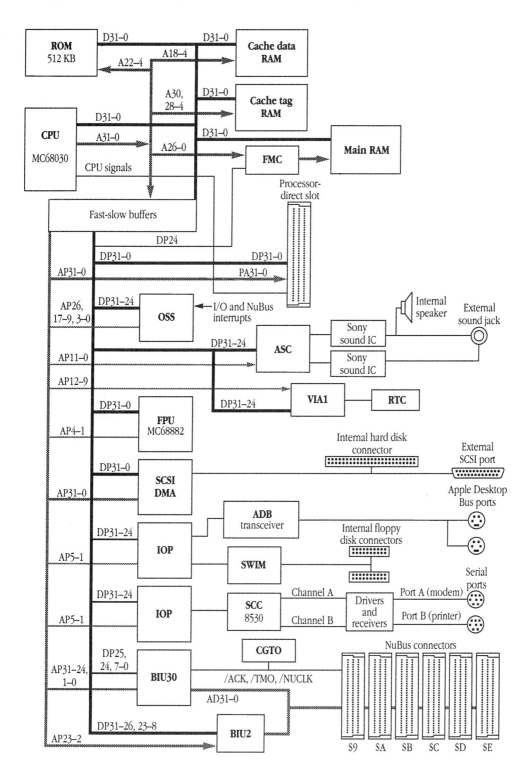

Data buses

As you can see from the block diagrams of the classic Macintosh computers (Figure 2-1 and Figure 2-2), all 16 data lines are connected to the main processor, the ROM, and the RAM data-bus buffers. In the Macintosh SE (Figure 2-3), all 16 data lines are connected to the processor-direct slot as well.

In the Macintosh Portable (Figure 2-5), all 16 data lines are connected to the RAM, the ROM, the VDI (Video Display Interface) IC, the processor-direct slot, and the RAM and ROM expansion connectors. The other devices in these computers are connected to either the high-order byte of the data bus (D15 through D8), or the low-order byte (D7 through D0).

In the Macintosh SE/30 (Figure 2-4) and Macintosh II–family computers (Figures 2-6, 2-7, 2-8, and 2-9), all 32 data lines are connected to the CPU, FPU, ROM, and RAM. In the Macintosh SE/30, all 32 data lines are also connected to the processor-direct slot. In the Macintosh II–family computers, the data lines are all connected to the NuBus interface. In the Macintosh II only, the AMU/PMMU is also connected to all 32 data lines.

The other devices in the Macintosh SE/30 and Macintosh II–family computers, including all I/O devices plus the video RAM and video ROM, are connected to the high-order byte of the data bus (D31 through D24). These devices can transmit or receive only 8 bits in parallel at one time.

RAM data-bus buffers

The classic Macintosh computers and the Macintosh SE use part of the main memory for the video display and for pulse-width-modulated (PWM) sound samples. RAM data-bus buffers can either connect the main data bus to the RAM data bus, or isolate the two buses and give the video and sound circuits direct access to RAM.

The Macintosh IIci has a similar arrangement for bank A of main RAM. Bank A is directly connected to the video controller (RBV) and is also connected to the main processor's data bus by way of a bus buffer. When the RBV is reading video data, the bus buffer disconnects bank A from the main processor's data bus. The MDU can generate two sets of RAM addresses and control signals at the same time: one set for a main-processor access to bank B and another for an RBV read from bank A. This independent address generation enables the main processor to read and write to RAM in bank B with no waiting or interruptions.

◆ *Note:* The sharing of bank A between the main processor and the video circuits affects the performance of the Macintosh IIci. How much the performance is affected depends on the kind and size of video monitor used. For details, please refer to the section "Video Circuits in the Macintosh IIci" in Chapter 12.

In the Macintosh IIfx, the clock for the main processor is much faster than in other Macintosh models. To enable the relatively slow I/O devices to operate effectively, the data and address buses to the I/O interfaces are buffered by fast/slow buffers controlled by a PAL. Most of the devices on the slow side of the bus operate at a clock speed half that of the main processor. The speed-shift PAL provides for two exceptions: it switches to the fast speed for PDS accesses in the address range $6000 0000–$6FFF FFFF and for accesses to the MC68882 FPU.

The Macintosh Portable, Macintosh SE/30, and Macintosh II–family computers have separate video RAM and use the RAM in the ASC for sound, so that it is not necessary for those computers to isolate the RAM from the main data bus.

Central processing units (CPUs)

The CPU executes programs stored in RAM and ROM, performing calculations, accessing hardware devices, and transferring data to and from memory and I/O devices. Device selection, RAM control, and some other functions—such as control of the video and sound circuits in the Macintosh SE—are handled by general logic circuits. (The PALs, BBU, and GLUE ICs are examples of general logic circuits.) The VIAs, SCSI, IWM, SWIM, ASC, and SCC ICs provide interfaces with I/O devices.

The CPU communicates asynchronously with all devices except the VIAs. Communications with the VIAs in the classic Macintosh and Macintosh SE computers are synchronized by a special signal generated by the MC68000 called the *Enable signal* or the *E clock.* In the Macintosh Portable, Macintosh SE/30, and Macintosh II–family computers, communications with the VIA are synchronized by a combination of a VIA clock signal and the VIA enable signal, both of which are generated by the general logic circuits.

The differences between asynchronous and synchronous (that is, MC6800-compatible) device accesses are detailed in the documentation for the Motorola MC68000-family microprocessors. The general logic circuits provide all device-select signals for internal devices and generate handshaking signals to the CPU for both synchronous and asynchronous devices.

The MC68000, MC68HC000, MC68020, and MC68030 microprocessors are described in more detail in Chapter 3.

◆ *Note:* Outside this book, the term *CPU* is sometimes used when referring to the main system unit of a computer; here the term is a synonym for *main processor*.

Interrupts

It is occasionally necessary for a device to interrupt the normal processing of the program being executed. For example, when a serial port receives some information, it interrupts the CPU, which can stop normal processing long enough to read the data in the SCC's receive buffer. The CPU can then return to the program it was executing while the SCC receives more data over the serial port.

The MC68000-family processors have three interrupt lines plus a Reset line. When a signal is received over one or more interrupt lines, the CPU determines the priority of the interrupt (determined by which interrupt lines are asserted). If the interrupt priority is higher than the current processor priority (set by the software), the CPU suspends execution of the currently running program.

In the Macintosh Portable, Macintosh SE, and classic Macintosh computers, each interrupt request line from an I/O device is connected directly or indirectly to one of the three processor interrupt lines.

The CPU in the Macintosh Portable receives its interrupt control (IPL) inputs from the custom GLU ICs: two from the CPU GLU IC and the third—and highest priority—from the Miscellaneous GLU IC.

In the Macintosh SE/30 and Macintosh II–family computers, the general logic circuits receive interrupt requests from the various devices, assign a priority to each, and assert one or more interrupt lines to the CPU.

In the Macintosh IIci, interrupt requests are handled by the RBV, which assigns a priority to each and asserts one or more interrupt lines to the CPU. The Macintosh IIci also has an additional interrupt: the built-in video generates an interrupt that is handled like a NuBus interrupt.

In the Macintosh IIfx, interrupts are processed by the OSS custom IC, which determines the priorities of interrupts under software control. The OSS allows different operating systems to use different interrupt priorities.

The CPU acknowledges the interrupt and, in response to a signal from the general logic circuits, reads an interrupt vector from a memory location determined by the level of the interrupt. The CPU then executes the code pointed to by that vector. This process is known as **automatic vectoring.** The code jumped to by the CPU in response to an interrupt is referred to as an **interrupt handler.**

When the Reset line is asserted, the CPU stops whatever it's doing and executes the code pointed to by the Reset vector. The Reset vector is always found at the first location in memory (address $00 0000 for the 24-bit processors and $0000 0000 for the 32-bit processors).

Interrupts are described in more detail in Chapter 3.

Unimplemented instructions

Interrupts are hardware signals, as opposed to **traps,** which are interruptions in the operation of the CPU generated by execution of instructions. A trap can be caused by a special instruction, the purpose of which is to cause a trap, or by an attempt to execute an unrecognized instruction. When a trap occurs, the CPU executes code pointed to by an exception vector.

Certain instructions unrecognized by the MC68000-family microprocessors are known as **unimplemented instructions** and cause a special type of trap known as an **unimplemented instruction exception.** Unimplemented instructions are used in Macintosh computers to cause the CPU to jump to Macintosh Toolbox and Operating System routines.

Mathematics coprocessors (FPUs)

The MC68881 and MC68882 mathematics coprocessors (also called *floating-point units,* or *FPUs*) perform fast and highly accurate floating-point arithmetic in parallel with the CPU. After the general control logic decodes the address and asserts the device select to the FPU, the FPU communicates directly with the CPU without further intervention of the memory management unit or logic circuits. To a programmer, the FPU appears to extend the capabilities of the CPU, adding several instructions, data types, and registers to the features of the MC68020 or MC68030. The FPU is described in more detail in Chapter 3.

Macintosh II memory management unit

Between the CPU and the GLUE IC in the Macintosh II computer is a memory management unit (MMU) IC. This IC can be the Apple proprietary Address Management Unit (AMU), or a Motorola MC68851 Paged Memory Management Unit (PMMU).

When you are running the Macintosh operating system in 24-bit mode, the memory management unit (either the AMU or the PMMU) translates the 24-bit address used by the operating system into the 32-bit equivalent that the GLUE IC decodes. When you are using a virtual-memory operating system, such as system software version 7.0 or A/UX, the memory management unit (in this case it must be the PMMU) translates between the 32-bit logical address used by software and the 32-bit physical address used by the GLUE IC.

◆ *Note:* In the Macintosh models that use the MC68030 microprocessor, the memory management function is built into the microprocessor. Those machines support operating systems with either 24-bit or 32-bit addresses, as described for the Macintosh II in the previous paragraph.

Power Manager microprocessor

The **Power Manager IC** in the Macintosh Portable computer is a Mitsubishi M50753 microprocessor, which contains its own RAM and ROM. The microcode in the Power Manager IC's ROM enables the Power Manager IC to control the power circuits in the Macintosh Portable, and to act as the real-time clock and as the ADB transceiver. The RAM in the Power Manager IC serves as the parameter RAM for the Macintosh Portable. The VIA provides the interface between the Power Manager IC and the CPU.

General logic circuits

A variety of ICs perform general logic functions in Macintosh computers. The Macintosh Plus and earlier Macintosh computers use PALs, which are programmable logic array devices. The other Macintosh computers have Apple custom ICs: the BBU in the Macintosh SE; the GLUE in the Macintosh SE/30, Macintosh II, and Macintosh IIx; the RBV and MDU in the Macintosh IIci; the CPU GLU, Miscellaneous GLU, and VDI in the Macintosh Portable; and the FMC, OSS, and PALs in the Macintosh IIfx.

The general logic circuits decode addresses, assert device-select signals to the internal devices being addressed, and assert signals to the CPU to acknowledge the receipt of data by the addressed device. Other functions performed by general logic circuits include refreshing RAM, controlling RAM addressing, and performing direct memory access for video and sound circuits in some of the Macintosh computers. They also generate clock signals and other control signals. In the Macintosh SE/30 and Macintosh II family, the general logic circuits monitor interrupt requests from internal devices, determine the priority of each, and assert the interrupt lines to the CPU.

The general logic circuits generate the control and handshaking signals that coordinate the various components in the computer. The general logic circuits are discussed in more detail in Chapter 3.

RAM

The RAM ICs in the Macintosh Portable and in the Macintosh 128K, 512K, and 512K enhanced computers are mounted on the main logic board of the computer. The RAM ICs in all other Macintosh computers (the Macintosh Plus, Macintosh SE, Macintosh SE/30, and Macintosh II–family computers) are mounted on SIMMs (Single In-line Memory Modules) that plug into connectors on the main logic board. The Macintosh Portable also has a connector for a RAM expansion card.

In the Macintosh SE and classic Macintosh computers, the video circuitry, the sound circuitry, the floppy disk motor-speed control circuitry, and the CPU can all read data from RAM, but only the CPU writes to RAM. The Macintosh IIci also has video circuitry that reads from RAM (bank A only). The other Macintosh II–family computers, along with the Macintosh Portable and the Macintosh SE/30, have separate RAM for the video and sound circuits; in those computers, only the CPU reads from and writes to system RAM. In addition, in the Macintosh SE, Macintosh SE/30, and Macintosh II–family computers, a card plugged into an expansion slot can both read from and write to RAM.

Macintosh RAM is described in more detail in Chapter 5.

Reading data from RAM

When the CPU reads data from RAM in the Macintosh SE, Macintosh Plus, and earlier Macintosh computers, the CPU sends an address to the RAM through the RAM address MUXs, and the RAM places the data on the RAM data lines. The RAM data-bus buffers transmit the data to the CPU data bus, where the CPU reads it. The CPU can read data from RAM at any time except when data is being read for video, sound, or disk-speed control.

When the CPU reads data from RAM in the Macintosh Portable computer, the CPU sends an address directly to the static RAM. The RAM places the data on the data bus, where the CPU reads it. The CPU in the Macintosh Portable can read data from RAM at any time (except when an expansion card has control of the bus).

In the Macintosh SE/30 and Macintosh II–family computers, when the CPU reads data from RAM, the CPU sends an address to the RAM through the RAM address MUXs, the RAM places the data on the system data bus, and the CPU reads it. The CPU can read data from RAM at any time (except when an expansion card has control of the bus).

In the Macintosh IIci computer, the MDU provides separate addresses for the processor and for the video circuitry. RAM is divided into two banks, A and B, with separate address and data buses. The screen buffer for the built-in video occupies a portion of memory bank A. When the CPU addresses bank A, an ongoing RAM access by the video circuits can cause the CPU to wait. However, the CPU can read or write to bank B at any time, even when the video circuits are fetching data from bank A. To minimize the effect of competition for bank A on performance, the Macintosh IIci computer normally has additional RAM over the 1 MB minimum installed in bank B. For more information about RAM operation, please refer to Chapter 5.

Video RAM

The video logic in the classic Macintosh, Macintosh SE, and Macintosh IIci computers reads data from a video screen buffer in system RAM and sends the data to the screen. When video data is being read, the RAM data-bus buffers isolate the RAM data bus from the CPU data bus.

The Macintosh SE and classic Macintosh computers have their video screen buffers in main memory. The logic circuits fetch the video data in bursts, two words at a time, so as to minimize the amount of RAM access time denied to the CPU.

The built-in video circuits in the Macintosh IIci computer use a screen buffer stored in bank A of main memory. The MDU (Memory Decode Unit) generates video addresses under the control of the RBV (RAM-Based Video controller). The RBV fetches video data in bursts, eight longwords at a time, so as to minimize the amount of bank-A access time denied to the CPU.

The video circuits in the Macintosh Portable and Macintosh SE/30 computers have their own RAM. Similarly, Macintosh II video cards installed in NuBus slots have their own RAM. In addition, the ASC has its own sound buffer. Therefore, in the Macintosh Portable, Macintosh SE/30, and Macintosh II family, the only time the CPU has to share RAM access time with any other device is when an expansion card has control of the bus or, in the Macintosh IIfx, when a DMA device is making DMA accesses.

There is more information about video circuits later in this chapter, in the section "Built-in Video," and in Chapter 12. For more information about DMA accesses, please refer to the sections "IOPs in the Macintosh IIfx Computer" in Chapter 3 and "SCSI DMA in the Macintosh IIfx Computer" in Chapter 11.

Cache RAM

The Macintosh IIfx computer has 32 KB of high-speed cache RAM on its main logic board. The Macintosh IIci computer has a connector for an optional RAM cache card. In both machines, the operation of the cache is similar: it provides faster access when the main processor is reading instructions or data.

Cache RAM in the Macintosh IIfx computer

In the Macintosh IIfx computer, the main processor can read a longword from the cache RAM in just two clock cycles, provided the required data is in the cache. If it is not, the processor requires an additional four clock cycles to read the data from main memory. While the processor reads data from main RAM, the FMC loads the new data into the cache.

Chapter 5 contains more information about cache RAM in the Macintosh IIfx.

Cache RAM in the Macintosh IIci computer

In the Macintosh IIci computer, the optional cache card provides a similar decrease in the time required for the processor to read from RAM.

With the optional cache card installed, the processor in the Macintosh IIci can read any longword in just two clock cycles, provided the data is in the cache. If it is not, the processor requires an additional seven clock cycles to retry the read operation. During the retry, while the processor is reading data from main RAM, the cache card also reads the data and updates the cache.

Chapter 5 contains more information about cache RAM in the Macintosh IIci.

ROM

The ROM ICs in the Macintosh Plus, Macintosh SE, Macintosh Portable, Macintosh II, Macintosh IIcx, and Macintosh IIci computers are mounted on the main logic board of the computer. The ROM ICs in the Macintosh SE/30, Macintosh IIx, and Macintosh IIfx computers are mounted on SIMMs that plug into connectors on the main logic board. The Macintosh IIcx and Macintosh IIci also have a connector for an optional SIMM, and the Macintosh Portable has an internal connector that can be used for additional ROM.

The ROM contains system routines, including most of the code for the Macintosh Toolbox, and the Reset handler that is executed each time the computer is started up or reset. The Macintosh SE/30, Macintosh IIcx, and Macintosh IIx computers all have identical code in system ROM. Each of the other Macintosh computers has ROM code unique to that computer.

The CPU can always access ROM without sharing access time with any other circuits.

In the Macintosh Portable, Macintosh SE, Macintosh Plus, and earlier Macintosh computers, the CPU always reads one word of data at a time from ROM; the low byte of each word is read from one ROM IC and the high byte is read from the other. In the Macintosh SE/30 and Macintosh II–family computers, each read operation makes a longword of data available from ROM, reading all four ROM ICs simultaneously; one byte of the longword is read from each ROM IC.

There is more information about the Macintosh ROM in Chapter 5.

Built-in video

The classic Macintosh, Macintosh SE, Macintosh SE/30, and Macintosh Portable computers have built-in video generation circuits and display screens. The Macintosh IIci computer does not have a built-in display, but it does have built-in video generation circuits for use with an external monitor.

◆ *Note:* The Macintosh II–family computers have no built-in displays. Instead, the user can select any available video card designed for their computer, and install it in a NuBus slot. The video card contains RAM for the screen buffer plus all of the logic circuitry needed to send horizontal and vertical blanking signals and video data to the monitor. The video card has its own connector for an external video monitor.

The Macintosh IIci computer has the equivalent of a built-in video card that generates a display on an external monitor. Like other members of the Macintosh II family, the Macintosh IIci can accept a video card in any of its NuBus slots. The video card can operate either instead of or along with the built-in video.

Video circuits

The video circuitry for the built-in monitor in the Macintosh SE and classic Macintosh computers is located on the analog board. This circuitry controls the horizontal and vertical motions of the electron beam that generates the picture on the screen, and turns the beam on and off according to the stream of data fed to it by the general logic circuits. A 0 is displayed as a white pixel and a 1 is displayed as black. The video circuitry on the analog board is coordinated by vertical and horizontal timing signals that are generated by the logic circuits on the main logic board.

In the Macintosh SE/30 computer, the vertical and horizontal synchronization signals are provided by special video circuits on the main logic board, rather than by the general logic circuits. The video circuits on the main logic board also contain their own RAM and ROM to provide video logic and data. The signals generated by the video logic circuits in the Macintosh SE/30 are identical to the video signals generated by the general logic circuits in the Macintosh SE. The operating system, however, addresses the video circuits on the Macintosh SE/30 main logic board in the same manner that it would address a NuBus video card in a Macintosh II–family computer.

The Macintosh Portable computer has separate RAM for its video screen buffer and a custom IC, the VDI, that provides data and control signals. The VDI provides the vertical and horizontal synchronization signals and video data to the flat-panel display and to the external video port.

In the Macintosh IIci computer, the vertical and horizontal synchronization signals are provided by the RBV custom IC on the main circuit board. The video buffer is in bank A of main memory; video addresses are generated in the MDU custom IC at the request of the RBV. The RBV fetches video data 8 longwords at a time and uses FIFO storage and shift registers to send pixel-sized chunks of video data on to the CLUT DAC IC, which generates the RGB video signals.

Screen-buffer sizes

A full-screen display for a built-in Macintosh CRT monitor—such as the one in the Macintosh SE or Macintosh Plus computers—consists of 342 horizontal scan lines and a vertical blanking interval. Each scan line consists of 512 pixels, each pixel corresponding to 1 bit of data. Thus, a full screen display requires 21,888 bytes of data. The screen image is refreshed approximately 60 times per second.

In the Macintosh Portable computer, a full screen on the built-in flat-panel display consists of 400 horizontal lines and a display synchronization signal. Each line consists of 640 pixels and each pixel corresponds to 1 bit of data. Thus, a full screen display requires 32,000 bytes of data. The screen image is updated approximately 60 times per second.

The Macintosh IIci computer has built-in video circuitry but uses an external video monitor. The size of the screen buffer depends on the number of bits per pixel and on the size of the monitor; pins in the monitor cable enable the computer to determine what kind of monitor is attached. On the standard-size Apple High-Resolution Monochrome Monitor or the AppleColor™ High-Resolution RGB Monitor, the video circuits in the Macintosh IIci can provide up to 8 bits per pixel for 256 colors or shades of gray. The display is made up of 480 lines of 640 pixels each. For a black-and-white display (1 bit per pixel), the screen buffer occupies 38,400 bytes. For 8 bits per pixel, the screen buffer occupies 307,200 bytes. The image is refreshed approximately 67 times a second.

◆ *Note:* The MMU in the Macintosh IIci allocates memory for the screen buffer in increments of 32 KB, so it takes 64 KB for 1 bit per pixel on a monochrome monitor, 320 KB for a color monitor with 8 bits per pixel.

On the Macintosh Portrait Display (with 870 lines of 480 pixels), the Macintosh IIci can provide up to 4 bits per pixel for 16 shades of gray. For a black-and-white display (1 bit per pixel) on the Portrait Display, the screen buffer occupies 69,600 bytes. For 4 bits per pixel, the screen buffer occupies 278,400 bytes. The image is refreshed approximately 75 times a second.

Sound circuits

Two different types of sound circuits have been used in Macintosh computers. The Macintosh SE and classic Macintosh computers use their general logic circuits plus a Sony sound IC to generate output for the internal speaker or external sound jack. The Macintosh SE/30, Macintosh Portable, and Macintosh II–family computers use the Apple Sound Chip (ASC) plus two Sony sound ICs to generate the sound signals.

Macintosh SE and classic Macintosh sound circuits

In the Macintosh SE and classic Macintosh computers, the general logic circuits read a word of data for the sound and disk-speed control just before each horizontal video line begins. The high-order byte of this word is used for sound and the low-order byte for disk-speed control. Every 44.93 μs, the pulse-width modulator (PWM) PAL in the Macintosh Plus, or the BBU in the Macintosh SE, generates a pulse, the width of which depends on the sound value read from RAM. This train of pulses is sent to the Sony sound IC, which integrates it into a smoothly varying waveform. The amplitude of the waveform is adjusted in the Sony sound IC according to a 3-bit value from the VIA, and the signal is sent by the sound IC to the internal speaker or external sound jack.

Apple Sound Chip

The Macintosh Portable, Macintosh SE/30, and Macintosh II–family computers have an Apple custom IC, the Apple Sound Chip (ASC), plus two Sony sound ICs. The ASC has four 512-byte buffers of its own, so computers that use it do not use system RAM for storing sound values. Although the data bus to the ASC is only 8 bits wide, the dynamic bus sizing feature of the MC68020 and MC68030 processors allows the sound driver to send longword (32-bit) data to the buffers. The CPU automatically performs four 1-byte accesses to the buffer and increments the addresses appropriately to accomplish the longword transfer.

The ASC can generate monophonic sound practically indistinguishable from that produced by the sound hardware in the Macintosh SE and classic Macintosh computers. However, the ASC also provides a variety of features not available in Macintosh computers that lack this IC. For example, the ASC has four independent channels that it can synthesize into monophonic or stereophonic sound. The features of the ASC are all available through the Macintosh Sound Manager.

In the Macintosh Portable and Macintosh II–family computers, the Sound Manager can read a bit in a VIA to determine whether the monophonic internal speaker or the stereophonic external sound jack is being used. In the Macintosh SE/30, the sound circuit includes a mixer to convert stereophonic to monophonic for the internal speaker; the Sound Manager always operates in stereophonic mode in the Macintosh SE/30.

The sound circuits are discussed in Chapter 13.

Disk-speed control

The logic circuits in the original Macintosh SE and in the classic Macintosh computers take the low-order byte of the word of data from the first sound buffer and generate a train of pulses with it just as the sound PWM does for sound. This train of pulses is fed directly to the motor of any single-sided (400 KB) floppy disk drive connected to the IWM port. The power to the motor is turned on and off by these pulses, so that the inertia of the motor itself integrates the pulses, controlling the motor speed. This signal is used to vary the disk speed of disks in 400 KB drives. Disk speed is varied by the disk controller to compensate for the fact that, at a given rotational speed, sectors near the disk's outer edge travel under the disk-drive head faster than sectors closer to the center of the disk.

◆ *Note:* Macintosh SE computers manufactured after August 1989 use the SWIM controller and support the FDHD drive. Those machines are identified by the letters *FDHD* on the front.

The Macintosh 512K enhanced and all later Macintosh computers are capable of driving double-sided disk drives. The double-sided disk drives have internal speed control circuitry and do not use the disk-speed control signal.

The disk-speed PWM signal is not provided by the Macintosh Portable, Macintosh SE FDHD, Macintosh SE/30, or Macintosh II–family computers, which do not use the 400 KB floppy disk drive.

VIAs

The Macintosh Plus and earlier Macintosh computers use a standard Rockwell or VTI 6522 Versatile Interface Adapter (VIA) IC. The Macintosh SE, Macintosh II, and all later Macintosh computers use an Apple custom version of this IC that is functionally identical to the Rockwell and VTI VIAs. The VIA contains internal control registers and data registers. System software can write to the registers to set the state of the VIA and to set bits that control outputs. System software can also read the registers to determine the state of the VIA and of signals that the VIA monitors. The VIA contains two timers. The operating system or a program loads an initial value into one of the timers and starts the timer; once started, the timer count is decremented once every 1.2766 µs. When the timer counts down to 0, the VIA generates an interrupt.

The VIA in the Macintosh Plus and earlier Macintosh computers is used primarily as the interface between the main logic board and the keyboard, mouse, and real-time clock. It also provides control lines for the floppy disk drives, video interface, sound circuitry, and serial interface.

The VIA in the Macintosh SE computers is used primarily as the interface between the main logic board and the Apple Desktop Bus and the real-time clock. It also provides control signals for the floppy disk drives, video interface, sound circuitry, serial interface, and SCSI interrupts.

The VIA in the Macintosh Portable computer is used primarily as the interface between the MC68HC000 CPU and the Power Manager IC. It also provides control signals for the floppy disk drives, sound circuitry, serial interface, and SCSI interrupts.

The Macintosh SE/30 and some members of the Macintosh II–family computers have two VIAs, known as *VIA1* and *VIA2*. In the Macintosh IIci and Macintosh IIfx, the functions of VIA2 are incorporated into an Apple custom integrated circuit (RBV in the Macintosh IIci, OSS in the Macintosh IIfx). VIA1 maintains compatibility with existing Macintosh software by supplying most of the signals used by Macintosh computers that have only one VIA. It provides control signals for the floppy disk drives, serial interface, and other I/O devices. VIA2 (or the corresponding custom IC) supports features not present in one-VIA Macintosh computers, such as interrupts from expansion cards, interrupts from the Apple Sound Chip, and other features.

The VIAs are described in detail in Chapter 4.

Non-ADB keyboard interface

In the Macintosh Plus and earlier Macintosh computers, the keyboard and mouse are connected directly to the VIA; this is in contrast to the later Macintosh computers, in which the keyboard and mouse are connected to the VIA through the Apple Desktop Bus (ADB).

The classic Macintosh keyboard contains a microprocessor that communicates with the VIA through a bidirectional serial data line. All data transfers are synchronized by the keyboard clock, which is generated by the keyboard processor. Each transmission consists of 8 bits. Each byte of data input to the computer is stored in a register in the VIA from which it is read over the parallel CPU data bus by the CPU.

Only the computer can initiate communication over the keyboard lines. The Keyboard Driver sends an inquiry command to the keyboard; the keyboard sends back either a key transition response if a key has been pressed or released, or a null response if nothing has happened since the last inquiry. The Keyboard Driver can then read the key transition code from the register in the VIA.

The classic Macintosh keyboards and keyboard interface are described in detail in Chapter 7.

Non-ADB mouse interface

The classic Macintosh mouse generates four square-wave signals that together indicate the magnitude and direction of mouse motion. Two of these signals go to the Serial Communications Controller (SCC), which interrupts the CPU and records the levels of the signals (high or low) as bits in a register; and two of the signals go to the VIA, which records the levels of the signals as bits in another register. Interrupt-driven routines in the classic Macintosh ROM convert this information into the corresponding motion of the pointer on the screen. The Macintosh mouse is a relative-motion device—that is, it doesn't report where it is, only how far and in which direction it's moving.

The mouse button is a switch that, when pressed, grounds a pin on the mouse connector. The state of the button is recorded as a bit in the VIA and is checked by software during each vertical blanking interrupt.

The classic Macintosh mouse and mouse interface are described in detail in Chapter 7.

Apple Desktop Bus

The Apple Desktop Bus (ADB) is an asynchronous serial communication bus used to connect keyboards, mouse devices, graphics tablets, and other input devices to Macintosh computers starting with the Macintosh SE and Macintosh II. It is a single-master, multislave bus; in other words, two or more input devices can be connected to the same ADB, but the computer controls the bus at all times. The devices can be connected in parallel or daisy-chained. The two ADB ports on the back of the Macintosh are connected in parallel to the same ADB.

The ADB is driven either by an ADB transceiver or a custom IC (see the note later in this section). The ADB transceiver is a microprocessor that communicates with the CPU through a VIA (VIA1 in the Macintosh SE/30 and Macintosh II–family computers; the single VIA in the Macintosh SE and Macintosh Portable computers). The ADB transceiver directly controls transactions with ADB input devices. The ADB Manager or device driver sends commands for an ADB device to the VIA 1 byte at a time. The VIA holds the byte in an internal register and shifts it out 1 bit at a time to the ADB transceiver, which sends it over the ADB to the appropriate device.

In the other direction, an ADB device that has information to send to the ADB Manager or device driver sends a service request when polled by the ADB transceiver in the computer. In response to the service request, the ADB transceiver sends an interrupt request to the VIA, which interrupts the CPU. The ADB Manager then polls the various ADB devices to determine the source of the service request and commands the device to send its data to the computer. Each byte of data from the device is shifted 1 bit at a time to the VIA over the ADB bus. The byte is held in a register in the VIA until it is read over data lines by the CPU. The ADB device drivers store all ADB data (such as key transitions and mouse motion information) in RAM on the main logic board, where it can be accessed by software.

In addition to the data line, there are several control lines between the VIA and the ADB transceiver. These lines are used to time and sequence transactions between the VIA and the ADB transceiver.

◆ *Note:* In the Macintosh Portable computer, the Power Manager IC provides the functions of the ADB transceiver. The Power Manager IC is connected to the VIA in the Macintosh Portable by an 8-bit parallel data bus. In the Macintosh IIfx computer, the ADB interface is part of one of the custom IOPs. The system software that controls the ADB is different for the two machines, but the operation of the ADB is the same as it is in machines with a separate ADB transceiver IC.

In the Macintosh Portable computer, the keyboard microprocessor is located on the main logic board, rather than in the keyboard as with other ADB keyboards. The keyboard microprocessor interprets the keyswitch transitions and supplies the serially encoded signal over a serial data line to the Power Manager IC. In the Macintosh Portable, the entire ADB interface, including the ADB transceivers for both the computer and the keyboard, is located on the main logic board.

▲ **Warning**   The Macintosh Portable computer cannot provide the power required by many ADB devices; only low-power-consumption devices should be connected to the ADB connector on the Macintosh Portable. Connecting any other ADB device to the ADB connector can result in improper operation of the Macintosh Portable computer. ▲

The Apple IIGS® computer also uses the Apple Desktop Bus. Any ADB device that works on one of the ADB-equipped computers works on the others (with the exception stated in the preceding warning), provided that there is a device driver for that device in the computer's system. The Apple Desktop Bus, Apple Standard Mouse, and ADB-compatible keyboards are described in detail in Chapter 8.

The Macintosh II–family computers include a Power On signal that comes into the computer through the ADB connector, but that goes directly to the power control circuits without going through the ADB transceiver. Power control is discussed in Chapter 6.

Real-time clock

In all Macintosh computers except the Macintosh Portable, the Macintosh real-time clock (RTC) is a custom integrated circuit controlled through a VIA. The VIA communicates with the CPU over eight parallel data lines and with the RTC over a single serial data line. In the Macintosh Portable, the Power Manager IC performs the functions of the RTC.

The RTC contains a 4-byte counter that is incremented once each second. The RTC sends an interrupt request to the VIA once each second and, if the interrupt is enabled in the VIA, the VIA interrupts the CPU.

The RTC in the Macintosh 128K and 512K computers also contains 20 bytes of RAM, called **parameter RAM.** The RTC in the 512K enhanced and later Macintosh computers contains 256 bytes of parameter RAM (except for the Macintosh Portable, which has 128 bytes of parameter RAM in the Power Manager IC). Parameter RAM contains important data—such as the sound volume setting—that must be preserved even when the computer is off or unplugged. To keep the clock running and preserve the data in the parameter RAM, the RTC is powered by a battery when the computer is off.

The user can change most of the values in parameter RAM by using the Control Panel desk accessory. While the computer is on, the operating system maintains a copy of parameter RAM plus the date and time in system RAM. Once each second, the operating system updates the time stored in RAM. This setting is stored as the number of seconds since midnight, January 1, 1904.

In the Macintosh Portable computer, the functions of the RTC and parameter RAM are provided by the Power Manager IC. The interface to the Power Manager IC therefore serves as the interface to the real-time clock as well. The Power Manager IC recognizes two real-time clock commands, one to set and one to read the clock.

Parameter RAM in the Macintosh Portable computer consists of a group of storage locations in the Power Manager IC. The Macintosh Portable has no power on/off switch, so the parameter RAM is supplied continuously with power by the built-in battery. The Macintosh Portable also has a 9-volt backup battery to preserve parameter RAM in case the main battery becomes discharged or is disconnected. The Power Manager IC has only 128 bytes of parameter RAM.

The Macintosh real-time clock is described in more detail in Chapter 3.

SCSI

The Macintosh Plus and later Macintosh computers include a 5380 or 53C80 Small Computer System Interface (SCSI) controller, which controls a high-speed parallel interface with hard disk drives and other peripheral devices. The Macintosh Plus has one external SCSI connector; the Macintosh SE, Macintosh SE/30, Macintosh Portable, and Macintosh II–family computers have one external and one internal SCSI connector. A total of seven SCSI devices in addition to the computer itself can be daisy-chained to the SCSI bus.

◆ *Note:* The Macintosh IIfx computer uses an Apple custom IC, the SCSI DMA, that supports direct-memory-access transfers to and from SCSI devices. Please refer to Chapter 11 for information about the SCSI DMA IC.

The Macintosh SCSI hardware and communication protocol conform to the standard proposed by the American National Standards Institute (ANSI) for SCSI devices. The Macintosh implementation differs from the standard in that only the internal connector is the type specified by ANSI. The external DB-25 connector carries all of the signals specified by ANSI, but is smaller and easier to connect and disconnect than the standard 50-pin flat-ribbon connector. In addition, the SCSI connector on the Macintosh Plus does not provide power for the terminator resistors.

The SCSI interface includes eight data lines, one parity line, and nine control lines. The computer is normally the initiator in any communication with a peripheral device, although in principle an intelligent peripheral device could take control of the bus and initiate communication. Each device on the bus has a permanent, unique ID from 0 to 7. The main logic board has ID number 7, giving it the highest priority in case of contention for the bus with another initiator. You assign an ID to any peripheral device (using switches or jumpers) before attaching it to the bus.

At startup time, the computer checks the SCSI bus for peripheral devices, starting with ID 6 or with the device the user specified in the Control Panel. Each time it finds a device, the system finds the device driver (which is stored on the device) and loads it into memory.

SCSI data transfers are controlled by the CPU and performed by the 5380 SCSI controller. In a typical SCSI data transfer, the CPU first sends commands to set up a transfer of information and then lets the SCSI controller use its built-in internal logic to carry out the actual transfer of a byte of data. The CPU then reads that byte of data from the SCSI controller and sets up the transfer of the next byte.

All Macintosh SCSI interfaces except for the one in the Macintosh Plus include hardware handshaking to prevent the CPU from reading invalid data or writing data faster than the peripheral device can accept it. The handshaking is handled by the general logic circuits, which do not acknowledge a successful transfer to the CPU until the SCSI controller indicates that it has finished transferring the byte of data to or from the peripheral device. The CPU does not initiate the next transfer until it has received this acknowledgment. This handshaking makes SCSI transfers very safe, even when done at maximum speed.

In the Macintosh SE, the SCSI controller can generate a hardware interrupt to the CPU (by way of the BBU). In the Macintosh Portable, Macintosh SE/30, and Macintosh II–family computers, the SCSI controller can generate a hardware interrupt request to a VIA. If the interrupt is enabled, the VIA passes it on to the CPU by way of the general logic circuits. This interrupt can be used for bus disconnect and reconnect operations. The VIA normally disables this interrupt. The SCSI controller in the Macintosh SE/30 and Macintosh II–family computers can also assert a DMA Request signal to VIA2, which in turn can interrupt the CPU. This signal can be used to initiate SCSI transfers in interrupt-driven operating systems, such as A/UX.

In the Macintosh IIfx, an Apple custom integrated circuit, the SCSI DMA, provides the functions of the SCSI controller. In addition to providing all the features and functions of the 53C80 IC, the SCSI DMA IC can handle data transfers to and from the main memory by direct-memory access (DMA). To initiate a DMA transfer, the SCSI driver writes control information to the DMA Address counter and DMA Byte Count register on the SCSI DMA IC and then writes to one of the IC's start registers.

Using the SCSI DMA, data transfers are handled by the DMA channel. In addition, the SCSI DMA automatically arbitrates for the SCSI bus. Other elements of SCSI bus protocol are under the control of software running on the main processor, just as on other Macintosh models. The SCSI DMA on the Macintosh IIfx can function as a conventional SCSI interface and transfer data under the control of the main processor.

The Macintosh SCSI interface, including SCSI DMA, is described in more detail in Chapter 11.

▲ **Warning**   Developers are advised not to try to use the SCSI DMA feature by direct access to the IC. Future versions of the SCSI Manager will enable your applications to take advantage of this feature of the hardware. ▲

IWM and SWIM

Communication with floppy disk drives is handled by the Apple custom IWM (Integrated Woz Machine) integrated circuit in the Macintosh II, the original Macintosh SE, and all earlier Macintosh computers. The same function is handled by another Apple custom IC, the SWIM (Super Woz Integrated Machine), in all later Macintosh computers and in the Macintosh SE FDHD.

The IWM, which is also used in Apple II computers, converts between the serial group-code recording (GCR) encoded data used by Apple disk drives and the parallel data bus used by the CPU. The IWM provides all control signals used to communicate with disk drives except for the register-select signal SEL, and, in the original Macintosh SE, the drive-select signal needed to select between the upper and lower internal floppy disk drives. These last two signals are provided by the VIA. In addition, the logic circuits in the original Macintosh SE, Macintosh Plus, and earlier Macintosh computers provide speed control for 400 KB (single-sided) disk drives.

The SWIM provides all of the signals and functions provided by the IWM. In addition, the SWIM can sustain a data-transmission rate twice that of the IWM's fastest rate, and supports disk drives that use the modified frequency modulation (MFM) method of encoding data as well as those that use the GCR method. The high data transmission rate and MFM compatibility allow Macintosh computers that have the SWIM IC to use 1.4 MB FDHD drives as well as the older 800 KB disk drives.

The classic Macintosh computers, Macintosh SE, Macintosh SE/30, Macintosh IIcx, and Macintosh IIci provide one internal connector and one external connector for floppy disk drives. You can connect a single-sided (400 KB) or double-sided (800 KB) floppy disk drive or a Hard Disk 20 to the external IWM connector of the classic Macintosh computers and the original Macintosh SE. You can connect an 800 KB floppy disk drive, an FDHD floppy disk drive, or a Hard Disk 20 to the external SWIM connector of the Macintosh SE FDHD, Macintosh SE/30, Macintosh IIcx, and Macintosh IIci; those computers do not support 400 KB disk drives.

◆ *Note:* The Apple Hard Disk 20 is an earlier, non-SCSI drive designed for use on classic Macintosh models that have no SCSI port. Although you can connect a Hard Disk 20 to the external SWIM connector of the Macintosh SE/30 and Macintosh IIcx computers, those computers do not have drivers for the Hard Disk 20 in ROM. Neither the Macintosh SE/30 nor the Macintosh IIcx can be started up from a Hard Disk 20. (The Macintosh IIci does have the requisite driver and can start up from a Hard Disk 20.)

The original Macintosh SE and the Macintosh Portable each provide two internal connectors and one external connector for floppy disk drives. There is room in the case for either a second floppy disk drive or an internal SCSI hard disk, not for both. You can connect a single-sided (400 KB) or double-sided (800 KB) floppy disk drive or a Hard Disk 20 to the external IWM connector of the Macintosh SE. You can connect an 800 KB floppy disk drive, a 1.4 MB floppy disk drive, or a Hard Disk 20 to the external SWIM connector of the Macintosh Portable and the Macintosh SE FDHD.

The Macintosh II and Macintosh IIx computers have two internal connectors for floppy disk drives. There is room in the case for both a second internal floppy disk drive and a SCSI hard disk. The Macintosh II and Macintosh IIx have no external floppy disk connectors.

The non-SCSI disk drives and disk drive interfaces used by the various Macintosh computers are summarized in Table 2-1. The Macintosh floppy disk interface is described in detail in Chapter 9.

■ **Table 2-1**   Non-SCSI disk drives used by Macintosh computers

Computer	Interface	Internal disk drives	External disk drives	Start up from HD20?
Macintosh 128K, Macintosh 512K	IWM	One 400 KB	400 KB	
Macintosh 512K enhanced, Macintosh Plus	IWM	One 800 KB	400 KB, 800 KB, or HD 20	Yes
Macintosh SE	IWM	One or two 800 KB	400 KB, 800 KB, or HD 20	Yes
Macintosh SE FDHD	SWIM	One or two FDHD	800 KB, FDHD, or HD 20	Yes
Macintosh SE/30	SWIM	One FDHD	800 KB, FDHD, or HD 20	No
Macintosh Portable	SWIM	One or two FDHD	800 KB, FDHD, or HD 20	Yes
Macintosh II	IWM	One or two 800 KB	None	
Macintosh IIx	SWIM	One or two FDHD	None	
Macintosh IIcx	SWIM	One FDHD	800 KB, FDHD, or HD 20	No
Macintosh IIci	SWIM	One FDHD	800 KB, FDHD, or HD 20	Yes
Macintosh IIfx	SWIM	One or two FDHD	None	No

SCC

The Macintosh has two independent serial ports controlled by a Zilog Z8530 Serial Communications Controller (SCC) IC. The SCC is a programmable, dual-channel, multiprotocol data communications controller as well as a parallel-to-serial and serial-to-parallel converter.

The two serial ports are independent and identical except that port A of the Macintosh SE, Macintosh II, and later Macintosh computers includes support for synchronous modems. For most purposes, the AppleTalk Manager uses only port B, but the hardware of either port can support the AppleTalk Personal Network.

The serial interface is supported by differential line-driver and receiver ICs. The serial I/O signals conform to the Electronic Industries Association (EIA) standard RS-422. The RS-422 standard differs from the commonly used RS-232 standard in that the value (high or low) of RS-422 signals is determined by comparing the voltage levels on two lines (referred to as a *differential signal*) rather than comparing the voltage level of a single line with ground, as done by the RS-232 standard. A differential signal is more immune to noise and degrades less with distance than a nondifferential signal.

The SCC generates the handshaking signals required for the serial interface and converts between the serial data stream and the 8-bit parallel data read and written by the CPU. The drivers and receivers convert between the RS-422 differential signals and standard logic-board voltage levels.

The SCC connectors on the Macintosh 128K, 512K, and 512K enhanced Macintosh computers include +5-volt and +12-volt power not available on the serial connectors on later Macintosh computers.

The SCC connectors on the Macintosh Plus and all later Macintosh computers provide an output handshake signal; starting with the Macintosh SE and Macintosh II, the SCC connectors provide a general-purpose input (GPi) signal as well. When enabled by the VIA, the GPi signal of port A is fed into the receive clock input of the SCC. This allows the external device to provide its own clock to the SCC, which makes synchronous communication possible. The GPi input can also be used for handshaking.

In the Macintosh Portable computer, the user can choose to connect serial channel A to the internal modem connector. (The choice is made in the Control Panel desk accessory.)

When the user exercises this option, the Macintosh Portable disables the serial port connector for serial channel A, connects the modem card (if one has been installed) to the channel, and makes the telephone connector at the rear of the Macintosh Portable (or other connector provided by the modem card) the serial communications port. If the user does not enable the modem slot, power is not supplied to it.

The Macintosh serial ports are described in detail in Chapter 10.

I/O Processors

The Macintosh IIfx computer has two Apple custom integrated circuits, the I/O Processors (IOPs), that control the SCC and SWIM ICs and the ADB. The IOPs relieve the main processor of routine tasks on the ports for the floppy disk, the ADB, serial I/O, and AppleTalk. Each IOP has its own built-in microprocessor and its own dedicated RAM, which it can use for DMA data transfers to and from the I/O interface it controls.

One IOP controls the 5830 SCC that is the interface to the serial I/O ports. For information about the IOP for the SCC, please refer to Chapter 10.

Another IOP controls the SWIM custom IC and contains the interface for the ADB. For information about the ADB, please refer to Chapter 8; for information about the SWIM and the floppy disk interface, please refer to Chapter 9.

Macintosh expansion interfaces

There are two kinds of multi-purpose expansion interfaces used in Macintosh computers: the processor-direct slot (PDS) connectors used in the Macintosh SE, Macintosh SE/30, Macintosh Portable, and Macintosh IIfx; and the NuBus interface used in the Macintosh II, Macintosh IIx, Macintosh IIcx, Macintosh IIci, and Macintosh IIfx.

There is more information on the NuBus and PDS expansion interfaces in Chapter 14. Guidelines for designers of NuBus and PDS expansion cards are given in the book *Designing Cards and Drivers for the Macintosh Family,* second edition.

Processor-direct expansion interfaces

The processor-direct slots in the Macintosh SE and Macintosh Portable computers are Euro-DIN 96-pin connectors providing unbuffered access to all the MC68000 signals. The processor-direct slots in the Macintosh SE/30 and the Macintosh IIfx are Euro-DIN 120-pin connectors providing unbuffered access to most of the MC68030 signals. In addition, the processor-direct slots in the Macintosh SE, Macintosh SE/30, and Macintosh IIfx provide extensive power and grounding, as well as critical timing and control signals from the general logic circuits.

The processor-direct slots support high-speed direct access to the Macintosh RAM, allow coprocessors to share the Macintosh address and data bus, and allocate generous portions of the address space to new peripherals.

△ **Developer tip** In addition to the processor-direct slot, the Macintosh Portable computer has expansion connectors for RAM cards and ROM cards that can be used for electronic disks. Although +5-volt and ground connections are available at the processor-direct slot in the Macintosh Portable, no power has been allotted in the Macintosh Portable power budget for a PDS expansion card. Furthermore, in order to comply with FCC regulations on radio-frequency emissions, no connector or cable attached to an expansion card can penetrate the case of the Macintosh Portable. The RAM and ROM expansion connectors in the Macintosh Portable are described in Chapter 5. For more information on PDS expansion cards for the Macintosh Portable, contact Apple Developer Programs as described in the Preface. △

NuBus expansion interfaces

The NuBus interface is used in all Macintosh II–family computers. The NuBus provides an expansion method compatible across many different models, as contrasted with PDS expansion cards, which are different on different models.

The NuBus interface provides access to all the main logic board's resources, including RAM, ROM, and I/O devices. In addition, NuBus provides extensive power and grounding. The NuBus supports direct access to the Macintosh RAM, allows coprocessors access to the main logic board, and allocates 2.5 GB of the processor's 4 GB address space for new peripheral devices. The Macintosh II, Macintosh IIx, and Macintosh IIfx each have six NuBus slots for expansion cards; the Macintosh IIcx and Macintosh IIci have three NuBus slots.

The NuBus has a 32-bit–wide multiplexed address and data bus, and operates synchronously on a 10 MHz clock. The bus interface comprises transceivers and control logic that multiplex and demultiplex the address and data lines and that interface the NuBus signals with the asynchronous processor bus.

Each NuBus slot has an interrupt line. Except in the Macintosh IIci and the Macintosh IIfx, all the slot interrupt lines go to the VIA2 and to the GLUE IC. The GLUE IC performs an OR operation on the slot interrupt lines and sends the result (called SLOTS) to VIA2. When one or more cards in NuBus slots require the attention of the CPU, each asserts its interrupt line. VIA2 receives the SLOTS interrupt signal and asserts an interrupt to the CPU. VIA2 also records in an internal register the states of the six individual slot interrupt lines. When the CPU receives the interrupt, it checks the register in VIA2 to find out which cards are requesting attention.

In the Macintosh IIci, individual interrupt lines go to the RBV custom IC. The RBV performs the OR operation and stores the generic slot interrupt along with the states of the individual interrupt lines in its VIA2-emulation registers.

In the Macintosh IIfx, individual interrupt lines go to the OSS custom IC. The OSS performs the OR operation and stores the resulting generic slot interrupt along with the states of the individual interrupt lines.

For specifications of the NuBus interface, please refer to the section "The NuBus Expansion Interface" in Chapter 14. If you intend to develop a card for the NuBus, you will find much useful information in the book *Designing Cards and Drivers for the Macintosh Family,* second edition.

Using third-party products that adhere to recommended expansion guidelines and do not require physical alteration of the expandable Macintosh computer will not void the Apple Limited Warranty.

Chapter 3 **Processors and General Logic**

Processing and general logic functions in Macintosh computers are handled by the main processor, by auxiliary processors, and by general logic circuits. This chapter describes the functions of the main and auxiliary processors and the general logic circuits in each of the Macintosh computers; it also describes the real-time clock (RTC). Because the address map for each Macintosh computer is created by the general logic circuits—which decode signals on the address bus to select internal devices—the address maps are also described in this chapter.

◆ *Note:* Many control functions are handled by the VIA ICs; they are described in Chapter 4.

	CPU	Other processors	Memory mgt. ICs	General logic ICs
Macintosh Plus	MC68000	(none)	PALs	PALs
Macintosh SE	MC68000	(none)	PALs	BBU
Macintosh SE/30	MC68030	MC68882	Part of MC68030	GLUE
Macintosh Portable	MC68000	Power Mgr.	Part of MC68030	VDI, CPU GLU & Misc. GLU
Macintosh II	MC68020	MC68881	AMU or PMMU	GLUE
Macintosh IIx	MC68030	MC68882	Part of MC68030	GLUE
Macintosh IIcx	MC68030	MC68882	Part of MC68030	GLUE
Macintosh IIci	MC68030	MC68882	Part of MC68030	MDU & RBV
Macintosh IIfx	MC68030	MC68882 & 2 IOPs	Part of MC68030	OSS & FMC

Some auxiliary processors, such as the MC68882 floating-point unit (FPU), are true coprocessors that communicate directly with the main processor and use the processor's data and address buses. Other auxiliary processors, such as the Power Manager microprocessor in the Macintosh Portable computer, communicate with the main processor in other ways.

The general logic circuits may be implemented as programmable array logic chips (PALs), Apple custom integrated circuits, or a combination of the two. Additional control signals are generated by the Versatile Interface Adapter (VIA) and real-time clock (RTC) ICs. The VIAs are described in Chapter 4.

Main processor

The main processor, often called the *central processing unit* or *CPU,* executes programs stored in RAM and ROM, performing calculations, controlling hardware devices, and transferring data to and from memory and I/O devices. The main processor in the Macintosh SE, Macintosh Plus, and earlier Macintosh computers is a Motorola MC68000 microprocessor. The main processor in the Macintosh Portable is a high-speed, low-power-consumption version of the MC68000, the MC68HC000. The main processor in the Macintosh II is a Motorola MC68020; the main processor in all the other members of the Macintosh II family and in the Macintosh SE/30 is a Motorola MC68030.

◆ *Note:* Outside this book, the abbreviation *CPU* is sometimes used when referring to a computer's main system unit; here the term is a synonym for *main processor.*

This section lists some of the features of the microprocessors used in Macintosh computers and describes the use of interrupts and traps in Macintosh computers. The processors discussed in this section are described in detail in Motorola's documentation for those devices.

MC68000 and MC68HC000 microprocessors

This section provides a summary of the features of the MC68000 microprocessor, which is used in the Macintosh SE, Macintosh Plus, and earlier Macintosh computers, and of the MC68HC000, which is used in the Macintosh Portable. Except where otherwise noted, the MC68HC000 is identical in architecture and function to the MC68000. This section also describes the use of interrupts in the classic Macintosh, Macintosh SE, and Macintosh Portable computers.

Features of the MC68000

The MC68000 processor has seventeen 32-bit internal registers, a 32-bit program counter, and a 16-bit status register. Instructions can use data up to 32 bits long. The external data bus is 16 bits wide, so for every 32-bit longword read or written, the MC68000 must perform two data transfers.

The MC68000 provides 56 different instruction types with 14 addressing modes. Each of these instructions is fairly simple, causing a transfer of data from the data bus into a register, for example, or adding the data in two registers. Each valid combination of instruction type and addressing mode is represented in machine language by a binary number.

The MC68000 can handle both asynchronous and synchronous data transfers. Synchronous data transfers are required for devices designed to work with the MC6800, the predecessor of the MC68000 microprocessor.

Asynchronous data transfers are controlled by several signals, including a Data Transfer Acknowledge signal (/DTACK), which indicates that a data transfer is complete. The processor also can assert a Read/Write signal (R/W) and upper and lower data strobes (/UDS and /LDS). In the MC68000, the /UDS and /LDS signals together serve as the external A0 address signal: when /UDS is asserted, A0 is considered to be 0, and when /LDS is asserted, A0 is considered to be 1. Therefore, even-addressed byte-wide reads and writes use the upper byte of the data bus and odd-addressed accesses use the lower byte of the data bus.

Synchronous data transfers are controlled by a set of three signals: the Enable (E) signal, also called the *E clock*, which times the data transfer; the Valid Peripheral Address (/VPA) signal, which indicates that the device addressed requires synchronous communication; and the Valid Memory Address (/VMA) signal, which indicates that there is a valid address on the address bus.

The /DTACK and /VPA signals are generated by the general logic circuits, which handle all handshaking between the main processor and internal devices.

The MC68000 microprocessor provides bus arbitration signals that enable it to share its external address and data buses with other microprocessors. Although no coprocessors share the processor buses in the Macintosh Portable, Macintosh SE, or classic Macintosh computers, developers have taken advantage of the bus arbitration capability to design accelerator cards for these computers.

At any given time, the MC68000 operates in one of two states: the *user state* or the *supervisor state*. Certain instructions, such as the Reset instruction, cannot be executed in the user state. The purpose of this design is to prevent application programs from accessing information or executing instructions that affect the operating system or other programs that might be running at the same time. Not all operating systems take advantage of this feature.

Normal sequential processing of instructions can be interrupted through the exception mechanism. Exceptions include resets and interrupts, which are hardware signals, and traps, which result from the execution of instructions. When the MC68000 detects an exception, it jumps to code pointed to by an exception vector. The lower 1 KB of address space of the MC68000 is reserved for up to 255 exception vectors. The use of MC68000 interrupts in Macintosh computers is described in the following section. For a general discussion of MC68000 exceptions, see the *MC68000 16-Bit Microprocessor User's Manual* from Motorola.

MC68000 interrupts

The MC68000 has three interrupt lines—/IPL0, /IPL1, and /IPL2—providing seven levels of interrupt priority. The status register in the MC68000 has a 3-bit field that indicates the current processor priority level; interrupts with a priority level equal to or lower than the current processor priority level are ignored.

When a signal is received over one or more interrupt lines, the main processor determines the priority of the interrupt and, if the interrupt priority is higher than the current processor priority (set by the software), the processor suspends execution of the currently running program.

The Macintosh computers use automatic vectoring for interrupts. The MC68000 acknowledges an interrupt by putting an address in the range $FF FFF0 through $FF FFFF on the address bus. The general logic circuits respond by asserting the Valid Peripheral Address (/VPA) signal, which causes the main processor to generate a vector number based on the level of the interrupt. The processor then jumps to the interrupt handler at the address calculated by multiplying the vector number by 4.

There are three interrupt sources in the Macintosh Plus and earlier Macintosh computers: the VIA, the SCC, and the programmer's interrupt switch. In the Macintosh SE, the SCSI controller can also generate an interrupt. The SCC interrupt and the programmer's interrupt switch are connected to their own separate MC68000 interrupt lines, and the VIA and SCSI both can cause an interrupt on the third processor interrupt line. In the Macintosh Portable computer, the SCSI IRQ line goes to the VIA; the ASC is connected to an MC68HC000 interrupt line. The programmer's interrupt switch in the Macintosh Portable is connected to the Miscellaneous GLU custom IC, which is connected to an MC68HC000 interrupt line. All these interrupts are discussed in more detail in the following sections.

Interrupts on classic Macintosh computers

Table 3-1 shows the interrupt levels associated with various interrupting sources and combinations of sources for the Macintosh Plus and earlier Macintosh computers.

■ **Table 3-1**   Interrupt levels in the classic Macintosh computers

Interrupt level	MC68000 interrupt lines			Interrupting source	Automatic vector number
	/IPL2	/IPL1	/IPL0		
0	1	1	1	None	None
1	1	1	0	VIA	$19
2	1	0	1	SCC	$1A
3	1	0	0	SCC + VIA*	$1B
4	0	1	1	Interrupt switch	$1C
5	0	1	0	Interrupt switch + VIA	$1D
6	0	0	1	Interrupt switch + SCC	$1E
7	0	0	0	Interrupt switch + SCC + VIA*	$1F

*Because /IPL0 is disconnected from the VIA interrupt line when the SCC interrupts on /IPL1, interrupt level 3 or 7 can appear only very briefly before reverting to level 2 or 6.

The lowest level interrupts in the classic Macintosh computers are generated by the VIA. The interrupt request line from the VIA goes to the PALs, which can assert an interrupt to the processor on line /IPL0. The PALs also monitor interrupt line /IPL1, and deassert /IPL0 whenever /IPL1 is asserted.

Several different events can cause the VIA to generate an interrupt request, including timeouts by the VIA timers, keyboard transactions, the start of the video display's vertical blanking interval, and the one-second tick from the real-time clock. To determine which device caused a VIA interrupt, the processor must read the VIA's Interrupt Flag register at vBase+vIFR. For details about the Interrupt Flag register and about enabling or disabling any of the VIA interrupt sources, see the section "Processor-Interrupt Registers" in Chapter 4.

Intermediate-level interrupts are generated by the SCC. The SCC interrupt output is connected directly to the MC68000's /IPL1 line. Sending or receiving serial port data, various handshaking events, and mouse motion events can cause the SCC to generate an /IPL1 interrupt. See the documentation for the Zilog Z8530 IC for details about the sources of interrupts and the software controls over those interrupts.

The highest-level interrupts in the classic Macintosh computers are generated by the programmer's interrupt switch (which the user can install, together with the Reset switch, at the left side of the Macintosh). This switch is connected directly to the MC68000's /IPL2 line. The programmer's switch is used as an aid to debugging programs; it allows a programmer to interrupt an executing program without resetting the computer. The programmer's switch generates level-4 interrupts, which can be inhibited by the MC68000's interrupt priority mask; you cannot generate nonmaskable (level-7) interrupts on the classic Macintosh computers.

◆ *Note:* Although the Macintosh Plus contains an NCR 5380 SCSI controller IC, the IRQ and DRQ interrupt signals provided by that IC do not generate MC68000 interrupts in the Macintosh Plus. Software must poll the SCSI controller's Bus and Status register to determine whether a SCSI interrupt is pending.

Interrupts on the Macintosh SE computer

Table 3-2 shows the interrupt levels associated with various interrupting sources and combinations of sources for the Macintosh SE computer.

■ **Table 3-2**   Interrupt levels in the Macintosh SE computer

Interrupt level	MC68000 interrupt lines			Interrupting source	Automatic vector number
	/IPL2	/IPL1	/IPL0		
0	1	1	1	None	None
1	1	1	0	VIA or SCSI	$19
2	1	0	1	SCC	$1A
3	1	0	0	SCC + VIA or SCSI*	$1B
4	0	1	1	Interrupt switch	$1C
5	0	1	0	Interrupt switch + VIA or SCSI	$1D
6	0	0	1	Interrupt switch + SCC	$1E
7	0	0	0	Interrupt switch + SCC + VIA or SCSI*	$1F

Note: All three interrupt lines are available at the processor-direct expansion connector.

*Because /IPL0 is disconnected from the VIA and SCSI interrupt lines when the SCC interrupts on /IPL1, interrupt level 3 or 7 can appear only very briefly before reverting to level 2 or 6.

The lowest level interrupts in the Macintosh SE can be generated by either the VIA or the SCSI IRQ line or both; these interrupt requests are connected to the BBU, which can assert an interrupt to the processor on line /IPL0. To determine which source has generated the /IPL0 interrupt, the software must poll both sources. However, software can set a bit in the VIA that causes the SCSI interrupt to be masked, that is, that prevents the SCSI interrupt from being passed on to the MC68000. When this mask bit is set to 1, only the VIA can originate an /IPL0 interrupt. For more information on the SCSI interrupt mask, see the section "Data Register B" in Chapter 4. The BBU also monitors interrupt line /IPL1 and deasserts /IPL0 whenever /IPL1 is asserted.

◆ *Note:* The SCSI controller can generate two types of interrupt requests: IRQ interrupts—which can be used to indicate error conditions on the SCSI bus—and DRQ interrupts, which the SCSI can assert when the first byte of a block of data is ready to be transferred. The DRQ interrupt signal provided by the SCSI controller does not generate an MC68000 interrupt in the Macintosh SE. Software in the Macintosh SE must poll the SCSI controller's Bus and Status register to determine whether a SCSI DRQ interrupt is pending. For more information about the various NCR 5380 interrupt conditions and about software control over these interrupts, see the NCR 5380 manual.

Several different events can cause the VIA to generate an interrupt request, including timeouts on the VIA timers, transactions on the Apple Desktop Bus, the video display's vertical blanking, and the one-second tick from the real-time clock. Software can enable or disable any of these interrupts by setting bits in the VIA's Interrupt Enable register. To determine which device caused a VIA interrupt, the processor must read the VIA's Interrupt Flag register. For details about the Interrupt Enable register and the Interrupt Flag register, see the section "Processor-Interrupt Registers" in Chapter 4.

Intermediate-level interrupts are generated by the SCC. The SCC interrupt output is connected directly to the MC68000's /IPL1 line. Sending or receiving serial port data and various handshaking events can cause the SCC to generate an /IPL1 interrupt. See the Zilog 8530 manual for details about the sources of interrupts and the software controls over those interrupts.

The highest-level interrupt in the Macintosh SE is generated by the programmer's interrupt switch, which is connected directly to the MC68000's /IPL2 line. The programmer's switch generates a level-4 interrupt, which can be inhibited by the MC68000's interrupt priority mask. You cannot generate nonmaskable (level-7) interrupts on the Macintosh SE computer.

Interrupts on the Macintosh Portable computer

Table 3-3 shows the interrupt levels associated with various interrupting sources and combinations of sources for the Macintosh Portable.

■ **Table 3-3**   Interrupt levels in the Macintosh Portable computer

Interrupt level	MC68000 interrupt lines			Interrupting source	Automatic vector number
	/IPL2	/IPL1	/IPL0		
0	1	1	1	None	None
1	1	1	0	VIA	$19
2	1	0	1	SCC or ASC	$1A
3	1	0	0	None	$1B
4	0	1	1	Misc. GLU	$1C
5	0	1	0	Misc. GLU + VIA	$1D
6	0	0	1	Misc. GLU + SCC	$1E
7	0	0	0	None	$1F

Note: All three interrupt lines are available at the processor-direct expansion connector.

The lowest level interrupts in the Macintosh Portable are generated by the VIA. The interrupt request line from the VIA goes to the CPU GLU custom IC, which can assert an interrupt to the processor on line /IPL0. The CPU GLU also monitors interrupt line /IPL1, and deasserts /IPL0 whenever /IPL1 is asserted. Notice that, whereas in the Macintosh SE, the SCSI IRQ line is connected to the general logic circuits, in the Macintosh Portable, that line is connected to the VIA.

Several different devices can cause the VIA in the Macintosh Portable to generate an /IPL0 interrupt, including the SCSI controller (through its IRQ line), the Power Manager IC, the VIA timers, Apple Desktop Bus, the video display circuitry (vertical blanking signal), and the real-time clock. Software can enable or disable any of these interrupts by setting bits in the VIA's Interrupt Enable register. To determine which device caused a VIA interrupt, the processor must read the VIA's Interrupt Flag register. For details about the Interrupt Enable register and the Interrupt Flag register, see the section "Processor-Interrupt Registers" in Chapter 4.

Intermediate-level interrupts are generated by either the SCC or the ASC, both of which are connected directly to the MC68HC000's /IPL1 line. Sending or receiving serial port data and various handshaking events can cause the SCC to generate an /IPL1 interrupt. See the Zilog 8530 manual for details about the sources of SCC interrupts and the software controls over those interrupts. The ASC generates an interrupt when the sound buffers are half empty and when they are completely empty. ASC interrupts are handled by the Sound Manager.

The highest-level interrupts are generated by the Miscellaneous GLU IC in response to an interrupt request from the programmer's interrupt switch (which the user can install, together with the Reset switch, at the left side of the computer). The programmer's switch (through the Misc. GLU) generates level-4 interrupts; you cannot generate nonmaskable (level-7) interrupts on the Macintosh Portable computer.

MC68020 microprocessor

The main processor in the Macintosh II computer is a Motorola MC68020 microprocessor. This section provides an overview of the architecture of this microprocessor and a summary of its features. The MC68020 is described in detail in the *MC68020 32-Bit Microprocessor User's Manual* from Motorola.

Features of the MC68020

The MC68020 processor has sixteen 32-bit data and address registers, five special-purpose control registers, a 32-bit program counter, and a 16-bit status register. Instructions can use data up to 32 bits long. The MC68020 has an on-board instruction cache that can hold 64 longwords of instruction data. Whenever the processor fetches an instruction, it first checks the cache to determine if the word required is in the cache. When the information is found in the cache, the operation is much faster than it is when the fetch has to be made from external memory.

The MC68020 microprocessor has a 32-bit data bus, but has support for devices that use smaller data buses in the form of a feature called **dynamic bus sizing.** This feature allows a device to inform the main processor of its data bus size when the processor transfers data. The processor transfers the data in as many pieces as necessary to accommodate the device's data bus. For example, a 32-bit longword transfer to or from the SCSI controller is done in four cycles, transferring 8 bits each time.

The MC68020 provides over 60 different instruction types with 18 addressing modes. Each of these instructions is fairly simple, causing a transfer of data from the data bus into a register, for example, or adding the data in two registers.

The MC68020 can handle both asynchronous and synchronous data transfers. Synchronous data transfers are required for devices designed to work with the MC6800, an 8-bit predecessor of the MC68020 microprocessor.

Asynchronous data transfers are controlled by several signals, including two Data Transfer and Size Acknowledge signals (/DSACK0 and /DSACK1), which signal that a data transfer is complete and indicate the size of the data bus of the addressed device. The processor also can assert a Read/Write signal (R/W) and a Data Strobe (/DS). In the MC68020, the number of bytes put on the data bus for each transfer cycle depends on both the amount of data to be transferred and the size of the data bus of the addressed device. In the case of a device that has an 8-bit data bus, such as the I/O devices in the Macintosh II computer, the MC68020 always uses bits D31 through D24 for the data.

Synchronous data transfers can be timed by the system clock and use the same /DSACK0 and /DSACK1 signals used by asynchronous transfers.

In the Macintosh II, the /DSACK0 and /DSACK1 signals are generated by the GLUE IC, which handles all handshaking between the main processor and internal devices.

The MC68020 microprocessor provides bus arbitration signals that enable it to share its external address and data buses with other microprocessors. A NuBus card can take advantage of this capability to add an alternate processor to the system.

Like the MC68000, the MC68020 can operate in either the user state or the supervisor state. In contrast to the MC68000, however, a program running on the MC68020 cannot determine which state the processor is in. This feature helps protect the supervisor resources from access by user programs, so that an application program cannot interfere with the operating system or with other programs running simultaneously. Not all operating systems take advantage of this feature.

Instructions that begin with 1111 (binary) are interpreted as coprocessor instructions and include information that specifies which coprocessor is to be addressed. The FPU operates as a coprocessor in the Macintosh II–family computers.

Exception processing by the MC68020 is similar to that of the MC68000. The exception vectors for the MC68020 are stored in 1 KB of address space pointed to by the Vector Base register. Up to 256 exception vectors can be stored in this address space.

MC68020 interrupts

Like the MC68000, the MC68020 has three interrupt lines providing seven levels of interrupt priority, and the status register has a 3-bit field that indicates the current processor priority level. In the Macintosh II, unlike the Macintosh SE or classic Macintosh computers, the interrupt signals from the various devices are not connected directly to the main processor.

The GLUE IC in the Macintosh II receives interrupt requests from the various devices, assigns a priority to each, and asserts one or more interrupt lines to the main processor. When the main processor receives a signal over one or more interrupt lines, it determines the priority of the interrupt (determined by which interrupt lines are asserted) and, if the interrupt priority is higher than the current processor priority (set by the software), the main processor suspends execution of the currently running program.

Like other Macintosh computers, the Macintosh II uses automatic vectoring for interrupts. The automatic-vectoring sequence is as follows:

1. The main processor acknowledges the interrupt by asserting all three function-code signals (FC2 through FC0) to indicate the main processor address space, and by putting an address in the range $FFFF FFF0 through $FFFF FFFF on the address bus.

2. The main processor checks the /AVEC signal, which is permanently asserted (tied low) in the Macintosh II.

3. The main processor generates a vector number based on the level of the interrupt and jumps to the interrupt handler pointed to by that vector. The address of the interrupt handler is calculated by multiplying the vector number by 4 and adding the result to the value in the Vector Base register.

There are several possible originators of interrupts in the Macintosh II, including both VIAs, the SCSI controller, the SCC, the ASC, the programmer's interrupt switch, and each NuBus slot. The SCSI, ASC, and NuBus interrupt lines are all connected to the VIAs, whereas the VIA1, VIA2, SCC, power switch, and interrupt switch interrupts all go to the GLUE IC. The GLUE IC assigns a priority to the interrupt and asserts the interrupt lines to the MC68020.

Table 3-4 shows the interrupt levels associated with various Macintosh II interrupting sources.

Table 3-4   Interrupt levels in the Macintosh II computer

| Interrupt | MC68020 interrupt lines | | | | Automatic |
level	/IPL2	/IPL1	/IPL0	Interrupting source	vector number
0	1	1	1	None	None
1	1	1	0	VIA1	$19
2	1	0	1	VIA2	$1A
3	1	0	0	None	$1B
4	0	1	1	SCC	$1C
5	0	1	0	None	$1D
6	0	0	1	Power switch*	$1E
7	0	0	0	Interrupt switch	$1F

*Only on early production machines. On the current Macintosh II, there is no power-off interrupt; the power-off switch is connected directly to the hardware.

In addition to the interrupt requests from the SCSI controller, ASC, and NuBus, there are several other possible sources of VIA interrupts, including the VIA timers, Apple Desktop Bus transactions, the 60 Hz clock, and the one-second tick from the real-time clock. To determine which device caused a VIA interrupt, the processor must read the VIA's Interrupt Flag register. For details about the Interrupt Flag register and about enabling or disabling any of the VIA interrupt sources, see the section "Processor-Interrupt Registers" in Chapter 4.

The SCSI controller can generate two types of interrupt requests to VIA2: IRQ interrupts—which can be used to indicate error conditions on the SCSI bus—and DRQ interrupts, which the SCSI controller can use to interrupt the processor when the first byte of a block of data is ready to be transferred. Both of these interrupts can be enabled or disabled by setting bits in the VIA2 Interrupt Enable register. For more information about the various interrupt conditions in the NCR 5380 SCSI controller and about software control over those interrupts, see the manual for the NCR 5380.

The ASC can also generate an interrupt request to VIA2. Like the SCSI interrupt requests, this interrupt can be enabled or disabled by setting a bit in the VIA2 Interrupt Enable register.

Each NuBus slot can generate an interrupt request. The GLUE IC performs an OR operation on the six NuBus interrupt lines and sends the result to a VIA2 interrupt request line. Each of the NuBus slot interrupt lines is also connected to a VIA2 data input. When the main processor receives a VIA2 interrupt, it polls the VIA2 Interrupt Flag register to determine the source and, if the interrupt was caused by a NuBus slot, the processor then polls VIA2 Data register A to determine which slot was the source.

The SCC interrupt output is connected directly to the GLUE IC. Sending or receiving serial port data and various handshaking events can cause the SCC to generate an interrupt. See the Zilog 8530 manual for details about the sources of interrupts and the software controls over those interrupts.

In early models of the Macintosh II, the power-switch interrupt is connected to the GLUE IC. That interrupt is a level-6 interrupt and can be inhibited by the MC68020's interrupt priority mask. The power-off interrupt starts the process by which the firmware disconnects power from the Macintosh II. In the current Macintosh II, the power-off switch is connected directly to the power-off hardware and does not generate an interrupt.

The highest-level interrupt is generated by the programmer's interrupt switch (which the user can install, together with the Reset switch, at the rear right side of the Macintosh II main system unit). This switch is connected directly to the GLUE IC. The signal from the programmer's switch generates a level-7 interrupt, which cannot be inhibited by the MC68020's interrupt priority mask.

MC68030 microprocessor

The main processor in the Macintosh SE/30, Macintosh IIx, Macintosh IIcx, Macintosh IIci, and Macintosh IIfx computers is the Motorola MC68030 microprocessor. This section discusses the differences between the MC68030 and the MC68020, which was described in the preceding sections. The MC68030 is described in detail in the *MC68030 Enhanced 32-Bit Microprocessor User's Manual* from Motorola.

MC68030 enhancements

To an application program running in the user state, the MC68030 appears identical to an MC68020: it has sixteen 32-bit data and address registers, five special-purpose control registers, a 32-bit program counter, and a 16-bit status register. Instructions can use data up to 32 bits long. To a system program running in the supervisor state, on the other hand, the MC68030 offers several enhancements, including five additional special-purpose control registers and an additional status register.

The MC68030 has a data cache in addition to the instruction cache found in the MC68020. The MC68030 checks the data cache to determine if the operand required for an instruction is in the cache before performing a read. When the operand is found in the cache, the operation is much faster than it is when the fetch has to be made from external memory.

The MC68030 has an on-chip memory management unit (MMU), which replaces the Address Management Unit (AMU) or the MC68851 Paged Memory Management Unit (PMMU) used with the MC68020 in the Macintosh II. Having the MMU built into the main processor saves one wait state over the use of an external MMU such as that in the Macintosh II. To control the internal MMU, the MC68030 has four instruction types not supported by the MC68020; these instructions are a subset of the instruction set provided by the MC68851 MMU. The MC68030's MMU can be programmed to perform an address translation—such as the 24-bit to 32-bit address translation required by the Macintosh operating system— or to act as a paged memory management unit to support virtual memory.

MC68030 interrupts

The MC68030-based Macintosh computers—Macintosh SE/30, Macintosh IIx, Macintosh IIcx, Macintosh IIci, and Macintosh IIfx—handle interrupts in much the same way as they are handled by the Macintosh II; the sources and levels of interrupts in the MC68030-based computers are similar to those in the Macintosh II computer. As in the current Macintosh II, the power-off switch in an MC68030-based computer is connected directly to hardware and does not generate an interrupt.

Table 3-5 shows the interrupt levels associated with various interrupt sources on the MC68030-based computers.

■ **Table 3-5**   Interrupt levels in Macintosh models with the MC68030 microprocessor

Interrupt level	MC68030 interrupt lines			Interrupting source	Automatic vector number
	/IPL2	/IPL1	/IPL0		
0	1	1	1	None	None
1	1	1	0	VIA1	$19
2	1	0	1	VIA2, RBV*, or OSS†	$1A
3	1	0	0	None	$1B
4	0	1	1	SCC	$1C
5	0	1	0	None	$1D
6	0	0	1	None	$1E
7	0	0	0	Interrupt switch‡	$1F

*In the Macintosh IIci, the interrupt functions are handled by the RBV custom IC.

†In the Macintosh IIfx, the interrupt functions are handled by the OSS custom IC.

‡In the Macintosh IIci and Macintosh IIfx, the parity checking circuits can also initiate a level-7 interrupt.

In addition to the interrupt requests from the SCSI, ASC, and NuBus, there are several other possible sources of VIA interrupts, including the VIA timers, Apple Desktop Bus transactions, the Vertical Blanking signal (VBL), and the one-second tick from the real-time clock. To determine which device caused a VIA interrupt, the processor must read the VIA's Interrupt Flag register. For details about the Interrupt Flag register and about enabling or disabling any of the VIA interrupt sources, see the section "Processor-Interrupt Registers," in Chapter 4.

The SCSI can generate two types of interrupt requests: IRQ interrupts—which can be used to indicate error conditions on the SCSI bus—and DRQ interrupts, which the SCSI can use to interrupt the processor when the first byte of a block of data is ready to be transferred. Both of these interrupts can be enabled or disabled by setting bits in the Interrupt Enable register inside VIA2 (RBV in the Macintosh IIci, OSS in the Macintosh IIfx). For more information about the SCSI controller's various interrupt conditions and about software control over those interrupts, see the reference manual for the NCR 5380.

The ASC can also generate an interrupt request. As for the SCSI interrupt requests, this interrupt can be enabled or disabled by setting a bit in the Interrupt Enable register.

Each NuBus slot can generate an interrupt request. In the Macintosh IIx and Macintosh IIcx computers, the GLUE IC performs an OR operation on all the NuBus interrupt lines and sends the result to an interrupt request line on VIA2. Each of the NuBus slot interrupt lines is also connected to a data input of VIA2. When the main processor receives an interrupt, it polls the Interrupt Flag register in VIA2 to determine the source and, if the interrupt was caused by a NuBus slot, the main processor then polls VIA2 Data register A to determine which slot was the source.

The NuBus slots in the Macintosh IIci and the Macintosh IIfx generate interrupt requests in the same way as the slots on the Macintosh IIx but the hardware that handles them is different. In the Macintosh IIci, the functions of the GLUE are incorporated into the RBV along with VIA2-emulation registers including the Interrupt Flag register. Similarly, in the Macintosh IIfx, the OSS performs both the recording of the interrupts from the individual slots and the OR operation that produces the slot IRQ. When the main processor in one of these machines receives an interrupt, it polls the Interrupt Flag registers in the RBV or the OSS to determine the source.

In the Macintosh SE/30 computer, the processor-direct slot (PDS) connector provides lines for the first three interrupt-request lines to the GLUE IC, so an expansion card can emulate a NuBus card in any of the first three NuBus slots (slots $9, $A, or $B). The video circuitry, which emulates a NuBus card in slot $E, generates an interrupt request to the GLUE IC on the last interrupt-request line (lines 4 and 5 are not used). In addition, the expansion connector is connected directly to the three MC68030 interrupt lines, for use by expansion cards that do not emulate NuBus cards.

The SCC's interrupt output is connected directly to the general-logic IC—the GLUE in the Macintosh IIx and Macintosh IIcx, RBV in the Macintosh IIci, or OSS in the Macintosh IIfx. Sending or receiving serial port data and various handshaking events can cause the SCC to generate an interrupt. See the Zilog 8530 manual for details about the sources of SCC interrupts and the software controls over those interrupts.

The highest-level interrupts are generated by the programmer's interrupt switch. This switch is connected directly to the general-logic IC—the GLUE in the Macintosh IIx and Macintosh IIcx, RBV in the Macintosh IIci, or OSS in the Macintosh IIfx. The programmer's switch generates level-7 interrupts, which cannot be inhibited by the MC68030's interrupt priority mask.

Traps

Traps can be caused by special instructions (the purpose of which is to cause traps), by illegal instructions, and by unimplemented instructions. An illegal instruction is one for which the first word of its bit pattern does not correspond to the bit pattern of any recognized instruction. For example, any instruction beginning with $4AFA is considered an illegal instruction. Unimplemented instructions are any instructions beginning with $A (1010 binary). For the MC68000, unimplemented instructions may also begin with $F (1111). For the MC68020 and MC68030, instructions beginning with $F normally address a coprocessor, but if the coprocessor addressed is not found, the instruction is treated as an unimplemented instruction.

The difference between instructions designated as illegal instructions and those designated as unimplemented instructions is that, whereas Motorola has reserved the right to define new instructions with opcodes that had been previously considered illegal, the unimplemented instructions are reserved for use by programmers as a mechanism for generating exceptions. When an MC68000-family processor reads an unimplemented instruction, it executes the code pointed to by the exception vector that corresponds to that instruction number.

Traps caused by unimplemented instructions are used to extend the number and power of instructions that can be executed by a machine-language program in an MC68000-family-based system. That is, these traps look like machine-language instructions, but actually cause the execution of software routines. Such traps are extremely important in Macintosh programming: all Macintosh Toolbox routines are implemented as 1010 instructions.

Exceptions and exception processing are described in detail in Motorola's *MC68020 32-Bit Microprocessor User's Manual* and *MC68030 Enhanced 32-Bit Microprocessor User's Manual.* The trap mechanism used by Macintosh computers is discussed in Chapter 2 of the *Technical Introduction to the Macintosh Family.*

Auxiliary processors

The Macintosh Portable, Macintosh SE/30, and Macintosh II–family computers have auxiliary processors that perform specialized processing functions that supplement the functions of the main processor. The auxiliary processors used in Macintosh computers include the Power Manager IC in the Macintosh Portable, the memory management unit (AMU or PMMU) in the Macintosh II, and the floating point unit (FPU) in the Macintosh II family and in the Macintosh SE/30. This section describes all these auxiliary processors. Table 3-6 summarizes the components discussed in this section.

■ **Table 3-6** Auxiliary processors used in Macintosh computers

Computer	Auxiliary processors
Classic Macintosh	None
Macintosh SE	None
Macintosh SE/30	MC68882*
Macintosh Portable	Power Manager IC
Macintosh II	MC68881* and AMU or PMMU
Macintosh IIx	MC68882*
Macintosh IIcx	MC68882*
Macintosh IIci	MC68882*
Macintosh IIfx	MC68882*, IOPs, and SCSI DMA

*The MC68881 and MC68882 are coprocessors.

Memory management units in the Macintosh II computer

The Macintosh II computer is designed to run both the Macintosh Operating System and the A/UX operating system. Because the Macintosh Operating System uses 24-bit addresses, the 24-bit addresses used by the software must be translated into the 32-bit addresses decoded by the GLUE IC. The standard memory management IC provided with the Macintosh II, the AMU, performs this function. Because system software version 7.0 and the A/UX operating system support virtual memory, the logical addresses used by these operating systems must be translated into physical addresses for the GLUE IC. The optional memory management IC, the PMMU, provides this capability.

◆ *Note:* In the Macintosh models that have an MC68030 processor, address translation and other memory management functions of the AMU and PMMU are handled by the processor's on-chip memory management unit.

Address Management Unit (AMU)

The Address Management Unit (AMU) is an Apple custom IC that takes the 24-bit addresses used by the Macintosh Operating System (in 24-bit mode) and translates them into 32-bit addresses for use by the GLUE IC. In order to do this, the AMU ignores the top 8 bits of the address from the main processor and translates bits LA24 through LA20 into bits A31 through A20. This address translation is discussed in detail in the section "Address Map for the Macintosh SE/30 Computer," later in this chapter.

Software uses a special operating-system call to switch the AMU to 32-bit mode. In 32-bit mode, the AMU performs no address translation; the full 32-bit address from the main processor is sent to the GLUE IC. When running under versions of the Macintosh Operating System prior to version 7.0, the only reason to switch to 32-bit mode would be to address a NuBus card that needs more than 1 MB of address space. See the chapter on the operating system utilities in *Inside Macintosh* for information about switching between 24-bit and 32-bit modes.

Paged Memory Management Unit (PMMU)

The AMU can be replaced by the optional Paged Memory Management Unit (PMMU), which is a Motorola MC68851 IC. The MC68851 plugs directly into the same socket used by the AMU on the main logic board.

The PMMU performs address translation, either from 24-bit to 32-bit addresses (as done by the AMU) or from logical to physical addresses, as required by the A/UX operating system and other virtual memory operating systems. System software version 7.0 can operate in 32-bit mode on the Macintosh II with either the AMU or the PMMU, but requires the PMMU in order to provide virtual memory.

In virtual memory operations, the PMMU checks each logical memory address it receives from the main processor (which can be any address in the 4 GB address space of the MC68020) to see if the data corresponding to that location is currently stored in physical memory. If it is, the PMMU translates the logical address into the physical address of that data and passes the address on to the GLUE IC for decoding. If the data is not in physical memory, the PMMU suspends the operation of the main processor and checks the page table to locate the data that corresponds to that address—the data might be on a hard disk, for example. The main processor then loads the necessary data into physical memory and processing continues. To the software, it appears that the data was addressed directly; the software never knows that the data was read from disk.

The MC68851 PMMU can act as a coprocessor to the MC68020. As a coprocessor, the PMMU appears to extend the capabilities of the main processor: it adds several instructions and a variety of control, status, and address-pointer registers to the features of the MC68020. The operating system programs and controls the PMMU through the MC68851 instruction set. In addition to its function as an address translator and paged memory controller, the PMMU provides provisions for protecting the memory space of one application from other applications.

When the MC68020 executes an MC68851 instruction, it uses the function code signals and address bits A19 through A13 to indicate that the PMMU is being addressed. The GLUE decodes the address and asserts the device select to the PMMU, after which the PMMU communicates directly with the main processor. In the Macintosh II, the PMMU operates on the same 15.6672 MHz clock as the main processor.

All control of the PMMU is handled by the operating system; unless you are writing an operating system, you should have no need to address the PMMU directly. The MC68851 is described in detail in the *MC68851 Paged Memory Management Unit User's Manual* from Motorola.

MC68881 and MC68882 mathematics coprocessors

The MC68881 and MC68882 mathematics coprocessors implement in hardware the Institute of Electrical and Electronics Engineers Standard 754: *IEEE Standard for Binary Floating-Point Arithmetic*. These ICs also support several functions not included in the IEEE standard, including trigonometric and transcendental functions. The MC68881 is used in the Macintosh II; the MC68882 is used in the other Macintosh II models and in the Macintosh SE/30. The MC68882 is a more efficient version of the MC68881; the MC68882 can run any program written to use the MC68881. In this book, the term *floating-point unit* (or *FPU*) is used to refer to either of these ICs.

When the main processor executes a coprocessor instruction (an instruction that begins with $F), it uses address bits A19 through A16 plus some control lines (called the *function code signals*) to indicate that a coprocessor is being addressed, and puts a coprocessor identification number on address bits A15 through A13. The GLUE decodes the address and asserts the device select to the FPU, after which the FPU communicates directly with the main processor without further intervention of the memory management unit or GLUE IC.

To a programmer, the FPU appears to extend the capabilities of the main processor: it adds several instructions and data types, eight 96-bit floating-point data registers, a 32-bit control register, a 32-bit status register, and a 32-bit instruction address register to the features of the main processor.

In the Macintosh SE/30, Macintosh II, Macintosh IIx, and Macintosh IIcx, the FPU operates on the same 16 MHz clock as does the main processor. Similarly, in the Macintosh IIci, the FPU uses the main processor's 25 MHz clock.

In the Macintosh IIfx, the FPU also runs at the full clock speed, 40 MHz, even though it is on the slow side of the bus buffers; the speed-change PAL detects accesses to the FPU and switches the slow-side clock as needed. Because the FPU clock is not synchronized to the main processor's clock, instructions and data sometimes take one extra clock cycle to reach the FPU.

All FPU data transfers are performed by the main processor at the request of the FPU. Therefore, memory management, bus arbitration, and error handling behave as if the FPU instructions were executed by the main processor. Similarly, traps are handled by the main processor at the request of the FPU.

Because the Standard Apple Numerics Environment (SANE®) package takes advantage of the FPU when it is available, the FPU automatically speeds up processing by 5 to 50 times for any program that uses the SANE routines. If you access the FPU directly by using MC68881/MC68882 instructions in your assembly-language programs or by using an MC68881/MC68882 compiler option, you can achieve a speed gain of from 40 to 700 times. However, a program written to use the FPU directly will not run on Macintosh models that don't have an FPU (classic Macintosh and Macintosh SE).

The FPU is described in detail in the *MC68881/MC68882 Floating-Point Coprocessor User's Manual* from Motorola. Information about the use of the FPU in applications is found in the *Apple Numerics Manual,* second edition.

Power Manager IC in the Macintosh Portable computer

The power management circuitry in the Macintosh Portable computer includes a Mitsubishi M50753 microprocessor. The M50753 is an 8-bit microprocessor that contains 6 KB of ROM, 192 bytes of RAM, three timers, and an 8-bit analog-to-digital converter. The ROM contains microcode, written by Apple Computer, Inc., that allows the M50753 to implement the following functions through its 36 general-purpose I/O lines:

- It puts the Macintosh Portable into sleep state when it receives the Sleep command from the Power Manager firmware.

- It returns the Macintosh Portable to the operating state when it detects a keystroke, when the wake-up timer matches the real-time clock, or when it receives a Ring Detect signal from an internal modem.

- It acts as the real-time clock for the Macintosh Portable, keeping track of the date and time, and saving system-setup parameters in its on-chip RAM.

- It acts as an Apple Desktop Bus (ADB) transceiver.

- It generates a signal that controls the contrast of the flat-panel display.

- It monitors the temperature inside the case and asserts a signal warning of high temperatures when necessary.

- It monitors the voltage level of the battery and asserts a signal warning of low voltage when necessary.

The Power Manager IC communicates with the main processor through the VIA over an 8-bit parallel data bus. The Macintosh Portable VIA is described in Chapter 4.

Although the M50753 is a microprocessor, it does not function as a true coprocessor in that it does not extend the instruction set of the MC68HC000. Instead, instructions are sent as data from the main processor to the VIA, and from the VIA to the M50753 over the VIA's programmable output lines.

IOPs in the Macintosh IIfx computer

The **I/O Processor** (IOP) integrated circuits are Apple custom ICs designed to provide processing support for I/O controllers. There are two IOPs in the Macintosh IIfx computer: one for the SWIM and ADB and one for the SCC. The IOPs sit between the main processor and the I/O controllers.

The features of the IOP include

- a built-in microprocessor

- a 16-bit timer

- two DMA controllers, one for each floppy disk channel or serial I/O channel

- address and data buses for RAM shared by the IOP and the host processor

- two I/O ports for controlling the ADB

This section describes the operation of the IOPs themselves. For information about the I/O interfaces controlled by the IOPs, please refer to the appropriate chapters: Chapter 8 for the ADB; Chapter 9, the section "FDHD Drive Interface," for the SWIM; and Chapter 10 for the SCC.

IOP interface

The main processor communicates with the IOPs through a set of control registers in each IOP that are mapped into the main processor's I/O address space. The main processor can interrupt an IOP using a bit in one of the control registers; an IOP can interrupt the main processor using an interrupt line.

Data transfers between each IOP and the main processor use an external static RAM that is time-shared between the two processors. Each IOP contains a 16-bit auto-incrementing address register and an 8-bit data port that the host processor uses for access to the RAM that is shared with that IOP. Each IOP's shared RAM can be up to 60 KB in size.

◆ *Note:* The RAM used with each IOP is not part of main memory and does not reside in the processor's address space. It is dedicated to the IOP and addressed by means of registers in the IOP.

In normal operation, the two DMA channels of each IOP handle data transfers between the I/O device and the IOP's RAM, thus reducing the work load on the IOP's processor. Each IOP DMA channel has its own Transfer Count register, RAM Address pointer, and I/O Address pointer.

The DMA cycles used by the IOPS are taken from the main processor's portion of the IOP's RAM cycle, thereby reducing the transfer rate between the main processor and the shared RAM. For example, when the SCC is receiving AppleTalk data at 230.4 KHz, the SCC IOP's DMA activity reduces the host transfer rate—that is, the transfer rate for data between the IOP's RAM and the main processor—from 2 MB/second to 1.97 MB/second. The worst-case host RAM transfer rate, assuming the maximum number of IOP DMA requests, is 1 MB/second.

IOP for the SCC

In the Macintosh IIfx, an IOP controls the SCC and handles all communication between the SCC and the main processor. An SCC driver written for a non-IOP system controls the SCC directly. In the Macintosh IIfx, an access by the MC68030 directly to the SCC register space causes a bus error.

△ **Developer tip** If you have problems making your SCC driver software work with the SCC IOP, contact Apple's Developer Technical Support department at the address given in the Preface. △

IOP for the SWIM and ADB

The IOP that controls the SWIM also controls the Apple Desktop Bus. This arrangement eliminates the need for the separate ADB transceiver used in earlier Macintosh models. The IOP also improves the machine's performance by handling the ADB operations, relieving the main processor of those tasks. For information about the operation of the ADB, please refer to Chapter 8.

General logic circuits

General logic functions in the Macintosh computers are handled by one or more ICs in each computer. These ICs are either programmable logic array chips (PALs), custom ICs, or a combination of both. This section describes the general logic circuits used in each Macintosh family member. Table 3-7 summarizes the components discussed in this section.

■ **Table 3-7**   General logic circuits used in Macintosh computers

Computer	General logic circuits
Classic Macintosh	PALs
Macintosh SE	BBU and GLU
Macintosh SE/30	GLUE and video PALs
Macintosh Portable	CPU GLU, Misc. GLU, and VDI
Macintosh II	GLUE
Macintosh IIx	GLUE
Macintosh IIcx	GLUE
Macintosh IIci	MDU and RBV
Macintosh IIfx	PALs, FMC, and OSS

PALs in the classic Macintosh computers

PALs are programmable logic array chips used to implement a variety of decoders and finite-state machines. Most of the PALs used in the earlier Macintosh computers are replaced in the Macintosh SE and Macintosh II computers by custom integrated circuit chips. In the earlier Macintosh computers, PALs perform the following functions:

■ They decode addresses to determine which device is being requested by the main processor.

■ They assert the device-select signal to the appropriate device.

■ They generate the RAM address strobes (/RAS and /CAS) and control the multiplexers (MUXs) that feed addresses to RAM.

■ They control the timing and sequence of video functions, read data directly from RAM, and direct the Video Shift register to send the data as a bit stream to the video board.

- They generate the vertical and horizontal blanking interrupt signals used to coordinate the video circuitry.
- They control the timing and sequence of sound generation, including reading data from RAM, converting it to a PWM signal, and sending it to the sound IC.
- They read disk-speed control data from RAM for 400 KB floppy disk drives, convert it to a PWM signal, and send it to the disk drives.
- They generate the 7.8336 MHz clock used by the main processor.
- They generate the 3.672 MHz clock used by the SCC to control communication rates.

General logic circuits in the Macintosh SE computer

There are two general logic ICs in the Macintosh SE: the BBU and the GLU.

BBU custom IC

The BBU is an Apple custom integrated circuit that performs a variety of logic functions in the Macintosh SE computer, as follows:

- It decodes addresses to determine which device is being requested by the main processor.
- It asserts the device-select signal to the appropriate device.
- It generates the RAM address strobes (/RAS and /CAS) and controls the multiplexers (MUXs) that feed addresses to RAM.
- It controls all video functions, including reading data directly from RAM and shifting it out as a bit stream to the video board.
- It generates the vertical and horizontal blanking interrupt signals used to coordinate the video circuitry.
- It controls all sound functions, including reading data from RAM and sending it to the sound IC.
- It provides a speed-control signal for single-sided floppy disk drives.
- It generates the 7.8336 MHz clock used by the main processor.
- It generates the 3.672 MHz clock used by the SCC to control communication rates and by the microprocessor in the ADB transceiver.
- It monitors data transfers and generates the Bus Error signal to halt the main processor if a transfer fails to complete successfully.
- It handles hardware handshaking with the SCSI controller, making SCSI transfers faster and more secure than in the Macintosh Plus computer.

- It asserts the /IPL0 interrupt to the main processor when it receives an interrupt request from the VIA or SCSI.

- It deasserts the /IPL0 interrupt to the main processor when the /IPL1 interrupt is asserted by the SCC.

GLU custom IC

The GLU is a programmable logic array IC in the Macintosh SE used to perform some logic functions not included in the BBU. The GLU performs the following tasks:

- It generates disk drive enable signals that choose between the upper and lower internal floppy disk drives.

- It controls whether interrupt requests from the SCSI are passed on to the BBU.

- It inverts the write data (WR) signal to the floppy disk drives.

- It buffers the 15.6672 MHz master clock used by the BBU and the IWM and provided to the processor-direct slot.

- ◆ *Note:* Do not confuse the GLU IC in the Macintosh SE with the GLUE IC in the Macintosh SE/30 and Macintosh II–family computers. The GLUE IC is described in the following section.

GLUE in the Macintosh SE/30, Macintosh II, and Macintosh IIx computers

The GLUE is an Apple custom integrated circuit that performs a variety of logic functions in the Macintosh SE/30, Macintosh II, and Macintosh IIx computers, as follows:

- It decodes addresses to determine which device or auxiliary processor is being requested by the main processor.

- It asserts the device-select signal to the appropriate device.

- It sends acknowledge signals to the main processor that indicate that a device is present and that specify the width of that device's data bus.

- It generates the RAM address strobes (/RAS and /CAS) and controls the multiplexers (MUXs) that feed addresses to RAM.

- It generates the signals that refresh dynamic RAM.

- It generates the 15.6672 MHz clock used by the main processor.

- It generates the 3.672 MHz clock used by the SCC to control communication rates and by the microprocessor in the ADB transceiver.

- It generates the 783.36 kHz clock (the E clock) used to synchronize communications between the VIAs and the main processor.

- It monitors data transfers and generates the Bus Error signal to halt the main processor if a transfer fails to complete successfully.

- It handles hardware handshaking with the SCSI controller, making SCSI transfers faster and more secure than in the Macintosh Plus.

- It performs an OR operation on the six slot interrupt signals and sends the result to VIA2, which generates the processor interrupt.

- It monitors the interrupt lines from the VIAs, the SCC, the power switch (early Macintosh II only), and the nonmaskable interrupt switch, assigns a priority to each interrupt, and asserts the appropriate interrupt lines to the main processor. If the GLUE IC receives more than one interrupt at the same time, it passes only the highest priority interrupt on to the main processor.

◆ *Note:* The name *GLUE* is a play on words, based on the acronym *GLU* for *general logic unit* and the fact that the GLUE IC "glues together" the other chips by providing handshaking between the I/O devices and the main processor. Do not confuse the GLUE IC with the GLU IC in the Macintosh SE, described in the preceding section.

Video PALs in the Macintosh SE/30 computer

The video PALs in the Macintosh SE/30 perform the video functions handled by the BBU in the Macintosh SE, plus the video functions performed by a NuBus video card in a Macintosh II–family computer. The Macintosh SE/30 video logic circuits perform the following functions:

- They generate the vertical and horizontal blanking interrupt signals used to coordinate the video circuitry.

- They implement the frame buffer controller (FBC) functions of a NuBus video card.

- They implement the declaration ROM functions of a NuBus video card.

Unlike the video circuits on a NuBus video card, the Macintosh SE/30 video circuits do not implement a color look-up table (CLUT).

For information about the operation of the video circuits in the Macintosh SE/30, please refer to the section "Video Display in the Macintosh SE/30 Computer" in Chapter 12. For information about NuBus video cards, see the section "Expansion Card Video" in Chapter 12.

General logic circuits in the Macintosh IIci computer

The Macintosh IIci computer has two custom ICs containing general logic circuits: the Memory Decode Unit (MDU) and the RAM-Based Video controller (RBV).

Memory Decode Unit (MDU)

The MDU is an Apple custom IC that performs many of the same functions as the GLUE in the Macintosh II, along with several other functions that are specific to the Macintosh IIci.

MDU functions specific to the Macintosh IIci

- The MDU provides separate memory addresses and strobes for the two banks of RAM (bank A and bank B), making it possible for the main processor and the video circuits to use RAM at the same time.

- It provides address decoding and device-select signals for new devices: the RBV, the video CLUT DAC, and the NuChip30 (NuBus controller).

The MDU provides the addressing for the video buffer, located in bank A, but it has nothing further to do with the generation of the video signals. For more information about video generation, refer to the sections "RAM-Based Video Controller (RBV)," later in this chapter, and "Features of the Built-in Video Circuits," in Chapter 12.

MDU functions similar to the GLUE

In addition to the functions listed above, the MDU also performs many of the same functions as the GLUE in the Macintosh II; those functions are listed here.

- It decodes addresses to determine which device or auxiliary processor is being requested by the main processor.

- It asserts the device-select signal to the requested device.

- It sends acknowledge signals to the main processor that indicate that a device is present and that specify the width of that device's data bus.

- It generates the signals that refresh dynamic RAM.

- It generates the 25 MHz clock used by the main processor.

- It generates the 783.36 kHz clock (the E clock) used to synchronize communications between the VIAs and the main processor.

- It monitors data transfers and generates the Bus Error signal to halt the main processor if a transfer fails to complete successfully.

- It handles hardware handshaking with the SCSI controller, making SCSI transfers faster and more secure than in the Macintosh Plus.

RAM-Based Video controller (RBV)

The RBV is an Apple custom integrated circuit that performs three different sets of functions in the Macintosh IIci: it performs some functions of the GLUE in the Macintosh II and Macintosh IIx, it contains the registers and other circuitry implemented in the second VIA in other models in the Macintosh II family, and it controls the built-in video circuitry.

RBV functions similar to the GLUE

The RBV performs some of the functions of the GLUE in the Macintosh II.

- It generates the 15.6672 MHz clock used by bus-error and RAM-refresh circuitry.

- It generates the 3.672 MHz clock used by the microprocessor in the ADB transceiver and used by the SCC to set communication rates.

- It performs an OR operation on the three slot interrupt signals and sends the result to a register in the VIA portion of the RBV.

- It monitors interrupt signals in its internal registers as well as interrupts from the VIA1, the SCC, and the nonmaskable interrupt switch; assigns a priority to each interrupt; and asserts the appropriate interrupt lines to the main processor. If the RBV IC receives more than one interrupt at the same time, it passes only the highest priority interrupt on to the main processor.

VIA registers in the RBV

The VIA portion of the RBV contains eight 8-bit registers that are used for several inputs and outputs in addition to video control signals and interrupts. The main processor communicates with these registers over an 8-bit bidirectional data bus that is separate from the 32-bit RAM data bus used by the video portion. Having separate data buses for the two parts of the RBV makes it possible for the main processor to read and write to the VIA registers while video activity is taking place on the other data bus.

The VIA registers in the RBV control the following functions:

- The RBV decodes the interrupts from the NuBus slots.

- It decodes NuBus errors and enables or disables NuBus access to main RAM.

- It provides two SCSI interrupts and the interrupt from the ASC (Apple Sound Chip).

- It detects the signal indicating that an external speaker or amplifier is plugged in.

- It controls the interrupt from the parity circuit.

- It controls flushing and disabling of the optional cache RAM card.

- It contains a signal used to turn off the computer.

For more information about the functions of the VIA registers in the RBV, please refer to the section "VIA2 Functions in the Macintosh IIci Computer" in Chapter 4.

Video functions of the RBV

For the built-in video circuits, the RBV performs the following functions:

- The RBV reads the ID lines from the video monitor to determine the type of monitor.

- It provides horizontal and vertical synchronizing signals with the appropriate timing for the video monitor.

- It requests video data by sending appropriate signals to the MDU, which generates the addresses for the screen buffer.

- It reads video data from the screen buffer in bursts of 8 longwords at a time and stores it in an internal FIFO buffer.

- It contains a bit-order arranger and shift register that take data from the FIFO buffer and arrange it into single pixels of 1, 2, 4, or 8 bits each, which it transmits to the CLUT DAC for conversion into video signals.

The RBV does not control the addressing of the video buffer; that function belongs to the MDU, which is described in the section "Memory Decode Unit (MDU)," earlier in this chapter.

For detailed information about the video signals and the operation of the CLUT DAC, please refer to Chapter 12.

General logic circuits in the Macintosh Portable computer

The general logic circuits in the Macintosh Portable are implemented as three Apple custom integrated circuits: the CPU GLU (CPU General Logic Unit), the Miscellaneous GLU, and the VDI (Video Display Interface).

CPU GLU custom IC

The CPU GLU integrated circuit performs the following functions:

- It decodes addresses to determine which device is being requested by the main processor and asserts the device-select signal to the appropriate device.

- It generates the 15.6672 MHz clock used by the main processor and generates clock signals for the SWIM, ASC, and VIA chips.

- It monitors data transfers and generates the Bus Error signal to halt the main processor if a transfer fails to complete successfully.

- It handles hardware handshaking with the SCSI controller.

- It asserts the /IPL0 interrupt to the main processor when it receives an interrupt request from the VIA.

- It deasserts the /IPL0 interrupt to the main processor when the /IPL1 interrupt is asserted by the ASC or SCC chips.

Miscellaneous GLU custom IC

The Miscellaneous GLU integrated circuit performs the following functions:

- It decodes addresses to determine which specific system RAM IC is being addressed.

- It generates disk-drive enable signals that choose between the upper and lower internal floppy disk drives.

- It provides an interface between channel A of the SCC and the internal modem connector.

- It generates the 60 Hz clock signal for the Power Manager IC.

- It generates clock and control signals to the keyboard processor.

VDI custom IC

The video logic circuits in the Macintosh Portable computer include an Apple custom integrated circuit, the VDI (Video Display Interface). The VDI IC controls all video functions, including reading data directly from system RAM and placing it in video RAM. It also generates the video data signals that are sent to the built-in flat-panel display and that are provided on the external video connector.

For more information about Macintosh Portable video circuits, see the section "Displays on the Macintosh Portable" in Chapter 12.

General logic circuits in the Macintosh IIfx computer

The general logic circuits used in the Macintosh IIfx computer are the OSS (Operating System Support) IC and FMC (Fast Memory Controller) IC.

Operating System Support (OSS)

The OSS IC is an Apple custom integrated circuit that provides operating-system services; hence the name. It performs many of the functions of the second VIA and the GLUE IC in the standard Macintosh II.

The features of the OSS include

- software-programmable interrupt priority levels
- address decoding for all I/O devices
- generating acknowledge signals (DSACKx) for appropriate address spaces
- bus time-out logic

The OSS provides an interface to the 65C22 VIA for compatibility with earlier Macintosh models.

The OSS controls all interrupts and provides a means for assigning interrupt priorities. The system's Start Manager sets up the interrupt priority levels by writing to control registers in the OSS and initializing the interrupt vectors to match the priorities.

The Shutdown Manager uses a control register in the OSS to turn off the machine.

The OSS performs the address decoding that maps the I/O devices into the main processor's address space. Figure 3-9, in the section "Address Map for the Macintosh IIfx Computer," later in this chapter, shows the address map for the Macintosh IIfx and identifies the address spaces allocated to the various I/O devices. The OSS generates acknowledge signals (DSACK0, DSACK1) for the I/O spaces shown shaded.

Fast Memory Controller (FMC)

The Fast Memory Controller (FMC) is an Apple custom integrated circuit designed to operate with the MC68030 and support cache RAM, main RAM, and ROM.

The features of the FMC include

- support for RAM cache using high-speed static RAM
- burst access to both RAM and ROM
- multiplexed address for dynamic RAM
- programmable RAM and ROM access times
- fast page mode and buffered write operations

The FMC supports fast cache memory in conjunction with separate static RAM for tags and for data. The cache memory stores both instructions and data.

For a description of how the RAM operates in the Macintosh IIfx, please refer to Chapter 5.

Address maps

All addressing, whether of memory, internal devices, interfaces to external devices, or expansion cards, is performed in Macintosh computers using the system address bus. Therefore, the address space available to the main processor—often referred to as the *memory space*—must be divided between memory and other devices. This section describes the way in which address space is assigned to different devices in each Macintosh family member.

Each Macintosh computer uses two address maps: the *ROM overlay address map* and the *normal address map*. The ROM overlay address map, used when the machine is turned on or reset, maps addresses in the lowest address space to locations in ROM rather than to RAM. This address map is used because, whenever an MC68000-family microprocessor is reset, it looks at the first location in memory (address $0) for a pointer to the Reset handler, and the normal contents of RAM might not be available during startup or reset. The normal address map is used during all normal processing.

Within the address space for a particular device, addresses are further decoded to access specific hardware within that device or to control specific features of that device. For example, the SCSI controller in the Macintosh Plus contains eight registers that can be selected by signals on address lines A6 through A4. Notice, however, that the address space allocated to each device is considerably larger than the minimum needed to access all of the features of the device. For example, signals on address lines A18 through A10, A8, A7, and A3 through A1 have no significance for the SCSI in the Macintosh Plus computer, so there are thousands of possible addresses that will access the same register in the SCSI controller.

Similarly, the contents of RAM and ROM are repeated throughout unused address space assigned to memory. For example, the address space from $00 0000 through $3F FFFF in the Macintosh Plus is allocated to RAM in the normal address map, providing enough addresses for 4 MB of RAM. If there is only 1 MB of RAM installed in the system, it appears to software as if there are four identical RAM "images" in memory; that is, the same data is fetched by a read to any of the addresses $00 1000, $10 1000, $20 1000, or $30 1000.

◆ *Address maps:* The address maps in this chapter include dark shading, light shading, and unshaded areas. Dark-shaded areas indicate addresses that are assigned to devices in the basic configuration of that computer. Light-shaded areas indicate addresses that are decoded but might not be used; some of these areas (as noted) are reserved for use by Apple Computer, Inc. Unshaded areas are not decoded.

Note that the address maps are not to scale; you must look at the actual addresses to determine the relative sizes of address ranges in the address maps.

△ **Developer tip** The addresses used for device selects differ from one member of the Macintosh family to another, and sometimes between different versions of the same machine. Therefore, a program that addresses Macintosh hardware directly will not be compatible with all current members of the Macintosh family, and probably won't run on new versions of the Macintosh. To avoid compatibility problems, always use the Macintosh Toolbox calls, system traps, and global variables listed and described in *Inside Macintosh* to communicate with hardware in Macintosh computers. △

Address map for the classic Macintosh computers

The MC68000 processor can directly access 16 MB of address space, which is divided into several blocks allocated to RAM, ROM, and the various I/O devices.

△ **Important**   The addresses shown in this section for device selects apply only to the Macintosh Plus and earlier Macintosh computers. Most of these addresses are different for other Macintosh computers.   △

The ROM overlay address map, used when the machine is turned on or reset, maps addresses from $00 0000 to $01 FFFF to locations in ROM rather than to RAM. The startup or Reset handler software switches from the ROM overlay address map to the normal address map by setting low the Overlay signal from the VIA.

Figure 3-1 shows the Macintosh 512K computer address maps. Figure 3-2 shows the Macintosh Plus computer address maps.

The PALs respond to any address in the range $00 0000 through $DF FFFF with a /DTACK signal and to any address in the range $E0 0000 through $FF FFFF with a /VPA signal. The /DTACK signal is used to acknowledge a transaction with a device that uses asynchronous communication, and the /VPA signal is used to acknowledge a transaction with a device that requires synchronous communication with the main processor.

At system startup, the operating system reads an address in the range $F0 0000 through $F7 FFFF (labeled *Phase read* in Figures 3-1 and 3-2) to determine whether the computer's high-frequency timing signals are correctly in phase. When the timing signals are not in phase, RAM accesses are not timed correctly, causing an unstable video display, RAM errors, and VIA errors. A word-wide access to any SCC address causes a phase shift in the processor clock, and is used by the operating system to correct the phase when necessary.

■ **Figure 3-1** Address map for the Macintosh 512K computer

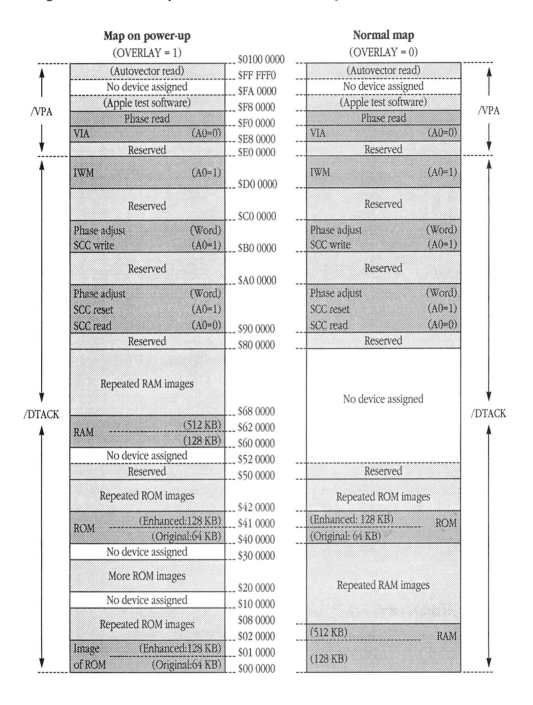

Figure 3-2 Address map for the Macintosh Plus computer

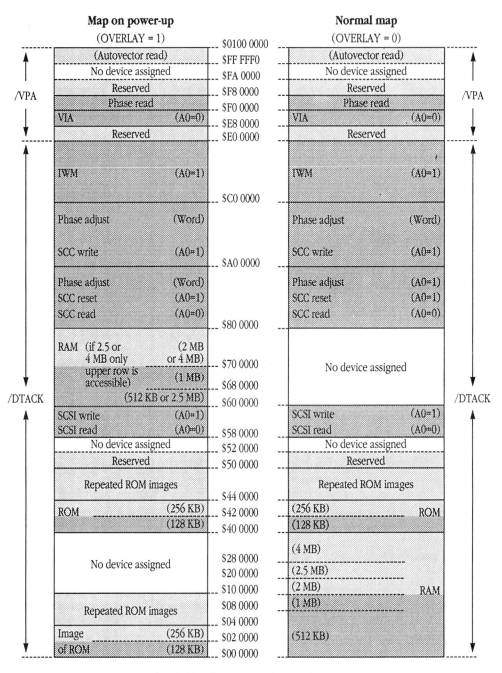

Note: 128 KB ROMs are disabled (no device assigned) everywhere A17=1.
Note: All unused RAM space is occupied by repeated RAM images.

When the main processor receives an interrupt, it performs a read operation with all address lines set to 1 except A3 through A1; lines A3 through A1 reflect the level of the interrupt. When the PALs receive an address in the range $FF FFF0 to $FF FFFF, they assert /VPA, which causes the main processor to jump to the location in memory containing the appropriate interrupt handler. When an address in this range is read, no device is activated and any data read from the data bus is ignored. Interrupts are discussed in the section "MC68000 Interrupts," earlier in this chapter.

◆ *Note:* The PALs always generate either /DTACK or /VPA in response to a memory access, even to an address space with no device. Of course, writing to an unoccupied address doesn't change anything, and reading fetches meaningless data from an undriven bus. Because every access is guaranteed by the design of the hardware to be successfully completed, the bus error signal (/BERR) is not used in the classic Macintosh.

Address map for the Macintosh SE computer

The MC68000 processor used by the Macintosh SE can directly access 16 MB of address space, which is divided into several blocks allocated to RAM, ROM, and the various I/O devices.

△ **Important**   The addresses shown in this section for Macintosh SE device selects apply only to the Macintosh SE, and only for the version of ROM current at the time of publication of this book. Most of these addresses are different for other Macintosh computers. Therefore, it is highly recommended that you use the Macintosh Toolbox calls, system traps, and global variables described and listed in *Inside Macintosh* to access all hardware in the Macintosh SE. △

Figure 3-3 shows the address map for the Macintosh SE computer.

The ROM overlay address map, used when the machine is turned on or reset, maps addresses from $00 0000 to $03 FFFF to locations in ROM rather than to RAM. The BBU switches from the ROM overlay address map to the normal address map the first time an access is made in the range $40 0000 through $5F FFFF.

The BBU responds to any address in the range $00 0000 through $DF FFFF with a /DTACK signal and to any address in the range $E0 0000 through $FF FFFF with a /VPA signal. The /DTACK signal is used to acknowledge a transaction with a device that uses asynchronous communication, and the /VPA signal is used to acknowledge a transaction with a device that requires synchronous communication with the main processor.

When the main processor receives an interrupt, it performs a read operation with all address lines set to 1 except A3 through A1; lines A3 through A1 reflect the level of the interrupt. When the BBU receives an address in the range $FF FFF0 to $FF FFFF, it asserts /VPA, which causes the main processor to transfer program control to the location in memory containing the appropriate interrupt handler. When an address in this range is read, no device is activated and any data read from the data bus is ignored. Interrupts are discussed in the section "MC68000 Interrupts," earlier in this chapter.

With two exceptions—noted in the next paragraph—the BBU always generates either /DTACK or /VPA in response to a memory access, even to an address space with no device. Of course, writing to an unoccupied address doesn't change anything, and reading fetches meaningless data from an undriven bus.

There are two cases in which the BBU does not issue a /DTACK signal promptly in response to an address in the range $00 0000 through $DF FFFF:

- During a SCSI access in pseudo-DMA mode, the BBU does not assert /DTACK until it receives a SCSI DRQ interrupt, indicating that the SCSI transaction is complete.

- During an access to the PDS, the BBU tri-states its /DTACK output if the /EXT.DTACK pin on the PDS is pulled low. This procedure allows expansion cards to delay the BBU's /DTACK or to generate their own.

If any access has not terminated within 265 ms, the BBU asserts the bus error signal /BERR.

■ **Figure 3-3** Address map for the Macintosh SE computer

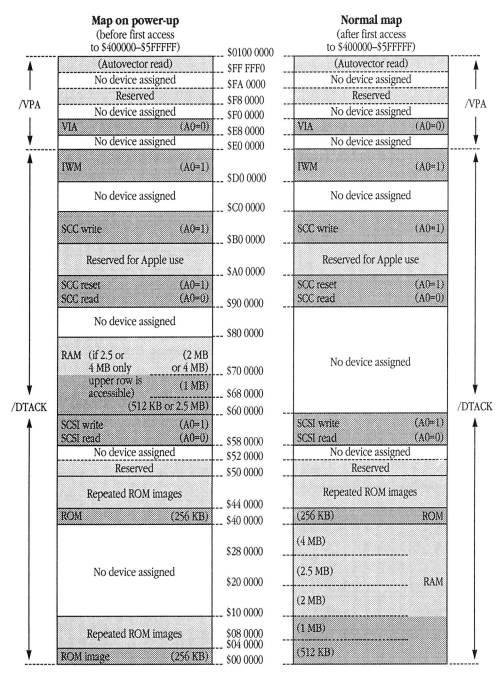

Note: All unused RAM space is occupied by repeated RAM images.

Chapter 3   Processors and General Logic   **127**

Address map for the Macintosh Portable computer

The MC68HC000 processor used by the Macintosh Portable computer can directly access 16 MB of address space, which is divided into several blocks allocated to RAM, ROM, and the various I/O devices.

△ **Important**   The addresses of device selects shown in this section apply only to the Macintosh Portable, and only for the version of ROM current at the time of publication of this book. Most of these addresses are different for other Macintosh computers. Therefore, it is highly recommended that you use the Macintosh Toolbox calls, system traps, and global variables described and listed in *Inside Macintosh* to access all hardware in the Macintosh Portable computer. △

The ROM overlay address map, used when the Macintosh Portable is turned on or reset, maps addresses from $00 0000 to $0F 0000 to locations in ROM rather than to RAM. The CPU GLU switches from the ROM overlay address map to the normal address map the first time an access is made in the range $90 0000 through $9F FFFF.

Figure 3-4 shows the address map for the Macintosh Portable computer.

The address space from $E0 0000 through $EF FFFF is not decoded by the general logic circuits in the Macintosh Portable. This address space is reserved for internal use by processor-direct slot expansion cards.

The CPU GLU IC responds to any address in the range $FF 0000 through $FF FFFF with a /VPA signal and to any other address with a /DTACK signal. The /DTACK signal is used to acknowledge a transaction with a device that uses asynchronous communication, and the /VPA signal is used to acknowledge a transaction with a device that requires synchronous communication with the main processor.

Notice that, unlike the classic Macintosh and Macintosh SE, the Macintosh Portable computer uses the /DTACK signal for communication with the VIA. Although the VIA is a synchronous device, the main processor in the Macintosh Portable can communicate asynchronously with the VIA. The CPU GLU IC makes this possible by providing a VIA clock signal in place of the E clock generated by the main processor, and by synchronizing the VIA clock with the VIA device-select signal, which is also generated by the CPU GLU.

■ **Figure 3-4** Address map for the Macintosh Portable computer

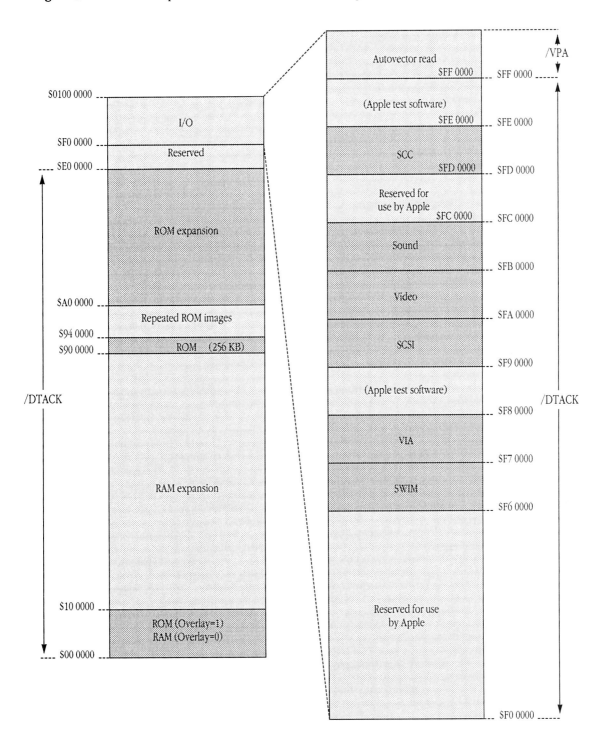

When the main processor receives an interrupt, it performs a read operation with all address lines set to 1 except A3 through A1; lines A3 through A1 reflect the level of the interrupt. When the CPU GLU receives an address in the range $FF 0000 to $FF FFFF, it asserts /VPA, which causes the main processor to jump to the location in memory containing the appropriate interrupt handler. Interrupts are discussed in the section "MC68000 Interrupts," earlier in this chapter.

With three exceptions—noted in the next paragraph—the CPU GLU always generates the /DTACK signal in response to a memory access, even a memory access to an address space with no device. Of course, writing to an unoccupied address doesn't change anything, and reading fetches meaningless data from an undriven bus.

There are three cases in which the CPU GLU does not immediately issue a /DTACK signal in response to an address:

- If the address is in the range $FF 0000 through $FF FFFF, the CPU GLU asserts the /VPA signal rather than the /DTACK signal.

- During a pseudo-DMA-mode SCSI access, the CPU GLU does not assert /DTACK until it receives a SCSI DRQ signal, indicating that the SCSI transaction is complete.

- The CPU GLU tri-states its /DTACK output if the /EXT.DTACK pin on the processor-direct slot is pulled low. This procedure allows expansion cards to delay the CAD GLU's /DTACK or to generate their own.

Address map for the Macintosh SE/30 computer

The MC68030 processor used by the Macintosh SE/30 can directly access 4 GB of address space, which is divided into several blocks allocated to RAM, ROM, expansion cards, and the various I/O devices.

△ **Important**   The addresses shown in this section for device selects apply only to the Macintosh SE/30, and only for the version of ROM current at the time of publication of this book. Most of these addresses are different for other Macintosh computers, and addresses will almost certainly change for future versions of the Macintosh SE/30. Therefore, it is highly recommended that you use the Macintosh Toolbox calls, system traps, and global variables described and listed in *Inside Macintosh* to access all hardware in the Macintosh SE/30. △

All addresses on the main logic board of the Macintosh SE/30 are 32 bits long. When operating in 24-bit mode, the Macintosh Operating System uses only the lower 24 bits of each address. In this case, the memory management unit in the MC68030 is programmed to ignore the high-order 8 bits from each address coming from the main processor and to translate the resulting 24-bit address into a 32-bit address for decoding by the GLUE. The firmware can switch the MMU to 32-bit mode, in which the full 32-bit address from the main processor is passed on to the GLUE. The 32-bit mode is used under versions of the Macintosh Operating System prior to version 7.0 only when necessary to access more than a megabyte of address space on an expansion card.

Other operating systems, such as system software version 7.0 and A/UX, can use disks and other storage devices as virtual memory. These operating systems program the MMU to translate between logical and physical addresses to support virtual memory.

The ROM overlay address map, used when the Macintosh SE/30 is turned on or reset, maps addresses from $0000 0000 to $3FFF FFFF to locations in ROM rather than to RAM. The RAM cannot be addressed at all when the ROM overlay address map is being used. The startup or Reset handler software switches from the ROM overlay address map to the normal address map by setting low the Overlay signal from VIA1.

Figure 3-5 shows the translation from the 24-bit address map to the normal 32-bit address map. Figure 3-6 shows the Macintosh SE/30 32-bit address map. Notice that the 24-bit address spaces map into a small portion of the 32-bit address space.

For your convenience, the 24-to-32-bit address translation is also shown in Table 3-8.

■ **Table 3-8**   Macintosh 24-bit to 32-bit address translation

24-bit address range		32-bit address range	
$00 0000	$7F FFFF	$0000 0000	$007F FFFF
$80 0000	$8F FFFF	$4000 0000	$400F FFFF
$90 0000	$9F FFFF	$F900 0000	$F90F FFFF
$A0 0000	$AF FFFF	$FA00 0000	$FA0F FFFF
$B0 0000	$BF FFFF	$FB00 0000	$FB0F FFFF
$C0 0000	$CF FFFF	$FC00 0000	$FC0F FFFF
$D0 0000	$DF FFFF	$FD00 0000	$FD0F FFFF
$E0 0000	$EF FFFF	$FE00 0000	$FE0F FFFF
$F0 0000	$FF FFFF	$5000 0000	$500F FFFF

■ **Figure 3-5** Translation from 24-bit address map to 32-bit address map

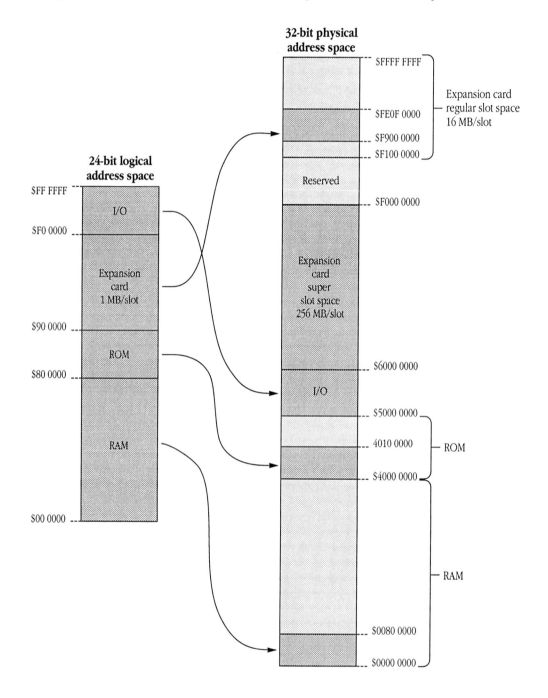

■ **Figure 3-6** Address map for the Macintosh SE/30 computer

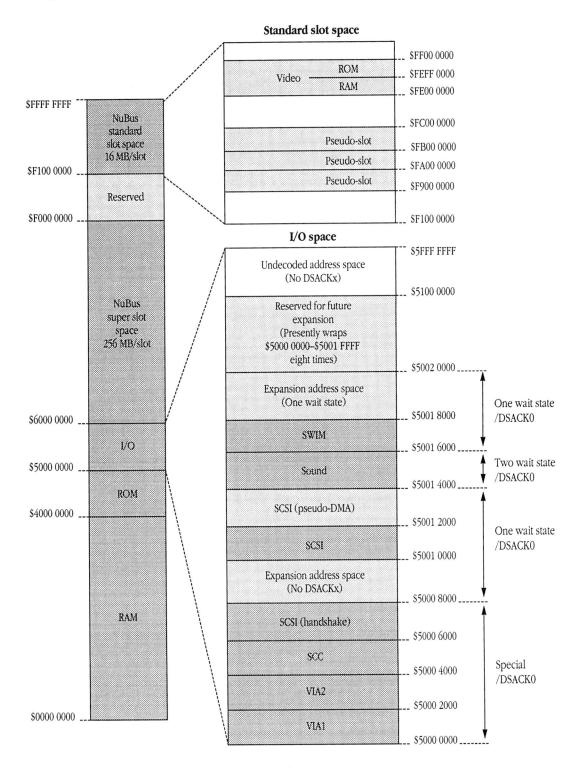

The GLUE responds to any I/O device address with a /DSACK0 signal. The /DSACK0 and /DSACK1 signals are used to acknowledge a transaction with a device and to indicate to the MC68030 the size of a device's data bus. As shown in Figure 3-6, the GLUE inserts one wait state for SWIM accesses and for SCSI accesses that do not involve hardware handshaking. The GLUE inserts two wait states for reads from the ASC and one for writes to the ASC. Accesses to the SCC and VIAs, and SCSI accesses that involve handshaking, require special control of the /DSACK0 signal, as follows:

- The SCC requires 2.2 μs between accesses for its internal lines to stabilize; in the case of back-to-back accesses to the SCC, the GLUE holds off the second access for that amount of time.

- The VIAs are MC6800-compatible peripheral devices that require synchronous communication with the MC68030.

- SCSI handshaking requires that the /DSACK0 signal be held off until a transaction is complete.

Hardware handshaking for SCSI transactions is described in the section "SCSI Data Transfers" in Chapter 11. For more information on the requirements of the SCC and VIA, see the manufacturers' specifications for those chips. For more information on the /DSACKx signals, see Motorola's documentation for the MC68030.

◆ *Note:* In the Macintosh SE/30, each access of RAM or ROM involves one wait state. This is in contrast to the Macintosh II, in which there are two wait states: one imposed by the AMU or the PMMU memory address translation, and the other imposed by the RAM or ROM access.

In the Macintosh SE/30, accesses to 32-bit addresses in the range $6000 0000 through $FFFF FFFF (except for $F0xx xxxx) can be used to communicate with an expansion card. The processor-direct slot provides three interrupt-request lines that go to VIA2 and are interpreted by the firmware as coming from the first three NuBus slots. In order for an expansion card to appear to the firmware as if it occupied one of these NuBus slots, it must respond to one of the address ranges shown in Table 3-9.

- **Table 3-9** Macintosh SE/30 expansion card address ranges

24-bit address	32-bit address	Equivalent NuBus slot
$90 0000–$9F FFFF	$F900 0000–$F9FF FFFF	$9
$A0 0000–$AF FFFF	$FA00 0000–$FAFF FFFF	$A
$B0 0000–$BF FFFF	$FB00 0000–$FBFF FFFF	$B

The translation from 24-bit addresses used by early versions of the Macintosh operating system to the 32-bit addresses shown in Table 3-9 is shown in Table 3-8. Notice that only the first 1 MB of each address range is available when the operating system is in 24-bit mode; you must switch to 32-bit mode to access the full 16 MB range of addresses reserved for each pseudo-slot.

▲ **Warning**   An access to any address range to which no device is assigned results in a bus error. ▲

The declaration ROM for a pseudo-slot expansion card must be located at the upper address limit of the 1 MB 24-bit address space in order for the Slot Manager firmware to recognize the card as a NuBus card. For more information about designing pseudo-slot expansion cards, see *Designing Cards and Drivers for the Macintosh Family,* second edition.

⚠ **Developer tip**   There is no requirement that an expansion card in the Macintosh SE/30 computer emulate a NuBus card. All the control, address, and data lines necessary for a card to perform direct memory addressing or to act as a coprocessor to the MC68030 are available at the processor-direct slot. ⚠

Address map for the Macintosh II, Macintosh IIx, and Macintosh IIcx computers

The MC68020 and MC68030 processors used by Macintosh II–family computers can directly access 4 GB of address space, which is divided into several blocks allocated to RAM, ROM, NuBus slots, and the various I/O devices.

The Macintosh II, Macintosh IIx, and Macintosh IIcx have the same address map, which is descibed in this section. Later sections describe the address maps for the Macintosh IIci and the Macintosh IIfx, which are different.

△ **Important**	The addresses shown in this section for device selects apply only to the Macintosh II, Macintosh IIx, and Macintosh IIcx computers, and only for the version of ROM current at the time of publication of this book. Most of these addresses are different for other Macintosh computers, including other members of the Macintosh II family. Therefore, it is highly recommended that you use the Macintosh Toolbox calls, system traps, and global variables described and listed in *Inside Macintosh* to access all hardware in Macintosh II–family computers. △

All addresses on the main logic board of Macintosh II–family computers are 32 bits long. When operating in 24-bit mode, the Macintosh Operating System uses only the lower 24 bits of each address. In this case, the MMU ignores the high-order 8 bits from each address coming from the main processor and translates the resulting 24-bit address into a 32-bit address for decoding by the GLUE. The firmware can switch the MMU to 32-bit mode, in which the full 32-bit address from the main processor is passed on to the GLUE. The 32-bit mode is used under versions of the Macintosh Operating System prior to system software version 7.0 only when necessary to access more than a megabyte of address space on a NuBus card.

Other operating systems, such as system software version 7.0 and A/UX, can use disks and other storage devices as virtual memory. System software version 7.0 and the A/UX operating system use the PMMU in the Macintosh II or the MC68030's on-chip MMU to translate between logical and physical addresses to support virtual memory. The PMMU and on-chip MMU can also be programmed to perform the same 24-to-32 bit address translation as done by the AMU in the Macintosh II.

The ROM overlay address map, used when the machine is turned on or reset, maps addresses from $0000 0000 to $3FFF FFFF to locations in ROM rather than to RAM. RAM cannot be addressed at all when the ROM overlay address map is being used. The startup or Reset handler software switches from the ROM overlay address map to the normal address map by setting low the Overlay signal from VIA1.

Figure 3-5 and Table 3-8 show the translation from the 24-bit address map to the normal 32-bit address map. Figure 3-7 shows the 32-bit address map for the Macintosh II, Macintosh IIx, and Macintosh IIcx. Notice that the 24-bit address spaces map into a small portion of the 32-bit address space. Notice, too, that whereas the 24-bit address map provides only 1 MB of address space for each NuBus slot, the 32-bit address map provides a 16 MB address space plus a 256 MB address space for each slot.

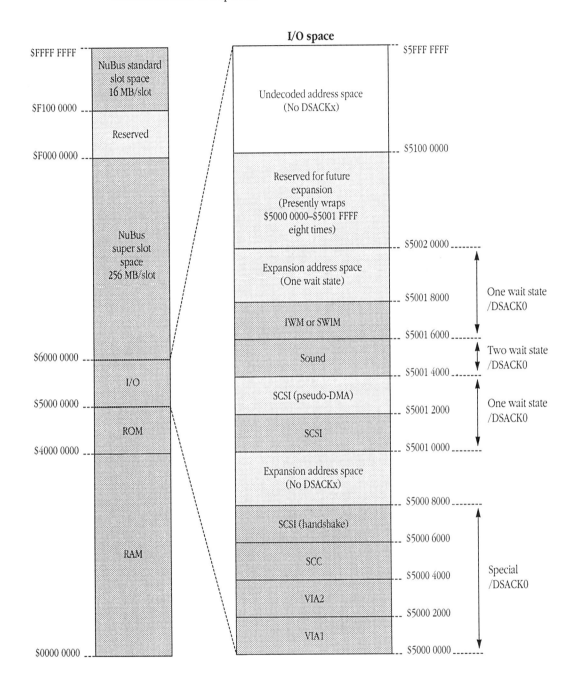

The GLUE responds to any I/O device address with a /DSACK0 signal. The /DSACK0 and /DSACK1 signals are used to acknowledge a transaction with a device and to indicate to the MC68020 or MC68030 the size of a device's data bus. As shown in Figure 3-7, the GLUE inserts one wait state for IWM accesses and for SCSI accesses that do not involve hardware handshaking. The GLUE inserts two wait states for reads from the ASC and one for writes to the ASC. Accesses to the SCC and VIAs, and SCSI accesses that involve handshaking, require special control of the /DSACK0 signal, as follows:

- The SCC requires 2.2 μs between accesses for its internal lines to stabilize; in the case of back-to-back accesses to the SCC, the GLUE holds off the second access for that amount of time.

- The VIAs are MC6800-compatible peripheral devices that require synchronous communication with the MC68020 or MC68030.

- SCSI handshaking requires that the /DSACK0 signal be held off until a transaction is complete.

Hardware handshaking for SCSI transactions is described in the section "SCSI Data Transfers" in Chapter 11. For more information on the requirements of the SCC and VIA, see the manufacturers' specifications for those chips. For more information on the /DSACKx signals, see Motorola's documentation for the MC68020 and MC68030.

◆ *Note:* Each access of RAM or ROM in the Macintosh II involves two wait states. One wait state is imposed by the AMU or the PMMU memory address translation, and the other is imposed by the RAM or ROM access. Because the MMU in the MC68030 requires no wait states, only one wait state is required for each ROM or RAM access in the Macintosh IIx and Macintosh IIcx.

Accesses to 32-bit addresses in the range $6000 0000 through $FFFF FFFF (except for $F0xx xxxx) initiate a NuBus transaction. Each NuBus slot is allocated two slot spaces: 16 MB within the range $F100 0000 through $FFFF FFFF (called the **standard slot space**), and 256 MB within the range $6000 0000 through $EFFF FFFF (called the **super slot space**).

A 32-bit address of the form $Fsxx xxxx accesses the standard slot space for NuBus slot *s*. A 32-bit address of the form $sxxx xxxx accesses the super slot space for NuBus slot *s*. Notice that the Macintosh II and Macintosh IIx have connectors for slots $9 through $E only, and the Macintosh IIcx has connectors for slots $9 through $B only.

▲ **Warning**   An attempt to read or write to an address in the range $F000 0000
through $F0FF FFFF from the main processor results in a bus error; this
address range is used by NuBus cards to address the I/O devices and
ROM on the main logic board. ▲

A 24-bit address of the form $sx xxxx, where *s* is a number in the range $9 through $E, is
translated to a 32-bit address of the form $Fs0x xxxx and accesses the card in the slot *s*.
Notice that only the lower 1 MB of each card's standard slot space can be addressed in
24-bit mode.

A card in a NuBus slot can address any other NuBus card, or it can address the main logic
board. If an address from $F000 0000 to $F07F FFFF is placed on NuBus by a NuBus card,
the NuBus controller (NuChip, NuChip30, or BIU30) translates it to an address in the range
$5000 0000 to $507F FFFF and makes an access to one of the main logic board I/O
devices. An address from $F080 0000 through $F0FF FFFF on NuBus causes the NuBus
controller to access ROM in the range $4080 0000 to $40FF FFFF. An address from $0000
0000 to $3FFF FFFF on NuBus results in a main logic board RAM access to the same
address. These translations from NuBus addresses to main logic board addresses are
summarized in Table 3-10.

■ **Table 3-10** Translations from NuBus addresses to main logic board addresses

NuBus address	Logic board address	Used to access
$0000 0000 to $3FFF FFFF	$0000 0000 to $3FFF FFFF	RAM
$6000 0000 to $8FFF FFFF	$6000 0000 to $8FFF FFFF	Presently unused super slot space
$9000 0000 to $EFFF FFFF	$9000 0000 to $EFFF FFFF	Super slot space, slots $9 to $E
$F000 0000 to $F070 FFFF*	$5000 0000 to $507F FFFF	Main logic board I/O devices
$F080 0000 to $F0FF FFFF*	$4080 0000 to $40FF FFFF	ROM
$F100 0000 to $F8FF FFFF	$F100 0000 to $F8FF FFFF	Presently unused standard slot space
$F900 0000 to $FEFF FFFF	$Fs00 0000 to $FsFF FFFF	Standard slot space, slots $9 to $E
$FF00 0000 to $FFFF FFFF	$FF00 0000 to $FFFF FFFF	Presently unused standard slot space

Note: *s* is a number in the range $9–$E.

*A NuBus card can use an address in this range to access the main logic board. If the main processor attempts to access addresses in this range, it immediately generates a bus error (/BERR) exception and no NuBus transaction takes place.

See *Designing Cards and Drivers for the Macintosh Family,* second edition, for more information about NuBus cards and the use of NuBus address space.

Address map for the Macintosh IIci computer

The MC68030 processor used by the Macintosh IIci computer can directly access 4 GB of address space, which is divided into several blocks allocated to RAM, ROM, NuBus slots, and the various I/O devices.

In most respects, the address map for the Macintosh IIci, shown in Figure 3-8, is identical to that for the Macintosh II, as described in the previous section.

△ **Important**   The addresses shown in this section apply only to the Macintosh IIci computer, and only for the version of ROM current at the time of publication of this book. It is highly recommended that you use the Macintosh Toolbox calls, system traps, and global variables listed in *Inside Macintosh* to access all hardware in Macintosh II–family computers. △

Address map for the Macintosh IIfx computer

The MC68030 processor used by the Macintosh IIfx computer can directly access 4 GB of address space, which is divided into several blocks allocated to RAM, ROM, NuBus slots, and the various I/O devices.

In most respects, the address map for the Macintosh IIfx computer, shown in Figure 3-9, is identical to that for the Macintosh II, as decribed in the earlier section "Address Map for the Macintosh II, Macintosh IIx, and Macintosh IIcx Computers."

△ **Important**   The addresses shown in this section for device-select signals apply only to the Macintosh IIfx computer, and only for the version of ROM current at the time of publication of this book. Most of these addresses are different for other Macintosh computers, including other members of the Macintosh II family. Therefore, it is highly recommended that you use the Macintosh Toolbox calls, system traps, and global variables listed in *Inside Macintosh* to access all hardware in Macintosh II–family computers. △

Figure 3-8 Address map for the Macintosh IIci computer

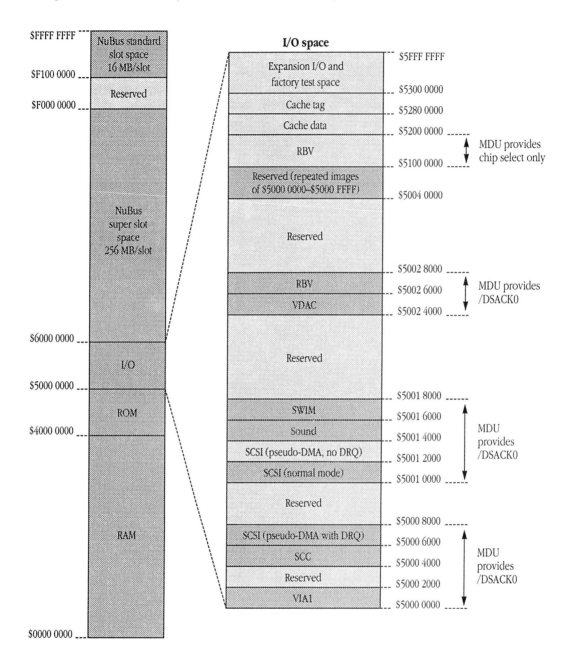

■ **Figure 3-9** Address map for the Macintosh IIfx computer

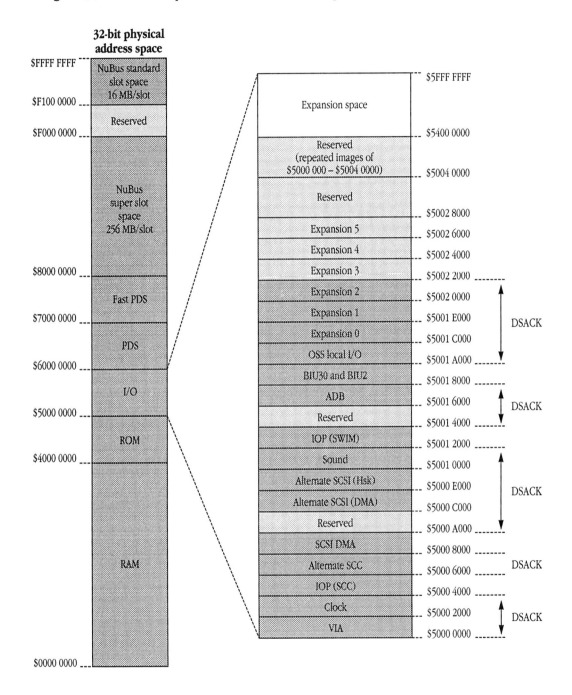

Real-time clock (RTC)

The Macintosh real-time clock (RTC) is a custom IC that is interfaced to the main logic board by a VIA. The real-time clock used in the Macintosh SE, Macintosh SE/30, and Macintosh II–family computers is an upgraded version of the custom IC used in the Macintosh Plus and earlier Macintosh computers. In the Macintosh Portable computer, the Power Manager IC performs the functions of the real-time clock.

The RTC contains a 4-byte counter incremented once each second. Each time the counter is incremented, the RTC sends an interrupt request signal to the VIA and (if this interrupt is enabled), the VIA sends an interrupt to the main processor. The RTC also contains 256 bytes of RAM (20 bytes in the Macintosh 512K and Macintosh 128K, 128 bytes in the Macintosh Portable), called *parameter RAM,* that is powered by a battery when the Macintosh is turned off (because system RAM in the Macintosh Portable is never switched off, a separate battery is not needed for the RTC in the Macintosh Portable). Parameter RAM contains important data that needs to be preserved even when the system power is not available. The Macintosh Operating System maintains in low memory a copy of parameter RAM that you can access.

△ **Developer tip** Although you can read from and write to the RTC as described in this section, it is much easier to use the copy of parameter RAM and the date and time kept in memory by the Macintosh Operating System. See the Operating System Utilities chapter in *Inside Macintosh* for information on these memory locations. In addition, note that the user can set or read the date, time, and most of the parameters in parameter RAM by using the Control Panel desk accessory. △

The RTC in all Macintosh computers except the Macintosh Portable is accessed by using bits 0 through 2 of Data register B of VIA1 (the only VIA in the Macintosh SE and classic Macintosh computers), as shown in Table 3-11.

■ **Table 3-11** RTC bits in Macintosh VIA1 Data register B

Bit	Direction	Software name	Description
2	Output	rtcEnb	0 = RTC is enabled
1	Output	rtcClk	RTC's data-clock line
0	In or out	rtcData	RTC's serial data line

These 3 bits constitute a simple serial interface. The rtcData bit is used as a bidirectional serial data line to send command and data bytes back and forth. The rtcClk bit is a data-clock line, driven by the processor, that regulates the transmission of the data and command bits. Software sets the rtcClk bit high or low by writing to register B of the VIA. The rtcEnb bit is the serial enable line, which signals the RTC that the processor is about to send it serial commands and data.

In the Macintosh Portable, the Power Manager IC performs the functions of the RTC. Communication with the Power Manager IC in the Macintosh Portable is through Data register A of the VIA; all 8 bits are used as a parallel data bus to the Power Manager IC.

Sending commands to the RTC

Programs can read or change the information in parameter RAM and read or set the date and time. See the Operating System Utilities chapter in *Inside Macintosh* for information about these functions.

The one-second interrupt

The RTC generates a VIA interrupt once each second (if this interrupt is enabled). This interrupt can be enabled or disabled by writing to bit 0 of the VIA's Interrupt Enable register (vBase+vIER). When you're reading the Interrupt Enable register, a 1 bit indicates that the interrupt is enabled, and a 0 means it's disabled. Writing $01 to the Interrupt Enable register disables the RTC's one-second interrupt (without affecting any other interrupts), whereas writing $81 enables it.

See the section "Processor-Interrupt Registers," in Chapter 4, for more information about enabling and disabling VIA interrupts.

△ **Developer tip**   The one-second interrupt is used by the Macintosh operating system to update the date and time and to blink the Apple icon on the menu bar when the alarm of the Alarm Clock desk accessory goes off. Because the timing of this interrupt is constant and does not depend on the type of processor or system clock speed, your program can use it to time any event that should be independent of the type of Macintosh on which your program is running. See *Inside Macintosh* for more information about writing your own interrupt handlers.

An even better way for applications to be independent of the different Macintosh models is to use the Time Manager in the system software. See the chapter on the Time Manager in *Inside Macintosh*. △

▲ **Warning**   When you write to bit 0 of the VIA's Interrupt Enable register, be sure that you don't change any of the other bits. ▲

Chapter 4 **Versatile Interface Adapter (VIA) ICs**

Macintosh computers use Versatile Interface Adapter (VIA) integrated circuits to provide a variety of control and interface functions. The Macintosh Plus, Macintosh SE, Macintosh Portable, and earlier Macintosh computers each have one VIA; the Macintosh SE/30, Macintosh II, Macintosh IIx, and Macintosh IIcx each have two.

In the Macintosh IIci and the Macintosh IIfx, each of which has one VIA, many functions handled by the VIAs in other models are incorporated into custom ICs: the RBV in the Macintosh IIci and the OSS, BIU30, and IOPs in the Macintosh IIfx. The custom ICs include registers that emulate the operation of the data and control registers of a VIA. The custom ICs are described in Chapter 3, but their VIA-emulation registers are described in this chapter.

Control ICs

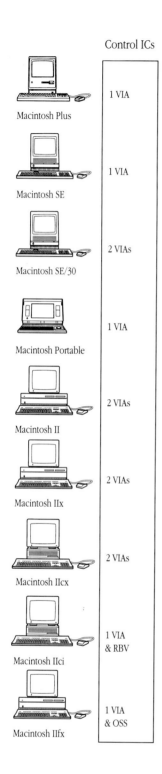

Macintosh Plus — 1 VIA

Macintosh SE — 1 VIA

Macintosh SE/30 — 2 VIAs

Macintosh Portable — 1 VIA

Macintosh II — 2 VIAs

Macintosh IIx — 2 VIAs

Macintosh IIcx — 2 VIAs

Macintosh IIci — 1 VIA & RBV

Macintosh IIfx — 1 VIA & OSS

The classic Macintosh computers use a Rockwell or VTI 6522 Versatile Interface Adapter integrated circuit. Other Macintosh computers use an Apple custom version of that IC. The Apple custom VIA is fully software compatible with the standard Rockwell or VTI 6522 VIA. The Macintosh SE/30 and Macintosh II family use two Apple custom VIAs called *VIA1* and *VIA2*. VIA1 performs functions similar to those handled by the VIA in the Macintosh SE or classic Macintosh. VIA2 handles the functions that are new in the Macintosh SE/30 or Macintosh II–family computers.

In the Macintosh IIci, an Apple custom IC, the RBV, includes registers that emulate the registers in the second VIA on other members of the Macintosh II family. This chapter describes the VIA-emulation registers of the RBV along with the functions of VIA2; for information about the other functions of the RBV, please refer to the sections "RAM-Based Video Controller (RBV)" in Chapter 3 and "Features of the Built-in Video Circuits" in Chapter 12.

In the Macintosh IIfx, Apple custom ICs—the OSS, the BIU30, and the IOPs—perform many functions that are performed by the VIAs on other members of the Macintosh II family. This chapter describes those functions along with the functions of the corresponding VIAs; for information about the other functions of the custom ICs, please refer to the sections "Operating System Support (OSS)" and "IOPs in the Macintosh IIfx Computer" in Chapter 3.

The VIA integrated circuit is designed to communicate synchronously with the main processor. In the Macintosh SE and classic Macintosh computers, communications between the main processor and the VIAs are timed by the E clock, a 783.36 kHz clock generated by the main processor. In the Macintosh SE/30, Macintosh Portable, and Macintosh II–family computers, communications with the VIAs are synchronized by the general logic circuits, which generate both the clock signal to the VIAs and the VIA device-enable signals.

In the classic Macintosh and Macintosh SE computers, the MC68000 has to wait for the phase of the relatively slow E clock signal to coincide with a normal processor-access cycle before it can access the VIA. In the Macintosh SE/30, Macintosh Portable, and Macintosh II–family computers, on the other hand, the general logic circuits synchronize the VIA clock signal with the accesses of the main processor so that the main processor can make VIA accesses without any delay. As a result, a VIA access for these computers takes an average of 0.5 μs as compared to 1.0 μs for the Macintosh SE and classic Macintosh. The general logic circuits maintain an average frequency for the E clock of 783.36 kHz, which is the same frequency as that used in the classic Macintosh and Macintosh SE computers.

△ **Developer tip** This chapter describes all the functions of each VIA used in a Macintosh computer. Many of these functions are of interest to programmers; for example, the VIAs can be used to enable or disable certain interrupts.

The information in this chapter will help you understand how the Macintosh Toolbox calls work, why some features are not available on every member of the Macintosh family, and why some functions differ between Macintosh family members.

Sometimes a function controlled by a VIA in one Macintosh computer is controlled by a different IC in other Macintosh family members; for example, sound volume is controlled by the VIA in the Macintosh Plus, but by the ASC in the Macintosh II. For this reason, it is never advisable to address the VIA directly; rather, you should use the Macintosh Toolbox calls described in *Inside Macintosh* whenever you want to control hardware. In any case, never use absolute addresses in your code; use instead the global variables and offsets provided here. △

Functions performed by the VIAs

As implied by its name, the VIA is a versatile IC, capable of performing a variety of functions. Some of the functions performed by the VIAs are consistent for the entire Macintosh family; other functions differ from computer to computer. This section summarizes the functions performed by the VIAs (or by VIA emulation in custom ICs) in each Macintosh computer. The sections that follow describe those functions in more detail.

VIA functions in the classic Macintosh computers

The VIA in a classic Macintosh computer performs the following functions:

- It provides the interface between the keyboard and the main logic board.

- It provides part of the interface between the mouse and the main logic board.

- It provides the interface between the RTC (real-time clock) IC and the main logic board.

- It monitors the vertical blanking interrupt request (/VSYNC) from the general logic circuits, and interrupts the main processor as appropriate. This signal provides a 60.15 Hz interrupt, used by a variety of firmware and software.

- It monitors the one-second interrupt request from the RTC, and interrupts the main processor as appropriate.

- It controls sound volume.

- It toggles sound on and off.

- It selects which of the two sound/disk-speed buffers is used.

- It selects which of the two screen buffers is used.

- It monitors the screen's horizontal retrace signal (H4).

- It controls whether the PALs decode addresses according to the ROM overlay address map or the normal address map. (ROM overlay is described in the section "Power Up, System Startup, and Power Down," in Chapter 6.)

- It enables software to monitor the SCC IC's Wait/Request output (/W/REQ) so that the software can detect activity on the serial port when interrupts are disabled.

- It provides the state-control line SEL to the floppy disk drives. Among other functions, in the Macintosh Plus this line selects which of the two heads is to be used in a double-sided floppy disk drive.

VIA functions in the Macintosh SE computer

The VIA in the Macintosh SE computer performs the following functions:

- It provides the interface between the Apple Desktop Bus transceiver and the main logic board.

- It provides the interface between the RTC (real-time clock) IC and the main logic board.

- It monitors the vertical blanking interrupt request (/VSYNC) from the general logic circuits, and interrupts the main processor as appropriate. This signal provides a 60.15 Hz interrupt, used by a variety of firmware and software.

- It monitors the one-second interrupt request from the RTC, and interrupts the main processor as appropriate.

- It controls sound volume.

- It toggles sound on and off.

- It controls whether SCC port A is used for synchronous or asynchronous I/O.

- It selects which of the two internal floppy disk drives is used.

- It provides the state-control line SEL to the floppy disk drives. Among other functions, this line selects which of the two heads is to be used in a double-sided floppy disk drive.

- It selects which of the two screen buffers is used.

- It enables software to monitor the SCC's Wait/Request output (/W/REQ) so that the software can detect activity on the serial port when interrupts are disabled.

- It controls whether the interrupt signal from the SCSI controller (SCSI.IRQ) is masked or is passed on to the main processor.

VIA functions in the Macintosh Portable computer

The VIA in the Macintosh Portable computer performs the following functions:

- It provides the interface between the Power Manager IC and the rest of the system. Among other things, the Power Manager IC performs the functions of the Apple Desktop Bus transceiver and the real-time clock in the Macintosh Portable.

- It monitors the 60.15 Hz interrupt request from the Power Manager IC (C.60HZ), and interrupts the main processor as appropriate.

- It monitors the one-second interrupt request from the Power Manager IC, and interrupts the main processor as appropriate.

- It controls whether SCC port A is used for synchronous or asynchronous I/O.

- It selects which of the two internal floppy disk drives is used.

- It monitors whether the external sound jack has a plug inserted in it. The Sound Manager can read a bit in the VIA to determine whether the mono internal speaker or the stereo external sound jack is being used.

- It provides the state-control line SEL to the floppy disk drives. Among other functions, this line selects which of the two heads is to be used in a double-sided floppy disk drive.

- It provides a test signal (VIA.TEST) that forces the Power Manager IC to turn on all power supplies.

- It enables software to monitor the SCC's Wait/Request output (/W/REQ) so that the software can detect activity on the serial port when interrupts are disabled.

- It monitors interrupt requests from the Power Manager IC (/PMINT) and the SCSI controller (SCSI.IRQ) and interrupts the main processor as appropriate.

VIA functions in the Macintosh SE/30 and Macintosh II–family computers

In Macintosh models that have two VIAs, VIA1 performs many of the functions of the VIA in one-VIA machines, while VIA2 performs functions that are not found on one-VIA machines.

◆ *Note:* In the Macintosh IIci and the Macintosh IIfx, custom ICs contain registers that emulate VIA registers. The functions of the VIA-emulation registers are listed below, by model.

Functions of VIA1

Many of the functions of VIA1 are the same for different Macintosh models. The following sections start by listing the VIA1 functions in the Macintosh II, Macintosh IIx, and Macintosh IIcx computers because those functions are shared by all the models in the group. Subsequent sections list additional functions found on individual machines.

Functions of VIA1 in the Macintosh II, Macintosh IIx, and Macintosh IIcx computers

In the Macintosh II, Macintosh IIx, and Macintosh IIcx computers, VIA1 performs the following functions:

- It controls whether the GLUE decodes addresses according to the ROM overlay address map or the normal address map. (In the Macintosh IIci, the MDU performs ROM overlay automatically. ROM overlay is described in the section "Power Up, System Startup, and Power Down," in Chapter 6.)

- It provides the interface between the Apple Desktop Bus transceiver and the rest of the system.

- It provides the interface between the RTC (real-time clock) IC and the rest of the system.

- It monitors the 60.15 Hz interrupt request (/VBLK) from VIA2 and interrupts the main processor as appropriate. This 60.15 Hz interrupt is used by a variety of firmware and software.

- It monitors the one-second interrupt request from the RTC (RTC.1HZ) and interrupts the main processor as appropriate.

- It controls whether SCC port A is used for synchronous or asynchronous I/O.

- It provides the state-control line SEL to the floppy disk drives. Among other functions, this line selects which of the two heads is to be used in a double-sided floppy disk drive.

- It enables software to monitor the SCC's Wait/Request output (/W/REQ) so that the software can detect activity on the serial port when interrupts are disabled.

Functions of VIA1 in the Macintosh SE/30 computer

In the Macintosh SE/30, VIA1 performs all the functions listed above; in addition, VIA1 also performs the following functions:

- It enables or disables an interrupt request from the video logic circuits to VIA2.

- It selects which of the two screen buffers is used.

Functions of VIA1 in the Macintosh IIci computer

In the Macintosh IIci, VIA1 performs all the functions listed above for the Macintosh II, Macintosh IIx, and Macintosh IIcx; in addition, VIA1 also performs the following functions:

- It controls the parity-enable signal and monitors the parity-error interrupt.

- Four of the inputs to VIA1 are permanently wired high or low to define a value, CPU.ID, that the ROM reads to determine which model Macintosh computer the system is running on.

Functions of VIA1 in the Macintosh IIfx computer

In the Macintosh IIfx, most of the functions listed above are performed by other ICs. The only functions still performed by VIA1 are these:

- It provides the interface between the RTC (real-time clock) IC and the rest of the system.

- It monitors the one-second interrupt request from the RTC (RTC.1HZ) and interrupts the main processor as appropriate.

- Four of the VIA1 inputs are permanently wired high or low to define a value, CPU.ID, that the ROM reads to determine which model Macintosh computer the system is running on.

VIA1 functions handled by IOPs in the Macintosh IIfx computer

In the Macintosh IIfx, the following functions of VIA1 on other models are performed by one of the IOPs.

■ An IOP provides the interface between the Apple Desktop Bus transceiver and the rest of the system.

■ An IOP provides the state-control line SEL to the floppy disk drives. Among other functions, this line selects which of the two heads is to be used in a double-sided floppy disk drive.

■ An IOP controls whether SCC port A is used for synchronous or asynchronous I/O.

■ An IOP enables software to monitor the SCC's Wait/Request output (/W/REQ) so that the software can detect activity on the serial port when interrupts are disabled.

VIA1 functions handled by the OSS in the Macintosh IIfx

In the Macintosh IIfx, one of the functions of VIA1 on other models is performed by the OSS.

■ The OSS monitors the 60.15 Hz interrupt request (/VBLK) and interrupts the main processor as appropriate. This 60.15 Hz interrupt is used by a variety of firmware and software.

Functions of VIA2

Many of the functions of VIA2 are the same for different Macintosh models. The following sections start by listing the VIA2 functions in the Macintosh SE/30, Macintosh II, Macintosh IIx, and Macintosh IIcx computers because those functions are shared by all the models in the group. Subsequent sections list additional functions found on individual machines.

In the Macintosh II only, VIA2 provides a signal (FC3) that can be used to switch the AMU to 32-bit mode so that the entire 32-bit longword address from the main processor is passed on to the GLUE IC for decoding. This signal is not needed in Macintosh computers that have the MC68030 processor.

Functions of VIA2 in the Macintosh SE/30, Macintosh II, Macintosh IIx, and Macintosh IIcx computers

The functions of VIA2 that are common to the Macintosh SE/30, Macintosh II, Macintosh IIx, and Macintosh IIcx computers are as follows:

- It monitors the slot interrupt signal from the GLUE IC (/SLOTIRQ). The GLUE IC performs an OR operation on the three or six interrupt lines from the expansion slots to generate this signal. When VIA2 receives this signal, it asserts the interrupt line to the processor.

- It monitors the interrupt lines from the expansion slots (/IRQ1 through /IRQ6) in a register where software can read the state of the interrupt lines. When the main processor receives a /SLOTIRQ interrupt from VIA2, software reads this register to find out which slot is generating the interrupt.

- It monitors interrupt lines from the ASC (/SNDINT) and the SCSI controller (SCSIIRQ), and interrupts the processor as appropriate.

- It monitors the Data Request line from the SCSI controller (SCSIDRQ) and can interrupt the main processor when the SCSI has received or sent a byte of data.

- It provides a signal (/BUSLOCK) that blocks NuBus cards from directly accessing the main logic board. This signal is used to protect time-critical operations from interruption by NuBus transactions. This signal is also available at the processor-direct slot in the Macintosh SE/30.

- It provides a signal (/POWEROFF) that shuts off the power supply. (In the Macintosh SE/30, this signal goes to the processor-direct slot only. An expansion card can use this signal to determine that it is about to lose power.)

- It records two status lines from the NuBus (/TM0A and /TM1A). If an error occurs during a NuBus access, a Bus Error signal is sent to the main processor by the NuBus controller (NuChip, NuChip30, or BIU30) and the error type is sent to VIA2 over these two lines. The main processor can read a register in VIA2 to find out the values of these two signals. These signals are available in the Macintosh SE/30 for use by an expansion card in the processor-direct slot.

- It monitors a signal (/SNDEXT) that indicates whether the external sound jack has a plug inserted in it. The Sound Manager can read a bit in VIA2 to determine whether the mono internal speaker or the stereo external sound jack is being used. This line is not available in the Macintosh SE/30 because the Macintosh SE/30 sound circuit includes a mixer to convert stereo to mono for the internal speaker; thus in the Macintosh SE/30, the Sound Manager always operates in stereo mode.

- It stores a value corresponding to the size of the RAM ICs installed in the SIMMs on the main logic board. That value drives two lines to the GLUE that determine how the GLUE addresses RAM.

- It provides a signal (/CDIS) that can be used to disable the data and instruction caches of the main processor. This feature is useful when debugging programs.

VIA2 functions in the Macintosh IIci computer

In the Macintosh IIci, there is no VIA2; the VIA2-emulation portion of the RBV performs all the functions listed above for the VIA2 in other machines; in addition, VIA2 emulation in the RBV also performs the following functions:

- It provides two signals used to enable and to flush the optional RAM cache.

- It provides a signal used for testing the parity circuits.

VIA2 functions in the Macintosh IIfx computer

In the Macintosh IIfx, there is no VIA2; its functions are handled by the OSS and BIU30 custom ICs. The OSS performs the following functions performed by VIA2 in other machines:

- It performs an OR operation on the six interrupt lines from the expansion slots to generate the /SLOTIRQ signal. When the OSS receives one of the slot interrupts, it asserts the interrupt line to the processor.

- It monitors the interrupt lines from the expansion slots (/IRQ1 through /IRQ6) and stores in a register the number of the slot generating the interrupt. When the main processor receives a /SLOTIRQ interrupt from the OSS, it reads this register to find out where the interrupt originated.

- It monitors interrupt lines from the ASC (/SNDINT) and the SCSI controller (SCSIIRQ), and interrupts the processor as appropriate.

- It monitors the Data Request line from the SCSI DMA (SCSIDRQ) and can interrupt the main processor when the SCSI DMA is ready to transfer data.

- It provides a signal (/POWEROFF) that shuts off the power supply.

- It monitors a signal (/SNDEXT) that indicates whether the external sound jack has a plug inserted in it. The Sound Manager can read a bit in the OSS to determine whether the mono internal speaker or the stereo external sound jack is being used.

- In machines fitted with the optional parity feature, the OSS controls the parity-enable signal and the parity-error interrupt.

The BIU30 in the Macintosh IIfx performs the following functions of the VIA2 on other machines:

■ It provides a signal (/BUSLOCK) that blocks NuBus cards from directly accessing the main logic board. This signal is used to protect time-critical operations from interruption by NuBus transactions.

■ It records status signals from the NuBus (/TM0A and /TM1A). If an error occurs during a NuBus access, the error type is sent to the BIU30 over these two lines and the BIU30 sends a Bus Error signal to the main processor. The main processor can read a register in the BIU30 to find out the values of those two signals.

Each VIA or custom IC carries out the functions listed in this section by way of several internal control and data registers. Those registers are described in the sections that follow.

VIA registers

There are two data registers in each VIA, called *Data register A* and *Data register B*, each with its own data direction register. A bit set as 1 in a data direction register causes the corresponding bit of the data register to be used for output, whereas a 0 causes it to be used for input. The Macintosh Operating System sets up the data direction registers at system startup or reset.

Other VIA registers include the Shift register, which holds keyboard data; two registers for control of VIA functions (called the *Auxiliary Control register* and the *Peripheral Control register*); a register that shows the source of an interrupt, called the *Interrupt Flag register*; and a register that enables or disables interrupts, called the *Interrupt Enable register*. Each VIA also has two event timers that are used by the operating system.

◆ *Note:* Applications should not write directly to the VIA timers but should use the Time Manager.

The base address of the VIA in the classic Macintosh computers, Macintosh SE, and Macintosh Portable, and of the VIA1 in other Macintosh computers, is available to assembly-language programs as the constant vBase and is also stored in the global variable VIA.

In the MC68000-based Macintosh computers, the VIA is on the upper byte of the 16-bit-wide data bus. In those computers, therefore, you must use even-addressed byte accesses only.

In those Macintosh computers that have two VIAs, the base address for the VIA2 registers is available as the constant vBase2.

From assembly language, low-level software can access the VIA registers by expressing addresses as offsets from the base address. A summary of these offsets is provided in Table 4-1. Each VIA register listed in this table is described in this chapter.

If you need more information about VIA registers and control structure, consult the technical specifications for the 6522 Versatile Interface Adapter, available from Rockwell or VTI.

■ **Table 4-1** Offsets of the VIA register locations

Offset from base address	VIA register
vBufA	Data register A
vBufB	Data register B
vDirA	Data Direction register A
vDirB	Data Direction register B
vPCR	Peripheral Control register
vACR	Auxiliary Control register
vTxx*	Event timers
vIFR	Interrupt Flag register
vIER	Interrupt Enable register
vSR	Shift register

*See Table 4-23 for a summary of the VIA event-timer offsets.

Data register A

VIA Data register A in Macintosh computers that have only one VIA, and VIA1 Data register A in Macintosh computers with two VIAs, have similar functions. In two-VIA Macintosh computers, VIA2 is used to implement features not present in the one-VIA computers. This section first describes the uses of the bits in VIA Data register A in one-VIA Macintosh computers, then the uses of the bits in VIA1 Data register A, and finally the bits in VIA2 Data register A.

◆ *Note:* Because the hardware and ROM of the Macintosh Portable computer are unique among Macintosh computers, the uses of the bits in the Macintosh Portable VIA are somewhat different from those of the Macintosh SE or any other Macintosh model.

Data register A in machines with only one VIA

The address of VIA Data register A is vBase+vBufA. The address of the corresponding Data Direction register A is vBase+vDirA.

VIA Data register A in the classic Macintosh computers

Table 4-2 shows the function of each bit in Data register A and the associated assembly-language name for controlling that bit in the Macintosh Plus and other classic Macintosh computers.

■ **Table 4-2**   Bits in VIA Data register A in the classic Macintosh computers

Bit	Direction	Bit name	Description
7	Input	vSCCWrReq	0 = SCC Wait/Request, channel A or B
6	Output	vPage2	0 = alternate screen buffer, 1 = main screen buffer
5	Output	vHeadSel	Floppy disk state-control line SEL
4	Output	vOverlay	1 = ROM overlay address map is used
3	Output	vSndPg2	0 = alternate sound buffer, 1 = main sound buffer
2	Output	vSound(2)	Sound volume
1	Output	vSound(1)	(111 = maximum, 000 = minimum;
0	Output	vSound(0)	bit 2 = most significant bit)

The vSCCWrReq bit monitors the /W/REQA and /W/REQB lines from the SCC, which are wired together on the main logic board. (Wiring together the two lines effectively performs an OR operation on the signals; that is, if either signal is asserted, the combined signal is asserted. Two lines connected in this way are said to be "wire ORed.") The Macintosh Operating System uses the vSCCWrReq bit to determine when the SCC has received a character (byte), thus enabling the operating system to maintain serial communications during floppy disk accesses, when the CPU's interrupts from the SCC are disabled. Serial communications is discussed in Chapter 10.

The vPage2 bit determines which of the two screen buffers is read by the video circuitry.

The vHeadSel bit is used to control the SEL line. This is one of the four disk state-control lines used by the disk interface. Among other things, this line is used to enable the upper or lower read/write head on a double-sided floppy disk drive.

The vOverlay bit (used only during system startup or reset) is used to switch the PALs to the ROM overlay address map.

The vSndPg2 bit determines which of the two sound buffers is read by the sound circuitry.

The vSound bits control the sound volume.

VIA Data register A in the Macintosh SE computer

Table 4-3 shows the function of each bit in Data register A and the associated assembly-language name for controlling that bit in the Macintosh SE.

■ **Table 4-3**   Bits in VIA Data register A in the Macintosh SE computer

Bit	Direction	Bit name	Description
7	Input	vSCCWrReq	0 = SCC Wait/Request, channel A or B
6	Output	vPage2	0 = alternate screen buffer, 1 = main screen buffer
5	Output	vHeadSel	Floppy disk state-control line SEL
4	Output	vDriveSel	0 = upper internal floppy disk drive, 1 = lower
3	Output	vSync	1 = synchronous modem support, channel A
2	Output	vSound(2)	Sound volume
1	Output	vSound(1)	(111 = maximum, 000 = minimum;
0	Output	vSound(0)	bit 2 = most significant bit)

The vDriveSel bit determines which of the two internal floppy disk drives will be used for the next floppy disk access. This signal goes to the BBU, which generates drive enable signals for the two internal floppy disk drives. When vDriveSel is set high, the /ENBL1 line of the IWM selects the lower internal floppy disk drive. When vDriveSel is set low, the /ENBL1 line selects the (optional) upper internal floppy disk drive.

The vSync bit supports a synchronous modem on channel A of the SCC. When vSync is set low, the SCC emulates the classic Macintosh configuration: the Receive Clock (RTxC) signal frequency for both channels is 3.672 MHz. When vSync is set high, the RTxC signal for SCC channel A is provided by the GPi pin from the modem serial port connector. The RTxC signal frequency for SCC channel B is always 3.672 MHz.

All the other bits in the Macintosh SE VIA Data register A have the same functions as the corresponding bits in the classic Macintosh computers.

VIA Data register A in the Macintosh Portable computer

Table 4-4 shows the function of each bit in Data register A and the associated assembly-language name for controlling that bit in the Macintosh Portable.

■ **Table 4-4**   Bits in VIA Data register A in the Macintosh Portable

Bit	Direction	Bit name	Description
7	In or out	PMD7	Power Manager data
6	In or out	PMD6	Power Manager data
5	In or out	PMD5	Power Manager data
4	In or out	PMD4	Power Manager data
3	In or out	PMD3	Power Manager data
2	In or out	PMD2	Power Manager data
1	In or out	PMD1	Power Manager data
0	In or out	PMD0	Power Manager data

In the Macintosh Portable, all the bits in Data register A of the VIA are used as an 8-bit bidirectional data bus used for communcation between the main processor and the Power Manager microprocessor.

Data register A in VIA1

VIA1 in two-VIA Macintosh computers performs most of the same functions as the VIA in the classic Macintosh computers and the Macintosh SE. The address of VIA1 Data register A is vBase+vBufA. The address of the corresponding Data Direction register A is vBase+vDirA.

VIA1 Data register A in the Macintosh SE/30, Macintosh II, Macintosh IIx, and Macintosh IIcx computers

Table 4-5 shows the function of each bit in VIA1 Data register A and the associated assembly-language name for controlling that bit in the Macintosh SE/30, Macintosh II, Macintosh IIx, and Macintosh IIcx computers.

- **Table 4-5** Bits in VIA1 Data register A in the Macintosh SE/30, Macintosh II, Macintosh IIx, and Macintosh IIcx computers

Bit	Direction	Bit name	Description
7	Input	vSCCWrReq	0 = SCC Wait/Request, channel A or B
6	Output	vPage2	0 = alternate screen buffer, 1 = main screen buffer (on Macintosh SE/30)
	Input	CPU.ID1	Identifies different models (except on Macintosh SE/30)
5	Output	vHeadSel	Floppy disk state-control line SEL
4	Output	vOverlay	1 = ROM overlay address map is used
3	Output	vSync	1 = synchronous modem support on SCC channel A
2			Reserved
1			Reserved
0			Reserved

The vSCCWrReq bit monitors the /W/REQA and /W/REQB lines from the SCC, which are wired together on the main logic board ("wire ORed"). The Macintosh Operating System uses the vSCCWrReq bit to determine when the SCC has received a character (byte), thus enabling the operating system to maintain serial communications during floppy disk accesses, when the CPU's interrupts from the SCC are disabled. The SCC is discussed in Chapter 10.

In the Macintosh SE/30, bit 6 is named *vPage2* and determines which of the two screen buffers is read by the video circuitry.

The CPU.ID1 line is used by the ROM code to identify which model it is running on. That line is tied low in the Macintosh II and Macintosh IIx computers.

The vHeadSel bit is used to set the level of the SEL line. This is one of the four disk state-control lines used by the disk interface. Among other things, this line is used to enable the upper or lower read/write head on a double-sided floppy disk drive.

The vOverlay bit (used only during system startup or reset) is used to switch the GLUE to the ROM overlay address map. Note that RAM is inaccessible until the Overlay signal is deasserted.

The vSync bit supports a synchronous modem on channel A of the SCC. When vSync is set low, the SCC emulates the classic Macintosh configuration: the Receive Clock (RTxC) signal frequency for both channels is 3.672 MHz. When vSync is set high, the RTxC signal for SCC channel A is provided by the GPi pin from the modem serial port connector. The RTxC signal frequency for SCC channel B is always 3.672 MHz.

On the classic Macintosh and Macintosh SE computers, bits 0, 1, and 2 are used to set the volume of the sound output. To maintain software compatibility on the two-VIA machines, those bits are either unused or are used only as machine-ID signals.

VIA1 Data register A in the Macintosh IIci computer

In the Macintosh IIci, many of the functions that are controlled by VIA registers in other models are controlled by registers in the RBV. Collectively, those registers are named the *VIA emulation registers;* individually, they are named for the equivalent registers in an actual VIA.

Table 4-6 shows the functions of VIA1 Data register A in the Macintosh IIci computer.

■ **Table 4-6** Bits in VIA1 Data register A in the Macintosh IIci computer

Bit	Direction	Bit name	Description
7	Input	vSCCWrReq	0 = SCC Wait/Request, channel A or B
6	Input	CPU.ID3	Bit 3 of 4-bit model-identity code
5	Output	vHeadSel	Floppy disk state-control line SEL
4	Input	CPU.ID2	Bit 2 of 4-bit model-identity code
3	Output	vSync	1 = synchronous modem support, channel A
2	Input	CPU.ID1	Bit 1 of 4-bit model-identity code
1	Input	CPU.ID0	Bit 0 of 4-bit model-identity code
0			Reserved

The vSCCWrReg, vHeadSel, and vSync bits in the Macintosh IIci are as described for the Macintosh SE/30 and earlier Macintosh computers. The ROM code uses bits CPU.ID0–CPU.ID3 to identify which model it is running on. The identity code values for the Macintosh IIci are shown in Table 4-8.

VIA1 Data register A in the Macintosh IIfx computer

In the Macintosh IIfx, many of the functions that are controlled by VIA registers in other models are controlled by registers in the OSS, IOP, and BIU30. Collectively, those registers are named the *VIA emulation registers;* individually, they are named for the equivalent registers in an actual VIA. Table 4-7 shows the functions of VIA1 Data register A in the Macintosh IIfx computer.

■ **Table 4-7** Bits in VIA1 Data register A in the Macintosh IIfx computer

Bit	Direction	Bit name	Description
7			Reserved
6	Input	CPU.ID3	Bit 3 of 4-bit model-identity code
5			Reserved
4	Input	CPU.ID2	Bit 2 of 4-bit model-identity code
3			Reserved
2	Input	CPU.ID1	Bit 1 of 4-bit model-identity code
1	Input	CPU.ID0	Bit 0 of 4-bit model-identity code
0			Reserved

The only bits used in VIA1 Data register A in the Macintosh IIfx are the model-identity bits
CPU.ID0–CPU.ID3. The ROM code uses those bits to identify which model it is running
on. The identity code values for the Macintosh IIfx are shown in Table 4-8.

■ **Table 4-8** Identity codes in the Macintosh IIci and Macintosh IIfx

Bit	Bit name	Value in Macintosh IIci	Value in Macintosh IIfx
6	CPU.ID3	1	1
4	CPU.ID2	0*	1
2	CPU.ID1	1	0
1	CPU.ID0	1	1

*This value is a 1 in a Macintosh IIci with the optional parity feature installed.

Data register A in VIA2

In Macintosh computers with two VIAs, VIA2 is used to implement features not present in
the Macintosh SE and classic Macintosh computers. The address of VIA2 Data register A is
vBase2+vBufA. The address of Data Direction register A is vBase2+vDirA. Table 4-9 shows
the function of each bit in VIA2 Data register A and the associated assembly-language
name for controlling that bit in the Macintosh SE/30 and Macintosh II–family computers.

The Macintosh IIci and Macintosh IIfx have no VIA2; for the functions of VIA2, those machines use registers in their custom ICs (RBV in the Macintosh IIci; OSS, IOPs, and BIU30 in the Macintosh IIfx). Collectively, those registers are named the *VIA emulation registers;* individually, they are named for the equivalent registers in an actual VIA. Some bits in the emulation registers are different from those in VIA2; the differences are indicated in the tables.

■ **Table 4-9**   Bits in VIA2 Data register A

Bit	Direction	Bit name	Description
7	Output	v2RAM1*	RAM-size bit 1 (except in the Macintosh IIci)
6	Output	v2RAM0*	RAM-size bit 0 (except in the Macintosh IIci)
5	Input	v2IRQ6	Interrupt request from expansion slot $E
4	Input	v2IRQ5	Interrupt request from expansion slot $D
3	Input	v2IRQ4	Interrupt request from expansion slot $C
2	Input	v2IRQ3	Interrupt request from expansion slot $B
1	Input	v2IRQ2	Interrupt request from expansion slot $A
0	Input	v2IRQ1	Interrupt request from expansion slot $9

*In the Macintosh IIci, memory mapping is taken care of by the MC68030, so RAM-size bits are not needed; instead, bit 6 is named *v2IRQ0* and is used for the interrupt from the internal video circuits; bit 7 is reserved.

The two RAM-size bits are set at system startup by the firmware to indicate the size of the RAM ICs being used in the RAM SIMMs in bank A. Table 4-10 shows how the bits reflect the size of the bank-A RAM ICs. The RAM-size bits determine the physical address at which the GLUE IC stops selecting bank A and starts selecting bank B.

In the Macintosh IIci, RAM bank B always starts at physical address $0400 0000, so the RAM-size bits are not needed. Instead, the startup firmware in the Macintosh IIci determines the amount of RAM in bank A by writing and reading, then sets up the MMU in the MC68030 to map bank B into the logical address space immediately after the last logical address in bank A.

■ **Table 4-10** VIA2 RAM size bits

Bit v2RAM1	Bit v2RAM0	Size of RAM ICs in bank A
0	0	256 Kbit
0	1	1 Mbit
1	0	4 Mbit
1	1	16 Mbit

Interrupt lines from the expansion slots appear as bits 0 through 5 in VIA2 Data register A. In addition, the GLUE IC performs an OR operation on the six interrupt requests, and the result is received as an interrupt request by VIA2. If this interrupt is enabled, VIA2 sends an interrupt to the main processor. The main processor polls the VIA2 Interrupt Flag register to determine the source of the interrupt and, upon determining that it is a NuBus interrupt, the main processor polls VIA2 Data register A to determine which slot or slots initiated the interrupt.

The Macintosh II and Macintosh IIx computers each have six NuBus slots, numbered $9, $A, $B, $C, $D, and $E. The Macintosh IIcx and Macintosh IIci have three NuBus slots: in the Macintosh IIcx, the slots are numbered $9, $A, and $B; in the Macintosh IIci, the slots are $C, $D, and $E. In the Macintosh SE/30 computer, an expansion card in the processor-direct slot can be addressed like a NuBus card in slot $9, $A, or $B, and can generate the corresponding interrupt. Also in the Macintosh SE/30, the interrupt for slot $E can be generated by the video logic circuits on the logic board.

Data register B

VIA Data register B in Macintosh computers that have only one VIA and VIA1 Data register B in Macintosh computers with two VIAs have similar functions. In two-VIA Macintosh computers, VIA2 is used to implement features not present in the one-VIA computers. This section first describes the uses of the bits in VIA Data register B in one-VIA Macintosh computers, then the uses of the bits in VIA1 Data register B, and finally the bits in VIA2 Data register B.

Data register B in machines with only one VIA

VIA Data register B is at vBase+vBufB. Data Direction register B is at vBase+vDirB. Table 4-11 shows the function of each bit in Data register B and the associated assembly-language name for controlling that bit for the Macintosh Plus and other classic Macintosh computers.

■ **Table 4-11** Bits in VIA Data register B in the classic Macintosh computers

Bit	Direction	Bit name	Description
7	Output	vSndEnb	0 = sound enabled
6	Input	vH4	0 = video beam in display portion of line
5	Input	vY2	Mouse Y2
4	Input	vX2	Mouse X2
3	Input	vSW	0 = mouse switch down
2	Output	rTCEnb	0 = real-time clock enabled
1	Output	rTCCLK	Real-time clock's data-clock line
0	In or Out	rTCData	Real-time clock's serial data line

The vSndEnb bit turns the sound generator on or off. This bit can be toggled between 0 and 1 by VIA timer T1, as discussed in the section "Auxiliary Control Register," later in this chapter.

The vH4 bit is set to a value of 1 when the video beam is in its horizontal blanking period. This bit can be used by software to count horizontal lines to keep track of the video beam's horizontal position on the screen.

The vY2 and vX2 bits read the mouse Y (vertical) and X (horizontal) quadrature signals.

The vSW bit reads the state of the mouse switch.

The rTCEnb, rTCClk, and rTCData bits are used for communication with the real-time clock.

Table 4-12 shows the function of each bit in Data register B and the associated assembly-language name for controlling that bit in the Macintosh SE.

■ **Table 4-12** Bits in VIA Data register B in the Macintosh SE computer

Bit	Direction	Bit name	Description
7	Output	vSndEnb	0 = sound enabled
6	Output	vH4	0 = SCSI IRQ interrupt enabled
5	Output	vFDesk2	ADB state input 1 (ST1)
4	Output	vFDesk1	ADB state input 0 (ST0)
3	Input	vFDBInt	0 = ADB interrupt
2	Output	rTCEnb	0 = real-time clock enabled
1	Output	rtcCLK	Real-time clock's data-clock line
0	In or Out	rtcData	Real-time clock's serial data line

The vH4 bit implements an interrupt mask for the SCSI interrupt line from the NCR 5380. When this bit is set high, interrupts on the SCSI controller's IRQ line are disabled. When bit vH4 is set low, a SCSI IRQ line generates a level-1 interrupt, which has the same priority as a VIA-generated interrupt. Interrupt-handling software then polls the VIA and SCSI to determine which device is generating the interrupt.

The vFDesk2 bit is ADB state input 1 (ST1), one of two state bits used to control a transfer between the ADB transceiver and the VIA.

The vFDesk1 bit is ADB state input 0 (ST0), one of two state bits used to control a transfer between the ADB transceiver and the VIA.

The vFDBInt bit is the ADB interrupt, which indicates that an ADB transaction is pending.

Bits 7 and 0 through 2 in VIA Data register B of the Macintosh SE have the same functions as the corresponding bits in the classic Macintosh.

Table 4-13 shows the function of each bit in Data register B and the associated assembly-language name for controlling that bit in the Macintosh Portable.

■ **Table 4-13** Bits in VIA Data register B in the Macintosh Portable computer

Bit	Direction	Bit name	Description
7	Input	vSCCWrReq	0 = SCC Wait/Request, channel A or B
	Output	vSndEnb	0 = sound enabled
6	Input	vSndExt	0 = plug is inserted in external sound jack
5	Output	vHeadSel	Floppy disk state-control line SEL
4	Output	vDriveSel	0 = upper internal floppy disk drive, 1 = lower
3	Output	vSync	1 = synchronous modem support, channel A
2	Output	vTest	Test signal
1	Input	vPMAck	Handshake signal for Power Manager IC
0	Output	vPMReq	Handshake signal for Power Manager IC

Bit 7 of Data register B in the Macintosh Portable serves two functions. When the CPU's interrupts from the SCC are disabled, this bit monitors the /W/REQA and /W/REQB lines from the SCC, which are wired together on the main logic board ("wire ORed"). The Macintosh Operating System uses the vSCCWrReq bit to determine when the SCC has received a character (byte), thus enabling the operating system to maintain serial communications during floppy disk accesses, when SCC interrupts are disabled. The SCC is discussed in Chapter 10.

When SCC interrupts are not disabled, bit 7 can be monitored by software as an aid in controlling the sound circuit. Once every 60th of a second (VBL interval), the operating system checks to see if this bit has been cleared. If it has, the Sound Manager sets up the ASC and sends a pulse to click the speaker. When used in this fashion, bit 7 emulates the function of the same bit in the VIA of the Macintosh SE and classic Macintosh computers and thereby helps to maintain compatibility with software written for those machines.

◆ *Note:* When writing new sound applications, you can ensure compatibility with the different models in the Macintosh family by using the Sound Manager.

The vSndExt bit indicates whether a plug has been inserted in the external sound jack. The internal speaker provides only monaural sound, so stereo output is possible only when the sound jack is being used.

The vHeadSel bit is used to control the SEL line, one of the four disk state-control lines used by the disk interface. Among other things, that line is used to enable the upper or lower read/write head on a double-sided floppy disk drive.

The vDriveSel bit determines which of the two internal floppy disk drives will be used for the next floppy disk access. This signal goes to the Miscellaneous GLU custom IC, which generates drive enable signals for the two internal floppy disk drives. When vDriveSel is set high, the /ENBL1 line of the SWIM selects the lower internal floppy disk drive. When vDriveSel is set low, the /ENBL1 line selects the (optional) upper internal floppy disk drive.

The vSync bit supports a synchronous modem on channel A of the SCC. When vSync is set low, the SCC emulates the classic Macintosh configuration: the Receive Clock (RTxC) signal frequency for both channels is 3.672 MHz. When vSync is set high, the RTxC signal for SCC channel A is provided by the GPi pin from the modem serial port connector. The RTxC signal frequency for SCC channel B is always 3.672 MHz.

The VTest bit sends a test signal to the Power Manager IC that forces it to turn on all power supplies; this signal is used only for testing by Apple service personnel.

The PMAck bit indicates the level of the acknowledge signal from the Power Manager IC. This signal is sent by the Power Manager IC to the main processor to acknowledge the receipt of a command or data.

The PMReq bit is used to set the level of the Power Manager IC request signal to the Power Manager IC. This signal is sent by the main processor to the Power Manager IC to indicate that there is valid data on the Power Manager IC data bus.

Data register B in VIA1

Table 4-14 shows the function of each bit in Data register B and the associated assembly-language name for controlling that bit in the Macintosh SE/30 and Macintosh II–family computers. Not all the bits in Data register B are used in all the models; differences are noted in the description column of the table.

In the Macintosh IIci, many of the functions that are controlled by VIA registers in other models are controlled by registers in the RBV. Similarly, the Macintosh IIfx uses registers in the OSS, IOP, and BIU30 for some of those functions. Collectively, those registers are named the *VIA emulation registers;* individually, they are named for the equivalent registers in an actual VIA. Some bits in the emulation registers are different from those in VIA1; the differences are indicated in the tables.

■ **Table 4-14** Bits in VIA1 Data register B in the Macintosh SE/30 and the Macintosh II family

Bit	Direction	Bit name	Description
7	Input	/Par.Err	0 = parity error (Macintosh IIci only)
	Output	vSndEnb	0 = sound enable (for software compatibility)
6	Output	/Par.En	0 = parity-checking enabled (Macintosh IIci only)
		vSyncEnA	0 = vertical synchronization interrupt enabled (Macintosh SE/30 only) (unused in other models)
5	Output	vFDesk2	ADB state input 1 (ADB.ST1) (Unused in Macintosh IIfx)
4	Output	vFDesk1	ADB state input 0 (ADB.ST0) (Unused in Macintosh IIfx)
3	Input	vFDBInt	0 = ADB interrupt (/ADB.INT) (Unused in Macintosh IIfx)
2	Output	rTCEnb	0 = real-time clock enabled
1	Output	rtcCLK	Real-time clock's data-clock line
0	In or Out	rtcData	Real-time clock's serial data line

On the Macintosh IIci, bit 7 is an input signal from the Parity Generator and Checker (PGC). When a nonmaskable interrupt (NMI) occurs, the interrupt service routine can read this bit to determine whether the cause of the interrupt was detection of a parity error.

◆ *Note:* In the Macintosh II family, bit 7 is used as an output only to maintain compatibility with the classic Macintosh and Macintosh SE computers, in which that bit is used as an output to enable or disable sound output.

In the Macintosh SE/30, bit 6 (vSyncEnA) enables or disables a slot $E interrupt request from the video logic circuits to VIA2. When enabled, this interrupt request is asserted each time the vertical blanking signal is asserted by the video logic circuits. If expansion slot interrupts are enabled, VIA2 then asserts an interrupt request to the GLUE, which interrupts the main processor. The vertical synchronization interrupt generated in this fashion is distinct from the 60.15 Hz interrupt (VBL) request, which is sent by VIA2 to VIA1. The 60.15 Hz interrupt in the Macintosh SE/30 and in the Macintosh II family emulates the VBL interrupt generated by the video circuits in the Macintosh SE and classic Macintosh computers.

⚠ **Developer tip** The 60.15 Hz interrupt is provided in the Macintosh SE/30 and Macintosh II–family computers to maintain compatibility with software that depends on this signal to time events. If you want your software to be synchronized with the actual vertical blanking of the screen, you must use the slot interrupt generated by a NuBus video card in the Macintosh II–family computers or by the video logic circuits in the Macintosh SE/30 and the Macintosh IIci. To learn more about using slot interrupts, read the chapter on the Deferred Task Manager in *Inside Macintosh*. ⚠

In the parity-equipped version of the Macintosh IIci, bit 6 enables or disables parity generation and checking by the PGC. Each time a byte of RAM is written, the PGC generates a parity bit and stores it in the ninth bit of the parity RAM SIMM for that byte. Each time a byte of RAM is read, the PGC generates an internal parity bit and compares it with the bit read from the RAM's parity bit for the byte. If the two parity bits are not the same and parity checking is enabled (bit 6 is 0), the PGC asserts two outputs: /NMI, which interrupts the main processor, and /PAR.ERR, which indicates a parity error. The interrupt service routine can turn off the /PAR.ERR and /NMI signals by setting the /Par.En bit to 1.

◆ *Note:* The parity feature is available in the Macintosh IIci only by special order; it is not available as as upgrade.

Bit 6 is not used in the other Macintosh II–family computers.

The vFDesk2 bit is ADB State input 1 (ST1), one of two state bits used to control a transfer between the ADB transceiver and VIA1.

The vFDesk1 bit is ADB State input 0 (ST0), one of two state bits used to control a transfer between the ADB transceiver and VIA1.

The vFDBInt bit is the ADB interrupt, which indicates that an ADB transaction is pending.

The rTCEnb, rTCClk, and rTCData bits are used for communication with the real-time clock.

Data register B in VIA2

VIA2 Data register B is at vBase2+vBufB. Data Direction register B is at address vBase2+vDirB. Table 4-15 shows the function of each bit in Data register B and the associated assembly-language name for controlling that bit in the Macintosh SE/30 and Macintosh II–family computers.

In the Macintosh IIci, many of the functions that are controlled by VIA registers in other models are controlled by registers in the RBV. Similarly, the Macintosh IIfx uses registers in the OSS, IOP, and BIU30 for some of those functions. Collectively, those registers are named the *VIA emulation registers;* individually, they are named for the equivalent registers in an actual VIA. Some bits in the emulation registers are different from those in VIA2; the differences are indicated in the tables.

■ **Table 4-15** Bits in VIA2 Data register B

Bit	Direction	Bit name	Description
7	Output	v2VBL	60.15 Hz interrupt request to VIA1
		/Par.Test	0 = parity test mode (Macintosh IIci only)
6	Input	v2SNDEXT	0 = plug is inserted in external sound jack (Macintosh II family)
			Tied low (Macintosh SE/30)
5	Input	v2TM0A	Transfer mode bit 0 acknowledge from NuBus
4	Input	v2TM1A	Transfer mode bit 1 acknowledge from NuBus
3	In or out	vFC3	AMU/PMMU control (Macintosh II)
			Tied low (Macintosh SE/30)
			0 = flush the cache card (Macintosh IIci)
			Not used (Macintosh IIx, Macintosh IIcx, Macintosh IIfx)
2	Output	v2PowerOff	0 = shut off power
1	Output	v2BusLk	0 = NuBus transactions are locked out
0	Output	/CEnable	1 = disable cache card (Macintosh IIci)
		v2CDis	0 = disable main processor's instruction and data caches (Macintosh SE/30 and Macintosh II–family machines)

The v2VBL bit is driven by timer T1 to send the 60.15 Hz interrupt request to VIA1 once every 16.63 ms. If enabled by the appropriate bit in the VIA1 Interrupt Enable register, this signal can be used by VIA1 to generate an interrupt to the main processor.

The v2SNDEXT bit indicates whether a plug has been inserted in the external sound jack. The internal speaker provides only monaural sound, so stereo output is possible only when the sound jack is being used. This bit is tied low in the Macintosh SE/30 so that the Sound Manager always operates in stereo mode in the Macintosh SE/30; the Macintosh SE/30 sound circuit includes a mixer to convert the stereo signal to mono for the internal speaker.

v2TM1A and v2TM0A are status bits returned from a NuBus access. If an error occurs during a NuBus access, a bus error is sent to the main processor and these bits are set to indicate what the error was, as shown in Table 4-16. The signals that control these bits are available to an expansion card in the processor-direct slot in the Macintosh SE/30 computer.

■ **Table 4-16** NuBus transfer acknowledge bits in VIA2 Data register B

Bits		
v2TM1A	**v2TM0A**	**Meaning**
0	0	No error
0	1	Read or write error, handled by bus master
1	0	Bus timeout
1	1	Try again later

The /TM0 and /TM1 signals controlled by these bits are also used, along with other signals, to indicate the transaction type and size during the NuBus start cycle. For more information on the /TM0 and /TM1 signals, see Chapter 3, "NuBus Data Transfer," of *Designing Cards and Drivers for the Macintosh Family,* second edition.

When the Macintosh II has the AMU installed, the vFC3 bit is used for output and controls whether 24-bit mode or 32-bit mode is used. When vFC3 is set to 0, the AMU performs a 24-bit to 32-bit address translation. When the PMMU is installed, this bit is used for input. When the PMMU is accessing the page table, it sets this bit to 1. This bit is tied low in the Macintosh SE/30 and is not used in the Macintosh IIx and Macintosh IIcx. In the Macintosh IIci, the vFC3 bit is an output that controls the /CFLUSH signal to the optional cache card.

When the v2PowerOff bit is set to 0, the power supply is shut off in the Macintosh II–family computers. The signal controlled by this bit is available at the processor-direct slot in the Macintosh SE/30 so that an expansion card can use it to shut down operations before losing power from the computer.

When the v2BusLk bit is set to 0 in a Macintosh II–family computer, NuBus transactions from a slot to the main logic board are blocked and a try-again-later response is sent to the NuBus controller (NuChip, NuChip30, or BIU30). That bit can be used to protect time-critical processor activity from NuBus direct-memory access transactions. This signal is available at the processor-direct slot in the Macintosh SE/30 for use by expansion cards that emulate NuBus cards.

In the Macintosh IIci, when the /CEnable bit is set to 0, the RBV asserts a signal that enables the optional cache card. When that bit is set to 1, the RBV disables the cache card. Applications should not set that bit directly, but should use the appropriate ROM traps to enable, disable, and flush the cache card. The traps, named *EnableExtCache, DisableExtCache,* and *FlushExtCache,* are available using selectors 4, 5, and 6 through the hardware priviledge trap HWPriv (A098).

On other Macintosh II–family machines and on the Macintosh SE/30, setting the v2VDis bit to 0 causes the VIA2 to assert a signal that disables the instruction and data caches in the main processor.

Peripheral Control register

The VIA Peripheral Control register allows software to set some very low-level parameters—such as positive-edge or negative-edge triggering—for certain VIA signals. The function of each of the bits in the Peripheral Control register is described fully in the manufacturers' documentation for the 6522 VIA IC.

▲ **Warning**   Do not change any of the bits in the Peripheral Control register. Changing these bits will interfere with the operation of the keyboard or with other computer functions. ▲

Peripheral Control register in VIA1 or VIA

The functions of the bits in the VIA Peripheral Control register in the classic Macintosh, at address vBase+cPCR, are shown in Table 4-17.

■ **Table 4-17**   Signals controlled by the VIA Peripheral Control register in the classic Macintosh computers

Bit	Signal controlled
7–5	Keyboard data
4	Keyboard clock
3–1	One-second interrupt
0	Vertical blanking interrupt

The keyboard data line is a bidirectional serial data line used to transfer data between the VIA Shift register and the keyboard.

The keyboard clock signal is the signal used to time communications over the keyboard data line. The keyboard clock signal is driven by the keyboard.

The one-second interrupt is a signal generated once every second by the RTC. If enabled by the appropriate bit in the VIA Interrupt Enable register, this signal can be used by the VIA to generate an interrupt to the main processor.

The 60.15 Hz interrupt (VBL) is a signal generated by a PAL once every 16.63 ms, at the start of the vertical blanking interval for the built-in video monitor. If enabled by the appropriate bit in the VIA Interrupt Enable register, this signal can be used by the VIA to generate an interrupt to the main processor.

The functions of the bits in the VIA Peripheral Control register in the VIA in the Macintosh SE and in VIA1 in the Macintosh SE/30 and Macintosh II family, at address vBase+cPCR, are shown in Table 4-18.

- **Table 4-18**   Signals controlled by the Peripheral Control register in VIA in the Macintosh SE/30 and in VIA1 in the Macintosh II–family computers

Bit	Signal controlled
7–5	Apple Desktop Bus data
4	Apple Desktop Bus clock
3–1	One-second interrupt
0	Vertical blanking interrupt

The ADB data line is a bidirectional serial data line used to transfer data between the VIA Shift register and the ADB transceiver.

The ADB clock signal is the signal used to time communications over the ADB data line. The ADB clock line is driven by the ADB transceiver.

As in the classic Macintosh, the one-second interrupt is a signal generated once every second by the RTC that can be used to generate an interrupt to the main processor.

The 60.15 Hz interrupt (VBL) is a signal generated by the BBU in the Macintosh SE and by VIA2 in the Macintosh SE/30 and Macintosh II family once every 16.63 ms. It serves many of the same software functions as the VBL interrupt in the classic Macintosh computers, although it is not sychronized to actual video signals generated on a video card in an expansion slot.

The functions of the bits in the VIA Peripheral Control register in the Macintosh Portable, at vBase+cPCR, are shown in Table 4-19.

- **Table 4-19**   Signals controlled by the VIA Peripheral Control register in the
  Macintosh Portable computer

Bit	Signal controlled
7–5	SCSI IRQ interrupt
4	Power Manager interrupt
3–1	One-second interrupt
0	60.15 Hz interrupt

The SCSI IRQ interrupt is generated by the SCSI controller to indicate an error condition.

The Power Manager interrupt is requested by the Power Manager IC microprocessor when it needs to communicate with the main processor.

The one-second interrupt is a signal generated once every second by the Power Manager IC that can be used to generate an interrupt to the main processor. It serves the same function as the one-second interrupt generated by the RTC in other Macintosh computers.

The 60.15 Hz interrupt is a signal generated by the Power Manager IC once every 16.63 ms that can be used to generate an interrupt to the main processor. It serves the same function as the 60.15 Hz interrupt in the Macintosh SE/30 and Macintosh II–family computers and the VBL interrupt in the classic Macintosh computers.

Peripheral Control register in VIA2

The VIA2 Peripheral Control register in the Macintosh SE/30 and Macintosh II family, at address vBase2+vPCR, controls parameters for SCSI, ASC, and slot interrupts. Table 4-20 shows the signals controlled by the VIA2 Peripheral Control register.

▲ **Warning**   Do not change any of the bits in the VIA2 Peripheral Control register. Changing these bits will interfere with the operation of the SCSI controller, sound IC, or NuBus. ▲

- **Table 4-20**   Signals controlled by the VIA2 Peripheral Control register

Bit	Signal controlled
7–5	SCSI IRQ interrupt
4	ASC interrupt
3–1	SCSI DRQ interrupt
0	Slot interrupt

All four of the signals controlled by the VIA2 Peripheral Control register are inputs to VIA2. If enabled by the appropriate bit in the VIA2 Interrupt Enable register, any of these signals can be used by VIA2 to generate an interrupt to the main processor.

The SCSI IRQ interrupt is generated by the SCSI controller to indicate an error condition.

The ASC interrupt can be used to control an interrupt-driven sound driver. It indicates when the buffer in the ASC is ready to be reloaded.

The SCSI DRQ interrupt indicates that the SCSI controller is ready to transfer data. This signal can be used to initiate a SCSI transaction for interrupt-driven SCSI communications.

The slot interrupt is the result of performing an OR operation on the interrupt outputs of all the NuBus slots. If the main processor receives this interrupt, it reads VIA2 Data register A to determine which slot initiated the interrupt request. The Macintosh IIcx and Macintosh IIci have only the first three NuBus slots; the Macintosh IIci can also generate a slot interrupt ($0) for its built-in video circuits. An expansion card in the processor-direct slot in the Macintosh SE/30 can generate any of the first three slot interrupts, and the video circuits on the logic board in the Macintosh SE/30 can generate an interrupt for slot $E.

Auxiliary Control register

The Auxiliary Control register controls various parameters pertaining to the VIA timers and the VIA Shift register. The VIA Auxiliary Control register in the classic Macintosh and Macintosh SE computers is at address vBase+vACR; the VIA1 Auxiliary Control register in the Macintosh SE/30 and Macintosh II family is also at address vBase+vACR. The VIA2 Auxiliary Control register in the Macintosh SE/30 and Macintosh II family is at address vBase2+vACR.

In the Macintosh IIci, parameters for the VIA2 portion of the RBV are fixed by the hardware so there is no Auxiliary Control register for VIA2 in that machine.

Table 4-21 shows the function of each bit in the Auxiliary Control register.

■ **Table 4-21**   Bits in the Auxiliary Control register

Bit	Function controlled
7,6	Timer T1 interrupts
5	Timer T2 interrupts
4–2	Keyboard data bit-shift operation (classic Macintosh) ADB data bit-shift operation (Macintosh SE, Macintosh SE/30 VIA1, and Macintosh II–family VIA1) Not used (Macintosh Portable, Macintosh SE/30 VIA2, and Macintosh II–family VIA2)
1	Enable/disable for input data latch for Data register B signal lines (1 = enable, 0 = disable)
0	Enable/disable for input data latch for Data register A signal lines (1 = enable, 0 = disable)

Timer T1 can operate either as a one-shot interval timer or as an automatically repeating pulse generator. In one-shot mode, timer T1 decrements one count every 1.2766 μs, generating an interrupt on the VIA interrupt line (if that interrupt is enabled by the appropriate bit in the Interrupt Enable register) when the count reaches 0. In automatic repeat (or free-running) mode, software can load the timer T1 latches with a value that T1 will reload automatically each time it counts down to 0. This mode can generate an interrupt each time the count reaches 0 and can also invert bit 7 in VIA Data register B each time. In the Macintosh II VIA2, this bit controls the 60.15 Hz interrupt, which is used as an interrupt-request input to VIA1.

⚠ **Developer tip**   In the past, some programmers working on the classic Macintosh computers have used timer T1 to toggle sound on and off, generating a square-wave sound signal. This technique does not work with recent Macintosh computers, however, because the sound enable/disable signal provided by the classic Macintosh and Macintosh SE computers is not available in Macintosh computers that have the Apple Sound Chip. Instead, you should use the Sound Manager routines described in *Inside Macintosh* to control sound output. ⚠

Bits 6 and 7 in the Auxiliary Control register control the mode of operation of timer T1, as shown in Table 4-22.

■ **Table 4-22**   Bits 6 and 7 in the VIA Auxiliary Control register

Bit 7	Bit 6	Operation	Effect on sound control
0	0	Timed interrupt each time T1 is loaded	No effect
0	1	Automatic loading of T1 from latches	No effect
1	0	Timed interrupt each time T1 is loaded	Negative pulse
1	1	Automatic loading of T1 from latches	Toggles on or off

Timer T2 can operate either as an interval timer (in the same fashion as the one-shot mode of timer T1) or can count negative pulses on VIA pin PB6. Because VIA1 pin PB6 is not used in the Macintosh II, Macintosh IIx, and Macintosh IIcx, this second function of VIA1 timer T2 is not available in those members of the Macintosh II family. In the Macintosh SE/30, VIA1 pin PB6 is used an an output, so the counting function of timer T2 is unavailable on that machine as well. VIA2 pin PB6 in the Macintosh II–family computers is used to detect when a plug is inserted in the external sound jack.

Bits 2, 3, and 4 of the Auxiliary Control register control the way the ADB data bits (or the keyboard data bits in the classic Macintosh) are shifted in and out of the VIA Shift register. The Macintosh Portable Shift register and the VIA2 Shift register are not used. The Macintosh Portable transfers ADB data over the Power Manager IC data lines to the VIA.

Bits 0 and 1 control whether bits in Data registers A and B that are used for input are latched or always reflect the voltage levels on the input pins.

▲ **Warning**   Do not change bits 0 through 5 in the Auxiliary Control register. Changing these bits will interfere with the operation of the keyboard, the ADB, or with other computer functions. ▲

Shift register

The Shift register, at vBase+vSR, contains the 8 bits of data that have been shifted in or that will be shifted out over the keyboard data line in the classic Macintosh computers, or over the ADB data line in the Macintosh SE, Macintosh SE/30, and Macintosh II family. The VIA Shift register is not used in the Macintosh Portable. In machines that have two VIAs, the VIA2 Shift register is not used.

Event timers

As discussed in the section "Auxiliary Control Register," earlier in this chapter, either VIA timer can be used to time a single event. In addition, software can cause timer T1 to repeat continuously by loading a value into the timer T1 latches and setting bits 6 and 7 of the Auxiliary Control register as shown in Table 4-22.

The VIA event timers use the Enable signal (E clock) as a reference; therefore, the timer counter is decremented once every 1.2766 ms. Timer T2 can be programmed to count down once each time the VIA receives an input for bit 6 of Data register B.

If the proper interrupt-enable bit has been set, an interrupt is generated when a VIA timer counts down to 0.

To start one of the timers, store the appropriate values in the high-order and low-order bytes of the timer counter (or, for a periodic interrupt, the timer T1 latches). Because the high-order and low-order bytes of a counter do not have adjacent addresses, software must explicitly do two stores, first for the low-order byte and then for the high-order byte. A program cannot simply store a full word to the high-order address to set a timer; it must write to the high-order byte last, because writing to the high-order byte starts the timer.

Table 4-23 shows the offsets from the VIA base value (vBase or vBase2) of the counters and latches used to start the timers.

■ **Table 4-23**   Offsets of Macintosh VIA timer latches

Offset	Contents
vT1C	Timer T1 counter (low-order byte)
vT1CH	Timer T1 counter (high-order byte)
vT1L	Timer T1 latch (low-order byte)
vT1LH	Timer T1 latch (high-order byte)
vT2C	Timer T2 counter (low-order byte)
vT2CH	Timer T2 counter (high-order byte)

Timer T1 of the classic Macintosh, Macintosh SE, and Macintosh Portable VIA, and of the Macintosh SE/30 and Macintosh II–family VIA1, is used by the Sound Driver and Sound Manager. Timer T2 is used by the Disk Driver to time disk I/O events. Timer T1 of the Macintosh SE/30 and Macintosh II–family VIA2 is used to generate the Vertical Blanking signal that goes to VIA1. VIA2 timer T2 is not currently used by the Macintosh Operating System.

△ **Developer tip** To avoid interfering with critical operating system routines, it is strongly recommended that you do not write to the VIA timers directly. Instead, use the Sound Driver and Sound Manager routines to control sound output, and use the routines provided by the Time Manager to time events. The Sound Driver, Sound Manager, and Time Manager are described in *Inside Macintosh*. △

Processor-interrupt registers

Low-level software can enable or disable each of the sources of VIA interrupts by setting or clearing a bit in the Interrupt Enable register. The main processor can then read the contents of the Interrupt Flag register to learn the cause of the interrupt.

The VIA in the classic Macintosh and Macintosh SE computers, or VIA1 in the Macintosh SE/30 and Macintosh II–family computers, can cause a level-1 processor interrupt whenever one of the following events occurs:

- Timer T1 or timer T2 counts down to 0.

- The keyboard clock signal is received (classic Macintosh); or the ADB clock signal is received (Macintosh SE or Macintosh II family).

- A bit is transferred over the keyboard data line (classic Macintosh) or over the ADB data line (Macintosh SE or Macintosh II family).

- The shift register for the keyboard serial interface (classic Macintosh) or for the ADB serial interface (Macintosh SE or Macintosh II family) finishes shifting 8 bits in or out.

- The vertical blanking interval is beginning (classic Macintosh, Macintosh SE) or the 60.15 Hz interrupt occurs (Macintosh II family).

- The one-second interrupt request is received.

The VIA in the Macintosh Portable can cause a level-1 processor interrupt whenever one of the following events occurs:

- Timer T1 or timer T2 counts down to 0.

- A SCSI IRQ interrupt request is received.

- A Power Manager IC interrupt request is received.

- The one-second interrupt request is received.

- The 60.15 Hz interrupt request is received.

VIA2 in the Macintosh II–family machines can cause a level-2 processor interrupt whenever one of the following events occurs:

- Timer T1 or timer T2 counts down to 0.

- A slot interrupt request is received.

- An ASC interrupt request is received.

- A SCSI IRQ interrupt request is received.

- A SCSI DRQ interrupt request is received.

See the sections "MC68000 Interrupts," "MC68020 Interrupts," and "MC68030 Interrupts" in Chapter 3 for more information on how Macintosh computers handle interrupts. For more information on how to use interrupts in your programs, see *Inside Macintosh.*

Interrupt Flag register

Each bit in the Interrupt Flag registers (at addresses vBase+vIFR and vBase2+vIFR) is set high whenever a specific interrupt has occurred, as shown in Tables 4-24 through 4-27. The Macintosh Operating System uses these flags to determine the cause of the interrupt. Bit 7 of the Interrupt Flag register remains set high (and the /IRQ line to the general logic circuits is held low) as long as any VIA interrupt flag is set.

■ **Table 4-24**   Bits in the Interrupt Flag register in the VIA in the classic
Macintosh computers

Bit	Cause of interrupt
7	IRQ (any enabled VIA interrupts)
6	Timer T1
5	Timer T2
4	Keyboard clock
3	Keyboard data
2	Keyboard data ready
1	Vertical blanking interrupt
0	One-second interrupt

■ **Table 4-25**   Bits in the Interrupt Flag register in the VIA in Macintosh SE and in VIA1
in the Macintosh SE/30 and Macintosh II–family computers

Bit	Cause of interrupt
7	IRQ (any enabled VIA interrupts)
6	Timer T1
5	Timer T2
4	ADB clock
3	ADB data
2	ADB data ready
1	Vertical blanking interrupt
0	One-second interrupt

Note: The Macintosh IIci uses registers in the RBV to control the interrupt functions. The Macintosh IIfx uses registers in the OSS to control the interrupt functions.

- **Table 4-26**   Bits in the Interrupt Flag register in the VIA in the
  Macintosh Portable computer

Bit	Cause of interrupt
7	IRQ (any enabled VIA interrupts)
6	Timer T1
5	Timer T2
4	Power manager interrupt
3	SCSI IRQ interrupt
2	Not used
1	60.15 Hz interrupt
0	One-second interrupt

- **Table 4-27**   Bits in the VIA2 Interrupt Flag register in the Macintosh SE/30 and
  Macintosh II–family computers

Bit	Cause of interrupt
7	IRQ (all enabled VIA interrupts)
6	Timer T1 (not used on the Macintosh IIci)
5	Timer T2 (not used on the Macintosh IIci)
4	ASC interrupt
3	SCSI IRQ
2	/EXP.IRQ (Macintosh IIci only)
1	Slot interrupt
0	SCSI DRQ

Note: The Macintosh IIci uses registers in the RBV to control the interrupt functions. The Macintosh IIfx uses registers in the OSS to control the interrupt functions.

Interrupt Enable register

The Interrupt Enable register lets software enable or disable the interrupts shown in
Table 4-24 through Table 4-27. If an interrupt is disabled, its corresponding bit in the
Interrupt Flag register continues to be set whenever the cause for that interrupt occurs,
but the IRQ flag (bit 7 in the Interrupt Flag register) is not affected and the VIA does not
assert the /IRQ line to the general logic circuits. Software can address the Interrupt Enable
register at address vBase+vIER for VIA1 or vBase2+vIER for the VIA2.

The lower 7 bits in the Interrupt Enable register are arranged in the same sequence as the bits in the Interrupt Flag register (Table 4-24 through Table 4-27). For example, bit 6 in the Interrupt Enable register enables or disables interrupts caused by timer T1.

When a program writes an 8-bit value to the Interrupt Enable register, if bit 7 is a 1, each 1 in bits 0 through 6 enables the corresponding interrupt; if bit 7 is a 0, each 1 in bits 0 through 6 disables the corresponding interrupt. In either case, 0's in bits 0 through 6 of the Interrupt Enable register have no effect on the status of the interrupts. For example, to enable interrupts caused by the classic Macintosh keyboard clock without affecting any other interrupt, software would write 1's to bits 7 and 4 of the Interrupt Enable register. To disable interrupts caused by the keyboard clock signal, it would write a 0 to bit 7 and a 1 to bit 4.

When software reads the Interrupt Enable register, bit 7 is always read as a 1.

Chapter 5 **Memory**

Macintosh computers contain both random-access memory (RAM) and read-only memory (ROM). This chapter describes the RAM and ROM hardware and connectors used in Macintosh computers. The way in which the address space is assigned to various devices in the different Macintosh family members is described in Chapter 3.

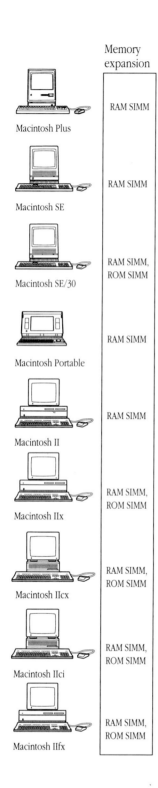

Memory
expansion

Macintosh Plus — RAM SIMM

Macintosh SE — RAM SIMM

Macintosh SE/30 — RAM SIMM, ROM SIMM

Macintosh Portable — RAM SIMM

Macintosh II — RAM SIMM

Macintosh IIx — RAM SIMM, ROM SIMM

Macintosh IIcx — RAM SIMM, ROM SIMM

Macintosh IIci — RAM SIMM, ROM SIMM

Macintosh IIfx — RAM SIMM, ROM SIMM

RAM

System RAM is the working memory of the system. The amount of RAM available and the memory addresses it occupies are different on the different models in the Macintosh family. The main reason for the differences is the use of different microprocessors and their different-sized address buses: the MC68000, with 24-bit addresses, and the MC68020 and MC68030, with 32-bit addresses.

RAM addresses in MC68000-based models

In the Macintosh computers that use the MC68000 processor, the address space from address $00 0000 through $3F FFFF ($00 0000 through $8F FFFF in the Macintosh Portable) is reserved for RAM, although the amount of that space actually used depends on the RAM available in the system, as shown in Table 5-1. The first 1024 bytes of RAM ($00 0000 through $00 03FF) are used by the MC68000 to store exception vectors. Of these locations, the first 256 bytes are reserved for use by the operating system and the remainder are available for use by applications. The first 256 bytes contain trap vectors, interrupt vectors for the I/O devices, and the Reset vector.

■ **Table 5-1**   RAM addresses in Macintosh computers with an MC68000 processor

Computer	Amount of RAM	Highest RAM address
Macintosh 128K	128 KB	$01 FFFF
Macintosh 512K	512 KB	$07 FFFF
Macintosh 512K enhanced	512 KB	$07 FFFF
Macintosh Plus	1 MB	$0F FFFF
	2 MB	$1F FFFF
	2.5 MB	$27 FFFF
	4 MB	$3F FFFF
Macintosh SE	1 MB	$0F FFFF
	2 MB	$1F FFFF
	2.5 MB	$27 FFFF
	4 MB	$3F FFFF
Macintosh Portable	1 MB	$0F FFFF
	2 MB	$1F FFFF
	5 MB	$4F FFFF
	9 MB	$8F FFFF

System RAM contains the system heap, a copy of parameter RAM, various global variables, application heaps, the stack, and other information used by applications. In addition, in the Macintosh SE and classic Macintosh computers, the following hardware devices share the use of system RAM with the MC68000:

- the video display, which reads the information for the display from one of two screen buffers in RAM

- the sound generator, which reads its information from one of two sound buffers in the classic Macintosh computers, or from one sound buffer in the Macintosh SE

- the disk-speed controller, which shares its data space with the sound buffers

The Macintosh Portable has RAM buffers for sound and video that are separate from system RAM, and does not provide a disk-speed signal. Therefore, the MC68HC000 in the Macintosh Portable does not share the use of system RAM with any other device.

RAM addresses in MC68020-based and MC68030-based models

In the Macintosh SE/30 and Macintosh II family, the 32-bit address space from address $0000 0000 through $3FFF FFFF is reserved for RAM. As in the MC68000-based Macintosh computers, the amount of address space actually used for memory depends on the RAM available in the system, as shown in Table 5-2. You must use a 32-bit operating system to make use of system memory beyond 8 MB.

Exception vectors are stored by the MC68020 and MC68030 in a 1024-byte-long table starting at the address in the Vector Base register. The Vector Base register is initialized to $0000 0000 when the system is started up or reset. The first 256 bytes of the exception vector table are reserved for use by the operating system; the remainder are available for use by applications. The first 256 bytes contain trap vectors, interrupt vectors for the I/O devices, and the Reset vector.

■ **Table 5-2** RAM addresses in the Macintosh SE/30 and Macintosh II–family computers

Amount of RAM	Highest RAM address
1 MB	$000F FFFF
2 MB	$001F FFFF
4 MB	$003F FFFF
5 MB	$004F FFFF
8 MB	$007F FFFF
16 MB	$00FF FFFF
32 MB	$01FF FFFF
64 MB	$03FF FFFF
128 MB	$07FF FFFF

System RAM in the Macintosh SE/30 and Macintosh II–family computers contains the system heap, a copy of parameter RAM, various global variables and trap handlers, application heaps, the stack, and other information used by applications. The video display and sound generator in the Macintosh SE/30 and Macintosh II family have their own dedicated memory buffers and do not use system RAM. In the Macintosh IIci, the built-in video generator uses system RAM for its screen buffer.

◆ *Note:* The second screen buffer and second sound buffer are not available in all versions of the Macintosh.

⚠ **Developer tip** To ensure that your software will run on all Macintosh computers— those with different memory configurations, as well as future models—use the addresses stored in the global variables listed in *Inside Macintosh.* ⚠

The contents of RAM and ROM are repeated throughout unused address space assigned to memory, as described in the section "Address Maps" in Chapter 3.

RAM access cycles

In the Macintosh SE and classic Macintosh computers, the main processor's RAM-access cycles are interleaved with the video display's access cycles. The video display access cycles occur only during the active portion of a screen scan line. The video logic scans the video screen buffer in RAM 60 times each second and sends the data to the screen. This process both refreshes the dynamic RAM and refreshes the image on the video screen.

In the Macintosh Portable, Macintosh SE/30, and Macintosh II family, the main processor's RAM access cycles are not interleaved with the video display's access cycles. The video circuitry has separate memory that is used exclusively by the video display.

Memory dedicated to sound generation in the Macintosh Portable, Macintosh SE/30, and Macintosh II family is located on the Apple Sound Chip in the form of FIFO (first-in-first-out) memories.

■ **Table 5-3**   RAM access rates in the Macintosh family computers

Macintosh model	CPU clock frequency	Average RAM access rate
Macintosh Plus	7.83 MHz	2.56 MB/sec.
Macintosh SE	7.83 MHz	3.22 MB/sec.
Macintosh SE/30	15.67 MHz	15.67 MB/sec.
Macintosh Portable	15.67 MHz	6.27 MB/sec
Macintosh II	15.67 MHz	12.53 MB/sec.
Macintosh IIx	15.67 MHz	15.67 MB/sec.
Macintosh IIcx	15.67 MHz	15.67 MB/sec.
Macintosh IIci	25 MHz	36.36 MB/sec. maximum*
Macintosh IIfx	40 MHz	60.69 MB/sec.

*Maximum rate on a Macintosh IIci with no cache card, using a NuBus video card. For details, see the section "RAM Access Rate in the Macintosh IIci Computer."

RAM access rate in the Macintosh Plus computer

In the Macintosh Plus and other classic Macintosh computers, one out of every two RAM access cycles is devoted to video data during a scan line. The last RAM access before the beginning of a scan line is used for sound and disk-speed control data. The Macintosh Plus has an average RAM access rate for the main processor of about 2.56 MB per second.

RAM access rate in the Macintosh SE computer

In the Macintosh SE, one longword video access is made for each four RAM access cycles during a scan line. The last RAM access before the beginning of a scan line is used for sound and disk-speed control data. The Macintosh SE has an average RAM access rate for the main processor of about 3.22 MB per second.

RAM access rate in the Macintosh Portable computer

Because the Macintosh Portable uses a faster system clock than the Macintosh SE, does not have to share processor RAM access cycles with video or sound circuitry, and does not have to refresh memory, it has a faster RAM access rate than the Macintosh SE. The Macintosh Portable has an average RAM access rate of 6.27 MB per second.

RAM access rate in the Macintosh SE/30, Macintosh II, Macintosh IIx, and Macintosh IIcx computers

As in the Macintosh Portable, the main processor in the Macintosh SE/30, Macintosh II, Macintosh IIx, and Macintosh IIcx computers does not share RAM accesses with video or sound circuitry. Except for memory refresh, which takes one access cycle every 15.6 μs, the main processors in those computers have uninterrupted access to RAM. The Macintosh II has an average RAM access rate of 12.53 MB per second; the Macintosh SE/30, Macintosh IIx, and Macintosh IIcx have an average RAM access rate of 15.67 MB per second.

RAM access rate in the Macintosh IIci computer

In the Macintosh IIci, the use of burst mode and fast page mode gives the processor a maximum RAM access rate of 36.36 MB per second. That access rate is always true for bank B; for bank A, it is achieved only when using a NuBus video card and not using the built-in video circuits.

The built-in video circuits use a screen buffer in RAM bank A. The effect of the video RAM cycles can decrease the processor's access to bank A by as little as 6% or as much as 65%, depending on the type of video display in use: larger displays and display modes with more bits per pixel have a greater effect. Please refer to the section "Built-in Video Display" in Chapter 12 for information about the effect of different display types and monitor sizes on CPU access to bank A.

The average RAM access rate actually achieved depends not only on the type of display in use but also on the amount of RAM in bank B. Remember that the processor always has immediate access to bank B, which is unaffected by the built-in video circuits. If most of the system's RAM is installed in bank B, then the majority of CPU accesses are in that bank and at the maximum rate, 36.36 MB per second. That is the reason for installing the larger RAM devices in bank B.

◆ *Note:* In a Macintosh IIci with a cache card installed, the maximum RAM access rate is 50 MB per second and is largely unaffected by the built-in video circuits.

RAM access rate in the Macintosh IIfx computer

In the Macintosh IIfx, the high-speed cache RAM gives the processor a maximum RAM access rate of 64.00 MB per second. Any time there is a cache hit—which occurs for over 90% of processor read operations—the effective rate is equal to the maximum rate. The additional time required for handling the occasional cache miss brings the overall average rate down to 60.95 MB per second. For more information about the operation of RAM in the Macintosh IIfx, please refer to the section "RAM Cache in the Macintosh IIfx Computer," later in this chapter.

RAM configuration in the Macintosh 128K, 512K, and 512K enhanced computers

RAM in the early Macintosh computers is provided in dynamic RAM (DRAM) ICs, which are arranged in two rows of 8 in the Macintosh 128K computer, Macintosh 512K computer, and Macintosh 512K enhanced computer. The Macintosh 128K RAM consists of 16 individual 64 Kbit DRAMs, and the Macintosh 512K and 512K enhanced use 16 individual 256 Kbit DRAMs. The DRAM ICs are mounted on the main logic board of the computer.

When the MC68000 writes data to RAM, it puts an address in the range $00 0000 to $07 FFFF on the address bus. The PALs in the Macintosh 128K, 512K, and 512K enhanced computers decode an address in this range as a request to address RAM and enable the data-bus buffers. The main processor places the data on the data bus. The address is further decoded by the RAM address MUXs, which divide the address into two 9-bit parts: the row address and the column address. First the row address is fed into the RAMs by the Row Address Strobe signal (RAS) generated by the PALs. Then the column address is fed into the appropriate RAM by a column address strobe signal generated by a PAL. There are two column address strobes: CAS1 and CAS2—one for each row of eight RAM ICs. In this way, up to 512 KB of RAM can be addressed through the nine RAM address lines.

Each time you turn on the Macintosh 128K, 512K, or 512K enhanced, system software does a memory test, then determines how much RAM is installed in the machine. Software stores this information in the global variable MemTop, which contains the address (plus 1) of the last byte in RAM.

RAM configuration in the Macintosh Plus and Macintosh SE computers

The RAM in the Macintosh Plus and Macintosh SE is provided in either two or four packages known as **Single In-line Memory Modules** (SIMMs). A SIMM consists of a small printed circuit board that contains several surface-mounted DRAM ICs. Along one edge of the SIMM are electrical finger contacts, which plug into the SIMM sockets that are mounted on the main logic board.

▲ **Warning**   Because the video monitor is built in, there are dangerous voltages inside the cases of the Macintosh Plus and Macintosh SE computers. The video tube and video circuitry may hold dangerous charges long after the computer's power is turned off. Opening the case of the Macintosh Plus and Macintosh SE computers requires special tools and may invalidate your warranty. Installation of RAM SIMMs in these computers should be done by qualified service personnel only. ▲

Each SIMM in the Macintosh Plus or Macintosh SE contains eight DRAM ICs. Each SIMM has ten address pins and eight data pins, and each data pin is connected to one of the eight DRAMs. The SIMMs are arranged in pairs; each pair is referred to as a *row*. Two SIMMs combined in a row provide a 16-bit-wide parallel data bus that is used by the MC68000. Row 1 comprises SIMM 1 and SIMM 2, whereas row 2 comprises SIMMs 3 and 4.

◆ *Note:* Other configurations of SIMMs can be used, such as two DRAM ICs with four data pins each. Nine-bit SIMMs can also be used in these machines; the ninth bit is simply ignored.

When the MC68000 writes data to RAM, it puts an address in the range $00 0000 to $3F FFFF on the address bus. The general logic circuits in the Macintosh Plus and Macintosh SE decode this address as a request to address RAM and enable the data-bus buffers. The main processor places the data on the data bus. The address is further decoded by the RAM address MUXs, which divide the address into two 10-bit parts: the row address and the column address. First the row address is fed into the RAMs by the Row Address Strobe signal (RAS) generated by the general logic circuits. Then the column address is fed into the appropriate RAM by a column address strobe signal generated by the logic circuits. There are four column address strobes: CAS1, CAS2, CAS3, and CAS4—one for each SIMM. In this way, 4 MB of RAM can be addressed through the ten RAM address lines.

Several RAM configurations are possible, depending on whether two or four SIMMs are used, and on the size of the RAM ICs mounted on the SIMMs. The size of a DRAM IC is sometimes referred to as its *density*.

In the Macintosh Plus and earlier Macintosh SE computers, there are two resistors on the main logic board (in the area labeled RAM SIZE) that tell the general logic circuits the number of SIMMs and size of the RAM ICs installed. In later Macintosh SE computers, there is a jumper on the main logic board that can be installed in either of two positions (labeled 2/4M and 1M) that provide this information to the general logic circuits.

You must follow these guidelines when installing RAM SIMMs in the Macintosh Plus and Macintosh SE:

- The RAM ICs in each SIMM must have 150 ns RAS access time or faster.

- All the RAM ICs in a row must have the same access time.

- Each SIMM must be filled with eight RAM ICs. (A nine-RAM SIMM will work in the Macintosh Plus or Macintosh SE, but the ninth RAM IC is not connected electrically to the main logic board.)

- All the RAM ICs in a row must be the same size.

- A row cannot contain only one SIMM. A row must either be empty or contain two SIMMs.

- In the Macintosh Plus and any Macintosh SE that has RAM size resistors, if the SIMMs in one row contain larger RAM ICs than the SIMMs in the other row, then the SIMMs with the larger RAM ICs must be installed in row 1. In the Macintosh SE that has a RAM size jumper, the SIMMs with larger RAM ICs must be installed in row 2.

The resistors in Macintosh Plus and earlier Macintosh SE computers must be arranged in the following manner:

- If only two SIMMs are installed, the resistor labeled ONE ROW (resistor R9 in the Macintosh Plus or R36 in the Macintosh SE) must be installed.

- If four SIMMs are installed, the resistor labeled ONE ROW must be removed.

- If all of the SIMMs contain 256 Kbit DRAMs, the resistor labeled 256K BIT (resistor R8 in the Macintosh Plus or R35 in the Macintosh SE) must be installed.

- If either two or four of the SIMMs contain 1 Mbit DRAMs, the resistor labeled 256K BIT must be removed.

The jumper in later Macintosh SE computers must be installed in the following manner:

- If only two SIMMs are installed, the jumper must be installed on the position labeled 2/4M.

- If four SIMMs containing 256 Kbit DRAMs are installed, the jumper must be installed on the position labeled 1M.

- If four SIMMs are installed and either two or four of them contain 1 Mbit DRAMs, the jumper must be left off.

The RAM SIMM socket pinout is shown in Figure 5-1. The RAM SIMM socket signal assignments for the Macintosh Plus and Macintosh SE are shown in Table 5-4.

- **Figure 5-1** Pinout of the RAM SIMM socket in the Macintosh Plus and Macintosh SE computers

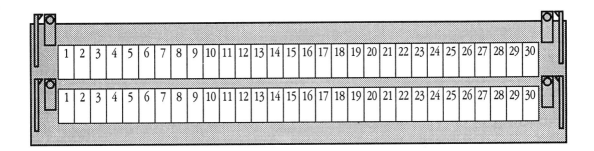

■ **Table 5-4** Signal assignments for the RAM SIMM socket in the Macintosh Plus and Macintosh SE computers

Pin number	Signal name	Signal description
1	+5V	+5 volts
2	/CAS1	Column Address Strobe for SIMM1; or
	/CAS2	Column Address Strobe for SIMM 2; or
	/CAS3	Column Address Strobe for SIMM 3; or
	/CAS4	Column Address Strobe for SIMM 4
3	RDQ0	RAM data bus, bit 0, SIMM 1 and SIMM 3; or
	RDQ8	RAM data bus, bit 8, SIMM 2 and SIMM 4
4	RA0	RAM address bus, bit 0
5	RA1	RAM address bus, bit 1
6	RDQ1	RAM data bus, bit 1, SIMM 1 and SIMM 3; or
	RDQ9	RAM data bus, bit 9, SIMM 2 and SIMM 4
7	RA2	RAM address bus, bit 2
8	RA3	RAM address bus, bit 3
9	GND	Ground
10	RDQ2	RAM data bus, bit 2, SIMM 1 and SIMM 3; or
	RDQ10	RAM data bus, bit 10, SIMM 2 and SIMM 4
11	RA4	RAM address bus, bit 4
12	RA5	RAM address bus, bit 5
13	RDQ3	RAM data bus, bit 3, SIMM 1 and SIMM 3; or
	RDQ11	RAM data bus, bit 11, SIMM 2 and SIMM 4
14	RA6	RAM address bus, bit 6
15	RA7	RAM address bus, bit 7
16	RDQ4	RAM data bus, bit 4, SIMM 1 and SIMM 3; or
	RDQ12	RAM data bus, bit 12, SIMM 2 and SIMM 4
17	RA8	RAM address bus, bit 8
18	RA9	RAM address bus, bit 9
19	n.c.	Not connected
20	RDQ5	RAM data bus, bit 5, SIMM 1 and SIMM 3; or
	RDQ13	RAM data bus, bit 13, SIMM 2 and SIMM 4
21	READ	RAM read
22	GND	Ground

(continued)

Pin number	Signal name	Signal description
23	RDQ6	RAM data bus, bit 6, SIMM 1 and SIMM 3; or
	RDQ14	RAM data bus, bit 14, SIMM 2 and SIMM 4
24	n.c.	Not connected
25	RDQ7	RAM data bus, bit 7, SIMM 1 and SIMM 3; or
	RDQ15	RAM data bus, bit 15, SIMM 2 and SIMM 4
26	n.c.	Not connected
27	/RAS	Row Address Strobe
28	n.c.	Not connected
29	n.c.	Not connected
30	+5V	+5 volts

The various combinations of SIMMs that can be installed in the Macintosh Plus computer are shown in Figure 5-2.

Two different SIMM configurations have been used in Macintosh SE computers. Earlier Macintosh SE computers have the SIMM configurations shown in Figure 5-3; later Macintosh SE computers have the SIMM configurations shown in Figure 5-4.

Each time you switch on the Macintosh Plus or Macintosh SE, system software does a memory test and detemines how much RAM is installed in the machine. Software stores this information in the global variable MemTop, which contains the address (plus one) of the last byte in RAM. Because the range of addresses in each SIMM row depends on the size of the DRAMs in the SIMM, the general logic circuits use the SIMM resistors or jumper to determine which row to access for each address range.

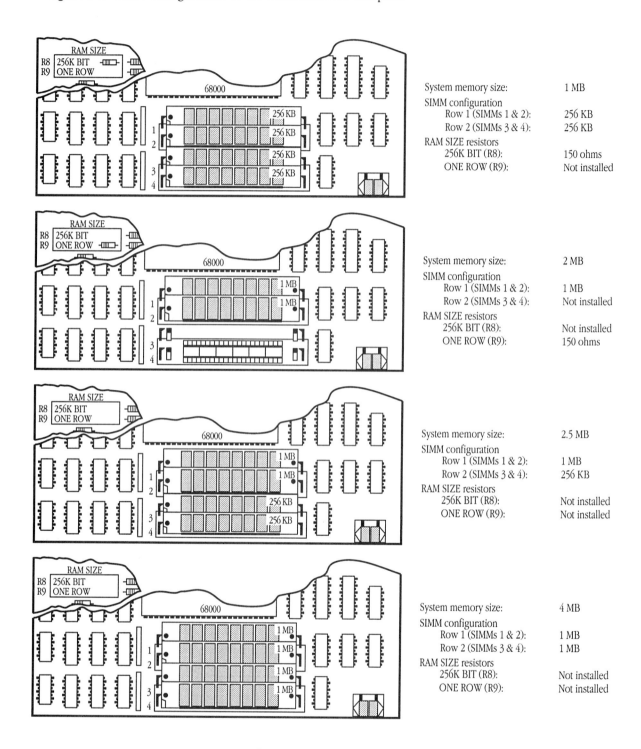

System memory size: 1 MB

SIMM configuration
  Row 1 (SIMMs 1 & 2): 256 KB
  Row 2 (SIMMs 3 & 4): 256 KB
RAM SIZE resistors
  256K BIT (R8): 150 ohms
  ONE ROW (R9): Not installed

System memory size: 2 MB

SIMM configuration
  Row 1 (SIMMs 1 & 2): 1 MB
  Row 2 (SIMMs 3 & 4): Not installed
RAM SIZE resistors
  256K BIT (R8): Not installed
  ONE ROW (R9): 150 ohms

System memory size: 2.5 MB

SIMM configuration
  Row 1 (SIMMs 1 & 2): 1 MB
  Row 2 (SIMMs 3 & 4): 256 KB
RAM SIZE resistors
  256K BIT (R8): Not installed
  ONE ROW (R9): Not installed

System memory size: 4 MB

SIMM configuration
  Row 1 (SIMMs 1 & 2): 1 MB
  Row 2 (SIMMs 3 & 4): 1 MB
RAM SIZE resistors
  256K BIT (R8): Not installed
  ONE ROW (R9): Not installed

■ **Figure 5-3** SIMM configurations in earlier Macintosh SE computers

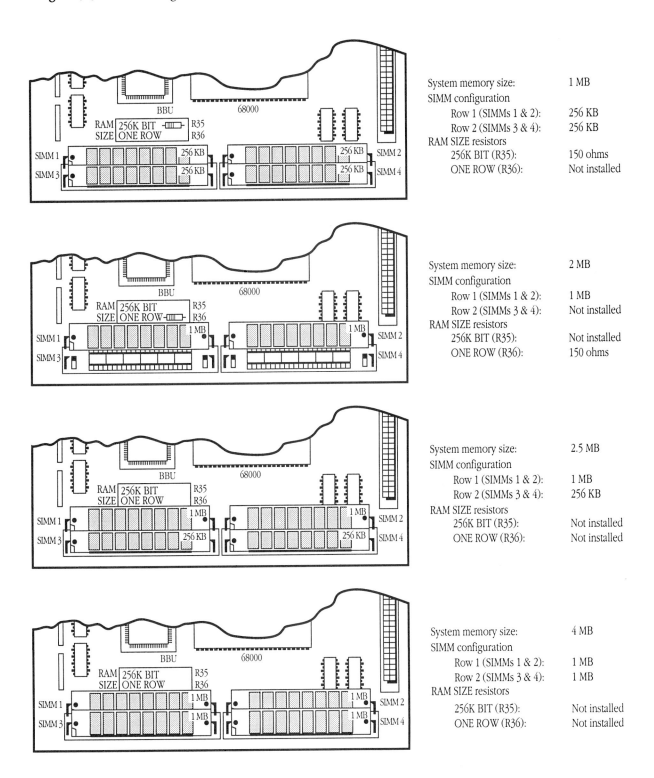

System memory size: 1 MB
SIMM configuration
    Row 1 (SIMMs 1 & 2):   256 KB
    Row 2 (SIMMs 3 & 4):   256 KB
RAM SIZE resistors
    256K BIT (R35):   150 ohms
    ONE ROW (R36):   Not installed

System memory size: 2 MB
SIMM configuration
    Row 1 (SIMMs 1 & 2):   1 MB
    Row 2 (SIMMs 3 & 4):   Not installed
RAM SIZE resistors
    256K BIT (R35):   Not installed
    ONE ROW (R36):   150 ohms

System memory size: 2.5 MB
SIMM configuration
    Row 1 (SIMMs 1 & 2):   1 MB
    Row 2 (SIMMs 3 & 4):   256 KB
RAM SIZE resistors
    256K BIT (R35):   Not installed
    ONE ROW (R36):   Not installed

System memory size: 4 MB
SIMM configuration
    Row 1 (SIMMs 1 & 2):   1 MB
    Row 2 (SIMMs 3 & 4):   1 MB
RAM SIZE resistors
    256K BIT (R35):   Not installed
    ONE ROW (R36):   Not installed

■ **Figure 5-4** SIMM configurations in later Macintosh SE computers

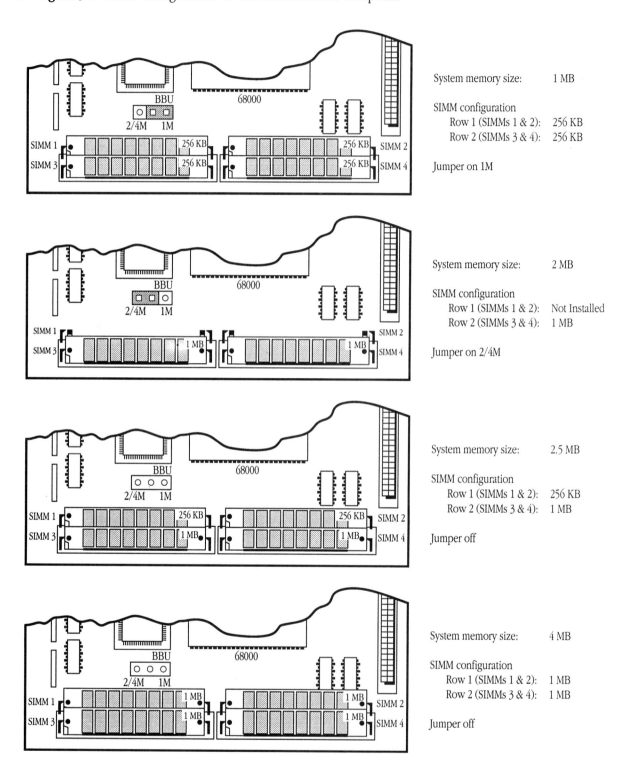

System memory size: 1 MB

SIMM configuration
   Row 1 (SIMMs 1 & 2): 256 KB
   Row 2 (SIMMs 3 & 4): 256 KB

Jumper on 1M

System memory size: 2 MB

SIMM configuration
   Row 1 (SIMMs 1 & 2): Not Installed
   Row 2 (SIMMs 3 & 4): 1 MB

Jumper on 2/4M

System memory size: 2.5 MB

SIMM configuration
   Row 1 (SIMMs 1 & 2): 256 KB
   Row 2 (SIMMs 3 & 4): 1 MB

Jumper off

System memory size: 4 MB

SIMM configuration
   Row 1 (SIMMs 1 & 2): 1 MB
   Row 2 (SIMMs 3 & 4): 1 MB

Jumper off

RAM configuration in the Macintosh Portable computer

RAM in the Macintosh Portable computer is provided in **static RAM** (SRAM) ICs, which do not have to be periodically refreshed and therefore consume less power than dynamic RAM ICs. The Macintosh Portable has 1 MB of SRAM on the logic board and has an internal connector for a memory expansion card.

◆ *Note:* The Macintosh Portable hardware and address map provide for up to 8 MB of expansion RAM, for a total of 9 MB of system RAM.

Each time you turn on the Macintosh Portable (that is, when the battery is recharged after being completely discharged, or a new battery is installed), system software does a memory test, then determines how much RAM is installed in the machine. Software stores this information in the global variable MemTop, which contains the address (plus one) of the last byte in RAM.

In addition to the system RAM, the Macintosh Portable contains 32 KB of RAM for use by the video circuits that is separate from system RAM.

Permanent RAM

The permanent memory of the Macintosh Portable consists of thirty-two 256 Kbit static RAM (SRAM) ICs mounted on the main logic board of the computer. These SRAM ICs have a 100 ns access time.

When the MC68HC000 writes data to permanent system RAM, it puts an address in the range $00 0000 to $0F FFFF on the address bus. The CPU GLU decodes this address as a request to address RAM, and asserts one of a pair of RAM Read/Write signals to select the upper half or lower half of permanent RAM. The address is further decoded by the Miscellaneous GLU, which uses one of 16 chip-select signals to enable a pair of RAM ICs. The RAM ICs in permanent RAM are arranged in pairs that are connected in parallel, using a 15-bit-wide RAM address bus (16 bits including the chip-select signal). In this way, 1 MB of RAM can be addressed through 15 RAM address lines.

An access to permanent RAM in the Macintosh Portable requires one MC68HC000 processor wait state. Because all the RAM used in the Macintosh Portable is static RAM, no refresh cycles are necessary. All permanent RAM is powered by the battery when the Macintosh Portable is in the sleep state.

Internal expansion RAM

The internal memory expansion card plugs into a 50-pin connector that provides for 23 address lines, 16 data lines, plus control signals and power. When the MC68HC000 writes data to the internal memory expansion card, it puts an address in the range $10 0000 to $8F FFFF on the address bus. The CPU GLU custom IC decodes this address as a request to address expansion RAM. Logic on the RAM expansion card further decodes the address and enables the appropriate RAM ICs. Because the Macintosh Portable hardware can address a maximum of 8 MB of expansion RAM, the 23 address lines are all that is needed to address all the RAM on the RAM expansion card.

The memory on a 1 MB RAM expansion card consists of either thirty-two 256 Kbit static RAM ICs or eight 1 Mbit static RAM ICs. The memory on a 4 MB RAM expansion card consists of thirty-two 1 Mbit static RAM ICs or eight 4 Mbit static RAM ICs. All SRAM ICs on RAM expansion cards must have an access time of 100 ns or faster.

Figure 5-5 shows the internal RAM connector pinout. The signal assignments for this connector are shown in Table 5-5.

■ **Figure 5-5** Pinout of the RAM expansion connector in the Macintosh Portable computer

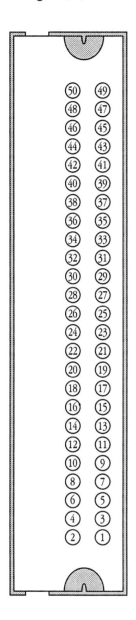

■ **Table 5-5** Signal assignments for the RAM expansion connector in the
Macintosh Portable computer

Pin number	Signal name	Signal description
1	+5V	+5 volts
2	A1	Address line A1
3	A2	Address line A2
4	A3	Address line A3
5	A4	Address line A4
6	A5	Address line A5
7	A6	Address line A6
8	A7	Address line A7
9	A8	Address line A8
10	A9	Address line A9
11	A10	Address line A10
12	A11	Address line A11
13	A12	Address line A12
14	A13	Address line A13
15	A14	Address line A14
16	A15	Address line A15
17	A16	Address line A16
18	A17	Address line A17
19	A18	Address line A18
20	A19	Address line A19
21	A20	Address line A20
22	A21	Address line A21
23	A22	Address line A22
24	A23	Address line A23
25	GND	Ground
26	GND	Ground
27	/SYS.PWR	Indicates whether system is in sleep state
28	/AS	Address strobe from MC68HC000
29	R/W	Read/Write line from MC68HC000
30	/UDS	Upper data strobe from MC68HC000
31	/LDS	Lower data strobe from MC68HC000
32	/DELAY.CS	Chip-select signal from CPU GLU
33	D0	Data line D0
34	D1	Data line D1

(continued)

Pin number	Signal name	Signal description
35	D2	Data line D2
36	D3	Data line D3
37	D4	Data line D4
38	D5	Data line D5
39	D6	Data line D6
40	D7	Data line D7
41	D8	Data line D8
42	D9	Data line D9
43	D10	Data line D10
44	D11	Data line D11
45	D12	Data line D12
46	D13	Data line D13
47	D14	Data line D14
48	D15	Data line D15
49	+5V	+5 volts
50	+5V	+5 volts

As for permanent RAM, an access to RAM on a Macintosh Portable internal memory
expansion card requires one MC68HC000 processor wait state. Because all the RAM used
in the Macintosh Portable is static RAM, no refresh cycles are necessary. All permanent and
internal expansion RAM is powered by the battery when the Macintosh Portable is in the
sleep state.

RAM configuration in the Macintosh SE/30 and Macintosh II–family computers

The RAM in the Macintosh SE/30 and in the Macintosh II family is provided in four or eight
SIMMs. All those machines use the same 30-pin SIMM except the Macintosh IIfx, which has
a different SIMM with 64 pins.

▲ **Warning**   Because the video monitor is built in, there are dangerous voltages
inside the case of the Macintosh SE/30 computer. The video tube and
video circuitry may hold dangerous charges long after the computer's
power is turned off. Opening the case of the Macintosh SE/30 requires
special tools and may invalidate your warranty. Installation of RAM in
the SIMM sockets in this computer should be done by qualified
service personnel only. ▲

Each SIMM in these computers contains eight DRAM ICs. Each SIMM has 12 address pins and 8 data pins, and each data pin is connected to one of the eight DRAMs. The SIMMs are arranged in groups of four; each group is referred to as a *bank*. Four SIMMs combined in a bank provide a 32-bit-wide parallel data bus that is used by the MC68020 or MC68030.

◆ *Note:* Other configurations of SIMMs can be used, such as two DRAM ICs with four data pins each.

In a Macintosh IIci or Macintosh IIfx equipped with the optional parity feature, each RAM SIMM contains nine bits. The ninth bit provides storage for the parity bits. See the sections "Parity RAM in the Macintosh IIci Computer" and "Parity RAM in the Macintosh IIfx Computer" later in this chapter.

When the main processor writes data to RAM in 24-bit mode, it puts an address in the range $xx00 0000 to $xx7F FFFF on the address bus. The memory management unit strips off the high byte and translates the address to one in the range $0000 0000 through $3FFF FFFF. The GLUE decodes this address as a request to address RAM, and the main processor places the data on the data bus. The RAM address MUXs divide the address into two 12-bit parts: the row address and the column address. First the row address is fed into the appropriate bank of RAMs by one of two Row Address Strobe (RAS) signals generated by the GLUE. Then the column address is fed into the appropriate SIMM by one of four Column Address Strobe (CAS) signals generated by the GLUE. In this way, up to 128 MB of RAM can be addressed through the 12 RAM address lines.

Several RAM configurations are possible, depending on whether one or two banks of SIMMs are used, and on the size of the RAM ICs mounted on the SIMMs.

You must follow these guidelines when installing RAM SIMMs in the Macintosh SE/30 or Macintosh II–family computers:

- The RAM ICs in each SIMM must have 120 ns RAS access time or faster (80 ns or faster in the Macintosh IIci and the Macintosh IIfx).

- All the RAM ICs in a bank must have the same access time.

- Each SIMM must be filled with eight RAM ICs. A nine-RAM SIMM will work in any Macintosh II–family computer, but the ninth RAM IC is not connected electrically to the main logic board except in the Macintosh IIci and the Macintosh IIfx. Those machines have an optional parity feature that uses the ninth RAM IC for the parity bit.

- All the RAM ICs in a bank must be the same size.

- The smallest SIMM that can be used in an Macintosh IIfx is 1 MB.

- A bank must either be empty or contain four SIMMs; a bank cannot contain one, two, or three SIMMs.

- If the SIMMs in one bank contain larger RAM ICs than do the SIMMs in the other bank, the SIMMs with the larger RAM ICs must be installed in bank A, except in the Macintosh IIci and the Macintosh IIfx. In those machines, you may install the larger SIMMs in either bank; in the Macintosh IIci, you obtain better performance when using the built-in video display circuitry by installing the larger RAM ICs in bank B. For more information, please refer to the section "Video RAM in the Macintosh IIci Computer" in this chapter and "Video Circuits in the Macintosh IIci Computer" in Chapter 12.

Except in the Macintosh IIfx, the RAM SIMM socket in the Macintosh II–family computers is identical to the one used in the Macintosh Plus and Macintosh SE and shown in Figure 5-1. The RAM SIMM socket signal assignments for the Macintosh SE/30 and Macintosh II family are shown in Table 5-6. The Macintosh IIfx uses a different SIMM socket with 64 pins; see Table 5-7 for the signal assignments.

■ **Table 5-6** Signal assignments for RAM SIMM sockets in the Macintosh SE/30 and Macintosh II–family computers (except the Macintosh IIfx)

Pin number	Signal name	Signal description
1	+5V	+5 volts
2	/CASLL	Column Address Strobe for data bits D7–0; or
	/CASLM	Column Address Strobe for data bits D15–8; or
	/CASUM	Column Address Strobe for data bits D23–16; or
	/CASUU	Column Address Strobe for data bits D31–24
3	D0	Data bus, bit 0; or
	D8	Data bus, bit 8; or
	D16	Data bus, bit 16; or
	D24	Data bus, bit 24
4	RAAF0	RAM address bus, bank A bit 0; or
	RABF0	RAM address bus, bank B bit 0;
5	RAAF1	RAM address bus, bank A bit 1; or
	RABF1	RAM address bus, bank B bit 1
6	D1	Data bus, bit 1; or
	D9	Data bus, bit 9; or
	D17	Data bus, bit 17; or
	D25	Data bus, bit 25
7	RAAF2	RAM address bus, bank A bit 2; or
	RABF2	RAM address bus, bank B bit 2
8	RAAF3	RAM address bus, bank A bit 3; or
	RABF3	RAM address bus, bank B bit 3
9	GND	Ground
10	D2	Data bus, bit 2; or
	D10	Data bus, bit 10; or
	D18	Data bus, bit 18; or
	D26	Data bus, bit 26
11	RAAF4	RAM address bus, bank A bit 4; or
	RABF4	RAM address bus, bank B bit 4
12	RAAF5	RAM address bus, bank A bit 5; or
	RABF5	RAM address bus, bank B bit 5
13	D3	Data bus, bit 3; or
	D11	Data bus, bit 11; or
	D19	Data bus, bit 19; or
	D27	Data bus, bit 27

(continued)

Pin number	Signal name	Signal description
14	RAAF6	RAM address bus, bank A bit 6; or
	RABF6	RAM address bus, bank B bit 6
15	RAAF7	RAM address bus, bank A bit 7; or
	RABF7	RAM address bus, bank B bit 7
16	D4	Data bus, bit 4; or
	D12	Data bus, bit 12; or
	D20	Data bus, bit 20; or
	D28	Data bus, bit 28
17	RAAF8	RAM address bus, bank A bit 8; or
	RABF8	RAM address bus, bank B bit 8
18	RAAF9	RAM address bus, bank A bit 9; or
	RABF9	RAM address bus, bank B bit 9
19	RAAF10	RAM address bus, bank A bit 10; or
	RABF10	RAM address bus, bank B bit 10
20	D5	Data bus, bit 5; or
	D13	Data bus, bit 13; or
	D21	Data bus, bit 21; or
	D29	Data bus, bit 29
21	RAMRWA	RAM Read/Write, bank A; or
	RAMRWB	RAM Read/Write, bank B
22	GND	Ground
23	D6	Data bus, bit 6; or
	D14	Data bus, bit 14; or
	D22	Data bus, bit 22; or
	D30	Data bus, bit 30
24	RAAF11	RAM address bus, bank A bit 11; or
	RABF11	RAM address bus, bank B bit 11
25	D7	Data bus, bit 7; or
	D15	Data bus, bit 15; or
	D23	Data bus, bit 23; or
	D31	Data bus, bit 31
26	n.c.	Not connected
27	/RASA	Row Address Strobe, bank A; or
	/RASB	Row Address Strobe, bank B
28	PU	Pull up
29	n.c.	Not connected
30	+5V	+5 volts

Pin number	Signal name	Signal description
1	GND	Ground
2	n.c.	Not connected
3	+5V	+5 volts
4	+5V	+5 volts
5	/CAS	Column address strobe
6	D0	Data input bus, bit 0
7	Q0	Data output bus, bit 0
8	/W0	Write-enable input for RAM IC 0
9	A0	Address bus, bit 0
10	n.c.	Not connected
11	A1	Address bus, bit 1
12	D1	Data input bus, bit 1
13	Q1	Data output bus, bit 1
14	/W1	Write-enable input for RAM IC 1
15	A2	Address bus, bit 2
16	n.c.	Not connected
17	A3	Address bus, bit 3
18	GND	Ground
19	GND	Ground
20	D2	Data input bus, bit 2
21	Q2	Data output bus, bit 2
22	/W2	Write-enable input for RAM IC 2
23	A4	Address bus, bit 4
24	n.c.	Not connected
25	A5	Address bus, bit 5
26	D3	Data input bus, bit 3
27	Q3	Data output bus, bit 3
28	/W3	Write-enable input for RAM IC 3
29	A6	Address bus, bit 6
30	n.c.	Not connected
31	A7	Address bus, bit 7
32	D4	Data input bus, bit 4

(continued)

Pin number	Signal name	Signal description
33	Q4	Data output bus, bit 4
34	/W4	Write-enable input for RAM IC 4
35	A8	Address bus, bit 8
36	n.c.	Not connected
37	A9	Address bus, bit 9
38	A10	Address bus, bit 10
39	A11	Address bus, bit 11
40	D5	Data input bus, bit 5
41	Q5	Data output bus, bit 5
42	/W5	Write-enable input for RAM IC 5
43	n.c.	Not connected
44	n.c.	Not connected
45	GND	Ground
46	D6	Data input bus, bit 6
47	Q6	Data output bus, bit 6
48	/W6	Write-enable input for RAM IC 6
49	n.c.	Not connected
50	D7	Data input bus, bit 7
51	Q7	Data output bus, bit 7
52	/W7	Write-enable input for RAM IC 7
53	/QB	Reserved (parity)
54	n.c.	Not connected
55	/RAS	Row address strobe
56	n.c.	Not connected
57	n.c.	Not connected
58	Q	Parity-check output
59	/WWP	Write wrong parity
60	PDCI	Parity daisy-chain input
61	+5V	+5 volts
62	+5V	+5 volts
63	PDCO	Parity daisy-chain output
64	GND	Ground

The locations of the RAM SIMMs on the main logic boards of the Macintosh SE/30, Macintosh II, Macintosh IIx, Macintosh IIcx, Macintosh IIci, and Macintosh IIfx are shown in Figures 5-6, 5-7, 5-8, 5-9, and 5-10. The numbering scheme used for the SIMMs in these computers is shown in Figure 5-11. Notice that each pair of SIMMs has a single number. For example, bank A comprises four SIMMs, labeled SIMM 3 (one pair) and SIMM 4 (one pair).

The different combinations of SIMMs that can be installed in the Macintosh SE/30 and in the Macintosh II–family computers are shown in Figure 5-11. The restrictions specified in Figure 5-11 do not apply to the Macintosh IIfx. On that machine, you may leave either bank empty and, when SIMMs larger than 1 MB become available, you may install them in either bank.

The RAM SIMMs used in all members of the Macintosh II family except the Macintosh IIfx have the same pinouts, but the DRAM ICs used in the SIMMs for different models have different speed requirements. The Macintosh SE/30, Macintosh II, Macintosh IIx, and Macintosh IIcx require DRAM with RAS access time of 120 ns or less; the Macintosh IIci and the Macintosh IIfx require a RAS access time of 80 ns or less. In addition, DRAM for the Macintosh IIci must have fast page mode.

■ **Figure 5-6** RAM SIMM locations in the Macintosh SE/30 computer

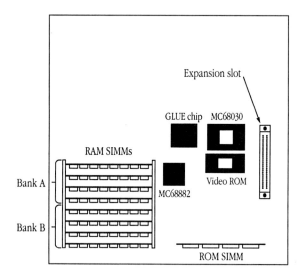

■ **Figure 5-7** RAM SIMM locations in the Macintosh II and Macintosh IIx computers

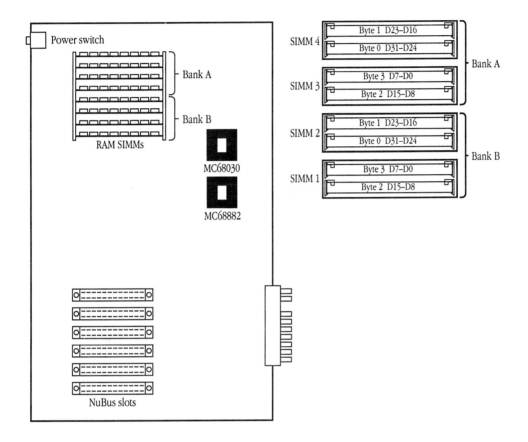

■ **Figure 5-8** RAM SIMM locations in the Macintosh IIcx computer

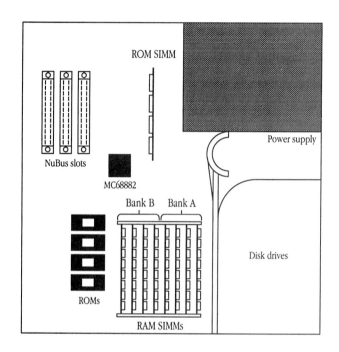

■ **Figure 5-9** RAM SIMM locations in the Macintosh IIci computer

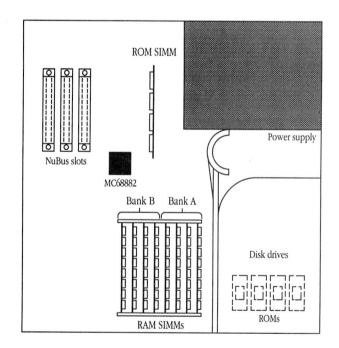

■ **Figure 5-10** RAM SIMM locations in the Macintosh IIfx computer

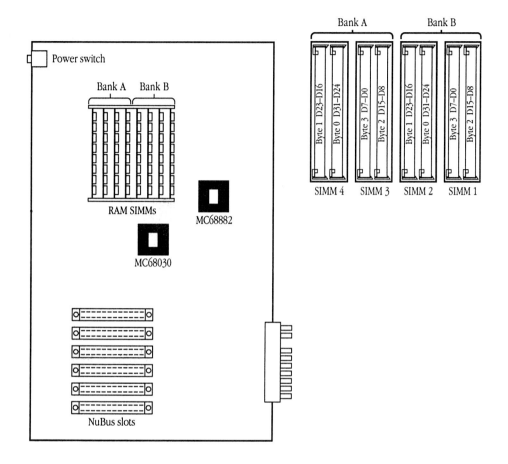

■ **Figure 5-11**   RAM SIMM configurations in the Macintosh SE/30 and
Macintosh II–family computers

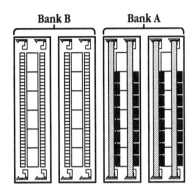

System memory size: 1 MB
Bank A: four 256 KB SIMMs
Bank B: empty

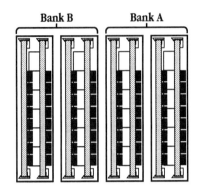

System memory size: 2 MB
Bank A: four 256 KB SIMMs
Bank B: four 256 KB SIMMs

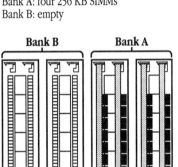

System memory size: 4 MB
Bank A: four 1 MB SIMMs
Bank B: empty

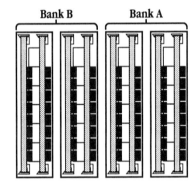

System memory size: 5 MB
Bank A: four 1 MB SIMMs [*]
Bank B: four 256 KB SIMMs [*]

[*] Note: For optimum performance on
a Macintosh IIci using built-in
video, put the larger-sized
SIMMs into bank B. Bank A
needs only 1 MB for video.

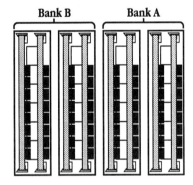

System memory size: 8 MB
Bank A: four 1 MB SIMMs
Bank B: four 1 MB SIMMs

Video RAM in the Macintosh IIci computer

The screen buffer for the built-in video display in the Macintosh IIci occupies physical addresses starting at $0000 0000 (bank A). The MMU in the MC68030 remaps the screen buffer into the logical address space allocated for NuBus slot $B so that the operating system can treat it the same as a video expansion card. At startup time, the operating system determines the size of the screen buffer depending on the maximum selected pixel size (bit depth) and on the type of monitor that is connected to the computer. The MMU maps the rest of bank A to the normal RAM address space.

◆ *Note:* The Macintosh IIci maps the portion of bank A used for main memory immediately above the memory in bank B. Even though the *physical* addresses of RAM bank B start at $0400 0000, the *logical* addresses start at $0000 0000, as required for software compatibility.

The RBV requests video data in bursts and the MDU generates the video addresses, automatically incrementing a pointer to the current location in the screen buffer. When the display scan reaches the end of a screen, the RBV sends a signal to the MDU causing it to set its pointer back to physical address $0000 0000.

◆ *Note:* All addresses from the MDU are physical addresses; logical memory mapping is performed by the MC68030's internal memory management unit.

RAM in bank A is connected directly to the RBV and is connected to the main processor's data bus by way of a bus buffer. When the RBV is reading video data, the bus buffer disconnects bank A from the main processor's data bus. The MDU can generate RAM addresses and control signals for a main-processor access to bank B and an RBV read from bank A at the same time, thus enabling the main processor to read and write to bank B with no waiting or interruptions.

For more information about the operation of the RBV and the rest of the built-in video circuitry, please refer to the section "Video Circuits in the Macintosh IIci computer" in Chapter 12.

Parity RAM in the Macintosh IIci computer

A special-order model of the Macintosh IIci comes equipped with an Apple custom IC, the Parity Generator and Checker (PGC), that enables it to use 9-bit RAM SIMMs and operate with parity checking.

At startup time, the system software first determines whether the system has the parity IC installed; it then tests for the presence of 9-bit RAM SIMMs and determines whether to enable parity checking. Bit 6 in VIA1 Data register B enables or disables parity generation and checking by the PGC. Before reading RAM with parity enabled, the system software must set the parity bits properly by writing using normal parity to all available RAM.

Each time a byte of RAM is read, the PGC generates an internal parity bit and compares it with the bit read from the RAM's parity bit for the byte. If the two parity bits are not the same and if parity is enabled (bit 6 of VIA1 Data register B set to 0), the PGC asserts two outputs: /NMI, which interrupts the main processor, and /PARERR, which indicates a parity error. The interrupt service routine can turn off the /PARERR and /NMI signals by setting /PAREN to 1.

Parity RAM in the Macintosh IIfx computer

A special-order model of the Macintosh IIfx comes equipped with an Apple custom IC, the RAM Parity Unit (RPU), and special 9-bit RAM SIMMs that enable the machine to operate with parity checking. The parity SIMMS include circuits that generate the parity bit and detect a hardware daisy-chain that enables the RPU to record whether parity SIMMs are installed.

At startup time, the system software first determines whether the system has the parity IC installed; it then reads the RPU and determines whether to enable parity checking. Bit 6 in VIA1 Data register B enables or disables parity generation and checking by the RPU. Before reading RAM with parity enabled, the system software must set the parity bits properly by writing using normal parity to all available RAM.

Each time a byte of RAM is read, the circuits on the parity SIMMs generate an internal parity bit and compare it with the bit read from the parity bit in the RAM. If the two parity bits are not the same and if parity is enabled, the RPU records the error condition and the SIMM that caused the error. The RPU then sends interrupt IRQ14 to the OSS.

System software writes the value 7 into the Interrupt Mask register in the OSS to enable parity interrupts as an NMI. When a parity interrupt occurs, the interrupt handler clears the interrupt by writing 0 to the Interrupt Mask register in the OSS.

RAM cache card in the Macintosh IIci computer

The Macintosh IIci has a connector for an optional RAM **cache card.** High-speed RAM on the cache card can improve the performance of the Macintosh IIci by as much as 50 percent, depending on the application and on the pixel size used by the built-in video display.

A cache card can be designed to achieve a large increase in the computer's performance at a small increase in cost. One way to increase performance is to use faster ICs for the entire RAM, but that would entail a large increase in cost. A cache card enables a small amount of fast RAM to provide a large performance increase.

The memory in the cache card duplicates small portions of the main memory. Each time the main processor starts to read data stored in the main memory, the cache card checks to determine whether it has the data. If it does, the cache card sends the data to the processor and the processor doesn't have to wait for the slower main memory to provide the data.

If the data the processor is reading is not stored in the cache card, the processor must get it from the main memory. When the main memory puts the data on the bus for the processor to read, the cache card also reads it; that is how the cache card brings new data into its RAM.

The time it takes to read data from main memory is longer than it would be without the cache because there is not only the time required for reading main memory but also the time it takes for the cache card to determine whether or not it has the data. The use of the cache provides an increase in overall performance because the data the processor needs is usually already in the cache.

Operation of a cache card

The cache card is an optional card that may not be installed. The information in this section describes the operation of a typical cache card.

The RAM on the cache card is divided into two parts called **tag RAM** and **data RAM.** To determine whether the requested data is already stored in the data RAM, the cache card uses the tag RAM to store a list of addresses. The addresses stored in the tag RAM are the main-memory addresses of the data that is stored in the data RAM.

If the cache contains the data the processor is requesting from main memory, the read operation is called a *hit.* If the cache does not contain the data, the operation is called a *miss.* Here are descriptions of three operations that can occur in a system with a typical cache card: a read operation with a hit, a read operation with a miss, and a write operation.

Reading with a cache hit

For a read operation, the main processor puts an address on the address bus and then asserts the Address Strobe signal (/AS). If the cache card is enabled, the card has the CACHE signal asserted; that signal inhibits the computer's Memory Decode Unit (MDU) from performing the memory access. The cache card compares the high-order address bits with the corresponding tag RAM to determine whether the data is held in the cache and checks the validity bits to determine whether the data is valid. The check for valid data is necessary because it is possible for the processor to write new data to main memory without the cache card being updated; that process is described in the next section.

If the addresses match and the data is valid, the read operation is a hit and the cache card puts its data onto the data bus.

Reading with a cache miss

If the addresses don't match or if the data is not valid, the operation is a miss and the cache card tells the processor to retry the read operation by asserting the /BERR and /HALT lines. The cache card also deasserts the CACHE signal so that the MDU can perform the access to main memory when the processor retries the read. After the main memory puts the data on the data bus, both the main processor and the cache card have access to the data. The cache card uses the data to update its data RAM and sets the appropriate validity bit in its tag RAM. That is the way locations in cache memory are filled or updated.

To fill the cache, read operations from main RAM use burst mode, which takes five clock cycles for the first read and two clock cycles each for three subsequent read operations. The five-clock read operation determines the address of a chunk of memory four longwords in size and aligned on a 4-longword boundary. Each subsequent read operation in the same 4-longword chunk takes only two clock cycles.

Writing

When the main processor performs a write operation, it can provide either 8, 16, or 32 bits of data. Depending on the design of the cache card, it may not be appropriate to update the cache each time the processor writes to main memory. If the cache card does not update its data RAM on a write operation, it must turn off the validity bit in its tag RAM to indicate that the data it holds is no longer valid.

To perform a write operation, the main processor puts an address on the address bus and deasserts the R/W signal. The processor then asserts the Address Strobe signal (/AS); after that, it puts the data on the data bus and the MDU writes to main memory. If the cache card does update its data RAM on a write operation, it does so in parallel with the main memory.

Controlling the cache card

Space has been allocated in the 32-bit address space of the Macintosh IIci for reading and writing to registers and testing memory in the cache card. This space includes addresses in the range $5200 0000 through $52FF FFFF. The cache card's address space is not accessible throught the 24-bit address map.

Bits in VIA2 Data register B in the RBV control enabling and disabling the cache card and flushing the cache. Applications should not set those bits directly, but should use the appropriate ROM traps to enable, disable, and flush the cache. The traps, named EnableExtCache, DisableExtCache, and FlushExtCache, are available using selectors 4, 5, and 6 through the hardware privilege trap HWPriv (A098).

△ **Developer tip** Normal operation of a cache card is transparent to applications running on the Macintosh IIci. System software makes no assumptions about the organization of the RAM on a cache card; applications should do likewise. Only test software for the card should address the cache card's data RAM and tag RAM directly. △

Cache card connector

The connector for the cache card is a 120-pin Euro-DIN connector, as shown in Figure 5-12. The signal assignments are shown in Table 5-8.

▲ **Warning** Do not plug a PDS expansion card into the cache card connector in the Macintosh IIci. Even though the connector for the cache card will accept a PDS expansion card, the pinouts are different. A PDS card will not work in the cache connector; attempting to operate the computer with a PDS card in the cache connector may damage both the computer and the card. ▲

△ **Developer tip** For information about designing a cache card for the Macintosh IIci, please refer to the manual *Designing Cards and Drivers for the Macintosh Family,* second edition. △

■ **Figure 5-12** Cache card connector in the Macintosh IIci computer

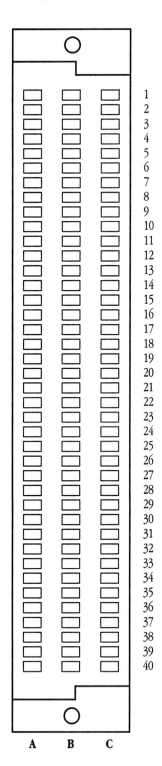

1
2
3
4
5
6
7
8
9
10
11
12
13
14
15
16
17
18
19
20
21
22
23
24
25
26
27
28
29
30
31
32
33
34
35
36
37
38
39
40

A   B   C

Pin	Row A	Row B	Row C
1	A30	/RESET	/R/W
2	/HALT	A29	/STERM
3	A31	A25	A28
4	A26	A27	+5V
5	/RMC	A24	/CFLUSH
6	D31	GND	+5V
7	D30	D29	n.c.
8	D28	D27	GND
9	D26	D25	+5V
10	D24	D23	GND
11	D22	D21	GND
12	D20	D19	/IPL2
13	D18	D17	/CENABLE
14	D16	+5V	+5V
15	A22	A21	+5V
16	A20	A19	GND
17	A18	A17	n.c.
18	A16	A15	GND
19	A14	A13	+5V
20	A12	A11	n.c.
21	A10	GND	GND
22	FC1	A9	+5V
23	A8	n.c.	GND
24	FC2	FC0	/CIOUT
25	D15	D14	/IPL1
26	D13	D12	/IPL0
27	D11	D10	/CBREQ
28	D9	D8	D7
29	D6	/BGACK	D5
30	D4	D3	D2
31	D1	D0	+5V
32	/ROMOE	A7	A6

(continued)

Pin	Row A	Row B	Row C
33	A5	A4	A3
34	A2	A1	A0
35	/BG	+5V	/CBACK
36	A23	CPUDIS	/BR
37	/DSACK0	/AS	/DS
38	CPUCLOCK	/DSACK1	/BERR
39	GND	+5V	SIZ1
40	GND	CACHE	SIZ0

RAM cache in the Macintosh IIfx computer

The Macintosh IIfx has an on-board RAM cache for 32 KB of data. The operation of the cache is controlled by the Fast Memory Controller (FMC). The cache uses high-speed static RAM: its access time is only 20 ns. The main processor can read from the cache with no wait states.

A cache is designed to achieve a large increase in the computer's performance at a small increase in cost. One way to increase performance would be to use faster ICs for the entire RAM, but that would entail a large increase in cost. A cache enables a small amount of high-speed RAM to provide a large performance increase.

The memory in the cache duplicates small portions of the main memory (either RAM or ROM). Each time the main processor starts a read operation, the FMC checks to determine whether the data is in the cache memory. If it is, the cache sends the data to the processor and the processor doesn't have to wait for the slower main memory to provide the data.

If the data the processor is reading is not stored in the cache memory, the processor must get it from the main memory. When the main memory puts the data on the bus for the processor to read, the cache also reads it; that is how the computer brings new data into the cache memory.

To determine whether the requested data is already stored in the cache memory, the cache uses a separate part of the cache called the tag RAM to store a list of addresses. The addresses stored in the tag RAM are the main-memory addresses of the data that is stored in the cache's data RAM.

Operation of the RAM cache

If the cache contains the data the processor is requesting from main memory, the read operation is called a *hit*. If the cache does not contain the data, the operation is called a *miss*. Here are descriptions of four operations that can occur in the Macintosh IIfx: a read operation with a hit, a read operation with a miss, filling the cache on burst reads, and a write operation.

Reading with a cache hit

For a read operation, the main processor puts an address on the address bus and then asserts the Address Strobe signal (/AS). The cache logic compares the high-order address bits with the corresponding tag RAM to determine whether the requested data is held in the cache and checks the validity bit to determine whether the data is valid. The check for valid data is necessary because when power is first turned on, the data in each cache location is invalid until loaded by a read operation.

If the addresses match and the data is valid, the read operation is a hit. Normally, the cache RAM is already enabled onto the data bus and the processor proceeds to read the data. The processor reads a longword of data in just two clock cycles. The FMC does not assert the Burst Acknowledge signal to the MC68030 on a cache hit, so only a single longword is read.

Reading with a cache miss

If the addresses don't match or if the data is not valid, the operation is a miss, as indicated by the negation of the MATCH signal from the tag RAM. The negated MATCH signal propagates to the /BERR and /HALT lines so that the processor ignores the invalid data and restarts the bus cycle in an operation called a *retry*.

The FMC responds to the miss by latching the address and initiating a read operation from main memory in parallel with the retry operation of the MC68030. It negates the CACHEN signal to remove the output of the cache RAM from the data bus. By the time the processor retries the read operation, the FMC will already have the data available from main memory. The overlapping of the main memory access with the retry operation eliminates much of the time penalty normally associated with a cache miss. The retry operation takes an additional four clock cycles.

If the main processor has requested a burst, the FMC loads the new data into the cache's data RAM. If no burst was requested, the FMC performs a single read from main memory and the cache is unaffected.

Filling the cache

To read valid data into the cache's data RAM, the FMC initiates a burst read consisting of four longwords from main memory. The FMC stores the address of the group of four longwords into the tag RAM. After the main memory puts the data on the data bus, both the main processor and the cache's data RAM read the data. Upon successful completion of the burst, the FMC sets the corresponding validity bit in the cache's tag RAM. There is only one tag location for each block of four longwords so the tag only allocates space on a burst read.

◆ *Note:* The FMC can perform burst reads from either RAM or ROM.

Writing

To perform a write operation, the main processor puts an address on the address bus and deasserts the R/W signal. The processor then asserts the Address Strobe signal (/AS); after that, it puts the data on the data bus and the FMC performs the write to main memory. While this is happening, the FMC uses the MATCH signal from the tag RAM to determine whether the data being written to main memory is also in the cache. If it is, the updated data is also written into the cache's data RAM. Write operations to cached memory always update the cache, regardless of bus mastership or the state of the Cache Control register, thus ensuring that the cache contains valid data.

△ **Developer tip**   Normal operation of the RAM cache is transparent to applications running on the Macintosh IIfx. System software makes no assumptions about the organization of the RAM cache; applications should do likewise. △

Buffered write operations in the Macintosh IIfx computer

Write operations in the Macintosh IIfx are always buffered writes. The FMC latches the data from the processor and terminates the processor's write cycle before the data has actually been written to memory. This technique allows the processor to continue with other operations: a write that would normally take six clock cycles occupies the processor for only two clock cycles. If the succeeding operation is anything other than another write, it can proceed while the FMC completes the write operation.

There is only one level of buffering on write operations, so that if there are two successive write operations, the second operation would normally have to wait until the first one was completed. The FMC handles this situation by comparing the latched address from the first write operation with the address of the second write. If the second address is in the same page of RAM, the FMC performs the second write operation as a page-mode write without inserting wait states, thus maintaining a high level of performance.

ROM

ROM is the Macintosh computer's permanent read-only memory. Its base address is available as the constant romStart and is also stored in the global variable ROMBase.

ROM contains the routines for the Macintosh Toolbox and Operating System, plus the various system traps. Because ROM access cycles are not interleaved with video or sound, the processor in a Macintosh computer can always access ROM at the same rate. Table 5-9 shows the ROM access rates for the different Macintosh models.

■ **Table 5-9**   ROM access rates

Macintosh model	CPU type	ROM access rate
Macintosh Plus	MC68000	3.92 MB/sec
Macintosh SE	MC68000	3.92 MB/sec
Macintosh SE/30	MC68030	15.67 MB/sec
Macintosh Portable	MC68HC000	7.86 MB/sec
Macintosh II	MC68020	12.53 MB/sec
Macintosh IIx	MC68030	15.67 MB/sec
Macintosh IIcx	MC68030	15.67 MB/sec
Macintosh IIci	MC68030	20.0 MB/sec
Macintosh IIfx	MC68030	64.0 MB/sec

ROM configurations

The Macintosh 128K and 512K computers each contain two 256 Kbit ROM ICs, forming a 16-bit-wide data bus and providing 64 KB of ROM.

The Macintosh 512K enhanced and the Macintosh Plus computers each contain two 512 Kbit ROM ICs, forming a 16-bit-wide data bus and providing 128 KB of ROM.

The 512 Kbit IC is the largest ROM IC that can be installed in the classic Macintosh computers.

The Macintosh Plus ROM sockets can handle 1 Mbit ROM ICs. A configuration of two 1 Mbit ROM ICs provides 256 KB of ROM.

Macintosh SE computers contain two 1 Mbit ROM ICs. These are the largest ROM ICs that can be installed in the Macintosh SE ROM sockets. This configuration provides 256 KB of ROM.

The Macintosh Portable computer contains two 1 Mbit ROM ICs on the logic board plus a connector for a ROM expansion card. The permanent ROM ICs provide 256 KB of ROM. A ROM expansion card can contain up to 4 MB of ROM, which can be used to supplement the system ROM (up to a total of 5 MB of ROM) or to replace it entirely.

The Macintosh II and Macintosh IIcx contain four 512 Kbit ROM ICs, forming a 32-bit-wide data bus, and providing 256 KB of ROM. The Macintosh II ROM sockets can accept ROM ICs up to 1 Mbit in size. A configuration of four 1 Mbit ROM ICs would provide 512 KB of ROM. In addition to the IC sockets, Macintosh IIcx computer also has SIMM sockets for upgrading or expanding ROM.

In the Macintosh SE/30 and Macintosh IIx computers, ROM is installed as a 64-pin ROM SIMM in a socket on the main logic board. The ROM SIMM makes it easy to upgrade ROM.

The Macintosh IIci contains four 1 Mbit ROM ICs on the main logic board, forming a 32-bit-wide data bus and providing 512 KB of ROM. The Macintosh IIci also has a 64-pin SIMM socket for upgrading or expanding ROM.

The Macintosh IIfx has one ROM SIMM that contains four 1 Mbit ROM ICs for 512 KB of ROM. Please refer to the section "ROM SIMMs" later in this chapter for more information.

ROM expansion in the Macintosh Portable computer

The ROM expansion connector in the Macintosh Portable is mechanically the same as the RAM expansion connector shown in Figure 5-5. The signal assignments for the ROM expansion connector are shown in Table 5-10.

The permanent ROM in the Macintosh Portable has an access time of 150 ns and requires two wait states. The ROM expansion card uses the /EXT.DTACK handshake signal to control the number of wait states for accesses to the ROM on the card.

A ROM expansion card can draw a maximum of 2 milliamps of power at +5 volts and must provide its own buffering, decoding circuits, and internal control signals.

⚠ **Developer tip** The ROM address space from $90 0000 through $9F FFFF in the Macintosh Portable is reserved for use by Apple Computer. You may use any portion of the remaining ROM address space for one or more read-only electronic disks (called *ROM EDisks* or *ROM disks*). Each ROM disk must start on a 64 KB boundary. Because you cannot tell into which ROM sockets the user will plug your ROM ICs, your code should be relocatable. You should use as little of the address space and as few ROM IC sockets as possible for your ROM disk, so that the user does not have to choose between your product and another that uses fewer resources. ⚠

■ **Table 5-10**   Signal assignments for the ROM expansion connector in the
Macintosh Portable computer

Pin number	Signal name	Signal description
1	+5V	+5 volts
2	A1	Address line A1
3	A2	Address line A2
4	A3	Address line A3
5	A4	Address line A4
6	A5	Address line A5
7	A6	Address line A6
8	A7	Address line A7
9	A8	Address line A8
10	A9	Address line A9
11	A10	Address line A10
12	A11	Address line A11
13	A12	Address line A12
14	A13	Address line A13
15	A14	Address line A14
16	A15	Address line A15
17	A16	Address line A16
18	A17	Address line A17
19	A18	Address line A18
20	A19	Address line A19
21	A20	Address line A20
22	A21	Address line A21
23	A22	Address line A22
24	A23	Address line A23
25	GND	Ground
26	GND	Ground
27	/DTACK	System ROM acknowledge signal to CPU GLU
28	/AS	Address Strobe from MC68HC000
29	/ROM.CS	Chip-select signal from CPU GLU (also used to select permanent ROM)
30	16M	15.6672 MHz system clock
31	/EXT.DTACK	Expansion ROM acknowledge signal to CPU GLU

(continued)

Signal assignments for the ROM expansion connector in the
Macintosh Portable computer (continued)

Pin number	Signal name	Signal description
32	/DELAY.CS	Chip-select signal from CPU GLU
33	D0	Data line D0
34	D1	Data line D1
35	D2	Data line D2
36	D3	Data line D3
37	D4	Data line D4
38	D5	Data line D5
39	D6	Data line D6
40	D7	Data line D7
43	D10	Data line D10
44	D11	Data line D11
45	D12	Data line D12
46	D13	Data line D13
47	D14	Data line D14
48	D15	Data line D15
49	+5V	+5 volts
50	+5V	+5 volts

ROM SIMMs

ROM is installed in SIMMs in the Macintosh SE/30 and Macintosh IIx computers. ROM
SIMMs are also present in the Macintosh II, Macintosh IIcx, Macintosh IIci, and
Macintosh IIfx for ROM upgrading or expansion.

△ **Important**   Only qualified service personnel should install ROM SIMMs in
Macintosh computers. △

The ROM SIMM socket pinouts are shown in Figure 5-13, and the signal assignments are
shown in Table 5-11.

■ **Figure 5-13**   Pinout of the ROM SIMM socket

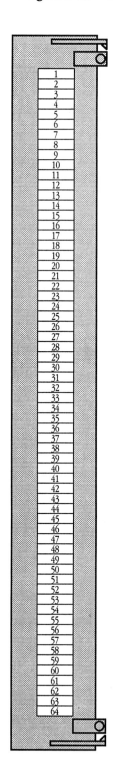

■ **Table 5-11**   Signal assignments for the ROM SIMM socket

Pin number	Signal name	Signal description
1	+5V	+5 volts
2	A0*	Address bus, bit 0
3	A1*	Address bus, bit 1
4	A2	Address bus, bit 2
5	A3	Address bus, bit 3
6	A4	Address bus, bit 4
7	A5	Address bus, bit 5
8	A6	Address bus, bit 6
9	A7	Address bus, bit 7
10	GND	Ground
11	/ROM or /CS0	ROM chip select
12	/ROMOE	ROM output enable
13	+5V	+5 volts
14	D0	Data bus, bit 0
15	D1	Data bus, bit 1
16	D2	Data bus, bit 2
17	D3	Data bus, bit 3
18	D4	Data bus, bit 4
19	D5	Data bus, bit 5
20	D6	Data bus, bit 6
21	D7	Data bus, bit 7
22	D8	Data bus, bit 8
23	D9	Data bus, bit 9
24	D10	Data bus, bit 10
25	D11	Data bus, bit 11
26	D12	Data bus, bit 12
27	D13	Data bus, bit 13
28	D14	Data bus, bit 14
29	D15	Data bus, bit 15
30	GND	Ground
31	A8	Address bus, bit 8

*A0 and A1 are used only on ROM SIMMs for the Macintosh IIcx and Macintosh IIci.

(continued)

Pin number	Signal name	Signal description
32	A9	Address bus, bit 9
33	A10	Address bus, bit 10
34	A11	Address bus, bit 11
35	A12	Address bus, bit 12
36	A13	Address bus, bit 13
37	A14	Address bus, bit 14
38	A15	Address bus, bit 15
39	A16	Address bus, bit 16
40	A17	Address bus, bit 17
41	A18	Address bus, bit 18
42	A19	Address bus, bit 19
43	A20	Address bus, bit 20
44	A21	Address bus, bit 21
45	A22	Address bus, bit 22
46	+5V	+5 volts
47	D16	Data bus, bit 16
48	D17	Data bus, bit 17
49	D18	Data bus, bit 18
50	D19	Data bus, bit 19
51	D20	Data bus, bit 20
52	D21	Data bus, bit 21
53	D22	Data bus, bit 22
54	D23	Data bus, bit 23
55	D24	Data bus, bit 24
56	D25	Data bus, bit 25
57	D26	Data bus, bit 26
58	D27	Data bus, bit 27
59	D28	Data bus, bit 28
60	D29	Data bus, bit 29
61	D30	Data bus, bit 30
62	D31	Data bus, bit 31
63	+5V (CS1)	+5 volts (alternate chip select)
64	GND	Ground

Chapter 6 **Power Supplies**

All power for components within the case of a Macintosh-family computer is provided by the power supply while the computer is switched on. This chapter first briefly describes the sequences of events that occur during system startup and power down. It then lists the specifications for the power supplies of the Macintosh Plus and all later Macintosh computers, discusses the power-on and power-off control circuits in the Macintosh II–family computers, and describes the battery charger and power circuit for the Macintosh Portable computer. The Power Manager IC in the Macintosh Portable is described in Chapter 3.

Power

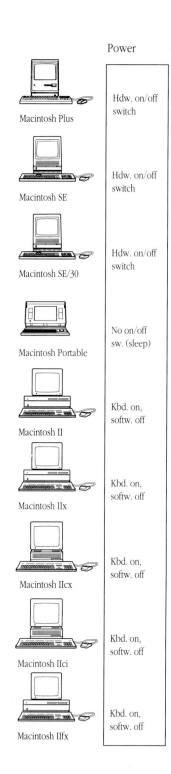

Macintosh Plus — Hdw. on/off switch

Macintosh SE — Hdw. on/off switch

Macintosh SE/30 — Hdw. on/off switch

Macintosh Portable — No on/off sw. (sleep)

Macintosh II — Kbd. on, softw. off

Macintosh IIx — Kbd. on, softw. off

Macintosh IIcx — Kbd. on, softw. off

Macintosh IIci — Kbd. on, softw. off

Macintosh IIfx — Kbd. on, softw. off

In the Macintosh Plus and earlier Macintosh computers, the power supply provides sufficient current to run the main logic board, the video display, the internal disk drive, and an external disk drive. The Macintosh SE and Macintosh SE/30 computers provide additional power for a fan, a second internal floppy disk drive or an internal hard disk, and any expansion card designed for the computer. The power supply in the Macintosh II, Macintosh IIx, Macintosh IIcx, Macintosh IIci, and Macintosh IIfx computers provides enough power to supply two floppy disk drives, one hard disk drive, and several NuBus expansion cards. The power supplies in all these computers provide power for the keyboard and the mouse.

Power for the Macintosh Portable computer is provided by a built-in battery, which is charged by an external battery charger. The Macintosh Portable uses components with low power requirements and employs special hardware and firmware to further reduce power consumption when the machine is not in use. The battery in the Macintosh Portable provides power for the main logic board, two internal disk drives, a flat-panel video display, the keyboard, and a trackball or other pointing device.

In the classic Macintosh computers, the power supply, video electronics, and internal speaker are all located on the analog board. In the Macintosh SE and Macintosh SE/30, the video electronics are on the analog board and the power supply is in a separate metal box, bolted onto the analog board. In the Macintosh II family, the power supply is in a separate metal box inside the main system unit. The Macintosh Portable has a battery charger and power transformer in a separate unit connected to the main system unit by a cable. The battery is in a compartment inside the main system unit.

The Macintosh SE/30, Macintosh SE, and classic Macintosh computers have a mechanical on/off switch located at the rear of the computer. The power supply in the Macintosh II–family computers is switched on by a signal line on the ADB connector and is switched off by a signal generated by software. The Macintosh Portable computer has no on/off switch; in the Macintosh Portable, the Power Manager IC puts the computer in a low-power-consumption state (the sleep state) when the computer is not being used.

Power up, system startup, and power down

The system startup sequence varies from one member of the Macintosh family to another. In addition, some Macintosh computers have firmware-controlled power-down sequences. This section describes the system startup sequence for all Macintosh computers, and the power-down sequences, where appropriate.

Classic Macintosh computers

When power is first applied to a classic Macintosh computer, the following sequence of events takes place:

1. The Sony sound IC monitors the voltage levels on the board and asserts the /RESET signal until 0.25 second after the voltage has stabilized.

2. The /RESET signal causes the CPU and all of the internal devices to come to a known initial state.

3. The Sony sound IC deasserts the /RESET signal and the CPU looks at the first four words in memory (starting at location $00 0000) to get the Reset vector. Because nothing has been loaded into RAM yet, it would not do for the CPU to try to get the Reset vector from RAM. Therefore, when the VIA is reset, it pulls the Overlay signal high, which causes the PALs to use an address decoding scheme that puts ROM at location $00 0000. This decoding scheme is referred to as the *ROM overlay*. In the ROM overlay address map, an address to a location in the range $40 0000 through $43 FFFF is also decoded by the PALs as an address to ROM.

4. The CPU goes to the memory address in ROM pointed to by the Reset vector and begins to execute the code it finds there (the Reset handler).

5. One of the first instructions in the Reset handler causes the Overlay signal to go low, which switches the PALs to the normal address map. In this address map, RAM is located at $00 0000 through $3F FFFF (for 4 MB of RAM) and ROM is located at $40 0000 through $43 FFFF (for 256 KB of ROM).

6. The Reset handler carries out the startup procedure described in *Inside Macintosh*.

Macintosh SE computer

When power is first applied to the Macintosh SE computer, the following sequence of events takes place:

1. The Sony sound IC monitors the voltage levels on the board and asserts the /RESET signal until 0.25 second after the voltage has stabilized.

2. The /RESET signal causes the CPU, the BBU, and all of the internal devices to come to a known initial state.

3. The Sony sound IC deasserts the /RESET signal and the CPU looks at the first four words in memory (starting at location $00 0000) to get the Reset vector. When the BBU is reset, it starts up with the ROM overlay address map, which puts ROM at location $00 0000. In the ROM overlay address map, an address to a location in the range $40 0000 through $43 FFFF is also decoded by the BBU as an address to ROM.

4. The CPU goes to the memory address pointed to by the Reset vector and begins to execute the code it finds there (the Reset handler).

5. One of the first instructions in the Reset handler is a jump to a location in the range normally assigned to ROM ($40 0000 through $43 E800). The first time the BBU receives an address in this range, it switches to the normal address map. In this address map, RAM is located at $00 0000 through $3F FFFF and ROM is located at $40 0000 through $43 FFFF.

6. The Reset handler carries out the startup procedure described in *Inside Macintosh.*

Macintosh Portable computer

The Macintosh Portable is the only Macintosh computer that is designed to be powered by a battery. In normal operation, the Macintosh Portable is never switched off; rather, it goes into a low-power-consumption state, the **sleep state,** when it is not in use. Whenever the Macintosh Portable returns to an active state after a period when a desktop machine would have been turned off, it automatically restores its presleep environment and resumes operation without going through the startup sequence. Ideally, the Macintosh Portable is switched on only when the battery is first installed by the dealer or after the batteries have been removed in order to install an expansion card in the machine.

When power is first applied to the Macintosh Portable, the Power Manager IC immediately puts the system into the sleep state. The first time a key is pressed, the Power Manager IC initiates a system reset and the Macintosh Portable goes through the same sequence of startup events as the Macintosh SE. In the Macintosh Portable, the ROM-overlay mapping is controlled by the CPU GLU, and is terminated by the first address in the range $90 0000 through $9F FFFF.

Macintosh SE/30 and Macintosh II–family computers

The Macintosh SE/30, Macintosh IIx, and Macintosh IIcx computers all use the same ROM, which has a startup routine almost identical to that used in the Macintosh II. These computers, like all other Macintosh computers, go through an elaborate series of hardware and software procedures to initialize the system when you turn them on or reset them. The power-down function in Macintosh II–family computers is normally under software control, unlike the other Macintosh computers, which have only a hardware power switch. This section describes the initialization sequence that takes place when you supply power to the Macintosh SE/30 or Macintosh II–family computers. The following section discusses the mechanism by which the Macintosh II–family firmware turns the power off.

Power up

When you press the power switch on the ADB keyboard of a Macintosh II–family computer, a capacitor discharges, generating a signal that causes the power supply to switch on within 2 seconds (assuming that AC current is present). The capacitor in the Macintosh II and Macintosh IIx is kept charged by two 3-volt lithium batteries; in the Macintosh IIcx and Macintosh IIci, it is kept charged by a trickle current from the power supply. The Macintosh II–family power-control circuit is shown and discussed in the section "Power-Control Circuit in the Macintosh II–Family Computers," at the end of this chapter. The Macintosh SE/30 has a hard-wired power switch, identical to the one used in the Macintosh SE.

System startup

When power is first applied to a Macintosh SE/30 or Macintosh II–family computer, the following sequence of events takes place:

1. One of the Sony sound ICs monitors the voltage levels on the board and asserts the /RESET signal until 0.25 second after the voltage has stabilized.

2. The /RESET signal causes the CPU, the general logic ICs, and all of the internal devices to come to a known initial state. The /RESET signal is also available to each expansion card slot so that expansion cards can be reset to a known initial state.

3. The Sony sound IC deasserts the /RESET signal and the CPU looks at the first four words in memory (starting at location $0000 0000) to get the Reset vector. When VIA1 is reset, it pulls the Overlay signal high, which causes the memory-control IC (GLUE or MDU) to use the ROM overlay address map. In the ROM overlay address map, an address to a location in either the range $0000 0000 through $0FFF FFFF or $4000 0000 through $4FFF FFFF is decoded as an address to ROM.

4. The CPU goes to the memory address pointed to by the Reset vector and begins to execute the code it finds there (the Reset handler).

5. One of the first instructions in the Reset handler causes the Overlay signal to go low, which switches the memory-control IC (GLUE or MDU) to the normal address map. In this address map, RAM is located at $0000 0000 through $3FFF FFFF and ROM is located at $4000 0000 through $4FFF FFFF.

6. The Reset handler carries out the startup procedure described in *Inside Macintosh*.

Macintosh II–family power down

In the Macintosh II–family computers, when you switch off power by choosing Shut Down from the Special menu, the computer first closes all files and finishes all pending activity. When the software is ready to turn off power to the computer, it causes a control IC (VIA2 or OSS) to assert the /POWEROFF signal. This signal causes the power supply to switch off after 2 ms.

◆ *Note:* There is a power switch on the back of the original Macintosh II that generates a level-6 interrupt to the CPU. The user can use this switch to shut down the computer, but it does not initiate the software shut-down procedures performed by the Shut Down menu command. If the computer hangs and ignores the interrupt generated by the power switch, you must press the nonmaskable interrupt switch (the "programmer's switch") to halt the CPU, and then press the power switch. If you do not have a programmer's switch installed on your Macintosh II and the power switch fails to turn off the machine, you must unplug the computer.

Later Macintosh II computers, the Macintosh IIx, and the Macintosh IIcx have hard-wired power-off switches on the back of the case. None of these switches initiates the software shut-down procedures performed by the Shut Down menu command.

In the Macintosh IIcx and Macintosh IIci, the power switch on the back can be locked in the "on" position with a screwdriver or a coin. If the switch is in the "on" position, the machine will turn itself back on after a power interruption. This feature is useful for machines operating as file servers, where automatic recovery after a power failure is desirable. When the switch is locked in the "on" position, choosing the Shut Down command from the Special menu while in the Finder causes the computer to restart.

▲ **Warning**   Never press the power switch, pull the plug, or otherwise remove power from your Macintosh computer while it is writing to disk. Doing so can cause loss of data on the disk, and could damage the disk directory, requiring you to reformat the disk. ▲

The power-control circuit is discussed in the section "Power-Control Circuit in the Macintosh II–Family Computers," at the end of this chapter.

Power connectors

Figure 6-1 shows the pinouts for the connector from the power supply to the main logic board in the Macintosh Plus and other classic Macintosh computers.

■ **Figure 6-1** Pinout of the power supply connector on the Macintosh Plus computer

Table 6-1 shows the signal assignments for the connector from the power supply to the main logic board in the classic Macintosh computers.

■ **Table 6-1** Signal assignments for the power supply connector on the Macintosh Plus computer

Pin number	Signal name	Signal description
1	/VIDEO	Video output
2	No pin	
3	/HSYNC	Horizontal synchronization
4	SPKR	Audio output
5	/VSYNC	Vertical synchronization
6	+5V	+5 volts
7	GND	Ground
8	–12V	–12 volts
9	GND	Ground
10	+12V	+12 volts
11	BAT	Battery for RTC

Figure 6-2 shows the pinouts for the connector from the power supply to the analog board in the Macintosh SE and Macintosh SE/30.

■ **Figure 6-2** Pinout of the power supply connector on the Macintosh SE and Macintosh SE/30 computers

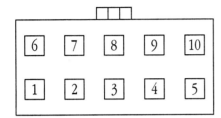

Table 6-2 shows the signal assignments for the connector from the power supply to the analog board in the Macintosh SE and Macintosh SE/30.

■ **Table 6-2** Signal assignments for the power supply connector on the Macintosh SE and Macintosh SE/30 computers

Pin number	Signal name	Signal description
1	GND	Ground
2	GND	Ground
3	GND	Ground
4	+5V	+5 volts
5	+12V disk	+12 volts for disk drives
6	−12V	−12 volts
7	GND	Ground
8	GND	Ground
9	+5V	+5 volts
10	+12V sweep	+12 volts for video circuits

Figure 6-3 shows the pinouts for the connector from the analog board to the main logic board in the Macintosh SE and Macintosh SE/30 computers.

■ **Figure 6-3** Pinout of the power and video connector from the analog board to the logic board in the Macintosh SE and Macintosh SE/30 computers

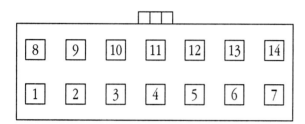

Table 6-3 shows the signal assignments for the connector from the analog board to the logic board in the Macintosh SE and Macintosh SE/30 computers.

■ **Table 6-3** Signal assignments for the power and video connector from the analog board to the logic board in the Macintosh SE and Macintosh SE/30 computers

Pin number	Signal	Signal description
1	GND	Ground
2	GND	Ground
3	GND	Ground
4	GND	Ground
5	GND	Ground
6	–5V	–5 volts
7	–12V	–12 volts
8	GND	Ground
9	VIDOUT	Video output
10	/HSYNC	Horizontal synchronization
11	/VSYNC	Vertical synchronization
12	+5V	+5 volts
13	+5V	+5 volts
14	+12V	+12 volts

Figure 6-4 shows the pinout for the power connector on the back of the
Macintosh Portable computer.

■ **Figure 6-4** Pinout of the power connector on the Macintosh Portable computer

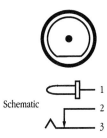

Table 6-4 shows the signal assignments for the power connector on the back of the
Macintosh Portable computer.

■ **Table 6-4** Signal assignments for the power connector on the Macintosh Portable computer

Pin number	Signal
1	+7.5 V nominal
2	Ground
3	Not connected

Figure 6-5 shows the pinouts for the connector from the power supply to the logic board in the Macintosh IIcx and Macintosh IIci computers.

■ **Figure 6-5** Pinout of the power supply connector on the Macintosh IIcx and Macintosh IIci computers

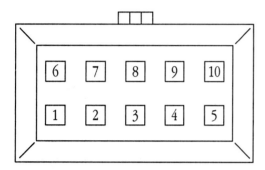

Table 6-5 shows the signal assignments for the connector from the power supply to the logic board in the Macintosh IIcx and Macintosh IIci computers.

■ **Table 6-5** Signal assignments for the power supply connector on the Macintosh IIcx and Macintosh IIci computers

Pin number	Signal	Signal description
1	+12V	+12 volts
2	+5V	+5 volts
3	+5V	+5 volts
4	+5V	+5 volts
5	GND	Ground
6	GND	Ground
7	GND	Ground
8	–12V	–12 volts
9	/PFW	Power fail warning
10	+5V.TRKL	Supply voltage for power-on circuit

Figure 6-6 shows the pinouts for the connector from the power supply to the main logic board in the Macintosh II, Macintosh IIx, and Macintosh IIfx computers.

■ **Figure 6-6** Pinout of the power supply connector in the Macintosh II, Macintosh IIx, and Macintosh IIfx computers

Table 6-6 shows the signal assignments for the connector from the power supply to the logic board in the Macintosh II, Macintosh IIx, and Macintosh IIfx computers.

■ **Table 6-6** Signal assignments for the power supply connector in the Macintosh II, Macintosh IIx, and Macintosh IIfx computers

Pin number	Signal	Signal description
1	+12V	+12 volts
2	+5V	+5 volts
3	+5V	+5 volts
4	+5V	+5 volts
5	+5V	+5 volts
6	+5V	+5 volts
7	GND	Ground
8	GND	Ground
9	GND	Ground
10	GND	Ground
11	GND	Ground
12	GND	Ground
13	n.c.	Not connected
14	–12V	–12 volts
15	/PFW	Power fail warning

Power input requirements

This section lists the power input requirements for the power supplies in Macintosh computers. In all Macintosh computers except the Macintosh Portable, the power supply converts AC line current into DC at the voltages required by the logic board and peripheral devices. In the Macintosh Portable, the battery charger converts the AC line current into DC, and the power supply converts the DC from either the battery charger or the battery into the voltages required by the logic board and peripherals.

Macintosh Plus computer

The Macintosh Plus power supply can accept any input AC line voltage from 85 to 135 V (rms), or from 170 to 270 V, at any single-phase input line frequency from 47 to 63 Hz. The input voltage range is configured by closing switch SW1 on the analog board for 120 V operation. All classic Macintosh power supplies generate output DC voltages of –12 V, +12 V, and +5 V. A three-terminal regulator IC on the main logic board converts from –12 V to –5 V for use by the serial port drivers.

△ **Important**   This section describes the power supply used in the Macintosh Plus computer. This power supply can be switched between configurations for 120 V and 240 V input line voltages. Some Macintosh 128K, 512K, and 512K enhanced computers may have power supplies that can use only 120 V nominal input voltage; some (configured for international use) can accept only 240 V nominal input voltage. △

Table 6-7 shows the AC input requirements for the Macintosh Plus computer.

■ **Table 6-7** AC input requirements for the Macintosh Plus computer

Parameter	Specification
Input voltage range	85–135 V (rms) and 170–270 V (rms)
Input surge voltage	150 V (rms) for 100 ms (120 V configuration) 300 V (rms) for 100 ms (240 V configuration)
Input line frequency	47–63 Hz, single phase
Line dropout immunity	16 ms minimum, for 95 V (rms, 120 V configuration) or for 190 V (rms, 240 V configuration), and maximum load
Starting voltage	70 V (rms, 120 V configuration), 140 V (rms, 240 V configuration), and maximum load
Input power under peak load	80 W (rms) maximum for all line conditions
Input/output power efficiency	65% minimum for all line conditions and maximum load

Macintosh SE and Macintosh SE/30 computers

The power supply in the Macintosh SE and Macintosh SE/30 can accept any input AC line
voltage from 85 to 135 V (rms) and 170 to 270 V at any single-phase input line frequency
from 47 to 63 Hz. This power supply does not have to be reconfigured when changing
from one input voltage range to the other. The power supply generates output DC voltages
of –12 V, +12 V, and +5 V. There is also a voltage regulator on the analog board that
provides a –5 V output.

Table 6-8 shows the AC input requirements for the Macintosh SE and Macintosh SE/30 computers.

■ **Table 6-8**   AC input requirements for the Macintosh SE and Macintosh SE/30 computers

Parameter	Specification
Input voltage range	85–270 V (rms)
Input surge voltage	300 V (rms) for 100 ms
Input line transient immunity	0–5 kV with no component failures
Peak inrush current	40 A for all load and line conditions
Input line frequency	47–63 Hz, single phase
Line dropout immunity	20 ms minimum, for 85 V (rms) 50 Hz input and maximum load
Input power under peak load	142 W (rms) maximum for all line conditions
Input/output power efficiency	70% minimum for all line conditions and maximum load

Macintosh Portable computer

The Macintosh Portable battery charger can accept any input AC line voltage from 85 to 270 V (rms) at any single-phase input line frequency from 48 to 62 Hz. The battery charger provides 5 ma to 1500 ma of DC current at 7.1 to 7.6 V to the battery. The voltage-control circuits on the main logic board can accept any input DC voltage from 5.12 V to 7.68 V from the battery. The voltage-control circuits supply DC voltages of +12 V, +5 V, and –5 V.

Table 6-9 shows the AC input requirements for the battery charger in the Macintosh Portable computer.

■ **Table 6-9** AC input requirements for the battery charger in the Macintosh Portable computer

Parameter	Specification
Input voltage range	85–270 V (rms)
Input surge voltage	300 V (rms) for 10 sec
Input line transient immunity	0–5 kV with no component failures
Peak inrush current	40 A for all load and line conditions
Input line frequency	48–62 Hz, single phase
Line dropout immunity	20 ms minimum, for 120 V (rms) 50 Hz input and maximum load
Input/output power efficiency	70% minimum for all line conditions and maximum load

Macintosh IIcx and Macintosh IIci computers

The power supply of the Macintosh IIcx and Macintosh IIci computers can accept any input AC line voltage from 85 to 135 V (rms) and 170 to 270 V at any single-phase input line frequency from 47 to 63 Hz. The power supply generates output DC voltages of –12 V, +12 V, and +5 V. There is also a voltage regulator on the logic board that provides a –5 V output.

The AC input requirements for the Macintosh IIcx and Macintosh IIci computers are shown in Table 6-10.

■ **Table 6-10** AC input requirements for the Macintosh IIcx and Macintosh IIci

Parameter	Specification
Input voltage range	85–135 V (rms) and 170–270 V (rms)
Input surge voltage	300 V (rms) for 100 ms
Input line transient immunity	0–6 kV with no component failures
Peak inrush current	40 A for all load and line conditions
Input line frequency	47–63 Hz, single phase
Line dropout immunity	20 ms minimum, for 85 V (rms) 50 Hz input and maximum load
Input/output power efficiency	70% minimum for all line conditions and maximum load

Macintosh II, Macintosh IIx, and Macintosh IIfx computers

The power supply of the Macintosh II, Macintosh IIx, and Macintosh IIfx computers can accept any input AC line voltage from 90 to 140 V (rms) and 170 to 270 V at any single-phase input line frequency from 47 to 63 Hz. The power supply generates output DC voltages of –12 V, +12 V, and +5 V. There is also a voltage regulator on the logic board that provides a –5 V output.

Table 6-11 shows the AC input requirements for the Macintosh II, Macintosh IIx, and Macintosh IIfx computers.

■ **Table 6-11** AC input requirements for the Macintosh II, Macintosh IIx, and Macintosh IIfx computers

Parameter	Specification
Input voltage range	90–140 V (rms) and 170–270 V (rms)
Input surge voltage	300 V (rms) for 100 ms
Input line transient immunity	0–5 kV with no component failures
Peak inrush current	60 A for all load and line conditions
Input line frequency	47–63 Hz, single phase
Line dropout immunity	20 ms minimum, for 90 V (rms) 50 Hz input and maximum load 20 ms minimum, for 180 V (rms) 50 Hz input and maximum load
Input power under peak load	230 W (rms) maximum for all line conditions
Input/output power efficiency	70% minimum for all line conditions and maximum load

DC output specifications

This section lists the power output specifications for the power supplies in Macintosh computers. It also describes the DC output of the Macintosh Portable battery charger, which is the input to the Macintosh Portable power supply.

Macintosh Plus computer

The Macintosh Plus power supply outputs remain within the limits shown in Table 6-12 under all input line voltage limits specified in the section "Power Input Requirements," earlier in this chapter, and under the load conditions shown in Table 6-13.

■ **Table 6-12**   Power supply output limits in the Macintosh Plus computer

Parameter	Specification
+5 volt supply	4.850 V to 5.150 V
+12 volt supply	11.90 V to 12.80 V
– 5 volt supply	–5.250 V to –4.750 V
–12 volt supply	–13.00 V to –11.30 V

■ **Table 6-13**   Total power at DC output loads for the Macintosh Plus computer

Load condition	+5 V	+12 V	–5 V	–12 V	Total power
Minimum load	3.0 A	0.50 A	5 mA	75 mA	21.9 W
Maximum load	4.5 A	1.5 A	50 mA	500 mA	46.8 W
Peak load*	4.5 A	2.2 A	50 mA	500 mA	55.2 W

*For a period of 15 seconds, maximum, 10% duty cycle.

Table 6-14 shows the maximum ripple and switching noise on the power supply outputs under all specified load conditions and for input voltages of 90 to 130 V (rms) or 180 to 260 V (rms).

■ **Table 6-14**   DC output ripple and switching noise for the Macintosh Plus computer

Parameter measured	+5 V	+12 V	–5 V	–12 V
Line frequency ripple	20 mV	30 mV	20 mV	30 mV
Switching noise	40 mV	40 mV	40 mV	40 mV

Note: All ripple and noise voltage measurements are peak-to-peak.

If the load on the +5 V supply is stepped from 3.5 A to 4.5 A or from 4.5 A to 3.5 A, the peak transient amplitude is 125 mV and the voltage recovers to +5 V ± 15 mV within 10 ms. All other outputs are assumed to be under maximum load with an input voltage of 120 V (rms) or 240 V (rms).

If the load on the +12 V supply is stepped from 0.50 A to 1.50 A or from 1.50 A to 0.50 A, supply voltages do not vary from the voltage ranges specified at the beginning of this section. All other outputs are assumed to be under maximum load with an input voltage of 120 V (rms) or 240 V (rms).

The adjustment potentiometer, R22, can vary the +5 V supply to be between 4.6 V and 5.4 V under all load conditions for an input voltage of 120 V (rms) or 240 V (rms).

Macintosh SE and Macintosh SE/30 computers

The outputs of the power supplies in the Macintosh SE and Macintosh SE/30 computers remain within the limits shown in Table 6-15 under all input line voltage limits specified in the section "Power Input Requirements," earlier in this chapter, and under the load conditions shown in Table 6-16.

■ **Table 6-15** Power supply output limits for the Macintosh SE and Macintosh SE/30 computers

Parameter	Specification
+5 volt supply	4.85 V to 5.20 V
+12 volt sweep supply	11.50 V to 12.50 V
+12 volt disk supply	11.50 V to 12.80 V
–12 volt supply	–13.20 V to –10.80 V

■ **Table 6-16** Total power at DC output loads for the Macintosh SE and Macintosh SE/30 computers

Load condition	+5 V	+12 V sweep	+12 V disk	–12 V	Total power
Minimum load	1.0 A	0.9 A	0.120 A	20 mA	17.0 W
Maximum load	6.0 A	1.25 A	2.1 A	0.5 A	76 W
Peak load*	6.0 A	1.25 A	4.0 A*	0.5 A	99 W

*For a period of 15 seconds, maximum, 10% duty cycle. The +12 V disk supply may drop to 11.0 V during the peak load; the +5 V and –12 V supplies conform to the limits listed previously in this section.

The maximum ripple and switching noise on the power supply outputs under all specified load and input-voltage conditions are shown in Table 6-17. Ripple and noise measurements assume resistive loads are bypassed only by a 0.1 µF ceramic capacitor for each output.

■ **Table 6-17**   DC output ripple and switching noise for the Macintosh SE and
                    Macintosh SE/30 computers

Parameter measured	+5 V	+12 V sweep	+12 V disk	−12 V
Line frequency ripple	20 mV	30 mV	30 mV	30 mV
Switching noise	40 mV	50 mV	50 mV	50 mV

Note: All ripple and noise voltage measurements are peak-to-peak.

If the load on the +5 V supply is stepped from 2.0 A to 6.0 A or from 6.0 A to 2.0 A, the peak transient amplitude is 125 mV and the voltage recovers to +5 V ± 15 mV within 5 ms. All other outputs are assumed to be under maximum load with an input voltage from 85 V to 135 V (rms) or 170 V to 270 V (rms).

If the load on the +12 V disk supply is stepped from 0.50 A to 2.1 A or from 2.1 A to 0.50 A, supply voltages do not vary from the voltage ranges specified in Table 6-15. All other outputs are assumed to be under maximum load with an input voltage from 85 V to 135 V (rms) or 170 V to 270 V (rms).

If the load on the −12 V supply is stepped from 0.02 A to 0.15 A or from 0.15 A to 0.02 A, supply voltages do not vary from the voltage ranges specified in Table 6-15. All other outputs are assumed to be under maximum load with an input voltage from 85 V to 135 V (rms) or 170 V to 270 V (rms).

If the load on any of the DC output supplies is stepped as specified in the preceding paragraphs, the +12 V sweep supply maintains a voltage of +12 V ± 10 mV.

With a ±10% instantaneous variation in the average input line voltage applied for 100 ms, and with the outputs loaded within the limits specified in Table 6-16, the +5 V supply voltage does not vary by more than 25 mV, and the voltage recovers to +5 V ± 15 mV within 5 ms.

Macintosh Portable computer

The outputs of the voltage control circuits on the main logic board in the Macintosh Portable remain within the limits shown in Table 6-18 for input of 5 mA to 1500 mA of DC current at 7.1 to 7.6 V, and under the load conditions shown in Table 6-19.

■ **Table 6-18**   Output limits for the voltage-control circuits in the
                    Macintosh Portable computer

Parameter	Specification
+5 volt supply	4.95 V to 5.05 V
+12 volt supply	11.40 V to 12.60 V
–5 volt supply	–4.95 V to –5.5 V

■ **Table 6-19**   Total power at DC output loads for the Macintosh Portable computer

Load condition	+5 V	+12 V	–5 V	Total power
Minimum load	0.0 A	0.0 A	0.0 A	0.0 W
Maximum load	1.5 A	0.5 A	0.2 A	14.5 W
Peak load	3.0 A	0.0 A*	0.0 A*	15.0 W

*The +12 V and –5 V power supplies are switched off during the power-on sequence.

Macintosh IIcx and Macintosh IIci computers

The output of the power supply used in the Macintosh IIcx and Macintosh IIci computers remains within the limits shown in Table 6-20 under all input line voltage limits specified in the section "Power Input Requirements," earlier in this chapter, and under the load conditions shown in Table 6-21.

■ **Table 6-20**   Power supply output limits in the Macintosh IIcx and
                    Macintosh IIci computers

Parameter	Specification
+5 volt supply	4.9 V to 5.2V
+12 volt supply	11.5 V to 12.8 V
–12 volt supply	–13.2 V to –10.8 V

- **Table 6-21**   Total power at DC output loads for the Macintosh IIcx and
  Macintosh IIci computers

Load condition	+5 V	+12 V	–12 V	Total power
Minimum load	2 A	20 mA	20 mA	10.5 W
Maximum load	12 A	1.5 A	1 A	90 W
Peak load*	12 A	3 A*	1 A	108 W

*For a period of 15 seconds, maximum, 10% duty cycle. The +12 V supply may drop to 11 V during the peak load; the +5 V and –12 V supplies conform to the limits listed previously in this section.

The maximum ripple and switching noise on the power supply outputs under all specified load and input-voltage conditions are shown in Table 6-22. Ripple and noise measurements assume resistive loads are bypassed only by a 0.1 µF ceramic capacitor for each output.

- **Table 6-22**   DC output ripple and switching noise for the Macintosh IIcx and
  Macintosh IIci computers

Parameter measured	+5 V	+12 V	–12 V
Line frequency ripple	20 mV	30 mV	30 mV
Switching noise	40 mV	50 mV	50 mV

Note: All ripple and noise voltage measurements are peak-to-peak.

If the load on the +5 V supply is stepped from 3.0 A to 6.0 A or from 6.0 A to 3.0 A, the peak transient amplitude is 125 mV and the voltage recovers to +5 V ± 15 mV within 5 ms. All other outputs are assumed to be under maximum load with an input voltage from 85 V to 270 V (rms).

If the load on the +12 V supply is stepped from 0.5 A to 1.0 A or from 1.0 A to 0.5 A, supply voltages do not vary from the voltage ranges specified in Table 6-20. All other outputs are assumed to be under maximum load with an input voltage from 85 V to 270 V (rms).

If the load on the –12 V supply is stepped from 0.5 A to 1.0 A or from 1.0 A to 0.5 A, supply voltages do not vary from the voltage ranges specified in Table 6-20. All other outputs are assumed to be under maximum load with an input voltage from 85 V to 270 V (rms).

With a ±10% instantaneous variation in the average input line voltage applied for 100 ms, and with the outputs loaded within the limits specified in Table 6-21, the +5 V supply voltage does not vary by more than 25 mV, and the voltage recovers to +5 V within 5 ms.

Macintosh II, Macintosh IIx, and Macintosh IIfx computers

The outputs of the power supplies of Macintosh II, Macintosh IIx, and Macintosh IIfx computers remain within the limits shown in Table 6-23 under all input voltage limits specified in the section "Power Input Requirements," earlier in this chapter, and under the load conditions shown in Table 6-24.

■ **Table 6-23** Power supply output limits for the Macintosh II, Macintosh IIx, and Macintosh IIfx computers

Parameter	Specification
+5 volt supply	4.90 V to 5.20 V
+12 volt supply	11.50 V to 12.80 V
–12 volt supply	–13.40 V to –10.80 V

■ **Table 6-24** Total power at DC output loads for the Macintosh II, Macintosh IIx, and Macintosh IIfx computers

Load condition	+5 V	+12 V	–12 V	Total power
Minimum load	3.0 A	20 mA	20 mA	15.5 W
Maximum load	18 A	2.5 A	1.0 A	132 W
Peak load*	18 A	4.5 A*	1.0 A	156 W
Maximum capacitive load	10,000 μF	4700 μF	4700 μF	

*For a period of 15 seconds, maximum, 10% duty cycle. The +12 V supply may drop to 11 V during the peak load; the +5 V and –12 V supplies conform to the limits listed previously in this section.

The maximum ripple and switching noise on the power supply outputs under all specified load and input-voltage conditions are shown in Table 6-25. Ripple and noise measurements assume resistive loads are bypassed only by a 0.1 μF ceramic capacitor for each output.

DC output ripple and switching noise for the Macintosh II, Macintosh IIx, and Macintosh IIfx computers

Parameter measured	+5 V	+12 V	–12 V
Line frequency ripple	20 mV	30 mV	30 mV
Switching noise	40 mV	50 mV	50 mV

Note: All ripple and noise voltage measurements are peak-to-peak.

If the load on the +5 V supply is stepped from 3.5 A to 7.0 A or from 7.0 A to 3.5 A, the peak transient amplitude is 125 mV and the voltage recovers to +5 V ± 15 mV within 5 ms. All other outputs are assumed to be under maximum load with an input voltage from 90 V to 270 V (rms).

If the load on the +12 V supply is stepped from 0.50 A to 1.50 A or from 1.50 A to 0.50 A, supply voltages do not vary from the voltage ranges specified in Table 6-23. All other outputs are assumed to be under maximum load with an input voltage from 90 V to 270 V (rms).

If the load on the –12 V supply is stepped from 0.50 A to 1.00 A or from 1.00 A to 0.50 A, supply voltages do not vary from the voltage ranges specified in Table 6-23. All other outputs are assumed to be under maximum load with an input voltage from 90 V to 270 V (rms).

With a ±10% instantaneous variation in the average input line voltage applied for 100 ms, and with the outputs loaded within the limits specified in Table 6-24, the +5 V supply voltage does not vary by more than 25 mV, and the voltage recovers to +5 V ± 15 mV within 5 ms.

Monitor power receptacle in the Macintosh II–family computers

The Macintosh II–family computers have a power receptacle on the back of the main system unit, identified as the *monitor power output receptacle* in the owner's manual. Table 6-26 shows the power available at this receptacle.

■ **Table 6-26**   Specifications for the monitor power output receptacle on the
Macintosh II–family computers

Parameter	Specification
Output voltage	Same as power-supply input voltage
Output current	3 A, maximum steady-state
Output power	300 VA, maximum
Peak output current	40 A
Fuse	6 A, 250 V

Responses to abnormal conditions

A crowbar circuit in the Macintosh Plus shorts out the power supply and stops the flyback oscillator when the +5 V output is between 5.35 V and 6.25 V.

If any output of the Macintosh SE, Macintosh SE/30, or Macintosh II–familty computer is short circuited to ground (that is, connected to ground through approximately 100 milliohm or less), the power supply shuts down within 25 ms. The Macintosh SE, Macintosh SE/30, and Macintosh IIcx power supplies shut down within 25 ms if for any reason the +5 V output exceeds +6.5 V, or either +12 V output exceeds +16 V, or the –12 V output exceeds –16 V.

If the heat sink of the primary switching devices in a Macintosh II–family power supply exceeds a temperature of 125° C, the power supply shuts down. Before shutting down, the power supply pulls the /PFW signal low for at least 2.2 ms.

The Macintosh II–family power supply also pulls the /PFW signal below +0.6 V when it detects an input voltage failure. The power supply keeps all output voltages within the limits specified in the previous section for at least 2.2 ms after it has pulled the /PFW signal low.

Power circuit in the Macintosh Portable computer

The Macintosh Portable power circuit includes the following components:

- an external transformer and voltage converter, referred to as the *battery charger,* that provides DC power to the main system unit

- voltage control circuits on the logic board that provide +5 V, +12 V, and –5 V to the rest of the system

- a battery monitor and battery charging circuit on the logic board

- a microprocessor, called the *Power Manager IC,* on the logic board

When the battery is initially connected to the power circuit, the Macintosh Portable computer starts up, and the Power Manager IC and battery monitor begin monitoring the state of the system. As long as the battery maintains a voltage of 5.74 volts or above, the system remains switched on. The Power Manager IC monitors battery voltage and shuts the system down when the voltage drops below 5.74 volts, maintaining power to system RAM and to itself. If the user plugs in the battery charger before the voltage drops below 5.65 volts, the Power Manager IC brings the system back up with no loss of data when the battery voltage reaches 5.74 volts. However, if the voltage continues to drop and reaches 5.65 volts, the battery monitor hardware removes power from all components, including RAM and the Power Manager IC, and all data (including parameter RAM) is lost.

Any time that the user chooses Sleep from the Special menu or from a desk accessory, or whenever the operating system determines that the system has been idle for too long, the Power Manager firmware puts the Macintosh Portable computer into a low-power-consumption state known as the **sleep state.**

Battery charger and voltage control circuits

The Macintosh Portable battery charger rectifies AC line power to DC and transforms it to 7.5 ± 0.1 V, which is input to the main system unit through the connector described in the section "Power Connectors," earlier in this chapter. The battery charger can accept input power of 85 V to 270 V, and limits output current to 1.5 A.

The Macintosh Portable voltage-control circuits on the logic board generate three voltages: +5 V, +12 V, and –5 V. The output specifications for the voltage control circuits are given in the section "DC Output Specifications," earlier in this chapter.

Battery monitor and battery charging circuit

The Macintosh Portable battery monitor consists of an operational amplifier, an analog-to-digital converter, and a comparator. The amplifier converts the battery voltage of 5.12 to 7.68 volts to a 0-to-5 volt input to the A to D converter. The comparator monitors the output of the A to D converter, and removes power from all circuitry except itself if the battery voltage drops below 5.65 volts. If the battery voltage rises to above 5.65 volts (as, for example, if the battery charger is connected), the comparator restores power to the system.

The input from the battery charger is also monitored by a comparator. If the charger input voltage is higher than the battery voltage—that is, if the battery charger is plugged in and connected to the computer—then the comparator applies voltage to the battery charge controller and asserts a signal that tells the Power Manager IC that the battery is being charged.

The battery charge controller is a voltage regulator with a switchable output. When the charger is initially connected to a Macintosh Portable computer with a low battery, the Power Manager IC connects the charger directly to the battery. The battery is therefore charged at the maximum rate (1.5 amps) until battery voltage reaches 7.2 volts. The Power Manager IC measures the time required to raise the battery voltage to this level, and maintains the connection for an equal amount of time to assure that the battery is fully charged. At the end of that time, the Power Manager IC switches the voltage regulator into the circuit.

The voltage regulator maintains the input voltage to the battery at a level that causes the battery to accept just enough charge to replace that lost through self-discharge. The maintenance voltage is 6.94 volts to 7.16 volts at 20° C, and decreases with increasing temperature at the rate of -7.5 ± 1.0 mV per degree C.

Sleep state in the Macintosh Portable computer

Whether the Macintosh Portable computer enters the sleep state is controlled by a firmware routine known as the BatteryMonitor routine. The BatteryMonitor routine is called by the interrupt handler each time a one-second interrupt occurs. The BatteryMonitor routine performs the following functions:

■ It checks the battery voltage to see if it is necessary to alert the user that the battery voltage is low.

■ It checks to see if the user has used the Control Panel desk accessory to change the length of time that the Macintosh Portable must be idle before the BatteryMonitor routine automatically invokes the sleep state. If the user has changed this time, the BatteryMonitor routine stores the new time in parameter RAM.

■ It turns off the sound circuit when it is not needed. The sound circuit uses a relatively large amount of power.

■ It updates the real-time clock function of the Power Manager IC.

■ It checks the internal temperature of the Macintosh Portable to see if it is necessary to alert the user that a high-temperature condition exists.

■ It monitors the amount of time the Macintosh Portable has been idle, and causes the Power Manager IC to put the system into the sleep state if the user-selected idle time has been reached.

The Macintosh Portable computer is not considered to be idle if any of the following kinds of activity are occurring:

■ any ADB routine other than routine monitoring of the bus

■ any I/O call to firmware (Read, Write, Control, Format, Status)

■ any change in the cursor (for example, the rotation of a hand in the clock icon)

■ any post-event call (for example, a call resulting from insertion of a disk)

■ any communication through a serial port

The Macintosh Portable is considered idle after 15 seconds without activity of any kind. When the BatteryMonitor routine determines that the Macintosh Portable is idle, it causes the CPU to insert 64 wait states into RAM and ROM accesses; this lowers the effective clock rate to approximately 1 MHz. Interrupts continue to be processed at the full speed of the CPU.

After the Macintosh Portable has been idle for the amount of time selected by the user, the BatteryMonitor routine puts the machine into the sleep state. When in sleep state, the Macintosh Portable maintains full power to system RAM, video RAM, and the Power Manager IC. The Power Manager IC stops the clocks to the SCC, the SWIM, and the ASC. By stopping the clocks to these devices, their power consumption is reduced almost to zero without requiring that they be reset, as would be necessary if all power were switched off. The Power Manager IC switches off power to the serial drivers, ROM, the flat-panel display, the ASC, the Sony sound ICs, the SCSI, and to a variety of pullup resistors and other components. The Power Manager IC sends a signal to the internal modem (if one is installed) that causes the modem to shut itself down.

After putting the rest of the system in the sleep state, the Power Manager IC does no processing except to monitor the 60 Hz interrupt signal. Each time the 60 Hz interrupt occurs, the Power Manager IC perfoms the following functions:

- It updates the real-time clock.
- It checks the wake-up timer to see if it matches the real-time clock.
- It checks for events that should return the machine to the operating state, such as a keystroke or a Ring Detect signal from the modem (when the modem feature has been enabled by the user).

The periodic functions take approximately 200 microseconds out of the 16.7 milliseconds between interrupts, so the Power Manager IC is inactive most of the time that the Macintosh Portable is in the sleep state.

When the Power Manager IC determines that the wake-up timer matches the real-time clock or detects an event, it asserts the /RESET signal to the CPU, restores the clocks and power to the other devices in the system, and then raises (deasserts) the /RESET signal.

Power-control circuit in the Macintosh II–family computers

The power-on switch on the Macintosh II–family computers does not simply connect and disconnect the AC power to the power supply. Instead, these computers have a power-control circuit that turns the power supply on in response to a signal from an ADB keyboard. To turn off the power to these computers, the user normally selects Shut Down from a menu, and the firmware causes a signal to be asserted that switches off the power. In early Macintosh II computers, the power switch on the back of the computer causes an interrupt, and the interrupt handler switches off the power. In later Macintosh II computers and the other members of the Macintosh II family, the power switch acts directly on the hardware.

When you press the power-on switch on the ADB keyboard, the Macintosh II–family power-control circuit sends a signal to the power supply that causes it to turn itself on and begin functioning normally within 1.5 seconds. This signal is also available to NuBus cards, so a NuBus card can be made that can turn on the computer.

When you choose Shut Down from a menu (or press the power switch at the back of the main system unit of an early Macintosh II), the power-switch interrupt signal is asserted to the GLUE IC. The GLUE IC interrupts the processor with a level-6 interrupt, and the processor causes the power-control circuit to shut down the power supply.

Figure 6-7 shows a block diagram of the power-control circuit in the Macintosh II, Macintosh IIx, and Macintosh IIfx computers; the other Macintosh II–family computers are similar. As you can see from the figure, when the computer is off, the /POWERON signal is held high by the same battery that runs the real-time clock. When you press the power-on switch on the ADB keyboard, the /POWERON signal is shorted to ground and pulled low. When /POWERON goes low, the power-on circuit connects the battery to the /PFW line. A voltage from +3 V to +6.5 V on the /PFW line causes the power supply to turn itself on. Once the power supply is on, +5 V from the power supply holds the /PFW signal high, keeping the power supply on.

The power-control circuit in the Macintosh IIcx and Macintosh IIci computers is the same as that shown in Figure 6-7, except that those machines have no thermal switch and the power supply for the power-on circuit is the +5V.TRKL line rather than the battery for the real-time clock.

The power-on function in the Macintosh IIx and Macintosh IIfx is the same as that in the Macintosh II. In the Macintosh IIcx and Macintosh IIci computers, when the computer is switched off, the /POWERON signal is held high by the +5V.TRKL line from the power supply.

◆ *Note:* In the Macintosh IIci, the power switch on the back can be locked in the "on" position with a screwdriver or a coin. If the switch is in the "on" position, the machine will turn itself back on after a power interruption. This feature is useful for machines operating as file servers, where automatic recovery after a power failure is desirable. When the switch is locked in the "on" position, choosing the Shut Down command from the Special menu in the Finder causes the computer to restart.

When the CPU receives a level-6 interrupt, it causes VIA2 to assert the /POWEROFF signal to the power-control circuit. The power-off circuit then pulls the /PFW signal low. When /PFW goes low, the power supply switches itself off.

The double-pole–double-throw switch at the back of the main system unit of Macintosh II–family computers simultaneously pulls /POWERON high (deasserting it) and pulls /PFW low, causing the power supply to switch itself off.

◆ *Note:* In early Macintosh II computers, the power switch pulls /POWERON high and pulls /PWRIRQ low. The /PWRIRQ signal causes the GLUE to send a level-6 interrupt to the CPU, thus turning off the computer. In this version of the Macintosh II computer only, the power switch does not work if level-6 interrupts are masked.

If some fault condition (such as an AC power-line failure) causes the power supply to turn off, the power supply pulls /PFW low at least 2 ms before the DC outputs turn off. The /PFW signal is not monitored by the CPU, but can be monitored by a NuBus card to detect the power-fail warning from the power supply.

If the temperature inside the computer gets too high, the thermal switch disconnects the /PFW signal from the +5 V pullup, causing the voltage to drop below +3 V, and thus causing the power supply to shut down.

■ **Figure 6-7** Power-control circuit in the Macintosh II–family computers

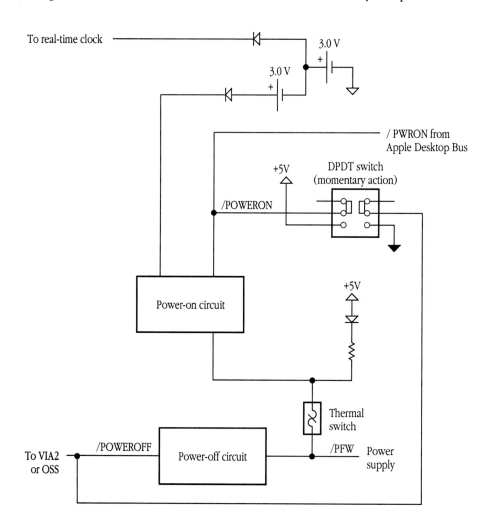

Chapter 7 **Macintosh Plus Mouse and Keyboard**

The Macintosh Plus computer communicates directly with the keyboard and the mouse through the Versatile Interface Adapter (VIA) and Serial Communications Controller (SCC) ICs. This chapter describes the operation of the mouse device and the keyboard used with the Macintosh Plus computer. It also describes the keyboards on the earlier Macintosh models where they are different from the one on the Macintosh Plus.

◆ *Note:* The interfaces to the mouse and the keyboard on the Macintosh Plus are similar to those on the earlier Macintosh models— Macintosh 128K, Macintosh 512K, and Macintosh 512K enhanced. On all other Macintosh models, the interface to the mouse and the keyboard is the Apple Desktop Bus, which is described in Chapter 8.

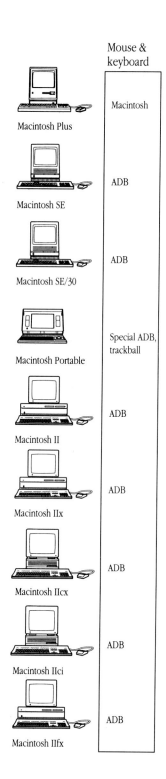

Mouse &
keyboard

Macintosh Plus — Macintosh

Macintosh SE — ADB

Macintosh SE/30 — ADB

Macintosh Portable — Special ADB, trackball

Macintosh II — ADB

Macintosh IIx — ADB

Macintosh IIcx — ADB

Macintosh IIci — ADB

Macintosh IIfx — ADB

Macintosh Plus mouse

The Apple mouse is a relative-motion input device. On the Macintosh Plus and earlier models, the mouse communicates with the CPU through the Versatile Interface Adapter (VIA) and Serial Communications Controller (SCC) chips. On other Macintosh models, the mouse communicates with the CPU by way of the Apple Desktop Bus (ADB), described in Chapter 8.

Macintosh Plus mouse mechanism

The mouse generates four square-wave signals that indicate the amount and direction of the mouse's travel. Interrupt-driven routines in the Macintosh Plus ROM convert this information into the corresponding motion of the pointer on the screen. Figure 7-1 shows the mouse mechanism and the signals to the VIA and SCC chips.

■ **Figure 7-1** Mouse mechanism in the Macintosh Plus computer

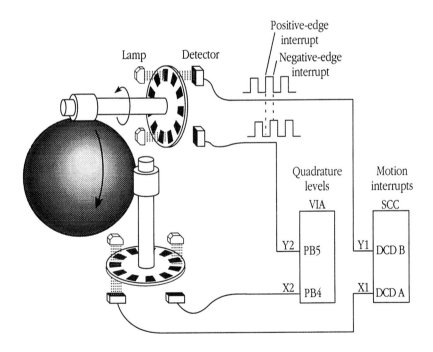

A rubber-coated steel ball in the mouse turns as the mouse is moved and contacts two capstans, each connected to a slotted wheel called an *interrupter wheel*. Motion in the mouse's X-axis direction (left and right) rotates one of the wheels and motion in the Y-axis direction (up and down) rotates the other wheel.

The Macintosh Plus uses a scheme known as *quadrature* to determine in which direction the mouse is moving along each axis. Two beams of infrared light shine through the slots in the interrupter wheel and strike one of two light detectors (phototransistors). The detectors are offset just enough so that, as the wheel turns, they produce two square-wave signals that are 90° out of phase. These signals are called the *interrupt signal* and the *quadrature signal*. The quadrature signal precedes the interrupt signal by 90° when the wheel turns one way, and trails it when the wheel turns the other way.

The interrupt signals, X1 and Y1, are connected to the DCDA and DCDB inputs, respectively, of the SCC chip. The quadrature signals, X2 and Y2, go to inputs of the VIA's Data register B. When the SCC receives a mouse-interrupt signal, it sends an interrupt signal to the CPU. The mouse driver can then read bits in the SCC to determine which mouse-interrupt signal caused the interrupt, and whether the interrupt was caused by a rising edge or a falling edge of the signal. The mouse driver also checks the VIA to determine the state of the quadrature signal for the axis (X or Y) corresponding to the interrupt signal.

The relative polarities of the interrupt and quadrature signals indicate the direction of the mouse motion, as shown in Table 7-1. When the interrupt is triggered by the rising edge of a mouse-interrupt signal, a low quadrature signal indicates that the mouse is moving to the left or down, and a high quadrature signal indicates that the mouse is moving to the right or up. When the SCC interrupt is triggered by the falling edge of the mouse-interrupt signal, a high quadrature level indicates motion to the left or down and a low quadrature level indicates motion to the right or up. For example, in Figure 7-1, the interrupt (Y1) and quadrature (Y2) signals indicate that the mouse is moving downwards.

■ **Table 7-1** Mouse-motion signals in the Macintosh Plus computer

Mouse interrupt	Mouse quadrature	Mouse motion
X1 rising edge	X2 low	Left
	X2 high	Right
Y1 rising edge	Y2 low	Down
	Y2 high	Up
X1 falling edge	X2 low	Right
	X2 high	Left
Y1 falling edge	Y2 low	Up
	Y2 high	Down

◆ *Note:* The mouse is a relative-motion device; that is, it doesn't report where it is, only how far and in which direction it's moving. Therefore, if you want to connect graphics tablets, touch screens, light pens, or other absolute-position devices to the mouse port of the Macintosh Plus computer, you must either convert their coordinates into motion information or install your own device-handling routines.

The user can change the amount of screen-pointer motion that corresponds to a given mouse motion by changing an option called *Mouse Tracking* in the Control Panel desk accessory. For more information about the rate of mouse motion, see the discussion of parameter RAM in the chapter on Operating System Utilities in *Inside Macintosh*.

The switch on the mouse is a push button that grounds pin 7 on the mouse connector when pressed. The state of the button is checked by software during each vertical blanking interrupt. The small delay between checks is sufficient to debounce the signal from the button (effectively ignoring the rapid multiple transitions produced each time the button is pressed or released). You can read the state of the mouse button by examining bit 3 of VIA Data register B. If the bit is zero, the mouse button is down.

△ **Developer tip** The mouse interface in the Macintosh Plus and earlier models is different from the Apple Desktop Bus used for the mouse in all other Macintosh computers. If you want your software to be compatible with all Macintosh computers, it is imperative that you deal with mouse events only through calls to the Macintosh Toolbox. Apple recommends that you let the Event Manager handle the task of reporting the state of the mouse button for you through the event mechanism. △

Macintosh Plus mouse interface

Figure 7-2 shows the pinout of the DB-9 mouse connector located on the back panel of the Macintosh Plus computer. The mouse socket signal assignments are shown in Table 7-2.

■ **Figure 7-2** Pinout of the DB-9 mouse connector in the Macintosh Plus computer

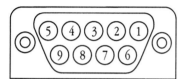

■ **Table 7-2** Signal assignments for the DB-9 mouse connector in the Macintosh Plus computer

Pin number	Signal name	Signal description
1	GND	Ground
2	+5V	+5 volts
3	GND	Ground
4	MSE.X2	Mouse X2 (quadrature signal)
5	MSE.X1	Mouse X1 (interrupt signal)
6	n.c.	Not connected
7	MSE.SW	Mouse Switch
8	MSE.Y2	Mouse Y2 (quadrature signal)
9	MSE.Y1	Mouse Y1 (interrupt signal)

▲ **Warning**   All devices connected to the Macintosh Plus unit must not draw a combined current of more than 200 milliamps at +5 volts from all connectors. ▲

Figure 7-3 shows a circuit diagram of the mouse port in the Macintosh Plus computer.

■ **Figure 7-3** Circuit diagram of the mouse port in the Macintosh Plus computer

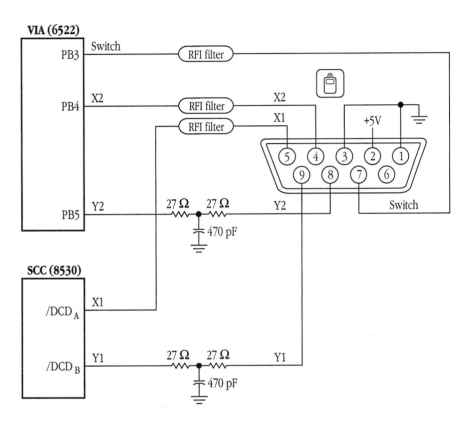

Note:

─(RFI filter)─ = R1 ∿ R2 ∿ ═╪═ C

(R1 + R2 = 40 to 60 ohms, C = 150 to 300 pF)

Macintosh Plus keyboard

The switches in the keyboard are wired in a two-dimensional array called a *keyswitch matrix*. The keyboard for the Macintosh Plus contains a microprocessor that scans the matrix to detect switch transitions as keys are pressed and released and reports those transitions as key-down and key-up events. The microprocessor contains its own ROM and RAM, and is programmed to conform to the interface protocol described later in this chapter.

The keyboard for the Macintosh Plus computer has a built-in numeric keypad and arrow keys not included on the keyboards of earlier Macintosh models (Macintosh 128K, Macintosh 512K, Macintosh 512K enhanced). In all other respects, the operation of the Macintosh Plus keyboard is identical to that of the earlier Macintosh keyboards.

The Macintosh Plus keyboard interface

The keyboard is connected to the Macintosh through a four-wire RJ-11 telephone-style connector, located on the front of the computer. Figure 7-4 shows the pinout for the keyboard connector used on the computer and the keyboard. Table 7-3 shows the keyboard connector signal assignments.

■ **Figure 7-4** Pinout of the RJ-11 keyboard connector in the Macintosh Plus computer

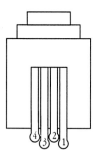

■ **Table 7-3** Signal assignments for the keyboard connector in the Macintosh Plus computer

Pin number	Signal name	Signal description
1	GND	Ground
2	CLOCK	Keyboard Clock (input to VIA)
3	DATA	Keyboard Data (serial)
4	+5V	+5 volts

▲ **Warning**   All devices connected to the Macintosh Plus must not draw a combined current of more than 200 milliamps at +5 volts from all connectors. ▲

Figure 7-5 shows the circuit diagram for the keyboard interface in the Macintosh Plus computer.

■ **Figure 7-5** Circuit diagram of the keyboard interface in the Macintosh Plus computer

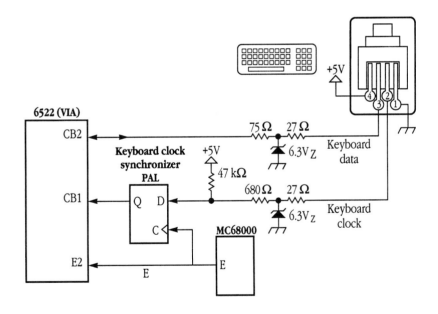

Macintosh Plus keyboard communication

On the Macintosh Plus and earlier Macintosh computers, the Keyboard Data line is bidirectional, driven at some times by the computer, and at other times by the keyboard, but the Keyboard Clock line is driven only by the keyboard. All data transfers are synchronous with the signals on the Keyboard Clock line, and each transmission consists of 8 bits, with the highest-order bit first.

When sending data to the computer, the keyboard transmits eight cycles of 330 µs each (160 µs low, 170 µs high) on the normally high Keyboard Clock line. It places a data bit on the data line 40 µs before the falling edge of each clock cycle and maintains it for 330 µs. The VIA in the computer latches the data bit into its Shift register on the rising edge of the Keyboard Clock signal.

When the computer is sending data to the keyboard, the keyboard transmits eight cycles of 400 µs each (180 µs low, 220 µs high) on the Keyboard Clock line. On the falling edge of each keyboard clock cycle, the Macintosh Plus places a data bit on the data line and holds it there for 400 µs. The keyboard reads the data bit 80 µs after the rising edge of the Keyboard Clock signal.

Only the computer can initiate communication over the keyboard lines. When the computer and keyboard are turned on, the computer is in charge of the keyboard interface and the keyboard is passive. The computer signals that it is ready to begin communication by pulling the Keyboard Data line low. Upon detecting this signal, the keyboard starts sending a Keyboard Clock signal, and the computer responds by sending an 8-bit command over the Keyboard Data line. The last bit of the command leaves the Keyboard Data line low; the computer then indicates that it is ready to receive the keyboard's response by setting the Keyboard Data line high.

The first command the computer transmits is the Model Number command. The keyboard's response to this command is to reset itself and send back its model number to the computer. If the computer does not receive a response within 0.5 second, it transmits the Model Number command again.

Once the computer has successfully received a model number from the keyboard, normal operation begins. The computer sends the Inquiry command; if a key has been pressed or released, the keyboard sends back a key transition response. If no key transition has occurred after 0.25 second, the keyboard sends back a Null response to let the computer know it's still there. The computer then sends the Inquiry command again. In normal operation, the computer sends an Inquiry command every 0.25 second. If it receives no response within 0.5 second, it assumes the keyboard is missing or needs resetting, so it begins again with the Model Number command.

There are two other commands that the Macintosh Plus computer can send: the Instant command, which gets an instant keyboard status without the 0.25 second timeout, and the Test command, to perform a keyboard self-test. Table 7-4 summarizes the commands that can be sent from the Macintosh Plus computer to the keyboard.

■ **Table 7-4**   Keyboard commands in the Macintosh Plus computer

Command name	Value	Keyboard response
Inquiry	$10	Key transition code or Null ($7B)
Instant	$14	Key transition code or Null ($7B)
Model Number	$16	Bit 0: 1
		Bits 1–3: keyboard model number, 1–8
		Bits 4–6: next device number, 1–8
		Bit 7: 1 if another device connected
Test	$36	ACK ($7D) or NAK ($77)

The key transition responses are sent out by the keyboard as a single byte: bit 7 high means a key-up transition, and bit 7 low means a key-down transition. Bit 0 is always high. The key transition responses for key-down transitions from the U.S. and international keyboards are shown (in hexadecimal) in Figure 7-6.

Macintosh Plus keyboard and keypad protocol

The Macintosh Plus keyboard produces all the key-down transitions produced by the keyboard and optional keypad used by earlier models of the Macintosh computer; the Macintosh Plus keyboard is completely compatible with those computers. (For descriptions, please refer to the next section, "Earlier Keyboard and Separate Keypad.")

Some keys on the Macintosh Plus keyboard reproduce the protocol of the separate keypad used with the earlier models, described in the later section "Communication Protocol for the Separate Keypad." If a key transition occurs for one of the arrow keys—which are lowercase keys on the separate keypad—the Macintosh Plus keyboard responds to an Inquiry command by sending back the Keypad response ($79) followed by the code shown in Figure 7-6. If a key transition occurs on the Macintosh Plus numeric keypad for the plus sign (+), asterisk (*), or slash (/) keys—which are uppercase keys on the separate keypad—the Macintosh Plus keyboard responds to an Inquiry command by sending back the Shift key–down transition response ($71), followed by the Keypad response ($79), followed by the code shown in Figure 7-6.

■ **Figure 7-6** Key-down transition codes in the Macintosh Plus computer (hexadecimal)

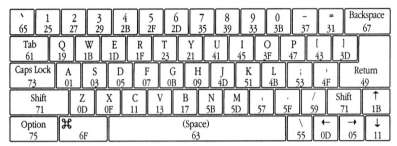

U.S. and international keyboard

These response codes are not the same as the key codes returned by the Keyboard Driver software. For the main keyboard, except for the arrow keys, the Keyboard Driver strips off bit 7 of the response code and shifts the result 1 bit to the right, removing bit 0. For example, a key transition response code of $33 from the keyboard is returned as $19 by the Keyboard Driver, and $2B is returned as $15.

For the numeric keypad and the arrow keys, the Keyboard Driver strips off bit 7 of the response code, shifts the result 1 bit to the right, removing bit 0, and adds $40 to the result. For example, a key transition response code of $33 from the numeric keypad is returned as $59 by the Keyboard Driver, and $2B is returned as $55.

Earlier keyboard and separate keypad

The earlier models of the Macintosh computer—the Macintosh 128K, 512K, and 512K enhanced—used a smaller keyboard with an optional separate keypad. Figure 7-7 shows the response codes for key-down transitions on that earlier keyboard (in hexadecimal). The next section describes the operation of the separate keyboard and keypad.

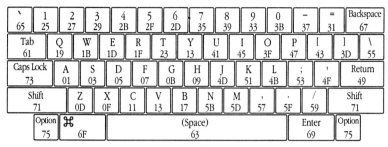

U.S. keyboard

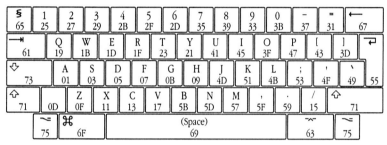

International keyboard (U.K. key caps shown)

Note that, as for the Macintosh Plus keyboard, these response codes are different from the key codes returned by the Keyboard Driver software. The Keyboard Driver strips off bit 7 of the response code and shifts the result 1 bit to the right, removing bit 0. For example, a key transition response code of $33 from the keyboard is returned as $19 by the Keyboard Driver software, and $2B is returned as $15.

Communication protocol for the separate keypad

Earlier models of the Macintosh computer (Macintosh 128K, 512K, and 512K enhanced) use an optional separate keypad. To install the keypad, the user inserts it between the keyboard and the computer; that is, the user plugs the keypad cable into the connector on the front of the computer and plugs the keyboard cable into a connector on the numeric keypad. In this configuration, the timings and protocol for the clock and data lines work a little differently from those for the keyboard alone: the keypad acts like a keyboard when communicating with the computer, and acts like a computer when communicating over the separate clock and data lines going to the keyboard. All commands from the computer are received by the keypad instead of the keyboard, and only the keypad can communicate directly with the keyboard.

When the computer sends an Inquiry command, one of two things may happen, depending on the state of the keypad. If no key transitions have occurred on the keypad since the last Inquiry command, the keypad sends an Inquiry command to the keyboard and, later, retransmits the keyboard's response back to the computer. But if a key transition has occurred on the keypad, the keypad responds to an Inquiry by sending back the Keypad response ($79) to the computer. In that case, the computer immediately sends an Instant command, and this time the keypad sends back its own key transition response. As with the keyboard, bit 7 high means key-up and bit 7 low means key-down.

The responses for key-down transitions for the keypad are shown in Figure 7-8.

■ **Figure 7-8** Key-down transition codes for the separate keypad (hexadecimal)

Note that these key-down transition response codes are different from the key codes returned by the Keyboard Driver software. The Keyboard Driver strips off bit 7 of the response code, shifts the result 1 bit to the right, removing bit 0, and adds $40 to the result. For example, a key transition response code of $33 from the optional keypad is returned as $59 by the Keyboard Driver software, and $2B is returned as $55.

Chapter 8 **Apple Desktop Bus**

The Apple Desktop Bus (ADB) is a serial bus used for input devices such as keyboards, mouse devices, and graphics tablets. The ADB is Apple's standard interface for input devices; it is used on the Apple IIGS as well as the following Macintosh models:

- Macintosh SE
- Macintosh SE/30
- Macintosh Portable
- Macintosh II
- Macintosh IIx
- Macintosh IIcx
- Macintosh IIci
- Macintosh IIfx

In addition to the ADB interface, this chapter describes the Apple Standard Mouse, the Macintosh Portable trackball, the Apple Standard Keyboard, and the Apple Extended Keyboard. This chapter also describes the protocols and signals used on the ADB for communications between the computer and ADB devices, and the internal registers used by ADB devices.

△ **Important**   Apple Computer, Inc. owns patents on the Apple Desktop Bus (ADB). If you wish to make a device that works with the Apple Desktop Bus software, you must obtain a license and Device Handler ID from Apple Computer, Inc. Write to this address:

Apple Software Licensing
Apple Computer, Inc.
20525 Mariani Avenue, Mail Stop 28-B
Cupertino, California 95014 △

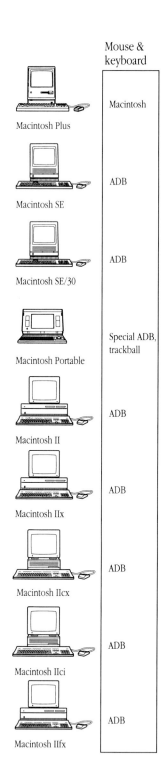

Mouse &
keyboard

Macintosh Plus — Macintosh

Macintosh SE — ADB

Macintosh SE/30 — ADB

Macintosh Portable — Special ADB,
trackball

Macintosh II — ADB

Macintosh IIx — ADB

Macintosh IIcx — ADB

Macintosh IIci — ADB

Macintosh IIfx — ADB

Overview

The Apple Desktop Bus is a single-master, multislave serial bus used to communicate with up to 16 low-speed input devices such as keyboards, mouse devices, and graphics tablets.

On all Macintosh models except the Macintosh Portable and the Macintosh IIfx, the Apple Desktop Bus hardware consists of the following components:

- ADB transceiver IC, a 4-bit microcontroller that drives the bus and reads the status of the ADB devices

- VIA IC that provides the interface between the ADB transceiver IC and the computer's CPU (an MC68000, MC68020, or MC68030, depending on the model)

- two ADB 4-pin connectors, hooked up in parallel; the ADB connectors are located on the rear panel of the computer and are used for attaching ADB input devices

In the Macintosh Portable, the Power Manager IC serves as the ADB transceiver. ADB devices on the Macintosh Portable must have low power consumption.

In the Macintosh IIfx, the functions of the ADB transceiver are incorporated into an Apple custom IC, the IOP. The IOP works with another custom IC, the OSS, and supports the ADB connectors in the same way that the ADB transceiver does on other members of the Macintosh II family. For information about the IOP, please refer to the section "IOPs in the Macintosh IIfx Computer" in Chapter 3.

The ADB hardware provided by peripheral devices on the ADB network consists of the following components:

- ADB transceiver IC in each ADB peripheral device

- four-conductor shielded cable used to connect the ADB device to the ADB

△ **Important**   Although the ADB transceiver is capable of addressing up to 16 different peripheral devices, daisy-chaining more than 3 devices is not recommended because of connector resistance and signal degradation. △

The ADB transceiver IC in the computer converts the computer's TTL signals to the variable-pulse-width open-collector signal used on the bus. When the bus is idle, the transceiver performs automatic polling of the ADB device that last sent data.

The computer transfers data to and from the ADB transceiver IC by using the Shift register in the VIA to send and receive the TTL signals. The Shift register contains the 8 data bits that have been shifted in from the ADB transceiver, or the 8 bits that are to be shifted out. In addition to the ADB data line, there are several control lines between the VIA and the ADB transceiver. These control lines are used to time and sequence transactions between the VIA and the ADB transceiver.

◆ *Note:* On Macintosh models that have two VIA ICs, VIA1 is the interface to the ADB.

When the computer is started up or reset, each ADB peripheral device defaults to an ADB device address from $00 through $0F. Certain default addresses are used by specific device types; for example, relative-position devices (such as a mouse device) always have a default ADB address of $03. In the case of two or more devices with the same default address, the Start Manager assigns a new (unique) address to one device at a time until all conflicts are eliminated.

▲ **Warning**   Do not unplug and reattach an ADB device while the computer is running—if you do, the device reverts to its default address while the computer continues trying to reach it at the address assigned at startup time. ▲

Each ADB device has a default identification code known as a *Device Handler ID,* stored in an internal register. The ADB Manager keeps track of the Device Handler ID and the default address of each device on the bus, and calls the appropriate device driver when that device has data to send to the computer.

An ADB device cannot initiate a data transaction. Instead, each device asserts a Service Request signal when it has data to send to the computer. The ADB Manager then attempts to read each device on the bus until one responds by sending data. When a device responds, the ADB Manager passes control to the appropriate device driver, which communicates with the device through the VIA and the ADB transceiver.

The ADB communication protocol and the functions of an ADB device's internal registers are described in detail in the sections "ADB Communications" and "ADB Peripheral Devices," later in this chapter. For more information on the VIA, see Chapter 4.

ADB interface

The ADB connector pinouts are shown in Figure 8-1. The ADB connector signal
assignments are listed in Table 8-1. The electrical characteristics of the ADB data line and
of ADB devices are listed in Table 8-2.

■ **Figure 8-1** Pinout of the ADB connector

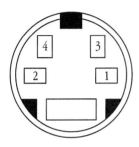

■ **Table 8-1** Signal assignments for the ADB connector

Pin Number	Signal name	Signal description
1	ADB	Bidirectional data bus used for input and output. It is an open-collector signal pulled up to +5 V through a 470 Ω resistor on the computer's main logic board.
2	POWER.ON	On the Macintosh II family, a key on the ADB keyboard momentarily grounds this pin to pin 4 to switch on the power supply. On other models, this pin is not connected.
3	+5V	+5 volts
4	GND	Ground

■ **Table 8-2** Electrical characteristics of the ADB transceiver

Parameter	Minimum	Maximum
Low input signal voltage	−0.2 V	0.8 V
High input signal voltage	2.4V	5.0V
Low output signal voltage	—	0.45 V (at 12 mA)
High output signal voltage	2.4 V	—
Device output current when off	—	−20 μA (at 0.4 V)
Device input capacitance	—	150 pF

ADB interface circuits

The ADB interface is functionally the same on all Macintosh models except the
Macintosh Plus and earlier models, which don't use it, and the Macintosh Portable, which
has its own unique ADB implementation. For a description of the ADB interface on the
Macintosh Portable, see the sections "Macintosh Portable Power Manager IC As ADB
Controller" and "Macintosh Portable Keyboard Processor," later in this chapter.

Figure 8-2 shows a circuit diagram for the ADB interface on the Macintosh models that do
not have the keyboard power-on feature (Macintosh SE and Macintosh SE/30 computers).
Figure 8-3 shows a circuit diagram for the ADB interface on the Macintosh II, Macintosh IIx,
Macintosh IIcx, and Macintosh IIci computers, which do have the keyboard power-on
feature. Figure 8-4 shows a circuit diagram for the ADB interface on the Macintosh IIfx
computer, which also has the keyboard power-on feature. Figure 8-6 shows a circuit diagram
for the ADB interface on the Macintosh Portable computer. Because the Macintosh
Portable is always on, it doesn't have the keyboard power-on feature.

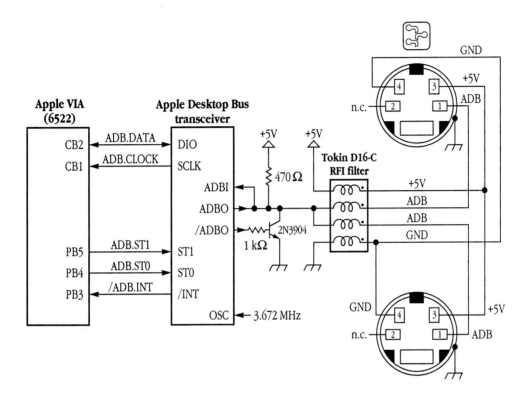

■ **Figure 8-2** Circuit diagram for the ADB interface on Macintosh SE and Macintosh SE/30 computers

■ **Figure 8-3** Circuit diagram for the ADB interface on Macintosh II, Macintosh IIx, Macintosh IIcx, and Macintosh IIci computers

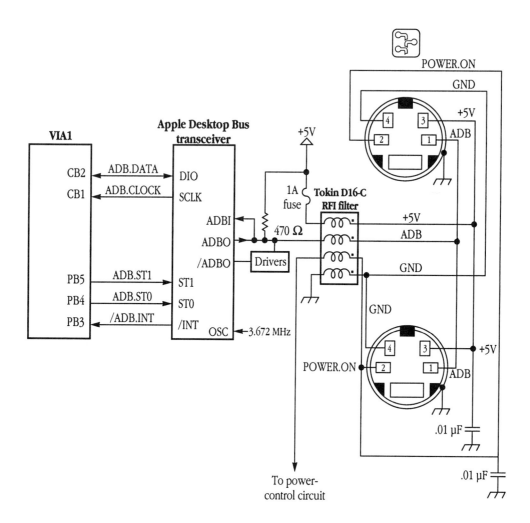

■ **Figure 8-4** Circuit diagram for the ADB interface on the Macintosh IIfx computer

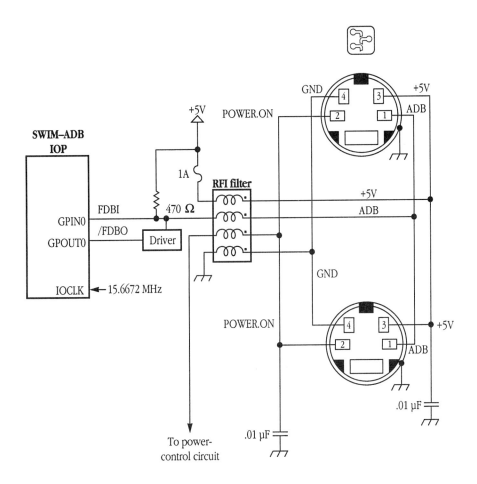

△ **Important**   ADB devices may use the +5 volts supplied by the bus, but all the ADB
devices combined must not draw more than a total of 500 mA. △

Cables should be no longer than 5 meters, and cable capacitance should not exceed 100
picofarads per meter. Although the ADB is capable of addressing up to 16 different
peripheral devices, daisy-chaining more than 3 devices on one ADB port is not
recommended because of connector resistance and signal degradation.

ADB interface circuits on the Macintosh Portable

In a departure from the usual Macintosh implementation, the ADB transceiver function on the Macintosh Portable is performed by the Power Manager IC and the keyswitch encoding is done by a separate keyboard processor IC. Both the Power Manager IC and the keyboard processor are located on the main logic board.

⚠ **Developer tip** The ADB device protocol and the device control commands are the same on all ADB-equipped Macintosh computers. However, different models may use different hardware to implement the ADB, as in the case of the Macintosh Portable. To ensure compatibility with all Macintosh computers, it is important that you use the routines and tools provided at the system level for controlling the ADB, as discussed in *Inside Macintosh.* ⚠

Macintosh Portable Power Manager IC as ADB controller

The Power Manager IC performs the functions that are performed by the ADB buffer, transceiver, and driver hardware in other members of the Macintosh family. The Power Manager IC transmits the ADB data through the VIA to the MC68HC000 CPU.

As in other Macintosh computers, the Macintosh Portable operating system implements a keyboard mapping resource to map key codes to Apple-extended ASCII codes (Return = $0D = 0000 1101 binary). Changes to this resource allow localization using various character sets. Refer to Chapter 3 in *Technical Introduction to the Macintosh Family* for a software-oriented discussion of the mapping operation.

Macintosh Portable keyboard processor

The keyboard processor is a Mitsubishi M50740 single-chip microcomputer. The M50740 is an 8-bit microcomputer in a 50-pin quad flat package (QFP). Its distinguishing features are

- 3072 bytes of ROM
- 96 bytes of RAM
- 15 mW power dissipation
- 8-bit timer
- 32 programmable I/O ports

The functions of the keyboard processor in the Macintosh Portable are the same as those performed by the microprocessors found inside other Apple keyboards. In the Macintosh Portable, however, the keyboard processor physically resides on the main logic board instead of on the circuit board in the keyboard.

The switches in the keyboard are wired in a two-dimensional array called a *keyswitch matrix*. The keyboard processor scans the matrix in the keyboard and numeric keypad to sense switch transitions as keys are pressed and released. The keyboard processor communicates with the CPU through the ADB, sending an 8-bit binary code characterizing the key transition. (For example, the Return key has the 8-bit transition code $24.)

Macintosh Portable keyboard and trackball connectors

The Macintosh Portable has two connectors in the keyboard area on the front part of the case. The connectors are positioned to permit the installation of the trackball on either side of the keyboard. Figure 8-5 shows the pinout of the 34-pin connectors used for the keyboard and trackball. Table 8-3 shows the signal assignments on those connectors.

■ **Figure 8-5** Pinout of the keyboard and trackball connectors on the Macintosh Portable computer

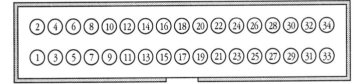

■ **Table 8-3**   Signal assignments for the keyboard and trackball connectors on the
Macintosh Portable computer

Pin number	Signal name	Signal description
1	GND3	Chassis ground
2	X0	Switch matrix line X0
3	X1	Switch matrix line X1
4	X2	Switch matrix line X2
5	X3	Switch matrix line X3
6	X4	Switch matrix line X4
7	X5	Switch matrix line X5
8	X6	Switch matrix line X6
9	X7	Switch matrix line X7
10	X8	Switch matrix line X8
11	X9	Switch matrix line X9
12	X10	Switch matrix line X10
13	Y0	Switch matrix line Y0
14	Y1	Switch matrix line Y1
15	Y2	Switch matrix line Y2
16	Y3	Switch matrix line Y3
17	Y4	Switch matrix line Y4
18	Y5	Switch matrix line Y5
19	Y6	Switch matrix line Y6
20	Y7	Switch matrix line Y7
21	CAPS.LOCK	Caps Lock key switch
22	SHIFT	Shift key switch
23	CONTROL	Control key switch
24	OPTION	Option key switch
25	COMMAND	Command key switch
26	GND1	Key-switch ground
27	GND2	ADB signal ground
28	(spare)	
29	ADB.DATA	Bi-directional serial data
30	BUTTON	Button switch (on trackball)
31	n. c.*	Not connected
32	n. c.*	Not connected
33	(spare)	
34	GND3	Chassis ground

*To identify ISO (European) keyboards, pins 31 and 32 are connected to each other on those keyboards.

Figure 8-6 shows the ADB interface through the Power Manager IC. The figure also shows how the keyboard processor reads the switch matrix and sends signals to the ADB interface.

■ **Figure 8-6** Circuit diagram of the ADB interface on the
Macintosh Portable computer

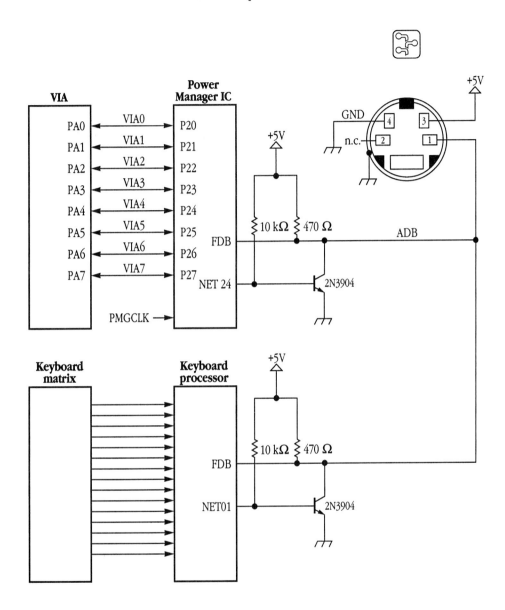

ADB keyboards and mouse

There are two ADB keyboard options available from Apple Computer, Inc.: the Apple Standard Keyboard and the Apple Extended Keyboard. Apple also provides an Apple Standard Mouse device with each ADB-equipped Macintosh computer. The mouse and keyboards communicate with the main logic board by way of the ADB interface.

⚠ **Developer tip** Your applications should read all keyboard and mouse data by using the Event Manager and Window Manager so that your program will be compatible with earlier Macintosh computers, which do not use the ADB, and with the Macintosh Portable, which uses different ADB hardware. The Event Manager and the Window Manager are described in *Inside Macintosh*. ⚠

Apple Standard Mouse

The Apple Standard Mouse is used by all Apple computers that have the Apple Desktop Bus except the Macintosh Portable, which uses a low-power model of the Apple mouse and also has a low-power trackball (see the section "Macintosh Portable Low-Power Trackball," later in this chapter).

A microprocessor in the Apple Standard Mouse provides position and status information to the computer. The mouse mechanism reports relative X (left and right) and Y (up and down) motion and indicates when the mouse button is pressed. This microprocessor also functions as an ADB transceiver chip, which communicates with the ADB transceiver chip in the computer. The computer's ADB transceiver chip receives the mouse information and sends it to the VIA. Routines in the ROM convert this information into the corresponding motion of the pointer on the screen.

The mouse operates by sending square-wave signals to the mouse microprocessor as the mouse moves. A rubber-coated steel ball in the mouse turns as the mouse is moved and contacts two capstans, each connected to a slotted wheel called an *interrupter wheel*. Motion in the mouse's X-axis direction rotates one of the wheels and motion in the Y-axis direction rotates the other wheel.

Beams of light are alternately transmitted and blocked by the slots in the interrupter wheel, and photo detectors pass the resulting square-wave signal to the mouse microprocessor. The microprocessor interprets these signals to determine the distance travelled in the X and Y directions and passes the information to the Mouse Driver software by way of the ADB transceiver and the VIA.

The mouse mechanism uses a scheme known as *quadrature* to determine the direction the mouse is moving along each axis. Two beams of infrared light shine through the slots in the interrupter wheel and strike one of two light detectors. The detectors are offset just enough so that, as the wheel turns, they produce two square-wave signals that are 90° out of phase. These signals are called the *interrupt signal* and the *quadrature signal.* The quadrature signal precedes the interrupt signal by 90° when the wheel turns one way, and trails it when the wheel turns the other way.

◆ *Note:* The mouse used in the Macintosh Plus and earlier Macintosh computers sends the square-wave signals generated by the interrupter wheels directly to the computer, where they are interpreted by the Mouse Driver software. The Macintosh Plus mouse is described in Chapter 7, "Macintosh Plus Mouse and Keyboard."

Figure 8-7 shows the Apple Standard Mouse mechanism. The square-wave signals in this figure are those generated when the mouse is moved downward.

The mouse motion information is stored in register 0 in the ADB transceiver IC in the mouse. (The registers in peripheral devices are described in the section "ADB Device Registers," later in this chapter.) The contents of ADB register 0 in the Apple Standard Mouse are shown in Table 8-4.

■ **Table 8-4**   ADB transceiver register 0 in the Apple Standard Mouse

Bit	Meaning
15	Button status; 0 = down
14–8	Y move counts*
7	Not used (always 1)
6–0	X move counts†

*Two's-complement form. Negative = up, positive = down.
†Two's-complement form. Negative = left, positive = right.

■ **Figure 8-7** Mechanism of the Apple Standard Mouse

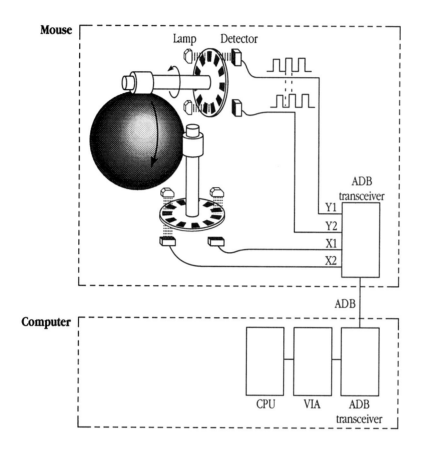

◆ *Note:* For a Device Handler ID of $0001, the mouse accumulates 100±10 counts on each axis for each inch of travel in that axis. For a Device Handler ID of $0002, the mouse accumulates 200±10 counts on each axis for each inch of travel in that axis. On startup or reset, the mouse has a Device Handler ID of $0001.

⚠ **Developer tip** The transfer of mouse data is handled automatically by the ADB Manager and the Mouse Driver. To ensure compatibility with all Macintosh computers, your software should always use Event Manager and Window Manager calls to determine mouse motion and the state of the mouse button. ⚠

The ADB transceiver in the mouse transmits the data to the ADB transceiver in the computer, which transmits it to the Shift register in the VIA. The Mouse Driver reads the information in the VIA's Shift register, interprets the data, and translates it into cursor motion on the screen as appropriate. Using the mouse-tracking option on the Control Panel desk accessory, the user can change the amount of screen-pointer motion that corresponds to a given mouse motion. For more information about the rate of mouse motion, see the discussion of parameter RAM in the chapter on Operating System Utilities in *Inside Macintosh*.

Macintosh Portable low-power trackball

Instead of a mouse, the Macintosh Portable uses a low-power trackball that works something like an upside-down mouse. The trackball is electrically compatible with the ADB, although it uses a few pins in a large shared connector instead of the dedicated mini-circular type.

The connector on the trackball is mechanically the same as the one on the keyboard, shown in Figure 8-5. The connectors are the same so that the trackball can be installed on either side of the Macintosh Portable computer. Table 8-5 shows the signal assignments for the trackball connector.

■ **Table 8-5**   Signal assignments for the connector on the trackball

Pin number	Signal name	Signal function
1	GND3	Chassis ground
2–26	n.c.	Not connected
27	GND2	ADB signal ground
28	+5V	5-volt power supply
29	ADB.DATA	Bi-directional serial data
30–33	n.c.	Not connected
34	GND	Ground

Note: All pins except 1, 27, 28, 29, and 34 are not connected.

▲ **Warning**   Any input devices connected to the Macintosh Portable ADB must be low-power versions. That means keyboards and mouse devices from other models in the Macintosh family are not usable with the Macintosh Portable. Connecting such input devices to the Macintosh Portable ADB could cause an unacceptable decrease in the +5 volt supply voltage and result in improper operation. ▲

The Power Manager IC in the Macintosh Portable controls the power to the trackball, removing the power when it puts the computer into the sleep state and restoring it when the computer resumes normal operation. The trackball is designed to be operational within 80 ms of the application of power. See the section "Sleep State in the Macintosh Portable Computer" in Chapter 6.

The trackball's default handler ID is $0001 and its address is $0011, the same as a mouse.

Movement of the top of the ball's surface to the right is in the positive X direction, and movement downwards is in the positive Y direction, as shown in Figure 8-8. Movement of the top surface of the ball to the right causes the display cursor to move to the right, and movement downward causes the cursor to move down on the display.

The trackball has one button, which is functionally equivalent to the mouse button.

■ **Figure 8-8** Trackball direction conventions

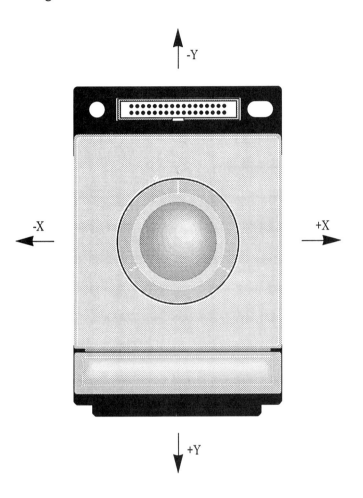

Apple Standard Keyboard

The switches in the keyboard are wired in a two-dimensional array called a *keyswitch matrix.* Like the keyboard on the Macintosh Plus, the Apple Standard Keyboard contains a microprocessor that scans the matrix to detect switch transitions as keys are pressed and released. The keyboard's microprocessor transmits the corresponding key-down and key-up events to the CPU by way of the Apple Desktop Bus (ADB), using the bus protocols described later in this chapter.

In addition to all the keys found on the Macintosh Plus keyboard (or their functional equivalents), the Apple Standard Keyboard has two additional keys: the Escape (Esc) key and the Control key.

The keyboard layout and the key-down transition codes are shown in Figure 8-9. The key-up transition codes are the same as the key-down transition codes, except that bit 7 is set to 1.

■ **Figure 8-9** Key-down transition codes generated by the Apple Standard Keyboard

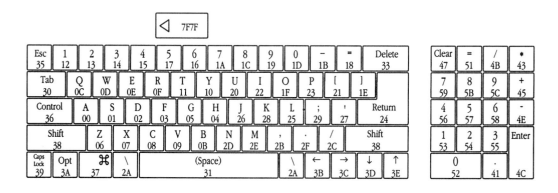

Notice that these response codes are not all the same as the key codes returned by the Keyboard Driver software. The standard 'KMAP' resource supplied in the System Folder reassigns several key codes, as shown in Table 8-6.

■ **Table 8-6** Key code reassignments for the Apple Standard Keyboard

Key	Transition code	Keyboard Driver code
Control	$36	$3B
Left Arrow	$3B	$7B
Right Arrow	$3C	$7C
Down Arrow	$3D	$7D
Up Arrow	$3E	$7E

The keyboard information is stored in register 0 in the ADB transceiver in the Apple Standard Keyboard. The statuses of two keys can be stored at the same time in keyboard register 0. In addition, the statuses of the modifier keys are stored in register 2 in the keyboard. The registers in peripheral devices are described in the section "ADB Device Registers," later in this chapter. The contents of Keyboard register 0 are shown in Table 8-7 and the contents of Keyboard register 2 are shown in Table 8-8.

■ **Table 8-7**   Register 0 in the Apple Standard Keyboard

Bit	Meaning
15	Key status for first key; 0 = down
14–8	Key code for first key; a 7-bit ASCII value
7	Key status for second key; 0 = down
6–0	Key code for second key; a 7-bit ASCII value

■ **Table 8-8**   Register 2 in the Apple Standard Keyboard

Bit	Key
15	None (reserved)
14	Delete
13	Caps Lock
12	Reset
11	Control
10	Shift
9	Option
8	Command
7–0	None (reserved)

Note: A 0 indicates that a key is down.

Upon a command from the ADB Manager, the ADB transceiver in the Apple Standard Keyboard transmits the data in register 0 to the ADB transceiver in the computer, which transmits it to the VIA's Shift register. The ADB Manager then passes control to the Keyboard Driver, which reads all the keyboard information, interprets it, and makes it available to applications.

Apple Extended Keyboard

The Apple Extended Keyboard is designed primarily for users who wish to run operating systems other than the Macintosh system. This keyboard is also useful with applications programs and data communications packages ported from other computers that use function keys.

The switches in the keyboard are wired in a two-dimensional array called a *keyswitch matrix*. Like the Apple Standard Keyboard, the Apple Extended Keyboard contains a microprocessor that scans the matrix to detect switch transitions as keys are pressed and released and transmits the corresponding key-down and key-up events to the CPU by way of the Apple Desktop Bus (ADB), using the bus protocols described later in this chapter.

Like the Apple Standard Keyboard, the Apple Extended Keyboard has all the keys (or their functional equivalents) found on earlier Macintosh keyboards, plus the modifier keys Escape (Esc) and Control. In addition, the Apple Extended Keyboard has function keys: twelve of the function keys (F1–F12) have no default definition; nine other function keys do have default definitions.

The Apple Extended Keyboard layout and key-down transition codes are shown in Figure 8-10. The key-up transition codes are the same as the key-down transition codes except that bit 7 is set to 1.

■ **Figure 8-10** Key-down transition codes generated by the Apple Extended Keyboard

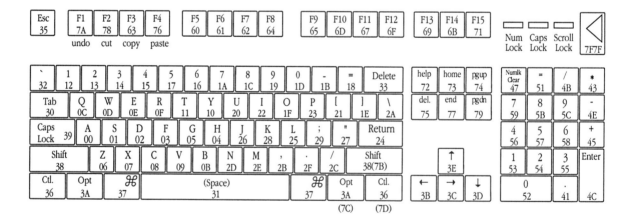

If your application needs to be able to distinguish the right-hand Option and Control keys from the corresponding keys on the left side of the keyboard, you can cause the keyboard to generate different transition codes for those keys (shown in parentheses in Figure 8-10) by changing the value of the Device Handler ID in Keyboard register 3 from $0002 to $0003. You can change this ID by sending a Listen Register 3 command to the keyboard. For more information, see the section "ADB Device Handler ID," later in this chapter, and the description of the Device Handler ID command in the chapter on the Apple Desktop Bus in *Inside Macintosh*.

Note that the transition codes shown in Figure 8-10 are not all the same as the key codes returned by the Keyboard Driver software. The standard 'KMAP' resource supplied in the System Folder reassigns several key codes, as shown in Table 8-9.

■ **Table 8-9**   Key code reassignments in the Apple Extended Keyboard

Key	Transition code	Keyboard Driver code
Control	$36	$3B
Left Arrow	$3B	$7B
Right Arrow	$3C	$7C
Down Arrow	$3D	$7D
Up Arrow	$3E	$7E
Right Shift	$7B*	$3C*
Right Option	$7C*	$3D*
Right Control	$7D*	$3E*

*These key codes are in effect only when the Device Handler ID in register 3 is set to $0003.

The keyboard information is stored in register 0 in the ADB transceiver in the Apple Extended Keyboard. The statuses of two keys can be stored at one time in keyboard register 0. In addition, the statuses of the modifier keys and LEDs are stored in register 2 in the keyboard. The registers in peripheral devices are described in the section "ADB Device Registers," later in this chapter. The contents of Keyboard register 0 are shown in Table 8-10 and the contents of Keyboard register 2 are shown in Table 8-11.

■ **Table 8-10**   Register 0 in the Apple Extended Keyboard

Bit	Meaning
15	Key status for first key; 0 = down
14–8	Key code for first key; a 7-bit ASCII value
7	Key status for second key; 0 = down
6–0	Key code for second key; a 7-bit ASCII value

■ **Table 8-11** Register 2 in the Apple Extended Keyboard

Bit	Meaning
15	None (reserved)
14	Delete
13	Caps Lock
12	Reset
11	Control
10	Shift
9	Option
8	Command
7	Num Lock/Clear
6	Scroll Lock
5–3	None (reserved)
2	LED 3 (Scroll Lock)*
1	LED 2 (Caps Lock)*
0	LED 1 (Num Lock)*

Note: A zero indicates that a key is down or that an LED is on.
*You can change the value of this bit with a Listen Register 2 command.

Upon a command from the ADB Manager, the ADB transceiver in the Apple Extended Keyboard transmits the data in register 0 to the ADB transceiver in the computer, which transmits it to the VIA's Shift register. The ADB Manager then passes control to the Keyboard Driver, which reads all the keyboard information, interprets it, and makes it available to applications.

Macintosh Portable low-power keyboard

The Macintosh Portable computer has a special low-power keyboard consisting of a keyswitch matrix only, with no active electronics. The keyswitches are supported by a steel plate and electrically connected to the keyboard connector by a PC board. The keyboard processor in the Macintosh Portable computer takes care of scanning the keyswitch matrix and sending the switch codes to the CPU by way of the ADB. See the earlier section "Macintosh Portable Keyboard Processor."

The Macintosh Portable keyboard has 63 keyswitches. The keyswitches are full-travel, low-profile type; the keytops are tapered style and platinum color. Figure 8-11 shows the layout of the keyboard; Figure 8-12 shows the layout of the optional keypad. The user can install the keypad in place of the trackball and use a low-power mouse.

The Macintosh Portable keyboard can be installed without opening the case. The user can perform the installation, placing the keyboard either to the left or right side of the case.

■ **Figure 8-11** Keyboard layout on the Macintosh Portable computer

U.S. keyboard

International keyboard (German key caps shown)

■ **Figure 8-12** Keypad layout on the Macintosh Portable computer

clear	=	/	*
7	8	9	-
4	5	6	+
1	2	3	
0		.	enter

U.S. key caps

⊠	=	/	*
7	8	9	-
4	5	6	+
1	2	3	
0		,	⊼

German key caps

ADB communications

Each ADB input device on the network may have up to four internal registers, which are referred to as *ADB device registers*. ADB devices are accessed over the network by reading from or writing to the appropriate ADB device register in that device. The registers of an ADB device may range in size from 2 bytes to 8 bytes.

Although each ADB device contains a microprocessor and can generate device identification and status information, an ADB device cannot initiate a command, nor can it interrupt the processor directly. The ADB transceiver in the computer automatically polls the last device to have sent data (known as the *active device*) for new data. If the active device has data to send, it shifts it out to the ADB transceiver in the computer, which sends it to the VIA. When the VIA receives ADB data, a bit in the VIA's Interrupt register is set. The ADB Manager can thus determine that the active device has sent data. The ADB Manager then passes control to the device driver for the active device, which communicates with the device through the VIA and the ADB transceiver.

◆ *Note:* On Macintosh models that have two VIA ICs, VIA1 is the interface to the ADB.

If an ADB device that is not the active device has data to send, the device asserts a Service Request signal to the computer. The ADB transceiver in the computer asserts its interrupt request signal to the VIA, which sets bit 3 in Data register B to 0. The operating system polls the VIA regularly; when it finds a 0 for this bit, the operating system passes control to the ADB Manager, which polls each device until it finds the one requesting service. The ADB Manager then passes control to the appropriate device driver, which communicates with the device through the VIA and the ADB transceiver.

Communications on the ADB are of two types: transactions and signals. Transactions consist of a command from the computer to the ADB device, followed by data sent by either the computer or the device. Each command is addressed to a specific device. Signals indicate the status of a device or cause all devices to perform a certain function. Signals are general; they are not addressed to a specific device.

The next sections define ADB transactions, describe each of the commands and signals, and list the timing specifications for ADB commands and signals.

ADB transactions

An ADB transaction is a bus communication between the computer and a device. A transaction consists of a command sent by the computer, followed by a data packet of several bytes sent by either the computer or a device. An ADB command consists of

■ an Attention signal

■ a Sync signal

■ one command byte

■ one stop bit

A data packet consists of

■ a start bit

■ two to eight (8-bit) data bytes

■ one stop bit

Figure 8-13 shows a typical transaction on the Apple Desktop Bus, consisting of a command followed by a data packet.

■ **Figure 8-13** A typical ADB transaction

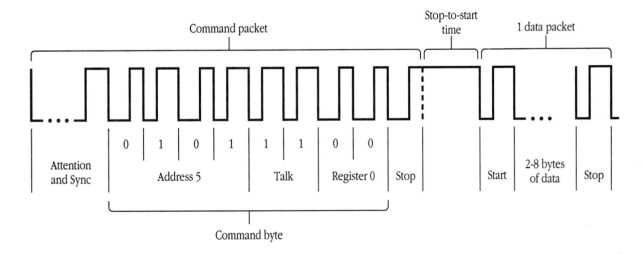

Two signal lines from the VIA to the transceiver—ST0 and ST1—define the ADB transaction state, which controls the sequence of operations performed by the ADB transceiver chip. After each part of an ADB command transaction is complete, the computer uses lines ST0 and ST1 to advance the ADB transceiver to the next transaction state, ready for the next part of the communication. There are four possible ADB transaction states, as shown in Table 8-12.

■ **Table 8-12** ADB transaction states

Signal ST1	Signal ST0	Transaction state
0	0	0: Start a new command
0	1	1: Transfer data byte (even)
1	0	2: Transfer data byte (odd)
1	1	3: Idle

To execute an ADB command, the ADB Manager sends the command byte to the VIA's Shift register, then sets the ADB transceiver to state 0. The transceiver shifts the command in from the VIA, converts it to ADB protocol, and puts it on the ADB. The VIA generates an interrupt when the entire byte has been transferred. When the processor receives the interrupt, the ADB Manager alternates the transaction state between 1 and 2 to transfer the data bytes from the VIA to the ADB transceiver and then over the ADB (for a Listen command), or from the device to the transceiver and then into the VIA (for a Talk command). (The Talk and Listen commands are described in the next section, "ADB Commands.") The VIA generates an interrupt after each byte is transferred.

After the last byte of data has been transferred, the ADB Manager sets the transaction state to 0 if the ADB Manager wants to send another command, or to 3, in which state the ADB transceiver automatically repeats the last Talk command every 11 ms. To abort a partially executed command, the ADB Manager sets the ADB transaction state to 0.

The default transaction state on startup or reset is 3.

ADB commands

An ADB command is sent by the computer to one specific device address. There are four commands:

- Talk
- Listen
- SendReset
- Flush

A command is an 8-bit word that has a specific syntax as shown in Table 8-13. Every command consists of

- a 4-bit field that specifies the address of the desired device
- a 2-bit command code
- a 2-bit register code

◆ *Note:* Although only the computer can initiate a command, the ADB transceiver can reissue a Talk command when the device addressed does not respond and there is no service request pending from another device. Therefore, the ADB Manager does not have to use processor time to monitor the bus continually.

■ **Table 8-13** Command byte syntax

Bit	Device address bits				Command code bits		Register code bits		Command
	7	6	5	4	3	2	1	0	
	X	X	X	X	0	0	0	0	SendReset
	A3	A2	A1	A0	0	0	0	1	Flush
	X	X	X	X	0	0	1	0	Reserved
	X	X	X	X	0	0	1	1	Reserved
	X	X	X	X	0	1	X	X	Reserved
	A3	A2	A1	A0	1	0	r1	r0	Listen
	A3	A2	A1	A0	1	1	r1	r0	Talk

Note: x = ignored; r = register number; A3 through A0 = bits 11 through 8 of register 3.

△ **Developer tip** To allow for future expansion of the command structure, Apple has reserved several commands. Applications that use commands listed as reserved in Table 8-13 may have compatibility problems on future Apple products. △

Talk command

The Talk command initiates a data transfer to the computer from a specific register (0 through 3) of an ADB input device. When the computer sends a Talk command to a device, the device must respond with data within 260 µs. The selected device performs its data transaction and releases the bus, leaving it high. If the device does not respond in time (the device times out), the computer takes control of the bus again to issue its next command. A device times out if it has no data to send; however, a device must respond to a Talk Register 3 command.

Listen command

The Listen command is a request for the device to receive data transmitted from the computer and store it in a specific internal register (0 through 3). When the computer sends a Listen command to a device, the device receives the next data packet from the computer and places it in the appropriate register. After the stop bit following the data is received, the transaction is complete and the computer releases the bus. If the addressed device detects another command on the bus (that is, receives an Attention signal and a Sync signal) before it receives any data, the original transaction is immediately considered complete.

SendReset command

The SendReset command causes all devices on the network to reset to their power-on states. Each device clears all pending service requests and returns to a state in which it can accept commands and assert Service Request signals.

Flush command

The action of the Flush command is defined for each device. Normally, it is used to clear any internal registers in the device. Any user input data being stored by the device—such as characters in a keyboard type-ahead buffer—are lost.

ADB signals

There are four global signals used in ADB communications:

■ Attention

■ Sync

■ Global Reset

■ Service Request

Signals are transmitted on the bus but do not address any specific device. The first three of these signals are always generated by the computer. The Service Request signal is always generated by a device.

Attention and Sync signals

The start of every command is indicated by a long low Attention signal that the computer sends on the bus. This is followed by a short high Sync pulse that establishes the timing of the data bits that follow. The first command bit follows immediately after the falling edge of the Sync signal. Figure 8-14 shows the format of the Attention and Sync signals.

■ **Figure 8-14**   Attention and Sync signals

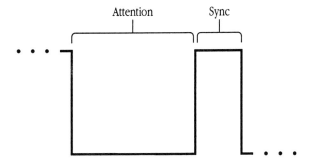

Global Reset signal

The computer initiates a reset of all devices on the ADB bus by holding the bus low for a minimum of 3.0 ms. Each device clears all pending service requests and returns to a state in which it can accept commands and assert Service Request signals.

Service Request signal

A Service Request signal is used by a device to inform the computer that the device has data to send. A device sends a Service Request signal by holding the bus low during the low portion of the stop bit of any command or data transaction. The device must lengthen the stop by a minimum of 140 μs beyond its normal duration, as shown in Figure 8-15.

■ **Figure 8-15**   ADB Service Request signal

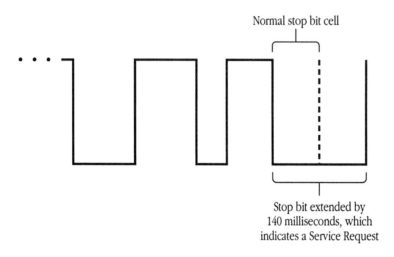

Normal stop bit cell

Stop bit extended by
140 milliseconds, which
indicates a Service Request

A device sends a Service Request signal repeatedly until it receives a command from the computer. When a device requests service, the computer does not know which device sent the request. Therefore, the computer polls each of the devices by sending a Talk Register 0 command, beginning with the last active device. Only a device that has data to send responds to the Talk command.

When the computer sends a Talk command to the requesting device, the device is considered served and does not send a Service Request signal again until it needs to be served again. The computer can set a bit in register 3 to enable or disable the ability of a device to send a Service Request signal. (See the section "Register 3," later in this chapter.)

ADB timing

Each command or data bit is encoded on the ADB as a short pulse known as a *bit cell*. Each bit cell consists of a low voltage on the ADB, a rising edge, a high voltage on the ADB, and a final falling edge. A 0 is distinguished from a 1 by the relative length of the low time in the bit cell, as illustrated in Figure 8-13.

Every command and data packet ends with a stop bit. A stop bit is a 0 bit that has a low time as long as any other 0 bit but that does not necessarily have a second falling edge to define the end of the bit cell. Note that the time from the stop bit to the next start bit is critical; the computer requires this minimum turnaround delay to allow for internal overhead.

ADB signals are distinguished from command and data bits by having low and high times different from those used for bit cells. Table 8-14 lists the timing parameters for ADB bit cells and signals.

■ **Table 8-14** ADB timing specifications

Parameter	Nominal	Host	Device
Bit-cell time	100 μs	±3%	±30%
"0" low time	65 μs	65% of bit-cell time ±5%	65% of bit-cell time ±5%
"1" low time	35 μs	35% of bit-cell time ±5%	35% of bit-cell time ±5%
Attention low time	800 μs	±3%	—
Sync high time	65 μs	±3%	—
Stop bit low time	70 μs	±3%	±30%
Global Reset low time	3 ms	3 ms minimum	3 ms minimum
Service Request low time	300 μs	—	±30%
Stop-bit-to-start-bit time	200 μs	140 μs minimum	140 μs minimum
		260 μs maximum	260 μs maximum

ADB error conditions

Two error conditions are defined for the ADB: when the bus remains low for an excessive amount of time, and when the bus is held high during a transaction.

If the bus level remains low for at least 3.0 ms, all devices interpret the low bus level as a Global Reset signal, release control of the bus, and reset themselves.

If a command or data transaction is incomplete, the ADB bus stays high beyond the maximum bit-cell time. In this case, all devices ignore the command and wait for an Attention signal.

ADB peripheral devices

All peripheral devices on the ADB are slaves; only the computer can send commands. ADB devices transmit data on the bus only after receiving a Talk command from the computer.

Each ADB device is required to have

- memory in which to store data
- a default ADB address
- a default Device Handler ID
- the ability to detect and respond to bus collisions
- the ability to assert a Service Request signal

In addition, some ADB devices have more than one functional mode; the device driver can select the mode by assigning a new Device Handler ID to the device.

The following sections describe each of these features of an ADB device.

ADB device registers

An ADB device may have up to four locations in which to store data, referred to as registers 0 through 3. Each Talk or Listen command is directed to a specific register. The following paragraphs describe the use of each of these registers.

Register 0

Register 0 is a data register. When the ADB Manager polls devices to determine which one sent a Service Request signal, it does so by sending a Talk Register 0 command to each device in turn. Therefore, it is essential that a device have data in register 0 when it requires service, even if the data of significance to the device handler is in another register.

The computer can send data to a device with a Listen Register 0 command if the device is designed to accept such data.

Table 8-4 shows the bits of register 0 as used in the Apple Standard Mouse. Tables 8-7 and 8-10 show the bits of register 0 as used in the Apple Standard Keyboard and Apple Extended Keyboard.

Register 1

Register 1 is a device-specific data register. This register can be used by the device for any data function.

Register 2

Register 2 is a device-specific data register. This register can be used by the device for any data function. For example, Tables 8-8 and 8-11 show the bits of register 2 as used by the Apple Standard Keyboard and the Apple Extended Keyboard.

Register 3

This register contains status and device identification information. A description of each bit in register 3 is shown in Table 8-15. For some devices, the computer can change the function of the device by addressing this register with a Listen Register 3 command. The functions of the bits in this register are described in more detail in the sections that follow.

■ **Table 8-15**   Bits in device register 3

Bit	Description
15	Reserved; must be 0
14	Exceptional event, device specific; always 1 if not used
13	Service Request enable; 1 = enabled
12	Reserved; must be 0
11–8	Device address
7–0	Device Handler ID

ADB device addresses

Each ADB device has a default 4-bit bus address. Certain device types have specified default addresses, as shown in Table 8-16. For example, all relative-position devices, such as a mouse, power up at address $03. Most devices have movable addresses; that is, the computer can assign a new address to the device. This is necessary because when two devices (such as a mouse device and a relative-position graphics tablet) have the same default address, one must be moved to a new address. Currently, eight addresses are predefined or reserved, leaving eight default addresses available for other types of devices.

■ **Table 8-16** Device addresses

Address	Device type	Example
$00–$01	Reserved	–
$02	Encoded devices	Keyboard
$03	Relative devices	Mouse
$04	Absolute devices	Graphics tablet
$05–$07	Reserved	–
$08–$0F	Any other	–

ADB Device Handler ID

The ADB Manager uses the 8-bit Device Handler ID—together with the default ADB address—to determine which device driver to call for a particular device. An ADB device driver is a system software routine that communicates with a particular ADB device or class of devices; ADB device drivers are located in 'ADBS' resources in the System file. At system startup, the Start Manager searches the System file for 'ADBS' resources, loads them into memory, and executes them. The Start Manager also reads register 3 in each ADB device, and places the device's default address and Device Handler ID into the ADB device table.

Each 'ADBS' resource includes a device type (corresponding to the Device Handler ID) and an ADB address (corresponding to the device's default address). In the case of more than one device on the ADB with the same default address, the Start Manager reassigns devices to new addresses until there are no more conflicts. (See the next section, "ADB Collision Detection.") The ADB device table contains both the original (default) address and the current address for each device. The ADB Manager uses the default ADB address and Device Handler ID to associate each device on the bus with a particular device driver.

Two or more devices can use the same device driver. For example, a relative-position graphics tablet could emulate a mouse, using the same default ADB address and Device Handler ID as used by a mouse, and providing the same information in response to Talk commands. In this case, both the mouse and the graphics tablet could be connected to the bus at the same time, and the ADB Manager would call the Mouse Driver when either device required service.

A device may have more than one functional mode; if it does, the device driver can use a Listen Register 3 command to change the Device Handler ID. If the device recognizes the new Device Handler ID, it changes functional modes accordingly. An example of such a device is a graphics tablet that can operate as either a relative-position device or as an absolute-position device; another example is a keyboard that can generate more than one set of key-down transition codes. For more information, see the description of the Device Handler ID command in the chapter on the Apple Desktop Bus in *Inside Macintosh*.

Certain Device Handler IDs are reserved; each device must respond in a prescribed manner to a Listen Register 3 command specifying these IDs, as shown in Table 8-17. One of these Device Handler IDs ($00) can also be returned by a device to indicate that the device failed a self-test. Other Device Handler IDs may be used for special functions, but any new Device Handler ID must be assigned by Apple Computer, Inc.

■ **Table 8-17**   Device Handler IDs reserved for special functions

ID value	Function definition
$FF	As Listen Register 3 data, initiates a self-test in the device.
$FE	As Listen Register 3 data, instructs the device to change the address field to the new address sent by the computer if no collision has been detected.
$FD	As Listen Register 3 data, instructs the device to change the address field to the new address sent by the computer if the activator is pressed. (The activator is explained in the next section, "ADB Collision Detection.")
$00	As Listen Register 3 data, instructs the device to change the address and enable fields to the new values sent by the computer.
$00	As data sent in response to a Talk Register 3 command, indicates that the device failed a self-test.

Upon receiving a reserved Device Handler ID, the device immediately performs the specified function. The device does not store the reserved Device Handler ID in register 3; only device-defined handler codes are stored. All unrecognized Device Handler IDs are ignored.

ADB collision detection

Each device waits to transmit data until it detects a free bus; that is, until the bus remains high for the stop-bit-to-start-bit time shown in Table 8-14. If a device is attempting to bring the bus high (for example; to complete a bit cell) and another device forces the line low, or if another device starts to send data before the device is able to assert its start bit, then the device is said to have lost a collision. All ADB devices must be able to detect collisions. The losing device immediately stops transmitting and preserves the data that was being sent. A device sets an internal flag if it loses a collision. This flag is cleared the next time the device successfully transmits data without detecting a collision.

◆ *Note:* Because a device could fail to detect a collision with another device that operates on a nearly identical internal clock, each device should attempt to assert its start bit at a random time within the stop-bit-to-start-bit time shown in Table 8-14.

Because all ADB devices are assigned unique addresses during startup, and because a device sends data only in response to a Talk command that is addressed specifically to that device, collisions do not ordinarily occur. When the bus is first started up or reset, however, there might be more than one device on the bus with the same default address.

At startup, the Start Manager sends a Talk Register 3 command to each ADB address. If there is more than one device at an address, each device that loses the collision sets its internal collision flag and disables its movable address function. The Start Manager then sends a Listen Register 3 command to that address with a Device Handler ID of $FE and a new device address. The device that did not detect the collision is moved to the new address. This process is repeated until the response to a Talk Register 3 command at that address is a timeout, that is, until there are no more devices at that address. Then one of the devices is moved back to the default address, and the Start Manager goes on to the next address.

An ADB device may have a key or button—called an *activator*—that can be used by multiuser applications to identify and locate individual devices. The activator might be a special key on a keyboard, for example, or a button on a mouse. An application can display a message requesting a user to press the activator. The device driver can then relocate the device to a new address by issuing a Listen Register 3 command with a Device Handler ID of $FD.

ADB polling protocol

After all address conflicts have been resolved, the Start Manager turns control of the ADB over to the ADB Manager and the ADB transceiver. If there are no service requests pending, the ADB Manager sends a Talk Register 0 command to address $03 (the default active device, usually the mouse) and the ADB transceiver repeats this command every 11 ms.

To send a Service Request signal, a device waits until the end of a command and then holds the bus low for 140 to 260 μs. Because the next command is normally a Talk Register 0 command addressed to the active device, the active device does not have to assert a Service Request signal to send data to the computer.

If another device has data to send, it sends a Service Request signal. When the ADB transceiver receives the Service Request signal, it sends an interrupt request to the VIA, which sets to 0 bit 3 in VIA Data register B. When the operating system finds a 0 in this bit, it passes control to the ADB Manager, which sends a Talk Register 0 command to each device on the bus until it finds the one requiring service. When a device responds to the Talk Register 0 command, the ADB Manager looks in the ADB device table to determine which device driver to call, and then passes control to the appropriate device driver.

The last device to send data to the computer becomes the active device, and the ADB transceiver addresses Talk Register 0 commands to that device every 11 ms until some other device asserts a Service Request signal.

Controlling the ADB Service Request

It is possible to control the ability of a device to transmit a Service Request signal. To disable a device's ability to send a Service Request signal, set bit 13 in register 3 to 0 by using a Listen Register 3 command with a Device Handler ID of $00, as shown in Table 8-17. To enable the Service Request ability, set this bit to 1. You can use this feature to improve service request response time when there are several devices on the bus and not all of them are required for a particular application.

Chapter 9 **Floppy Disk Interfaces**

Current Macintosh computers use two types of floppy disk drives: the Apple 800 KB drive and the Apple FDHD (floppy disk, high density) drive, also called the *SuperDrive*. This chapter describes two types of drives on the current machines and also discusses the 400 KB drive used on earlier Macintosh models.

Two different Apple custom ICs, the IWM (Integrated Woz Machine) and the SWIM (Super Woz Integrated Machine), are used in the interfaces for the two types of drives. This chapter describes the custom ICs and the other hardware used in those interfaces, gives pinouts for the internal and external connectors, and provides some information about how software communicates with the custom ICs.

Floppy
drive

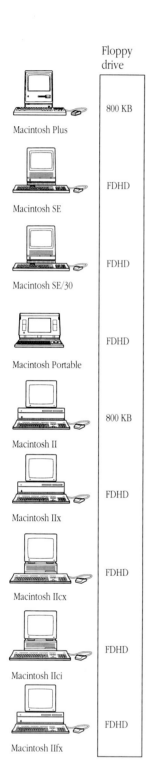

Macintosh Plus — 800 KB

Macintosh SE — FDHD

Macintosh SE/30 — FDHD

Macintosh Portable — FDHD

Macintosh II — 800 KB

Macintosh IIx — FDHD

Macintosh IIcx — FDHD

Macintosh IIci — FDHD

Macintosh IIfx — FDHD

The two types of disk drives

Current Macintosh computers use two types of floppy disk drives: the Apple 800 KB drive, a double-sided drive with storage capacities of 400 KB and 800 KB, and the Apple FDHD (floppy disk, high density) drive, with storage capacities of 400 KB, 800 KB, and 1.4 MB. The FDHD drive, also called the *SuperDrive,* can read and write MS-DOS files in addition to standard Macintosh files. Early Macintosh models used a single-sided version of the Apple 800 KB drive that has a storage capacity of 400 KB.

The drives used on the current Macintosh models are

- Apple 800 KB drive: Macintosh Plus, original Macintosh SE, and Macintosh II

- Apple FDHD drive: Macintosh SE FDHD, Macintosh SE/30, Macintosh Portable, Macintosh IIx, Macintosh IIcx, Macintosh IIci, and Macintosh IIfx

◆ *Note:* Macintosh SE computers manufactured before September of 1989 use the Apple 800 KB drive; newer Macintosh SE computers use the Apple FDHD drive and are identified by the letters *FDHD* on the front.

△ **Developer tip** This chapter does not contain information about the internal operation of the disk interface ICs (IWM and SWIM) used in the Macintosh computers. Apple recommends that applications use the routines and ROM tools provided by the Macintosh system software to communicate with hardware devices. If you are developing a device that requires its own disk driver, you should communicate directly with Apple to obtain technical assistance. See the section "Apple Developer Services" at the end of the Preface. △

Basic features of the disk drives

Table 9-1 shows the basic features of the two types of drives.

■ **Table 9-1** Basic features of Macintosh floppy disk drives

Type of drive	Interface IC	Disk type	Disk capacity	File system	Method of data encoding
800 KB drive	IWM	3.5-inch single sided	400 KB	MFS	Apple GCR
		3.5-inch double sided	800 KB	HFS	Apple GCR
FDHD drive	SWIM	3.5-inch single sided	400 KB	MFS	Apple GCR
		3.5-inch double sided	800 KB	HFS	Apple GCR
		3.5-inch double sided	720 KB	MS-DOS	MFM
		3.5-inch high density	1.4 MB	HFS	Apple GCR
		3.5-inch high density	1.4 MB	MS-DOS	MFM

Note: The terms GCR and MFM are defined in the next section.

Data encoding methods

A disk drive records data on a magnetic disk in somewhat the same way that a cassette recorder records sounds on a magnetic tape. The drive causes changes in the current flowing through a tiny electromagnet—the read-write head—that is held very close to the magnetic coating on the rotating disk. The changes in the current through the head cause changes in the magnetization of the disk coating. Those changes are called *magnetic transitions,* and they remain on the disk until written over. When reading the disk, the magnetic transitions on the rotating disk cause changing currents in the head. Appropriate circuitry in the disk drive converts those currents to digital signals.

There are many possible ways of encoding digital data as magnetic transitions on a disk, that is, of expressing a pattern of ones and zeros as a series of magnetic transitions. Two different encoding methods are used with Macintosh disk drives: group-code recording (GCR) and modified frequency modulation (MFM). Table 9-1 shows the encoding methods for the different types of disk drives.

Group-code recording (GCR)

Prior to the introduction of the Apple FDHD drive, all Apple II and Macintosh disk drives used **group-code recording** (GCR) with NRZI (non-return-to-zero, inverted) encoding.

With **NRZI encoding,** magnetic transitions represent digital data according to the following rules.

- A transition always occurs for a one in the data stream.
- No transition occurs for a zero in the data stream.

Groups of three or more zeros would be difficult to distinguish using this encoding, so the disk drivers use GCR to format the data in such a way that more than two adjacent zeros don't occur. With GCR formatting, each group of three data bytes is formatted as four 8-bit patterns.

Figure 9-1 shows the relationship between data bits and magnetic transitions written on the disk using NRZI encoding.

- **Figure 9-1** NRZI encoding (used with GCR formatting)

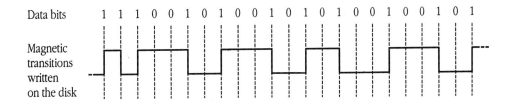

Modified frequency modulation (MFM)

Another standard encoding method is **modified frequency modulation** (MFM), which is used on many different kinds of computer disk drives in addition to the Apple FDHD drive. With MFM encoding, magnetic transitions represent digital data according to the following rules.

- A transition always occurs for a one in the data stream.
- No transition occurs for an isolated zero in the data stream.
- A transition always occurs for two adjacent zeros in the data stream.

Figure 9-2 shows the relationship between data bits and magnetic transitions written on the disk.

■ **Figure 9-2** MFM encoding

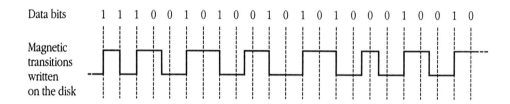

800 KB drive interface

Table 9-2 lists the Macintosh models that use the Apple 800 KB drives. The 800 KB drive can format, read, and write both 800 KB double-sided and 400 KB single-sided floppy disks.

The Macintosh Plus computer has an internal 800 KB drive and an external disk drive connector to which you can connect an 800 KB drive, a single-sided 400 KB floppy disk drive, or an Apple Hard Disk 20.

The Macintosh SE is equipped with an internal 800 KB drive and may be equipped with a second internal 800 KB drive. In addition, the Macintosh SE has an external disk drive connector to which you can connect an 800 KB drive, a single-sided 400 KB floppy disk drive, or an Apple Hard Disk 20.

◆ *Note:* Macintosh SE computers manufactured after August 1989 use the Apple FDHD Drive. They are identified by the letters *FDHD* on the front. For information about the Apple FDHD Drive, please refer to the section "FDHD Drive Interface," later in this chapter.

The Macintosh II is equipped with an internal 800 KB drive and may be equipped with a second internal 800 KB drive. The Macintosh II computer has no connector for an external floppy disk drive.

■ **Table 9-2** Macintosh models that use the 800 KB floppy disk drive

Macintosh model	Number of internal floppy disk drives	Number of external floppy disk drives
Macintosh Plus	1	1
Macintosh SE*	1 or 2	1
Macintosh II	1 or 2	0

*Macintosh SE computers manufactured after August 1989 use the Apple FDHD Drive.

The interface between the floppy disk drive connector and the Macintosh computer's main logic board is an Apple custom integrated circuit called the **IWM** (Integrated Woz Machine). The IWM controls four of the disk state-control lines, generates an internal/external drive-select signal, and generates the read-data and write-data signals for the disk drives. In addition, the VIA provides a disk state-control line to help select disk drive internal registers.

◆ *Note:* On Macintosh models that have two VIA ICs, VIA1 is the interface to the IWM.

The IWM converts between the NRZI serial data used to communicate with disk drives and the 8-bit parallel data used to communicate with the CPU. The Disk Driver software converts between the group-code recording (GCR) data format used by disk drives and the normal 8-bit bytes used by the application.

The clock used by the IWM in the Macintosh Plus and earlier models is the C8M signal, whose frequency is 7.8336 MHz. The clock used by the IWM in the Macintosh SE and Macintosh II computers is the C16M signal, whose frequency is 15.6672 MHz—twice as fast as the C8M clock. During the startup sequence, software sets a bit in the IWM to divide this faster clock by two when using the 800 KB drive, the single-sided 400 KB drive, or the Hard Disk 20.

The IWM can send data to the disk drive at a maximum rate of approximately 500 Kbits per second. Because 4 bytes of GCR-encoded data correspond to 3 bytes of data in system RAM, the effective maximum data transmission rate is approximately 375 Kbits per second. Notice, however, that the throughput of data to the disk depends on the amount of time spent seeking the correct location on the disk, reading RAM, and taking care of other system tasks in addition to the time spent actually transmitting data.

800 KB drive connectors

The figures and tables in this section specify the signals on the connectors for the 800 KB drive. The signals on the internal and external connectors are functionally the same, but on some machines they are electrically different, as shown in the circuit diagrams in the section "Circuit Diagrams for the 800 KB Drive Interface," later in this chapter.

Internal 800 KB drive connectors

Figure 9-3 shows the pinout for the 20-pin connector used for internal 800 KB drives on all Macintosh models that use that drive. There are slight differences in the signal assignments on different Macintosh models: please refer to Tables 9-3 and 9-4 for details.

■ **Figure 9-3** Pinout of the connector for the internal 800 KB floppy disk drive

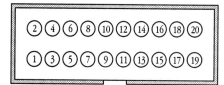

Table 9-3 shows the signal assignments for the 20-pin internal floppy disk drive connector on the Macintosh Plus.

Signal assignments for the internal floppy disk drive connector on the
Macintosh Plus computer

Pin number	Signal name	Signal description
1	GND	Ground
2	PH0	State-control line
3	GND	Ground
4	PH1	State-control line
5	GND	Ground
6	PH2	State-control line
7	GND	Ground
8	PH3	Register Write Strobe
9	–12V	–12 volts
10	/WRREQ	Write Data Request
11	+5V	+5 volts
12	SEL	State-control line SEL
13	+12V	+12 volts
14	/ENBL.INT	Internal Drive Enable
15	+12V	+12 volts
16	RD	Read Data
17	+12V	+12 volts
18	WR	Write Data
19	+12V	+12 volts
20	PWM	Motor-speed control

▲ **Warning**   The combined load of all devices connected to a Macintosh Plus
computer must not exceed 600 milliamps at +12 volts, 700 milliamps
at +5 volts, and 10 milliamps at –12 volts. A Macintosh single-sided
floppy disk drive requires 500 milliamps at +12 volts and 500 milliamps
at +5 volts. An Apple 800 KB drive requires 600 milliamps at +12 volts
and 360 milliamps at +5 volts. ▲

Table 9-4 shows the signal assignments for the 20-pin internal floppy disk connector used
on the Macintosh SE and Macintosh II.

Pin number	Signal name	Signal description
1	GND	Ground
2	PH0	State-control line
3	GND	Ground
4	PH1	State-control line
5	GND	Ground
6	PH2	State-control line
7	GND	Ground
8	PH3	Register Write Strobe
9	n.c.	Not connected
10	/WRREQ	Write Data Request
11	+5V	+5 volts
12	SEL	State-control line
13	+12V	+12 volts
14	/ENBL	Drive enable*
15	+12V	+12 volts
16	RD	Read Data
17	+12V	+12 volts
18	WR	Write Data
19	+12V	+12 volts
20	n.c.	Not connected

*On models that can have two internal drives, each drive has its own 20-pin connector and its own /ENABL signal on pin 14.

The signals PH2 through PH0, from the IWM, together with the signal SEL, from the VIA, make up the state-control lines used by the disk interface to select registers in the floppy disk drives. The signal PH3, from the IWM, is used to write data to the registers.

The signal /WRREQ is a programmable output of the IWM that is used for handshaking.

On models that have up to two floppy-disk drives, each drive has its own enable signal, which is generated by the IWM. On the Macintosh Plus, the enable signals for the internal and external drives are /ENBL.INT and /ENBL.EXT. On the Macintosh II, the drive-enable signals are called /ENBL.1 and /ENBL.2.

The Macintosh SE can have as many as three drives, two internal and one external. The enable signal for the external drive comes directly from the IWM. The enable signals for the internal drives are called /ENBL.HI and /ENBL.LO; they are generated by the GLU using the /ENBL1 signal from the IWM and the /HI.DRIVE signal from the VIA. If the /ENBL.INT and /HI.DRIVE signals are both asserted, the GLU asserts the /ENBL.HI signal to the upper internal drive; if the /ENBL.INT signal is asserted but the /HI.DRIVE signal is not, the GLU asserts the /ENBL.LO signal to the lower internal drive.

The RD and WR lines are the data lines used to transfer data between the disk drive and the IWM.

The PWM line carries a speed-control signal used only by 400 KB single-sided drives. For more information, refer to the section "Compatibility With Single-Sided Disk Drives," later in this chapter.

External 800 KB drive connectors

Figure 9-4 shows the pinout for the DB-19 external disk connector on the Macintosh Plus and Macintosh SE; Table 9-5 shows the signal assignments.

■ **Figure 9-4** Pinout of the connector for the external floppy disk drive on the Macintosh Plus and Macintosh SE computers

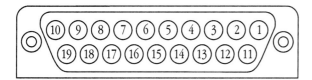

The signals available on the external floppy disk connector are the same as those available on the internal floppy disk connector, and are described just after Table 9-4, earlier in this section.

■ **Table 9-5** Signal assignments for the connector for the external floppy disk drive on the Macintosh Plus and Macintosh SE computers

Pin number	Signal name	Signal description
1	GND	Ground
2	GND	Ground
3	GND	Ground
4	GND	Ground
5	–12V	–12 volts
6	+5V	+5 volts
7	+12V	+12 volts
8	+12V	+12 volts
9	n.c.	Not connected
10	PWM	Motor-speed control
11	PH0	State-control line
12	PH1	State-control line
13	PH2	State-control line
14	PH3	Register Write Strobe
15	/WRREQ	Write Data Request
16	SEL	State-control line
17	/ENBL.EXT	External Drive Enable
18	RD	Read Data
19	WR	Write Data

▲ **Warning** The combined load of all devices connected to a Macintosh Plus computer must not exceed 600 milliamps at +12 volts, 700 milliamps at +5 volts, and 10 milliamps at –12 volts. A Macintosh single-sided floppy disk drive requires 500 milliamps at +12 volts and 500 milliamps at +5 volts. An Apple 800 KB drive requires 600 milliamps at +12 volts and 360 milliamps at +5 volts. ▲

Circuit diagrams for the 800 KB drive interface

Figure 9-5 shows a circuit diagram for the floppy disk interface on the Macintosh Plus computer. Figure 9-6 shows a circuit diagram for the floppy disk interface on the Macintosh SE computer.

■ **Figure 9-5** Circuit diagram of the floppy disk drive interface on the
Macintosh Plus computer

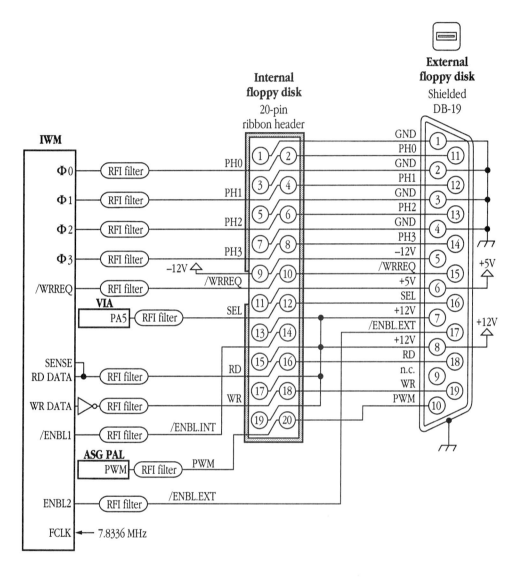

Note:

—(RFI filter)— = 〜〜⏚〜〜

(R1 + R2 = 40 to 60 ohms, C = 150 to 300 pF)

■ **Figure 9-6** Circuit diagram of the floppy disk drive interface on the original Macintosh SE computer

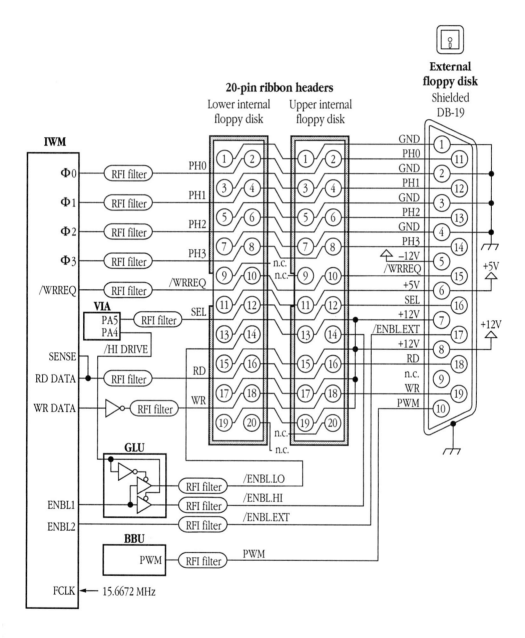

Note:
— RFI filter — = R1 R2 resistors with C capacitor to ground

(R1 + R2 = 40 to 60 ohms, C = 150 to 300 pF)

The Macintosh II has no external floppy disk drive connector and no disk-speed control line for use with single-sided 400 KB floppy disk drives.

Figure 9-7 shows a circuit diagram for the floppy disk drive interface on the Macintosh II computer.

■ **Figure 9-7** Circuit diagram of the floppy disk drive interface on the Macintosh II computer

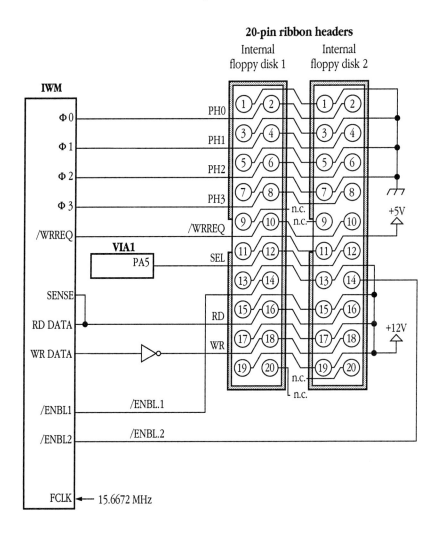

Compatibility with single-sided disk drives

The external disk connector on the Macintosh Plus and Macintosh SE computers supports the single-sided 400 KB external floppy disk drive. That drive requires a pulse-width-modulated (PWM) signal to control the speed of its drive motor.

A general logic IC (PAL in the Macintosh Plus, BBU in the Macintosh SE) uses values it reads from the disk-speed buffer in RAM to generate this PWM speed-control signal. By running the disk motor at slower speeds, the computer is able to store more sectors of information in the tracks closer to the edge of the disk.

On the Macintosh SE, the speed-control signal is required only for the 400 KB external floppy disk drive and is not available for internal disk drives. The 800 KB drive controls its own motor speed and ignores the speed-control signal.

△ **Developer tip** Because some disk drives ignore the speed-control signal, applications should never depend on that signal (for instance, in their copy-protection schemes). △

The Macintosh II has no external floppy disk connector and no disk-speed control line for use with single-sided 400 KB floppy disk drives.

Compatibility with the Hard Disk 20

On the Macintosh Plus and the Macintosh SE computers, the external disk drive connector can also be used for an Apple Hard Disk 20. (The Macintosh II has no external floppy disk drive connector.)

To use both the Hard Disk 20 and an external floppy disk drive, plug the Hard Disk 20 into the connector on the back of the computer and plug the external floppy disk drive into the DB-19 connector on the back of the Hard Disk 20. The pinout of the DB-19 connector on the Hard Disk 20 is identical to that of the DB-19 disk drive connector on the back of the computer.

△ **Developer tip** For compatibility with earlier Macintosh models, the Hard Disk 20 startup software contains a device driver for the Hard Disk 20 disk drive along with the hierarchical (128 KB ROM) version of the File Manager. The Hard Disk 20 startup software is part of the ROM in the Macintosh Plus, Macintosh SE, Macintosh Portable, and Macintosh IIci. The machines that do not have the Hard Disk 20 startup software in ROM—that is, the rest of the Macintosh II family and the Macintosh SE/30—can use the device driver from the Hard Disk 20 startup disk as an Init file, enabling them to read and write to the Hard Disk 20. That arrangement does not enable those machines to start up (boot) from the Hard Disk 20. △

FDHD drive interface

Table 9-6 lists the Macintosh models that use the Apple FDHD drive, also called the *SuperDrive*. The Macintosh SE FDHD, Macintosh SE/30, Macintosh IIcx, Macintosh IIci, and Macintosh Portable computers are equipped with an internal FDHD drive and an external disk drive connector to which you can connect a second FDHD drive. The Macintosh IIx and Macintosh IIfx are equipped with an internal FDHD drive and may be equipped with a second internal FDHD drive.

◆ *Note:* Macintosh SE computers manufactured before September 1989 use the Apple 800 KB drive.

■ **Table 9-6** Macintosh models that use the Apple FDHD drive

Macintosh model	Number of internal floppy disk drives	Number of external floppy disk drives
Macintosh SE FDHD	1	1
Macintosh SE/30	1	1
Macintosh Portable	1 or 2	1
Macintosh IIx	1 or 2	0
Macintosh IIcx	1	1
Macintosh IIci	1	1
Macintosh IIfx	1 or 2	0

*Macintosh SE computers manufactured before September 1989 use the Apple 800 KB drive.

◆ *Note:* On all Macintosh models that support an external FDHD drive, you can connect an external 800 KB drive instead.

The interface between the floppy disk drive connector and the Macintosh computer's main logic board is an Apple custom integrated circuit called the **SWIM** (Super Woz Integrated Machine). The SWIM controls four of the disk state-control lines, generates signals to select either the internal or external drive, and generates the read-data and write-data signals for the disk drives. In addition, the VIA provides a disk state-control line to help select disk drive internal registers.

◆ *Note:* On Macintosh models that have two VIA ICs, VIA1 is the interface to the SWIM.

In the Macintosh IIfx, the SWIM is controlled by an Apple custom IC, the IOP (I/O Processor). The IOP transfers disk data between the main memory and its own dedicated RAM using DMA transfers. The IOP controls the SWIM to perform the actual disk transfers. For information about the operation of the IOP, please refer to the section "IOPs in the Macintosh IIfx Computer" in Chapter 3.

The SWIM converts between the NRZI serial data used to communicate with disk drives and the 8-bit parallel data used to communicate with the computer. The Disk Driver software converts between the data formats (GCR and MFM) used by disk drives and the normal 8-bit bytes used by the application.

The SWIM uses a clock frequency of 15.6672 MHz. (That frequency is twice that used for the IWM interface IC that supports the 800 KB drive.) During the startup sequence, software sets a bit in the SWIM to divide the clock by two when reading and writing to the 800 KB drive or the Hard Disk 20. (The SWIM does not support the single-sided floppy disk drive.)

The SWIM can send data to the disk drive at a maximum rate of approximately 500 Kbits per second. Because 4 bytes of GCR-encoded data correspond to 3 bytes of data in system RAM, the effective maximum data transmission rate in GCR mode is approximately 375 Kbits per second. Notice, however, that the throughput of data to the disk depends on the amount of time spent seeking the correct location on the disk, reading RAM, and taking care of other system tasks in addition to the time spent actually transmitting data.

FDHD drive connectors

The figures and tables in this section specify the signals on the FDHD drive connectors. The signals on the internal and external connectors are functionally the same, but on some machines they are electrically different, as shown in the circuit diagrams in the section "FDHD Interface Circuit Diagrams," later in this chapter.

Internal FDHD drive connectors

Figure 9-8 shows the pinout for the 20-pin connector used for internal FDHD drives on all Macintosh models that use that drive. There are slight differences in the signal assignments on different Macintosh models: please refer to Tables 9-7 and 9-8 for details.

■ **Figure 9-8** Pinout of the connector for the internal FDHD drive

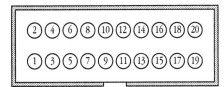

Table 9-7 shows the signal assignments for the 20-pin internal connector for the FDHD drive on the Macintosh IIx, Macintosh IIcx, Macintosh IIci, and Macintosh IIfx. Table 9-8 shows the signal assignments for the 20-pin internal connector for the FDHD drive on the Macintosh SE FDHD, Macintosh SE/30, and Macintosh Portable.

■ **Table 9-7**   Signal assignments for the internal FDHD drive connectors on the Macintosh IIx, Macintosh IIcx, Macintosh IIci, and Macintosh IIfx computers

Pin number	Signal name	Signal description
1	GND	Ground
2	PH0	State-control line
3	GND	Ground
4	PH1	State-control line
5	GND	Ground
6	PH2	State-control line
7	GND	Ground
8	PH3	Register Write Strobe
9	–12V	–12 volts
10	/WRREQ	Write Data Request
11	+5V	+5 volts
12	SEL	State-control signal (from VIA1)
13	+12V	+12 volts
14	/ENBL1	Drive Enable*
15	+12V	+12 volts
16	RD	Read Data
17	+12V	+12 volts
18	WR	Write Data
19	+12V	+12 volts
20	PWMPU	Pull-up resistor to +5V

*On the Macintosh IIx and Macintosh IIfx, which can have two internal drives, there are two 20-pin connectors. Pin 14 of each connector carries its respective enable signal; the signals are named /ENABL1 and /ENABL2.

■ **Table 9-8** Signal assignments for the internal FDHD drive connector on the Macintosh SE FDHD, Macintosh SE/30, and Macintosh Portable computers

Pin number	Signal name	Signal description
1	GND	Ground
2	PH0	State-control line
3	GND	Ground
4	PH1	State-control line
5	GND	Ground
6	PH2	State-control line
7	GND	Ground
8	PH3	Register Write Strobe
9	–12V*	–12 volts*
10	/WRREQ	Write Data Request
11	+5V	+5 volts
12	SEL	State-control signal (from VIA1)
13	+12V	+12 volts
14	/ENBL1†	Internal-drive Enable†
15	+12V	+12 volts
16	RD	Read Data
17	+12V	+12 volts
18	WR	Write Data
19	+12V	+12 volts
20	n.c.	Not connected

*On the Macintosh Portable, pin 9 is not connected.

†On the Macintosh Portable, which has provisions for two internal drives, there are two 20-pin connectors. Pin 14 of each connector carries its respective enable signal; the signals are named /INDISK1 and /INDISK2.

The signals PH2 through PH0, from the SWIM, together with the signal SEL, from the VIA, make up the state-control lines used by the disk interface to select registers in the floppy disk drives. The signal PH3, from the SWIM, is used for writing data to the registers in the floppy disk drives.

The SWIM supports two drives, each with its own enable signal; the signals are named /ENABL1 and /ENABL2. On machines with only one internal drive, the enable signal for the internal drive is /ENBL1 and the enable signal for the external drive is /ENBL2.

In the Macintosh Portable, which can have three drives, the /ENBL2 line from the SWIM selects the external floppy disk drive. Additional logic in the Miscellaneous GLU IC uses signals /ENBL1 from the SWIM and DRIVE.SEL from the VIA to generate separate select lines /INDISK1 and /INDISK2 for the two internal drives.

The signal /WRREQ is a programmable output of the SWIM that can be used for handshaking.

The RD and WR lines are the data lines used to transfer data between the disk drive and the SWIM.

External FDHD drive connectors

Figure 9-9 shows the pinout for the DB-19 external FDHD drive connector. Table 9-9 shows the signal assignments for the external FDHD drive connector on the Macintosh IIcx and Macintosh IIci computers. Table 9-10 shows the signal assignments for the external FDHD drive connector on the Macintosh SE FDHD, Macintosh SE/30, and Macintosh Portable computers.

■ **Figure 9-9** Pinout for the connector for the external FDHD drive

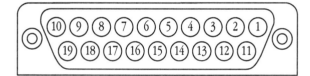

■ **Table 9-9**   Signal assignments for the external FDHD drive connector on the
Macintosh IIcx and Macintosh IIci computers

Pin number	Signal name	Signal description
1	GND	Ground
2	GND	Ground
3	GND	Ground
4	GND	Ground
5	–12V	–12 volts
6	+5V	+5 volts
7	+12V	+12 volts
8	+12V	+12 volts
9	n.c.	Not connected
10	PWMPU	Pull-up resistor to +5V
11	PH0	State-control line
12	PH1	State-control line
13	PH2	State-control line
14	PH3	Register Write Strobe
15	/WRREQ	Write Data Request
16	SEL	State-control line
17	/ENBL2	External Drive Enable
18	RD	Read Data
19	WR	Write Data

The functions of the signals on the external floppy disk connector are the same as those
on the internal floppy disk connector, and are described just after Table 9-8 in the section
"Internal FDHD Drive Connectors."

◆ *Note:* On the Macintosh IIcx and Macintosh IIci, pin 10 of the external connector is
tied to +5 V through a pull-up resistor. On the Macintosh SE FDHD and
Macintosh SE/30, pin 10 is tied directly to a +5 V supply. On the Macintosh Portable,
pin 10 is not connected. Please refer to Figures 9-10, 9-11, 9-12, and 9-13.

■ **Table 9-10**　Signal assignments for the external FDHD drive connector on the Macintosh SE FDHD, Macintosh SE/30, and Macintosh Portable computers

Pin number	Signal name	Signal description
1	GND	Ground
2	GND	Ground
3	GND	Ground
4	GND	Ground
5	n.c.	Not connected
6	+5V	+5 volts
7	+12V	+12 volts
8	+12V	+12 volts
9	n.c.	Not connected
10	+5V*	+5 volts*
11	PH0	State-control line
12	PH1	State-control line
13	PH2	State-control line
14	PH3	Register Write Strobe
15	/WRREQ	Write Data Request
16	SEL	State-control line
17	/ENBL2	External Drive Enable
18	RD	Read Data
19	WR	Write Data

*On the Macintosh Portable, pin 10 is not connected.

FDHD interface circuit diagrams

Figure 9-10 shows a circuit diagram for the disk drive interface on the Macintosh SE FDHD and Macintosh SE/30 computers. Figure 9-11 shows a circuit diagram for the disk drive interface on the Macintosh Portable. Figure 9-12 shows a circuit diagram for the disk drive interface on the Macintosh IIx. Figure 9-13 shows a circuit diagram for the disk drive interface on the Macintosh IIcx and Macintosh IIci. Figure 9-14 shows a circuit diagram for the disk drive interface on the Macintosh IIfx.

■ **Figure 9-10** Circuit diagram of the FDHD drive interface on the Macintosh SE FDHD and Macintosh SE/30 computers

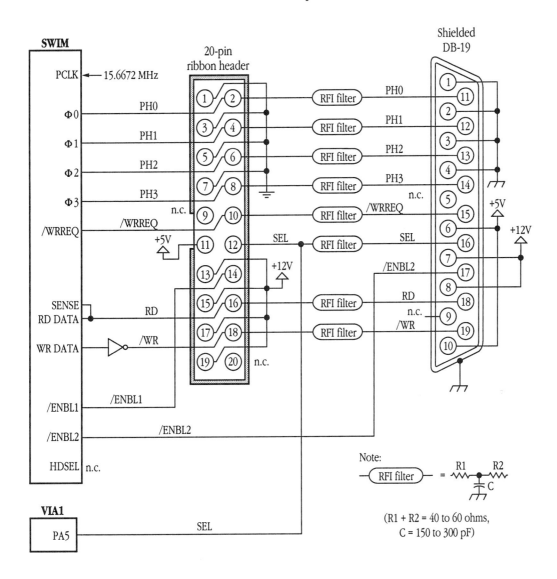

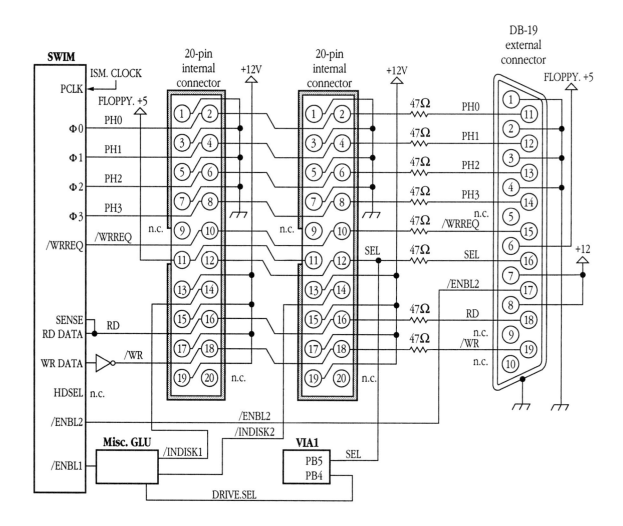

■ **Figure 9-11** Circuit diagram of the FDHD drive interface on the
Macintosh Portable computer

■ **Figure 9-12**   Circuit diagram of the FDHD drive interface on the Macintosh IIx computer

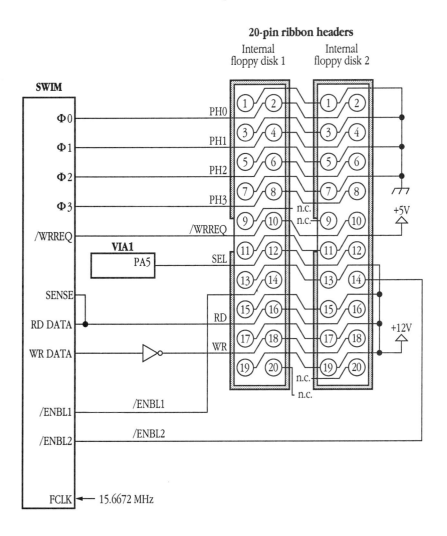

- **Figure 9-13**   Circuit diagram of the FDHD drive interface on the Macintosh IIcx and
  Macintosh IIci computers

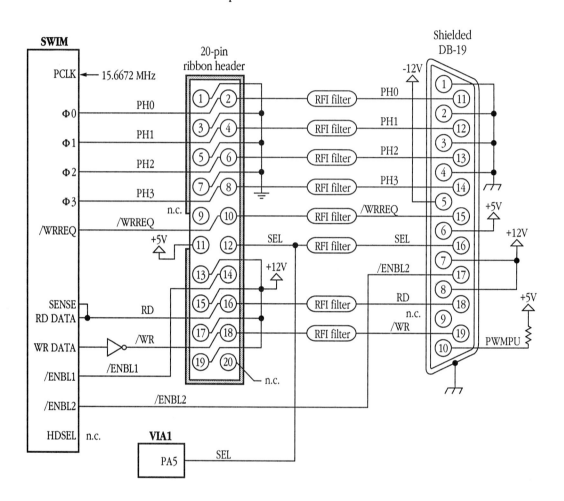

Note:

─(RFI filter)─ = ─R1\/\/\─

(R1 = 40 to 60 ohms)

■ **Figure 9-14** Circuit diagram of the FDHD drive interface on the
Macintosh IIfx computer

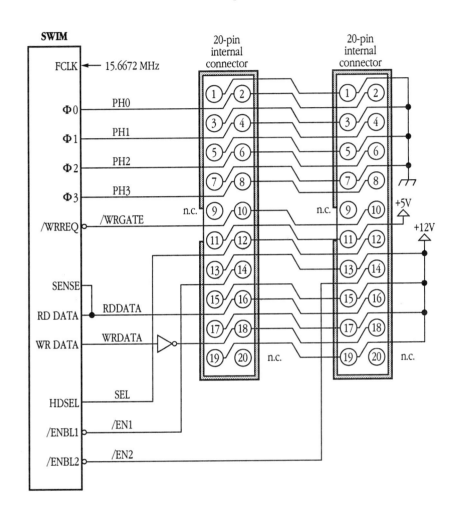

Incompatibility with the single-sided disk drive

Even though some of the Macintosh models with the SWIM interface have external disk-drive connectors, none of them support the 400 KB single-sided disk drive, which requires computer control of motor speed through a signal named PWM. On the SWIM-equipped machines, that signal is permanently high; a single-sided drive will not work.

Compatibility with the Hard Disk 20

On the Macintosh SE/30, Macintosh IIcx, Macintosh IIci, and Macintosh Portable computers, the external disk connector can be used for an external 800 KB drive, an external FDHD drive, or an Apple Hard Disk 20. (The external disk connector does *not* support the older, single-sided 400 KB external floppy disk drive.)

To use both the Hard Disk 20 and an external floppy disk drive on those machines, plug the Hard Disk 20 into the connector on the back of the computer, and plug the external floppy disk drive into the DB-19 connector on the back of the Hard Disk 20. The pinout of the DB-19 connector on the Hard Disk 20 is identical to that of the DB-19 disk drive connector on the back of the computer.

△ **Developer tip** For compatibility with earlier Macintosh models, the Hard Disk 20 startup software contains a device driver for the Hard Disk 20 disk drive along with the hierarchical (128 KB ROM) version of the File Manager. The Hard Disk 20 startup software is part of the ROM in the Macintosh Plus, Macintosh SE, Macintosh Portable, and Macintosh IIci. The machines that do not have the Hard Disk 20 startup software in ROM—that is, the rest of the Macintosh II family and the Macintosh SE/30—can use the device driver from the Hard Disk 20 startup disk as an Init file, enabling them to read and write to the Hard Disk 20. That arrangement does not enable those machines to start up (boot) from the Hard Disk 20. △

Chapter 10 **Serial I/O Ports**

All models of the Macintosh computer contain hardware interfaces for two RS-422 serial ports. In addition, the Macintosh Portable computer contains an internal slot for the installation of a modem card. This chapter describes the hardware used in each of these interfaces, gives pinouts for the connectors, and provides some information about how software communicates with the SCC devices that control the ports.

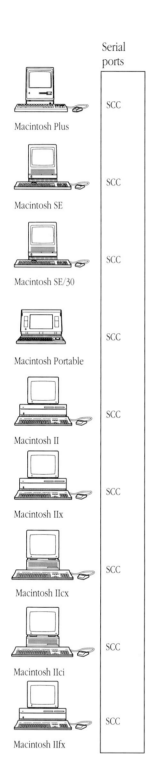

Serial
ports

Macintosh Plus — SCC

Macintosh SE — SCC

Macintosh SE/30 — SCC

Macintosh Portable — SCC

Macintosh II — SCC

Macintosh IIx — SCC

Macintosh IIcx — SCC

Macintosh IIci — SCC

Macintosh IIfx — SCC

The Macintosh serial interface is controlled by a Zilog Z8530 Serial Communications Controller (SCC) integrated circuit. The SCC provides two serial ports: SCC port A—the modem port—and SCC port B—the printer port. Each SCC port has a connector, located on the back panel, for connecting serial peripheral devices and for connecting the computer to the AppleTalk network.

△ **Developer tip** Even though this chapter describes the operation of the hardware that controls the serial ports, your programs should not communicate directly with that hardware. It is much easier and safer to use the tools provided by the Macintosh system software for this purpose. To ensure compatibility with other Macintosh computers, Apple strongly recommends that you follow the interface guidelines and philosophies described in *Inside Macintosh.* △

◆ *Note:* In the Macintosh IIfx, the SCC is controlled by an Apple custom IC, an IOP (I/O Processor). That IOP transfers disk data between the main memory and its own dedicated RAM using DMA transfers. The IOP controls the SCC to perform the serial I/O transfers. For information about the operation of the IOP, please refer to the section "IOPs in the Macintosh IIfx Computer" in Chapter 3.

Serial port connectors

All current Macintosh models use miniature 8-pin connectors for their serial ports. Those mini 8-pin connectors provide an output handshake signal not available on the DB-9 connectors for the serial ports of the earlier Macintosh computers (Macintosh 128K, 512K, and 512K enhanced); on the other hand, the mini 8-pin connectors do not provide the +5 volts and +12 volts provided by the serial ports of the earlier Macintosh computers.

Figure 10-1 shows the pinout for the mini 8-pin connectors used for the Macintosh serial ports; Table 10-1 shows the signal assignments. These signals are described in the next section, "Signals on the Serial Ports."

■ **Figure 10-1** Pinout of the mini 8-pin serial port connectors

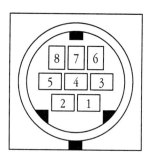

■ **Table 10-1** Signal assignments for the mini 8-pin serial port connectors

Pin number	Signal name	Signal description
1	HSKo	Handshake output. Driven inverted from SCC's /DTR. Voh = 3.6V; Vol = –3.6V; Rl = 450Ω
2	HSKi	Handshake input or external clock. Received uninverted at SCC's /CTS and /TRxC. Vih = 0.2V; Vil = –0.2V; Ri = 12KΩ
3	TxD–	Transmit data (inverted). Driven inverted from SCC's TxD; tri-stated when SCC's /RTS is not asserted. Voh = 3.6V; Vol = –3.6V; Rl = 450Ω
4	GND	Signal ground. Connected to logic and chassis ground.
5	RxD–	Receive data (inverted); received inverted at SCC's RxD. Vih = 0.2V; Vil = –0.2V; Ri = 12KΩ
6	TxD+	Transmit data. Driven uninverted from SCC's TxD; tri-stated when SCC's /RTS is not asserted. Voh = 3.6V; Vol = –3.6V; Rl = 450Ω
7	GPi*	General-purpose input.* Received inverted at SCC's DCD. Vih = 0.2V; Vil = –0.2V; Ri = 12KΩ
8	RxD+	Receive data. Received uninverted at SCC's RxD. Vih = 0.2V; Vil = –0.2V; Ri = 12KΩ

Note: Absolute values of specified voltages are minimums; Ri is a minimum, Rl is a maximum.

* On the serial port of the Macintosh Plus, pin 7 is not connected.

Signals on the serial ports

The transmit-data and receive-data lines of the Macintosh serial interface conform to the EIA standard RS-422, which differs from the more commonly used RS-232-C standard in that, whereas an RS-232-C transmitter modulates a signal with respect to a common ground, an RS-422 transmitter modulates the signal against an inverted copy of the same signal (to generate a differential signal). The RS-232-C receiver senses whether the received signal is sufficiently negative with respect to ground to be a logical 1, whereas the RS-422 receiver simply senses which line is more negative than the other. An RS-422 signal is therefore more immune to noise and interference, and degrades less over distance, than an RS-232 signal.

The serial data inputs and outputs of the SCC are connected to the external connectors through differential line drivers and receivers. On the Macintosh Plus, Macintosh SE, and Macintosh Portable, the drivers are 26LS30 and 9636A ICs and the receivers are 26LS32 ICs; on the Macintosh II, Macintosh IIx, Macintosh IIcx, and Macintosh SE/30, the line drivers are all 26LS30 ICs and the receivers are 75175 ICs. The line drivers can be put in the high-impedance mode between transmissions to allow other AppleTalk devices to transmit over those lines. A line driver is enabled by lowering the SCC's Request To Send (RTS) output for that port.

Inside the SCC IC, port A (the modem port) has a higher interrupt priority than port B, making port A more suitable for high-speed communication. Whenever interrupts are turned off for longer than 100 microseconds, the serial driver stores any data received through port A for later handoff to the port-A input driver. The higher interrupt priority of port A affects only the internal operations of the SCC, and has no effect on the interrupt priority of the SCC in the Macintosh device-interrupt scheme.

On the Macintosh SE, Macintosh II, and more recent models, serial port A supports synchronous transmission, but port B does not; see the discussion of the GPi signal, later in this section. The Macintosh Plus and earlier models do not support synchronous transmission on either port.

Other than the two differences just described, port A and port B are identical.

The Output Handshake signal (HSKo) for each Macintosh Plus serial port originates at the SCC's Data Terminal Ready (DTR) output for that port and is driven by an RS-422 line driver. On the Macintosh Plus and the Macintosh SE, it's a 3488A or 9636A; on the Macintosh SE/30 and the Macintosh II–family computers, it's a differential line driver (26LS30).

Each port's Input Handshake signal (HSKi) is connected to the SCC's Clear To Send (CTS) input for that port, and is designed to accept an external device's Data Terminal Ready (DTR) handshake signal. This line is also connected to the SCC's Transmit/Receive Clock (TRxC) input for that port, so that an external device can perform high-speed synchronous data exchange. Note that you can't use the HSKi line for receiving DTR if you're using it to receive a high-speed data clock.

Except on the Macintosh Plus and earlier models, each serial port also has a general-purpose input (GPi, pin 7), connected to the SCC's Data Carrier Detect (DCD) input for that port. This input can be used to provide a handshake signal from an external device to the computer. The DCD input to the SCC can be polled by software or can be used to generate a CPU interrupt.

◆ *Note:* On the Macintosh Plus and earlier Macintosh computers, the GPi signal is not connected. On those computers, the DCD inputs to the SCC are used to generate mouse interrupts, as described in the section "Macintosh Plus Mouse" in Chapter 7. In the other Macintosh models, each DCD input to the SCC is brought out to a pin on a serial port connector.

On port A only, the GPi line can be connected to the SCC's Receive/Transmit Clock (RTxCA). This feature supports devices that provide separate transmit and receive data clocks, such as synchronous modems. Bit 3 (vSync) of Data register A in the VIA (VIA1 in machines with two VIAs), when set low, connects GPiA to RTxCA. When the VIA vSync bit is set high, RTxCA is connected to a 3.672 MHz clock. Port B's Receive/Transmit clock (RTxCB) is always connected to the 3.672 MHz clock, as in the classic Macintosh configuration. Note that you can't use the GPi line to receive a DCD input when you are using it to receive a high-speed clock. This input is noninverting for compatibility with the classic Macintosh configuration. The general-purpose input (GPi) is received by means of the negative (inverting) input of one of the same differential receivers, with the positive input grounded.

△ **Developer tip** Because the 26LS32 is a differential receiver, any handshake or clock signal driving it must be bipolar, alternating between a positive voltage and a negative voltage with respect to the internally grounded input. If a device uses ground (0 volts) as one of its handshake logic levels, the receiver interprets that level as an indeterminate state, with unpredictable results. △

The SCC chip generates level-2 processor interrupts (/IPL1) during I/O over the serial lines. During disk accesses, the disk controller disables all interrupts of level 3 and lower to prevent any loss of data that might occur when the CPU pauses to service an interrupt. Because the SCC chip cannot store more than 3 bytes of incoming data, however, and because serial data (such as an AppleTalk message) might come in at any time, it may be necessary to service the SCC before a floppy disk transaction is complete. To allow software to determine whether there is a byte of serial data waiting to be read, the VIA monitors the SCC's Wait/Request line. Whenever there is a pause in a floppy disk transaction, the disk driver can check bit 7 in Data register A in the VIA (VIA1 in machines with two VIAs) to determine the state of the Wait/Request line. If there is data waiting in the SCC, the driver reads it during the next pause in the disk transaction.

The maximum nominal data transmission rate that you can select through the Macintosh Toolbox is 57,600 baud. This is the maximum rate that the classic Macintosh computers can maintain for transmission of serial data when the SCC port is operating in an asynchronous, interrupt-driven fashion, timed by the 3.672 MHz clock.

AppleTalk operates at a nominal data transmission rate of 230.4 Kbaud. This higher rate is possible because AppleTalk communications are not interrupt driven; during AppleTalk communications, the AppleTalk Driver has complete control of the computer. Although AppleTalk uses a synchronous communication protocol, the AppleTalk Driver runs the SCC chip in asynchronous mode, timed by the 3.672 MHz clock.

The maximum possible transmission rate for serial data ranges from approximately 500 Kbaud on the Macintosh Plus and Macintosh SE to 900 Kbaud on the Macintosh II family. To achieve such data transmission rates, the SCC would have to be operated in synchronous mode timed by an external clock, and the serial driver would have to have complete, uninterrupted control of the computer.

SCC addresses

This section describes the way low-level programs—serial drivers—control the serial interface. It is provided for the sake of completeness only. Unless you are writing your own driver software, you should never need to use the information is this section. For more information about the SCC chip, see the product specification for the Zilog Z8530 Serial Communications Controller.

△ **Developer tip** Unless you need to write your own driver software, it is much easier and safer to use the driver routines and ROM tools provided by the Macintosh Operating System to access the hardware devices in the Macintosh. If you do need to write drivers, you should communicate directly with Apple to obtain technical assistance. See the section "Apple Developer Services," at the end of the Preface. △

▲ **Warning** In the Macintosh IIfx computer, an IOP controls the SCC and handles all communication between the SCC and the main processor. An access by the MC68030 directly to the SCC register space causes a bus error. ▲

The addresses of the SCC control and data registers are given in Table 10-2 as offsets from the constant sccWBase for writes, or sccRBase for reads. These base addresses are also available in the global variables SCCWr and SCCRd.

■ **Table 10-2** Addresses of SCC registers

Location	Register
sccWBase+aData	Write Data register A
sccRBase+aData	Read Data register A
sccWBase+bData	Write Data register B
sccRBase+bData	Read Data register B
sccWBase+aCtl	Write Control register A
sccRBase+aCtl	Read Control register A
sccWBase+bCtl	Write Control register B
sccRBase+bCtl	Read Control register B

Note: On the Macintosh models with MC68000 microprocessors, using the address offsets shown in this table automatically supplies the correct even or odd address for each access.

△ **Developer tip** On the Macintosh Plus and earlier Macintosh models, it is necessary to let the SCC lines stabilize for 2.2 μs between accesses. On later models, it is not necessary to do so because the general logic IC (GLU or BBU) delays the acknowledge signal (/DTACK or /DSACK0) until the SCC lines have stabilized. △

On Macintosh models with MC68000 microprocessors, you must use even-addressed byte-wide accesses to read data from the SCC and odd-addressed byte-wide accesses to write data to the SCC. Although the SCC is on only the upper byte of the data bus, this scheme works because the MC68000 CPU reads from the upper byte of the data bus when reading from an even address, and puts the same data on both bytes of the data bus when writing to an odd address. A byte-wide read from an odd address resets the SCC.

△ **Developer tip** In Macintosh models with MC68000 microprocessors, be careful never to make a word-wide access to the SCC. A word-wide access to any SCC address causes a phase shift in the processor clock in those models (a feature used by the operating system during system startup to ensure correct RAM-access timing). An incorrect phase shift causes an unstable video display, RAM errors, and VIA errors. △

Serial I/O interface circuit diagrams

Although all current Macintosh models use the same SCC IC and external connectors for serial I/O, the serial I/O interface is not implemented in the same way in all of them. This section shows the circuit diagrams for the different implementations. Figures 10-2 through 10-6 are circuit diagrams for the serial I/O interface on the following models of Macintosh computers:

- Macintosh Plus: Figure 10-2
- Macintosh SE: Figure 10-3
- Macintosh SE/30: Figure 10-5
- Macintosh Portable: Figure 10-4
- Macintosh II: Figure 10-5
- Macintosh IIx: Figure 10-5
- Macintosh IIcx: Figure 10-5
- Macintosh IIci: Figure 10-5
- Macintosh IIfx: Figure 10-6

- **Figure 10-2** Circuit diagram of the serial I/O interface in the Macintosh Plus computer

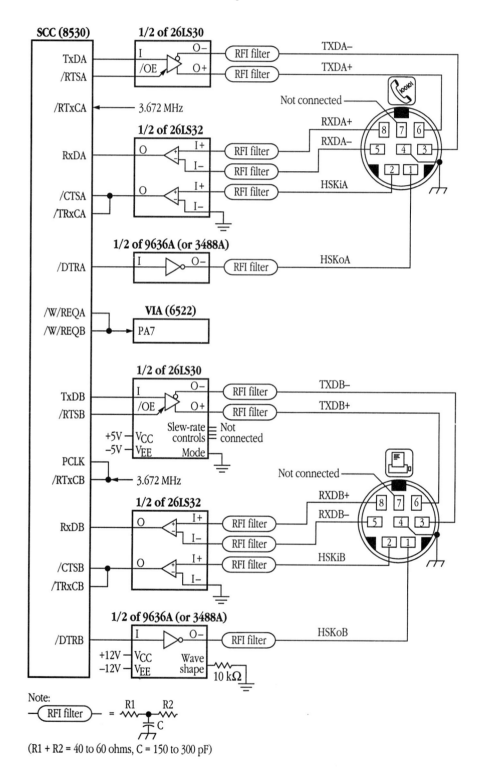

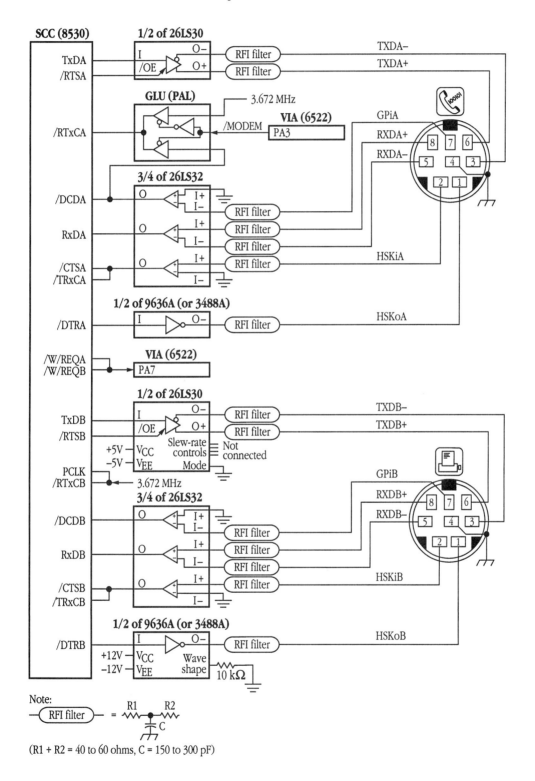

■ **Figure 10-3** Circuit diagram of the serial I/O interface in the Macintosh SE computer

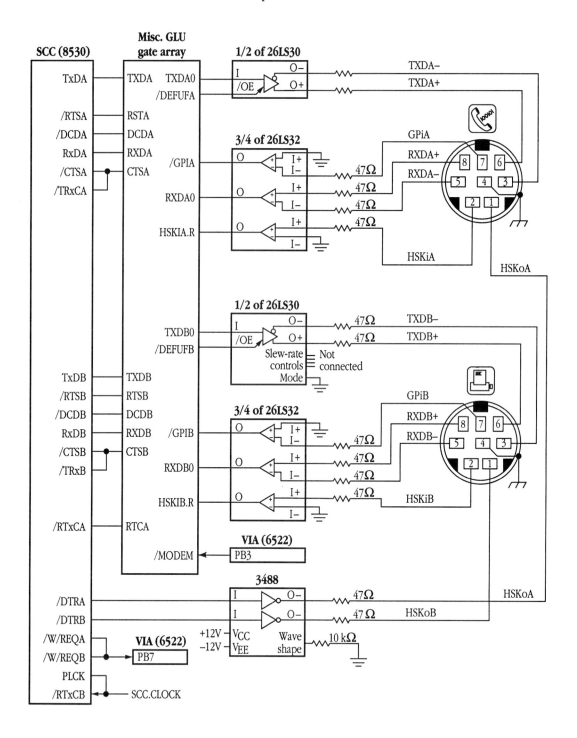

Circuit diagram of the serial I/O interface in the Macintosh SE/30, Macintosh II, Macintosh IIx, Macintosh IIcx, and Macintosh IIci computers

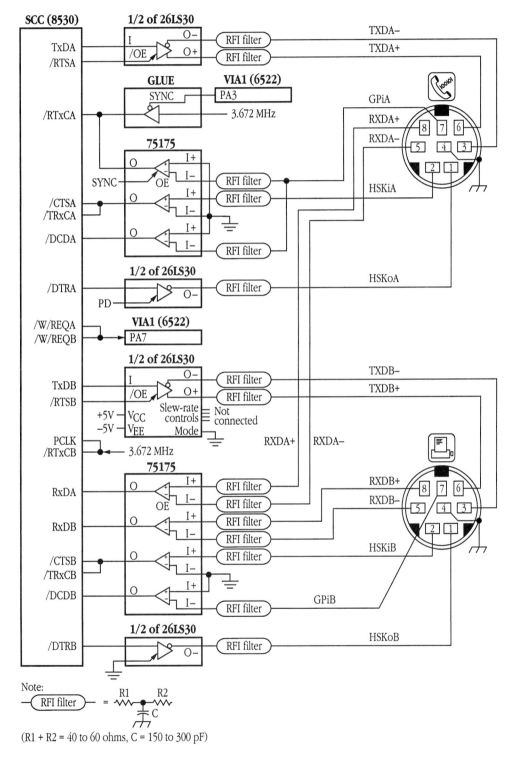

Note:
—(RFI filter)— = R1 R2 ...with C

(R1 + R2 = 40 to 60 ohms, C = 150 to 300 pF)

Figure 10-6   Circuit diagram of the serial I/O interface in the Macintosh IIfx computer

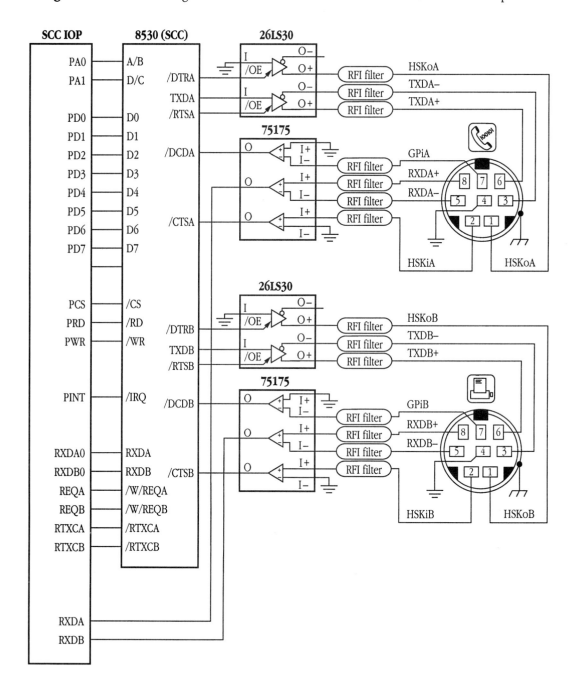

Modem slot in the Macintosh Portable

The Macintosh Portable can assign its internal modem slot to serial I/O channel A, the modem port. Figure 10-8 (on the next page) shows the hardware interface between serial channel A and the modem expansion slot in the Macintosh Portable.

The modem slot in the Macintosh Portable is an 18-pin dual in-line socket connector on the main circuit board. The data is at CMOS levels (that is, V_{IL} = 0 to 0.8 V; V_{IH} = 3.5 V to V+; I_{OL} = 1.6 mA; I_{OH} = –25 μA). Figure 10-7 shows the pinouts of the modem connector. Table 10-3 gives the signal names and functional descriptions.

■ **Figure 10-7** Pinout of the modem connector on the Macintosh Portable computer

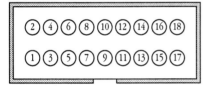

■ **Figure 10-8** Circuit diagram of the modem interface on the
Macintosh Portable computer

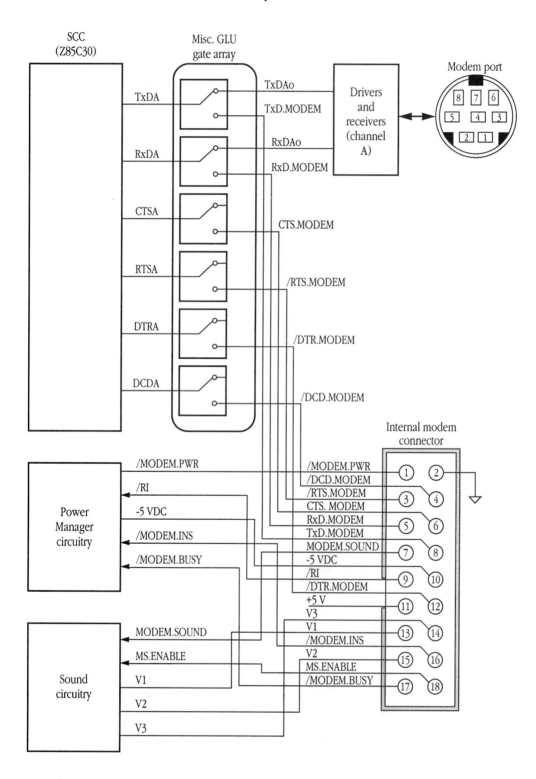

■ **Table 10-3** Signal assignments for the modem connector in the
Macintosh Portable computer

Pin number	Signal name	Signal direction	Signal description
1	/MODEM.PWR	Output	Active-low signal from the Power Manager IC; see the next section "Modem Power Control."
2	GND	—	Ground
3	/RTS	Output	Request to Send signal from the computer to the modem
4	/DCD	Input	Data Carrier Detect; the behavior of the Data Carrier Detect signal depends on the state of the &C command.
5	RxD	Input	Data Received; data received by the computer from the modem.
6	CTS	Input	Clear to Send; asserted by the modem whenever it has power.
7	MODEM.SOUND	Input	Analog sound; output from the modem
8	TxD	Output	Transmit Data; data and commands transmitted from the computer to the modem.
9	/RI	Input	Ring Detect Interrupt; the signal to the computer that a ring is present. If the computer is in the sleep state, assertion of this signal causes the computer to return to the operating state and power-up the modem.
10	–5 VDC*	—	–5 volt power; the –5 volt supply is guaranteed to be present whenever the /MODEM.PWR signal is asserted. This signal may float or go to ground any time following the negation of /MODEM.PWR.
11	+5 VDC	—	VCC power; whenever the host has power available, this pin supplies +5.2 VDC ± 5%.
12	/DTR	Output	Data Terminal Ready; the behavior of the Data Terminal Ready signal depends on the state of the &D command.
13	V1	Output	Least significant volume-control bit. This signal may remain high following the negation of /MODEM.PWR.
14	V3	Output	Most significant volume-control bit. This signal may remain high following the negation of /MODEM.PWR.
15	V2	Output	Second volume-control bit. This signal may remain high following the negation of /MODEM.PWR.
16	/MODEM.INS	Input	Modem Installed; always asserted by the modem while the modem is installed in the computer.
17	/MODEM.BUSY	Input	Modem Busy; asserted by the modem when the modem is busy.
18	MS.ENABLE	Input	Modem Sound Enable; asserted by the modem to enable the computer's speaker.

*Power on pin 10 is controlled by the Power Manager IC.

Modem power control

Control of the power to the modem slot is signaled by the lines /MODEM.PWR and /MODEM.BUSY. A modem card can use the /MODEM.BUSY signal to indicate to the CPU that any of the following is true:

■ The modem is executing its power-up sequence.

■ The modem is off-hook (for any reason).

■ The modem is executing a command, where command execution begins with the carriage return at the end of an AT command sequence or the repeat-last-command sequence (a/ or A/).

If the modem is executing any of its self-tests, it is considered to be executing a command and therefore busy.

The Power Manager IC controls the /MODEM.PWR signal. If /MODEM.PWR is negated (high), the modem must immediately initiate its power-off sequence regardless of what it is doing. The modem must enter its sleep state within 500 ms following the negation of /MODEM.PWR; by that time the modem must reduce its power consumption to meet the maximum power limitation for sleep state. The modem can also use that 500 ms to set its outputs to a default state and store its operating parameters and register values so that it can restore them when operation resumes. Two of the lines to the modem, /DTR and TxD, go to ground potential within 50 ns of the negation of /MODEM.PWR. While the computer is in the sleep state, the volume-control bits, V1, V2, and V3, are floating.

◆ *Note:* On Apple's modem card for the Macintosh Portable, the CTS line is always asserted (pulled high) because flow control is not provided. The /RI signal always reflects the status of the incoming ring signal. The /RTS signal, which is meaningless in full-duplex operation, is not connected. When /MODEM.PWR is negated and the modem card prepares itself for the sleep state, the card forces two of its outputs high (/DCD and RxD) and one of its outputs low (MS.ENABLE).

Usually, the Power Manager IC does not negate /MODEM.PWR if the modem has /MODEM.BUSY asserted. However, there are times when the Power Manager IC must turn the modem off even though it is busy; for example, when the battery reserve is too low. If this occurs, the modem must stop its activity (for example, go on-hook) and perform the necessary activities to prepare for switching to its sleep state. If the modem is executing a command when /MODEM.PWR is negated, the modem can do one of two things before switching to its sleep state: either finish executing the command, or abort execution and restore the state prior to the command, whichever takes the least amount of time.

Chapter 11 **SCSI Ports**

All current models of the Macintosh have the Small Computer System Interface (SCSI). The Macintosh Plus computer has an external SCSI parallel port. All other current Macintosh models have both internal and external SCSI ports. On models with internal SCSI ports, an internal hard disk, if present, is connected to the SCSI port.

- external SCSI port only: Macintosh Plus computer
- internal and external SCSI ports: Macintosh SE, Macintosh SE/30, Macintosh Portable, Macintosh II, Macintosh IIx, Macintosh IIcx, Macintosh IIci, and Macintosh IIfx computers

This chapter describes the hardware used in the SCSI interfaces, gives pinouts for the internal and external connectors, and provides some information about how software communicates with the SCSI devices. The chapter concludes with a brief description of SCSI data transfers.

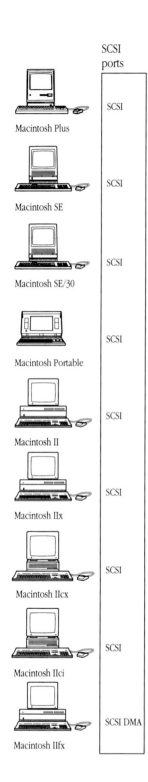

SCSI
ports

SCSI

Macintosh Plus

SCSI

Macintosh SE

SCSI

Macintosh SE/30

SCSI

Macintosh Portable

SCSI

Macintosh II

SCSI

Macintosh IIx

SCSI

Macintosh IIcx

SCSI

Macintosh IIci

SCSI DMA

Macintosh IIfx

Using the Small Computer System Interface (SCSI)

All current Macintosh models provide a high-speed parallel communication port controlled by an NCR 5380 Small Computer System Interface (SCSI) IC. The NCR 5380 is capable of communicating with up to seven SCSI peripheral devices such as the Apple Hard Disk SC, other SCSI hard disk drives, streaming tape drives, and high-speed printers.

△ **Developer tip** This chapter does not contain information about the internal operation of the SCSI controller ICs (5380 and SCSI DMA) used in the Macintosh computers. Apple recommends that applications use the routines and ROM tools provided by the Macintosh system software and described in *Inside Macintosh* to communicate with hardware devices. If you are developing a device that requires its own SCSI driver, you should communicate directly with Apple to obtain technical assistance. See the section "Apple Developer Services," at the end of the Preface. △

All current Macintosh models have an external SCSI port: a DB-25 connector located on the back panel for attaching SCSI peripheral devices. In addition, all Macintosh models except the Macintosh Plus and earlier models have an internal connector, connected in parallel with the external one, for attaching an internal SCSI hard disk drive. The internal SCSI connector is a 50-pin flat-ribbon connector (except on the Macintosh Portable, which uses a 34-pin internal SCSI connector).

The Macintosh SCSI port interface can be used to implement all of the protocols, arbitration, interconnection, and other features of the IEEE SCSI standard, defined by the ANSI X3T9.2 committee. For more information on the SCSI standard, consult the IEEE specification: Section D, ANSIX3T9.2 (Version 17B).

Each device on the SCSI bus has a unique device ID from 0 through 7; the ID of the Macintosh computer is always 7 and the ID of the internal SCSI device—if one is installed—is always 0.

If the SCSI network has any peripheral devices connected, at least one set of termination resistors must also be connected. The SCSI network uses open-collector logic, and the termination resistors are required to bring the SCSI bus lines up to their correct inactive levels of approximately 3 volts.

If an internal SCSI device is installed in the computer, a set of termination resistors is also installed, either in or near the internal SCSI device. An external SCSI device may contain built-in termination resistors, or—more commonly—it may require an external set of termination resistors called a *termination block*.

If an internal or external device does not provide termination resistors, at least one termination block must be installed at the appropriate location in the SCSI network. A SCSI network with multiple peripheral devices, or more than approximately 3 feet of total cable length, may require two sets of termination resistors: one set at either end of the SCSI network.

▲ **Warning**   Never connect more than two sets of termination resistors to a Macintosh SCSI network. Connecting more than two sets of termination resistors will overload the NCR 5380 line drivers. Keep in mind that any Macintosh computer that has an internal SCSI hard disk already has one set of termination resistors installed. ▲

The termination block receives its power from the Terminator Power (TPWR) pin on the SCSI connector.

◆ *Note:* Because of power supply limitations, the Macintosh Plus and the Macintosh Portable do not provide power for termination resistors at the SCSI connector. If you want your SCSI device to be usable with those machines, the device must provide power for the termination resistors.

The DB-25 external SCSI connectors on the Macintosh computers do not match the ANSI X3T9.2 standard, which calls for a 50-pin flat-ribbon connector. Even though the external connectors use only 25 pins, all the ANSI X3T9.2–defined signals and control lines are available; only the extra ground lines have been removed (except on the Macintosh Plus and Macintosh Portable models, where the termination power line was also removed).

The standard 50-pin connector is used for internal SCSI devices in all Macintosh models that support SCSI except the Macintosh Portable, which uses a 34-pin internal connector. The signals on the DB-25 external connector are identical to the corresponding signals on the internal connector. The internal and external connectors are wired in parallel, both controlled by the same NCR 5380 IC; there is no difference in data transfer rate or device performance between the two connectors.

◆ *Note:* If a SCSI peripheral device requires a standard 50-pin connector, the user can attach an Apple adapter cable to connect the external DB-25 connector to a standard 50-pin connector.

SCSI connectors

Macintosh computers use different connectors for internal and external SCSI devices.

External SCSI connector

Figure 11-1 shows the pinout for the DB-25 external SCSI connector, located on the back panel of the computer.

▲ **Warning**   Do not connect an RS-232 device to the DB-25 SCSI port connector. The SCSI interface uses standard TTL logic levels of 0 and +5 volts, whereas RS-232 devices can impose levels of –25 and +25 volts on some lines. These voltage levels will damage the NCR 5380 IC on the computer's main logic board. ▲

■ **Figure 11-1** Pinout of the external SCSI connector on the Macintosh computers

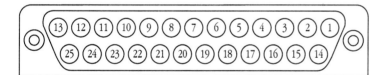

Table 11-1 shows the signal assignments for the SCSI DB-25 external connector. These signals are described in detail in the *NCR 5380 SCSI Interface Chip Design Manual* and the IEEE specification: Section D, ANSIX3T9.2 (Version 17B).

■ **Table 11-1** Signal assignments for the external SCSI connector on the Macintosh computers

Pin number	Signal name	Signal description
1	/REQ	Request for a REQ/ACK data transfer handshake
2	/MSG	Indicates the message phase
3	/I/O	Controls the direction of data movement
4	/RST	SCSI data bus reset
5	/ACK	Acknowledge for a REQ/ACK data transfer handshake
6	/BSY	Indicates whether SCSI data bus is busy
7	GND	Ground
8	/DB0	Bit 0 of SCSI data bus
9	GND	Ground
10	/DB3	Bit 3 of SCSI data bus
11	/DB5	Bit 5 of SCSI data bus
12	/DB6	Bit 6 of SCSI data bus
13	/DB7	Bit 7 of SCSI data bus
14	GND	Ground
15	/C/D	Indicates whether control or data is on the SCSI bus
16	GND	Ground
17	/ATN	Indicates an attention condition
18	GND	Ground
19	/SEL	Selects a target or an initiator
20	/DBP	Parity bit for SCSI data bus
21	/DB1	Bit 1 of SCSI data bus
22	/DB2	Bit 2 of SCSI data bus
23	/DB4	Bit 4 of SCSI data bus
24	GND	Ground
25	TPWR	+5 volts terminator power*

*On the Macintosh Plus, this pin is not connected. On other Macintosh models, this line is provided for powering termination resistors only, not for powering SCSI devices.

Internal SCSI connector

Figure 11-2 shows the pinout for the 50-pin flat-ribbon internal SCSI connector used in all models except the Macintosh Portable.

Table 11-2 shows the signal assignments for the SCSI 50-pin flat-ribbon internal connector. These signals are described in detail in the *NCR 5380 SCSI Interface Chip Design Manual* and the IEEE specification: Section D, ANSIX3T9.2 (Version 17B).

■ **Figure 11-2**   Pinout of the internal SCSI connector on the Macintosh computers

■ **Table 11-2**   Signal assignments for the internal SCSI connector on the
Macintosh computers

Pin number	Signal name	Signal description
1	GND	Ground
2	/DB0	Bit 0 of SCSI data bus
3	GND	Ground
4	/DB1	Bit 1 of SCSI data bus
5	GND	Ground
6	/DB2	Bit 2 of SCSI data bus
7	GND	Ground
8	/DB3	Bit 3 of SCSI data bus
9	GND	Ground
10	/DB4	Bit 4 of SCSI data bus
11	GND	Ground
12	/DB5	Bit 5 of SCSI data bus
13	GND	Ground
14	/DB6	Bit 6 of SCSI data bus
15	GND	Ground
16	/DB7	Bit 7 of SCSI data bus
17	GND	Ground
18	/DBP	Parity bit for SCSI data bus

(continued)

■ Table 11-2   Signal assignments for the internal SCSI connector in the
Macintosh computers (continued)

Pin number	Signal name	Signal description
19	GND	Ground
20	n.c.*	Not connected*
21	GND	Ground
22	n.c.*	Not connected*
23	GND	Ground
24	n.c.*	Not connected*
25	GND	Ground
26	TPWR	+5 volts termination power
27	GND	Ground
28	n.c.*	Not connected*
29	GND	Ground
30	n.c.*	Not connected*
31	GND	Ground
32	/ATN	Indicates an attention condition
33	GND	Ground
34	n.c.*	Not connected*
35	GND	Ground
36	/BSY	Indicates whether SCSI data bus is busy
37	GND	Ground
38	/ACK	Acknowledge for a REQ/ACK data transfer handshake
39	GND	Ground
40	/RST	SCSI data bus reset
41	GND	Ground
42	/MSG	Indicates the message phase
43	GND	Ground
44	/SEL	Selects a target or an initiator
45	GND	Ground
46	/C/D	Indicates whether control or data is on the SCSI bus
47	GND	Ground
48	/REQ	Request for a REQ/ACK data transfer handshake
49	GND	Ground
50	/I/O	Controls the direction of data movement

*Pins 20, 22, 24, 28, 30, and 34 are connected to ground on the Macintosh SE and Macintosh II.

Internal SCSI connector in the Macintosh Portable

Figure 11-3 shows the pinout for the 34-pin flat-ribbon internal SCSI connector used in the Macintosh Portable computer.

■ **Figure 11-3** Pinout of the internal SCSI connector in the Macintosh Portable computer

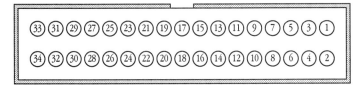

Table 11-3 shows the signal assignments for the SCSI 34-pin internal connector in the Macintosh Portable computer. These signals are described in detail in the *NCR 5380 SCSI Interface Chip Design Manual* and the IEEE specification: Section D, ANSIX3T9.2 (Version 17B).

Pin number	Signal name	Signal description
1	/REQ	Request for a REQ/ACK data transfer handshake
2	GND	Ground
3	/MSG	Indicates the message phase
4	/C/D	Indicates whether control or data is on the SCSI bus
5	/I/O	Controls the direction of data movement
6	GND	Ground
7	/ACK	Acknowledge for a REQ/ACK data transfer handshake
8	/ATN	Indicates an attention condition
9	/BSY	Indicates whether SCSI data bus is busy
10	/RST	SCSI data bus reset
11	GND	Ground
12	/SEL	Selects a target or an initiator
13	/DBP	Parity bit for SCSI data bus
14	/DB0	Bit 0 of SCSI data bus
15	/DB1	Bit 1 of SCSI data bus
16	GND	Ground
17	/DB2	Bit 2 of SCSI data bus
18	/DB3	Bit 3 of SCSI data bus
19	/DB4	Bit 4 of SCSI data bus
20	/DB5	Bit 5 of SCSI data bus
21	/DB6	Bit 6 of SCSI data bus
22	/DB7	Bit 7 of SCSI data bus
23	+5V	+ 5V power
24	+5V	+ 5V power
25	+12V	+12V power
26	+12V	+12V power
27	GND	Ground
28	GND	Ground
29	GND	Ground
30	GND	Ground
31	+12V	+12V power
32	+12V	+12V power
33	+5V	+ 5V power
34	+5V	+ 5V power

Circuit diagrams of the SCSI interface

While the SCSI interface is functionally the same on all Macintosh models, there are differences in details, as shown in the circuit diagrams on the following pages. Figures 11-4 through 11-9 are circuit diagrams for the following models of Macintosh computers:

- Macintosh Plus: Figure 11-4
- Macintosh SE: Figure 11-5
- Macintosh SE/30: Figure 11-8
- Macintosh Portable: Figure 11-6
- Macintosh II: Figure 11-7
- Macintosh IIx: Figure 11-8
- Macintosh IIcx: Figure 11-8
- Macintosh IIci: Figure 11-8
- Macintosh IIfx: Figure 11-9

■ **Figure 11-4** Circuit diagram of the SCSI interface on the
Macintosh Plus computer

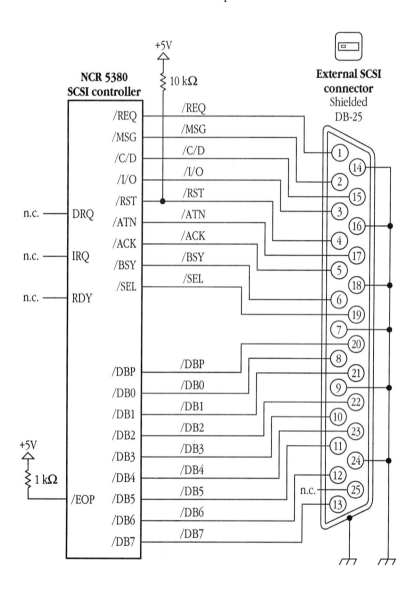

Figure 11-5 Circuit diagram of the SCSI interface on the Macintosh SE computer

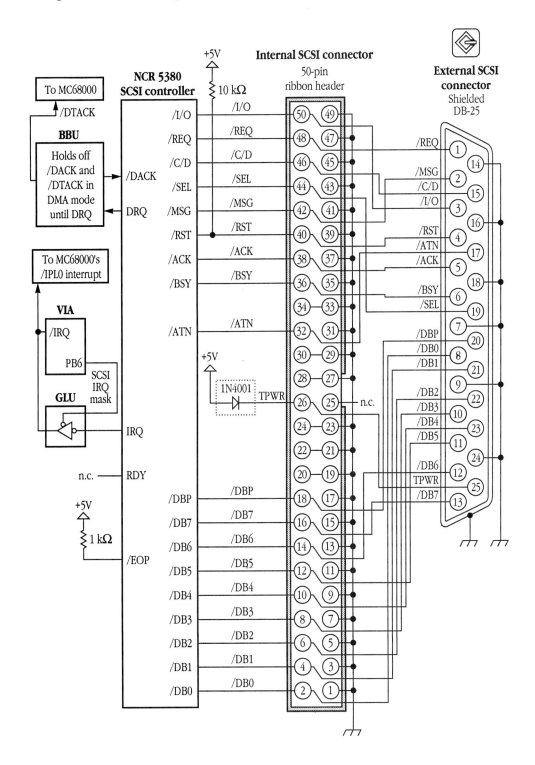

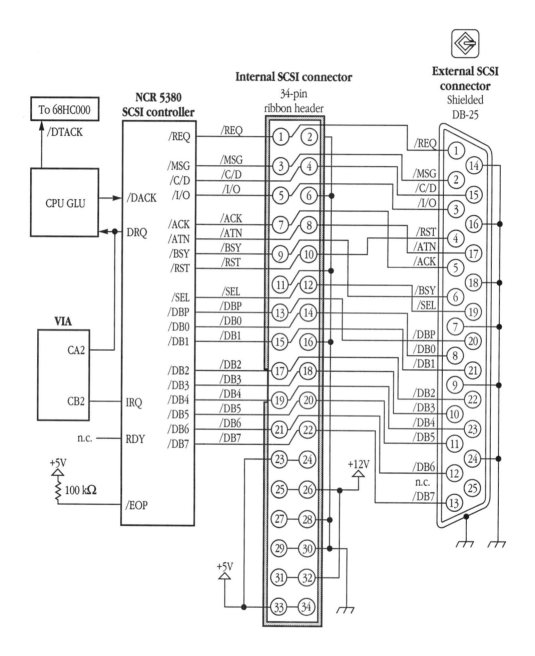

■ **Figure 11-6** Circuit diagram of the SCSI interface on the Macintosh Portable computer

■ **Figure 11-7** Circuit diagram of the SCSI interface on the Macintosh II computer

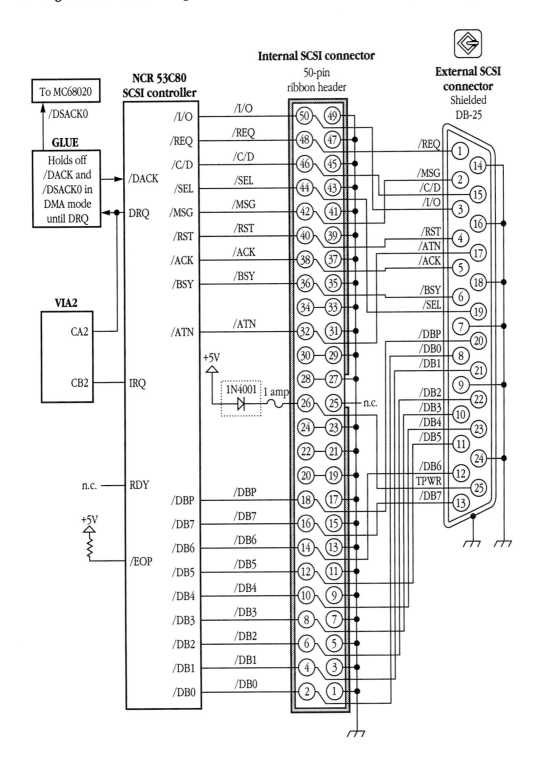

Figure 11-8 Circuit diagram of the SCSI interface on the Macintosh SE/30, Macintosh IIx, Macintosh IIcx, and Macintosh IIci computers

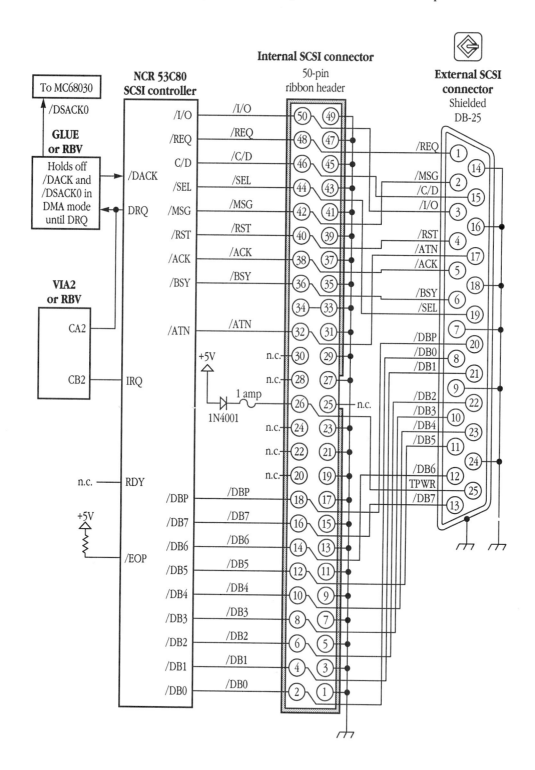

■ **Figure 11-9** Circuit diagram of the SCSI interface on the Macintosh IIfx computer

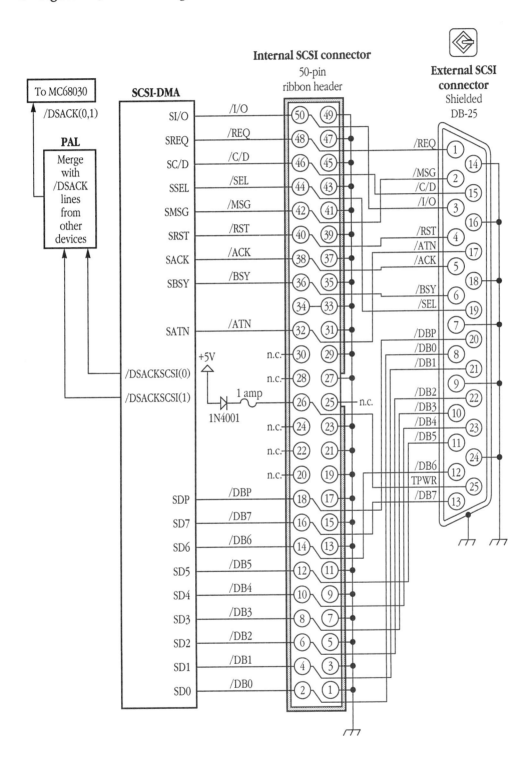

SCSI data transfers

SCSI data transfers are controlled by the CPU and performed by the NCR 5380 SCSI controller IC. The SCSI controller can operate in three modes: normal mode, pseudo-DMA mode, and true DMA mode. In normal mode, the SCSI driver software has to manage all the handshaking necessary to communicate with a peripheral SCSI device. In pseudo-DMA mode, the SCSI controller's internal logic automatically handles all the SCSI handshake signals. (All three modes are described in detail in NCR's documentation for the 5380.)

The SCSI controller's normal mode is always used for commands; also, a SCSI driver can use normal mode to perform SCSI bus data transfers if the peripheral device requires nonstandard handshaking or nonstandard timing of handshaking signals. Because pseudo-DMA mode transfers are faster and easier to implement, however, most SCSI drivers perform SCSI bus data transfers in pseudo-DMA mode.

◆ *Note:* DMA stands for *direct-memory access.* Macintosh models other than the Macintosh IIfx do not support true direct-memory access by the SCSI controller, but they do support the SCSI controller's pseudo-DMA mode. For a description of true DMA operation of the SCSI interface in the Macintosh IIfx, please refer to the section "SCSI DMA in the Macintosh IIfx Computer" later in this chapter.

In a typical SCSI data transfer, the CPU first uses the SCSI controller's normal mode to set up a block transfer of information, and then uses pseudo-DMA mode to carry out the actual transfer of data. Once the data transfer has begun, the SCSI controller uses the DRQ bit in its Bus and Status register to indicate when it has received a byte from, or written a byte to, the peripheral device.

The CPU can use either of two methods to respond: polling or blind transfer. In the polling method, the SCSI driver polls the DRQ bit in normal mode to determine when each byte is ready to be read or written; then the actual read or write is performed in pseudo-DMA mode. In the blind transfer method, the Bus and Status register is checked in normal mode only to determine when the first byte of a block is ready to be transferred; the remaining bytes in the block are read or written in pseudo-DMA mode at the maximum rate possible for the interface.

Handshaking for SCSI data transfers

All Macintosh models since the Macintosh Plus—that is, the Macintosh SE,
Macintosh SE/30, Macintosh Portable, Macintosh II, Macintosh IIx, Macintosh IIcx,
Macintosh IIci, and Macintosh IIfx—include hardware handshaking in pseudo-DMA mode
to prevent the CPU from reading invalid data or writing data faster than the peripheral can
accept it. The handshaking is handled by the computer's general logic IC, which does not
complete each byte transfer until the SCSI controller's DRQ line goes high. This
handshaking makes read and write operations safe in pseudo-DMA mode, even when using
the blind transfer method.

◆ *Note:* The different Macintosh models use a different general logic IC to control the
SCSI: the BBU in the Macintosh SE computer; the CPU GLU in the Macintosh Portable;
the GLUE in the Macintosh SE/30, Macintosh II, Macintosh IIx, and Macintosh IIcx;
and the MDU in the Macintosh IIci. In the Macintosh IIfx, the SCSI DMA IC controls all
SCSI functions except interrupts, which are handled by the OSS. The next section
describes the SCSI DMA in the Macintosh IIfx.

On all models more recent than the Macintosh Plus, if the read or write operation over the
SCSI bus is not completed within certain time (different for different machines), the
general logic IC asserts a bus error (/BERR) to the CPU. This timeout does not occur in the
Macintosh Plus, whose SCSI operations never wait for DRQ.

On Macintosh models with two VIAs, the IRQ line from the NCR 5380 goes to VIA2. If
enabled by the appropriate bit in the VIA2 Interrupt Enable register, the IRQ line causes a
VIA2 interrupt to the CPU. This interrupt can be used for bus disconnect and reconnect
operations and to indicate bus errors.

On Macintosh models with two VIAs, the DRQ line also goes to VIA2 (as well as to the
GLUE IC). If enabled by the appropriate bit in the VIA2 Interrupt Enable register, the DRQ
line causes a VIA2 interrupt to the CPU. This interrupt can be used to initiate a data
transfer for an interrupt-driven operating system like A/UX.

On the Macintosh IIci, both the IRQ and DRQ signals from the 5380 are stored in the
Interrupt Flags register in the VIA2 portion of the RBV. As on Macintosh models with two
VIAs, the SCSI controller's IRQ and DRQ signals can be used to generate appropriate
interrupts to the main processor.

On the Macintosh IIfx, the IRQ and DRQ signals from the SCSI DMA are stored in the
Interrupt Flags register in the OSS. Under the control of the system software, the OSS uses
the IRQ and DRQ signals to generate appropriate interrupts to the main processor.

On Macintosh models that have an MC68020 or MC68030, the CPU uses longword instructions for reading and writing to the SCSI controller, thus taking advantage of the dynamic bus sizing feature to achieve a faster data transfer rate. Because the CPU can tell by the /DSACK0 and /DSACK1 signals that the SCSI controller has an 8-bit data bus, it makes four back-to-back 8-bit data transfers for each longword. Transmission of each byte can be delayed until permitted by the hardware handshaking. On those Macintosh models, the approximate maximum SCSI transfer rate within a block is 1.4 MB per second for blind transfers.

△ **Developer tip** In the Macintosh Plus computer, neither of the NCR 5380 interrupt signals (IRQ and DRQ) is connected to the CPU: there is no hardware handshaking on the SCSI port. Instead, software must poll the Bus and Status register in the NCR 5380 to detect interrupt requests. Approximate maximum SCSI transfer rates within a block are 170 KB per second for polled transfers and 263 KB per second for blind transfers. △

SCSI DMA in the Macintosh IIfx computer

In the Macintosh IIfx, an Apple custom integrated circuit, the SCSI DMA, provides the functions of the SCSI controller. In addition to providing all the features and functions of the 53C80 IC, the SCSI DMA IC can handle data transfers to and from the main memory by direct-memory access (DMA).

Some features of the SCSI DMA IC include

- built-in 53C80 SCSI adapter
- DMA bypass mode for compatibility with software written for the 53C80
- hardware handshake mode (software-controlled data transfer with no polling for available bytes)
- DMA transfers of 32-bit longwords
- direct addressing of the entire memory (32 address lines)
- block transfers of up to 4 GB
- support for misaligned data buffer addresses (nonzero modulo 4)
- asynchronous data transfer rate of 3 MB per second
- automatic SCSI bus arbitration as well as program-controlled arbitration

Only data transfers are handled by the DMA channel; SCSI bus protocol is under the control of software running on the main processor. The main processor sends control and command bytes to the SCSI DMA IC a byte at a time. Using DMA, data transfers usually consist of four bytes (32 bits) at a time.

Operation of the SCSI DMA IC

Using the SCSI DMA IC, only data transfers are handled by the DMA channel; SCSI bus protocol is under the control of software running on the main processor, just as it is on other Macintosh models. In addition, the SCSI DMA IC on the Macintosh IIfx can also function as a conventional SCSI interface and transfer data under the control of the main processor.

The SCSI DMA IC has four modes of operation: slave mode, master mode, test mode, and reset mode. Slave and master modes are the modes used in normal operation of the Macintosh IIfx computer.

Slave mode

The main processor uses slave mode to set up the registers on the SCSI DMA IC and to transfer data to and from the IC. The main processor reads and writes to the IC's registers by reading or writing to the address space assigned to the SCSI DMA IC. In slave mode, the main processor communicates with the SCSI DMA IC in the same way that it does with any other asynchronous memory controller.

△ **Developer tip** Existing drivers that don't use hardware handshaking will run on the Macintosh IIfx as is. Drivers that do use hardware handshaking must be modified to set up the SCSI DMA for hardware handshaking in order to run on the Macintosh IIfx. △

Master mode

The SCSI DMA IC uses master mode to perform DMA data transfers. In master mode, the SCSI DMA IC uses the normal bus-arbitration procedures of the MC68030 to transfer data to and from main memory without assistance from the MC68030.

To initiate a DMA transfer, the SCSI driver writes control information to the DMA address counter and DMA Byte Count register on the SCSI DMA IC and then writes to one of the IC's start registers.

The SCSI DMA IC handles addresses that are nonzero modulo 4 by adjusting for them on the first and last MC68030 bus transfer. Similarly, the SCSI DMA IC handles byte counts that are nonzero modulo 4 by adjusting for them on the first and last MC68030 bus transfer. The SCSI DMA IC keeps track of the number of bytes transferred and places the data in the correct byte lanes as it is transferred to or from memory.

Chapter 12 **Displays**

Different Macintosh models provide different displays. Some machines have both the display device and the display circuits built in, as in the original Macintosh. Other models require an expansion card for the video circuits and an external video monitor. The Macintosh IIci, which has built-in display circuits for an external monitor, can also use a video expansion card.

The types of displays used on the different models are as follows:

- built-in display circuits and CRT display: Macintosh Plus, Macintosh SE, and Macintosh SE/30 computers

- built-in display circuits and flat-panel display: Macintosh Portable computer

- video expansion card and external monitor: Macintosh II, Macintosh IIx, Macintosh IIcx, and Macintosh IIfx computers

- built-in display circuits for an external monitor, or video expansion card: Macintosh IIci computer

For the Macintosh models that have built-in video display devices and circuits, this chapter describes the video signals generated on the main logic board and the use of the video buffers in RAM. For the Macintosh SE/30, this chapter also describes the way the display is functionally similar to a video card in an expansion slot.

For the Macintosh models that require a video card in an expansion slot, this chapter describes the Macintosh II Video Card as a typical example.

For the Macintosh Portable, this chapter describes the flat-panel display and provides information about its interface to an optional external video display.

Display

Macintosh Plus — Built-in B&W video

Macintosh SE — Built-in B&W or exp. card

Macintosh SE/30 — Built-in B&W or exp. card

Macintosh Portable — Flat panel or ext. video

Macintosh II — B&W or color on exp. card

Macintosh IIx — B&W or color on exp. card

Macintosh IIcx — B&W or color on exp. card

Macintosh IIci — Built-in B&W or color, or exp. card

Macintosh IIfx — B&W or color on exp. card

Built-in video display

The Macintosh Plus, Macintosh SE, and Macintosh SE/30 (and earlier Macintosh models) have built-in video circuits and a built-in monitor. The video display on those machines is an array of black and white pixels approximately 4.6 by 7 inches. This section describes that display and the hardware that generates it.

◆ *Note:* The built-in display on the Macintosh SE/30 computer has the same appearance as that on the Macintosh Plus and Macintosh SE computers—black and white, 512 by 342 pixels—but the hardware that generates it has some of the features of a video expansion card. For a description of a video expansion card, please refer to the next major section, "Expansion Card Video"; for information about the way the Macintosh SE/30 emulates an expansion card, refer to the next major section after that, "Video Display in the Macintosh SE/30 Computer."

⚠ **Developer tip** Macintosh models that accept a processor-direct expansion card can support a video display card and an external monitor in addition to their built-in display (Macintosh SE and Macintosh SE/30 models). The Macintosh Portable computer can also support an external monitor. The system software supports multiple displays as parts of an extended desktop. ⚠

Video display scanning

The video display is created by a moving electron beam that scans across the screen, turning on and off as it scans in order to create black and white pixels. Each pixel is a square, approximately 1/72 inch on a side.

To create a screen image, the electron beam starts at the upper-left corner of the screen (see Figure 12-1). The beam scans horizontally across the screen from left to right, creating the top line of graphics. When it reaches the last pixel on the right end of the top line, it turns off and continues past the last pixel to the physical right edge of the screen. Then it flicks invisibly back to the left edge, moving down one scan line. After tracing across the black border, it begins displaying the data in the second scan line. The time between the display of the rightmost pixel on one line and the leftmost pixel on the next is called the **horizontal blanking interval.**

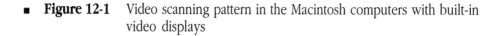

■ **Figure 12-1**　Video scanning pattern in the Macintosh computers with built-in video displays

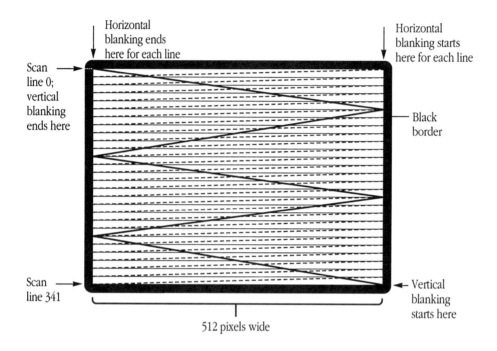

When the electron beam reaches the last pixel of the last (342nd) line on the screen, it traces out to the right edge and then moves back up to the upper-left corner (continuing to scan horizontally several times as it does so). There it traces the left border and then begins once again to display the top line. The time between the last pixel on the bottom line and the first one on the top line is called the *vertical blanking interval.* At the beginning of the vertical blanking interval, the VIA generates a vertical blanking interrupt (VBL).

◆ *Note:* On the Macintosh SE/30 (as well as all models that do not have a built-in display) the VBL interrupt is driven by a 60.15 Hz clock and is not synchronous with the blanking of the screen. See the next major section, "Expansion Card Video," for information about synchronizing software with vertical blanking on those models.

The pixel clock rate (the frequency at which pixels are displayed) is 15.6672 MHz, or about 0.064 μs per pixel. For each scan line, 512 pixels are drawn on the screen, requiring 32.68 μs. The horizontal blanking interval takes the time of an additional 192 pixels, or 12.25 μs. Thus, each full scan line takes 44.93 μs, making the horizontal scan rate 22.25 kHz.

The visible portion of a full-screen display consists of 342 horizontal scan lines and requires 15367.65 μs, or about 15.37 ms, to scan. During the vertical blanking interval, the turned-off beam—while moving from the bottom of the screen back to the top—invisibly traces out an additional 28 scan lines, taking 1258.17 μs or about 1.26 ms to do so. This means the full frame is redisplayed every 370 scan lines, or once every 16625.8 μs. That's about 16.6 ms per frame and makes the vertical scan rate (the full-screen display frequency) equal to 60.15 Hz.

Video display circuits

The video generator uses 21,888 bytes of RAM to compose a bit-mapped video image 512 pixels wide by 342 pixels tall. Each bit in this range controls a single pixel in the image: a 0 bit is white, and a 1 bit is black.

◆ *Note:* The display on the Macintosh SE/30 model has the same appearance as that on the Macintosh Plus and Macintosh SE computers, but the hardware that generates it is quite different. For a description of the display hardware on the Macintosh SE/30, please refer to the next two major sections, "Expansion Card Video" and "Video Display in the Macintosh SE/30 Computer."

Two areas of memory are reserved for use by the video circuitry: the main screen buffer and the alternate screen buffer. A bit in VIA Data register A determines which screen buffer is read by the video circuitry.

To make a video access to RAM, the general logic circuits (PAL in the Macintosh Plus, BBU in the Macintosh SE) first disable the RAM data bus buffers so that the main processor cannot read data from the RAM, and then generate a RAM address in the video-screen-buffer range. Next, the general logic circuits switch the RAM address MUXs to put the video address they generate onto the address bus, rather than the address generated by the processor. When the RAMs respond by putting the video data on the RAM data bus, the general logic circuits signal the Video Shift register on the main logic board to take the data and send it in a serial stream to the video display circuits.

During a video-data access, the general logic circuits in the Macintosh Plus and earlier models read one word from RAM and store the data in the Video Shift register. The circuits in the Macintosh SE read two consecutive words during a video access. The main processor then has full access to the RAM during the time it takes the video circuits to send the 16 bits or 32 bits of data to the screen. The main processor also has full access to RAM during horizontal and vertical blanking.

◆ *Note:* On the Macintosh SE, Macintosh Plus, and earlier Macintosh models, the general logic circuits use one access to RAM during each horizontal scan line to read sound and disk-speed data. For more information, please refer to Chapter 13, "Sound."

Video display buffers

The starting addresses of the screen buffers depend on the amount of memory installed in the system. The base address of the main screen buffer is stored in the global variable ScrnBase and the base address of the alternate screen buffer is ScrnBase – $8000. The base address of the bit map currently being displayed on the screen is available in the QuickDraw™ global variable ScreenBits.

⚠ **Developer tip** To ensure that your software will run on Macintosh computers that use different display hardware, you should never write directly to the screen buffer, but always use QuickDraw calls to send data to the screen. ⚠

Each scan line of the screen displays the contents of 32 consecutive words of memory, each word controlling 16 horizontally adjacent pixels. In each word, the high-order bit (bit 15) controls the leftmost pixel and the low-order bit (bit 0) controls the rightmost pixel. The first word of data for each scan line follows the last word for the line above it. The starting address of the screen is thus in the upper-left corner, and the addresses progress from there to the last byte in the extreme lower-right corner.

The screen is refreshed frequently enough that the video display normally doesn't flicker. However, the display may appear to flicker if the electron beam displays the image when your program hasn't finished updating it, showing some of the new image and some of the old in the same frame. This effect can become noticeable when you're creating an animated image by repeatedly drawing the graphics in quick succession.

One way to prevent flickering when you're updating the screen repeatedly is to use the vertical blanking interrupt (VBL) to synchronize your updates to the scanning of video memory. Small changes to your screen can be completed entirely during the interval between frames (the first 1.26 ms following a vertical blanking interrupt), when nothing is being displayed on the screen. To find out how to specify tasks to be performed during a vertical blanking interval, see the chapter on the Vertical Retrace Manager in *Inside Macintosh*.

When making larger changes, the trick is to keep your changes happening ahead of the spot being displayed by the electron beam. If you start changing your image when the vertical blanking interrupt occurs, you have 1.26 ms of unrestricted access to the image. After that, you can change progressively less and less of your image as it's scanned onto the screen, starting from the upper-left corner (the lowest video memory address). From the vertical blanking interrupt, you have only 1.26 ms in which to change the first (lowest address) screen location, but you have almost 16.6 ms to change the last (highest address) screen location.

Notice that changes you make in the memory already passed over by the scan spot won't appear until the next frame.

Another way to create smooth, flicker-free graphics, especially useful with changes that may take more than 16.6 ms, is to use the two screen buffers as alternate displays. If you draw into the one that's currently not being displayed, and then switch the buffers during the next vertical blanking interval, your graphics will change all at once, producing a clean animation.

To use the alternate screen buffer, you have to specify that choice to the Segment Loader as described in *Inside Macintosh*. To switch to the alternate screen buffer, clear bit 6 of VIA Data register A to 0. To switch back to the main buffer, set the same bit to 1. The VIA is described in Chapter 4. The alternate screen buffer is not available in all Macintosh models.

△ **Developer tip** The VBL interrupt is guaranteed to be synchronized with the screen's vertical blanking interval only in Macintosh models that use the built-in video display described above. On Macintosh models with other types of displays, the VBL interrupt is replaced by the 60.15 Hz interrupt that is used for general timing functions. In those machines, the Vertical Retrace Manager maintains a separate VBL queue for each slot and executes the tasks in each queue when the corresponding slot interrupt occurs. Please refer to *Inside Macintosh* for information about the Vertical Retrace Manager. △

Expansion card video

The Macintosh II family of computers—except for the Macintosh IIci—do not contain any built-in video electronics. Instead, those machines use a video expansion card in a NuBus slot to produce a display on an external video monitor. The Macintosh IIci, which has built-in video circuits, can also use a video expansion card.

The standard video expansion card available from Apple Computer, Inc., is called the Macintosh II Video Card and is fully described in *Designing Cards and Drivers for the Macintosh Family,* second edition. To show how such cards operate, this section provides a brief overview of the Macintosh II Video Card. Other video expansion cards are different in detail, but operate in a similar fashion.

△ **Developer tip**   Macintosh models that use video expansion cards can support multiple cards and multiple monitors. The system software supports multiple displays as parts of an extended desktop. △

Video card features

The Macintosh II Video Card is a high-performance color video card that provides the following features:

- support for several different screen sizes
- up to 256 colors out of 16 million possible
- support for 1-bit, 2-bit, 4-bit, and 8-bit per pixel display modes
- frame buffer sizes of 256 KB and 512 KB, upgradable by the user
- full support for RS-170 video monitors
- ability to recognize different monitors at startup time and automatically configure itself appropriately
- video driver with software support for compatibility with genlock and overlay devices
- full support for A/UX system software in the card's ROM

◆ *Note:* An early version of the Macintosh II Video Card did not have the last five features in this list.

Video card components

The Macintosh II Video Card contains the following components:

- timing generation circuitry
- Frame Buffer Controller (FBC, also called TFB)
- video RAM
- color look-up table and digital-to-analog converter (CLUT DAC)
- declaration ROM

The following sections describe these components.

△ **Developer tip** To ensure that your software will run on Macintosh computers with different screen sizes and different video cards, you should always use QuickDraw calls to address the screen. △

Timing generation

The timing generation circuitry on the video card generates these signals:

- the Frame Buffer Controller interface signals, including the video card clock
- the NuBus handshake and control signals
- other video card control signals

The Macintosh II Video Card generates a NuBus slot interrupt corresponding to the vertical blanking signal used on the video card. The Vertical Retrace Manager uses this signal to maintain a separate VBL queue for each slot, executing the tasks in each queue when the corresponding slot interrupt occurs. By making use of this feature of the Vertical Retrace Manager, applications can make changes to the display during the vertical blanking interval, thereby avoiding flicker. For more information, please refer to the chapter on the Vertical Retrace Manager in *Inside Macintosh*.

Frame Buffer Controller (FBC)

The **Frame Buffer Controller** (FBC) is an Apple custom IC that controls the operation of the video card. The FBC contains several control registers that are mapped into Macintosh II main memory in the slot space assigned to the video card. The control address space is separate from the frame buffer address space occupied by the video RAM.

The FBC uses the parameters stored in the control registers to generate and control video data and timing signal output. The various inputs on the FBC are used to execute RAM read, write, and refresh operations.

Video RAM

The Macintosh II Video Card has its own RAM so that the video circuitry does not have to share RAM access time with the main processor. Both the main processor and the video display must have access to this RAM—that is how the processor puts display data into the video memory. To make that possible, the video card uses a special dual-ported RAM that allows the video data to be sent to the display at the same time that the processor is writing new data to memory. The main processor has access to video RAM more than 95 percent of the time. The base address of the bitmap currently being displayed on the screen is available in the QuickDraw global variable ScreenBits.

The video RAM consists of eight or sixteen 256 Kbit, 150 ns RAM ICs for a memory configuration of 256 KB or 512 KB.

CLUT DAC on the video card

One IC contains the **color look-up table** (CLUT) and the **digital-to-analog converter** (DAC). Working together, the CLUT and DAC make up the electrical interface between the video RAM and the video monitor. Digital video data is passed to the CLUT through the FBC. The CLUT expands the digital data (1-bit, 2-bits, 4-bits, or 8-bits per pixel) to 24-bit-per-pixel RGB color values by means of a table in its own RAM (hence the name *color look-up table*). The 24-bit RGB color values comprise three 8-bit values that correspond to the intensities of the red, green, and blue primary colors for each pixel.

The digital-to-analog converter (DAC) portion of the CLUT DAC IC comprises three 8-bit DACs that convert the digital RGB color values to analog color signals. The DACs provide RS-343-A–compatible RGB video signals to the video connector at the rear of the video card.

Color QuickDraw software initializes the color-table RAM within the CLUT with default color values, using the video driver loaded from the declaration ROM (see the next section). Color QuickDraw also uses the video driver to provide utilities for reading and modifying the color table.

Declaration ROM

Every NuBus card includes ROM, called **declaration ROM,** that contains all the information required for the Macintosh II system software to identify and make use of the capabilities of that card. Some Apple publications refer to the declaration ROM as the *configuration ROM.* The information in the declaration ROM for the Macintosh II Video Card includes

- device type (video card), manufacturer (Apple), and model number
- specifications of the predefined video modes
- video driver code
- initialization code

The declaration ROM in the Macintosh II Video Card identifies the card as a video device manufactured by Apple and specifies its model number. The declaration ROM also provides a list of predefined video modes and the specifications of the displays for each mode.

Many of the operating parameters of the video card are programmable; as a result, the number of possible video modes is enormous. A useful subset, optimized for the Apple displays, is included in the declaration ROM. The list characterizing each video mode also specifies a software driver, specific to the card hardware and also stored in the declaration ROM, that is loaded into main memory by the Slot Manager at startup time.

The declaration ROM also includes special code, called *initialization code,* that is executed at startup time to initialize both the hardware on the card and the system software that will be using the card. The initialization code performs such tasks as selecting the appropriate pixel clock rate for the display monitor connected to the video card, checking the amount of video RAM on the card, and providing the Slot Manager and Color Quickdraw with information about the size of the display and the amount of memory available.

External connector

The Macintosh II Video Card has a DB-15 connector at the rear of the card that provides the video output signals for the video monitor. The pinout of this connector is shown in Figure 12-2.

■ **Figure 12-2**   Pinout of the external connector on the Macintosh II Video Card

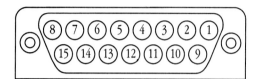

The signal assignments for the video card's external connector are listed in Table 12-1.

■ **Table 12-1**   Signal assignments for the external connector of the
              Macintosh II Video Card

Pin number	Signal name	Signal description
1	RED.GND	Red ground
2	RED.VID	Red video signal
3	/CSYNC	Composite synchronization signal
4	SENSE0	Monitor sense signal 0
5	GRN.VID	Green video signal
6	GRN.GND	Green ground
7	SENSE1	Monitor sense signal 1
8	n.c.	Not connected
9	BLU.VID	Blue video signal
10	SENSE2	Monitor sense signal 2
11	C&VSYNC.GND	Ground for CSYNC and VSYNC
12	/VSYNC	Vertical synchronization signal
13	BLU.GND	Blue ground
14	HSYNC.GND	HSYNC ground
15	/HSYNC	Horizontal synchronization signal

◆ *Note:* The external video connector on the early version of the Macintosh II Video Card
did not have the signals SENSE0, SENSE1, and SENSE2.

Detecting monitor type

The initialization code in the declaration ROM reads the state of the three sense lines to determine the type of monitor that is connected to the card. Table 12-2 shows the values of the sense lines and the different monitor types.

■ **Table 12-2**   Sense line values for different types of monitors

Sense line values	Monitor type
000	(Reserved by Apple)
001	Portrait monitor (monochrome)
010	(Reserved by Apple)
011	Two-page monitor (monochrome)
100	(Reserved by Apple)
101	(Reserved by Apple)
110	640 × 480-pixel monitor (monochrome or RGB)
111	(No monitor connected)

Video display in the Macintosh SE/30 computer

Although the Macintosh SE/30 computer has a built-in black-and-white video display identical in appearance to the built-in display on a Macintosh Plus or Macintosh SE, its video interface hardware simulates some features of a Macintosh II Video Card in a NuBus expansion slot, making it considerably different from the built-in video hardware in other Macintosh models.

The main logic board of the Macintosh SE/30 contains a separate 64 KB video display RAM and a separate 8192-byte video declaration ROM. The video display RAM occupies physical address space $FE00 0000 to $FEFF FFFF. This address space was chosen because it is the same as the address space used by expansion slot $E in the Macintosh II family.

The use of expansion-slot address space and other features of a NuBus video expansion card is called *pseudo-slot video*. By simulating the features of an expansion card in a NuBus slot, the Macintosh SE/30 can share common system ROM with the other Macintosh models that use the MC68030 processor and NuBus video cards.

The pseudo-slot video on the Macintosh SE/30 has the following features:

- 512 × 342 black and white pixels, like other Macintosh built-in video displays
- 60.15 Hz video frame rate, like other Macintosh built-in video displays
- independent RAM: 64 KB of RAM containing two screen buffers

The video buffer occupies RAM that is separate from the main memory. The video buffer uses the address multiplexing method described in the section "Built-in Video Display," earlier in this chapter.

Like the Macintosh II Video Card, the pseudo-slot video has a declaration ROM containing a video driver and initialization routines. Because pseudo-slot video in the Macintosh SE/30 supports only the built-in black-and-white monitor, it does not need a programmable video timing controller or a color look-up table.

Video circuits in the Macintosh IIci computer

In addition to the NuBus slots that can accept a video expansion card, the Macintosh IIci computer also has built-in video circuits to drive an external video monitor. The built-in video circuits support the standard-size Macintosh II monitors, either monochrome or color, and the Macintosh Portrait Display.

Features of the built-in video circuits

The features of the built-in video circuits include

- screen sizes of 640 × 480 and 640 × 870 pixels
- 1, 2, 4, and 8 bit-per-pixel displays with 640 × 480 monitors
- 1, 2, and 4 bit-per-pixel displays with 640 × 870 monitors
- detection of type of monitor connected and setting of appropriate display parameters
- memory addresses in slot $B of NuBus address space
- accessibility as pseudo-slot video in slot $0

Detection of monitor type

The Macintosh IIci can detect monitors with different display sizes, such as the AppleColor High-Resolution RGB Monitor (640 × 480 pixels) and the Macintosh Portrait Display (640 × 870). Apple monitors for the Macintosh include three sense lines that enable the computer to determine the monitor type. At startup time, logic in the RBV reads the sense lines and sets the display parameters to the appropriate values for the monitor that is connected. See the section "Video Connector on the Macintosh IIci," later in this chapter, for information about the sense lines.

Pixels and colors

The number of bits per pixel determines the number of different colors (with a color monitor) or the number of different shades of gray (with a monochrome monitor) in the video display. With 1 bit per pixel, the display is black and white. With 2 bits per pixel, the display has 4 colors or black, white, and 2 shades of gray. With 4 bits per pixel, the display has 16 colors or shades of gray (again including black and white). With 8 bits per pixel, a monochrome display can have 256 shades of gray; a color display can have 256 colors on the screen at a time. No matter how many bits per pixel are being used, the displayed colors or shades of gray are selected from a palette of over 16 million possible colors or shades that can be specified by 24-bit color values.

Sizes of monitors and screen buffers

The amount of memory required for the screen buffer depends on the size of the monitor screen and the number of bits per pixel used for the display. Table 12-3 shows the different screen sizes and screen-buffer sizes for the Apple monitors that the Macintosh IIci supports.

■ **Table 12-3** Screen sizes and buffer sizes supported by the Macintosh IIci computer

Name of monitor	Screen size (in pixels)	Buffer size for given pixel size			
		1 bpp	2 bpp	4 bpp	8 bpp
High-Resolution Monochrome Monitor	640 × 480	38 KB	75 KB	150 KB	300 KB
AppleColor High-Resolution RGB Monitor	640 × 480	38 KB	75 KB	150 KB	300 KB
Macintosh Portrait Display	640 × 870	68 KB	136 KB	272 KB	—*

*The built-in video circuits on the Macintosh IIci do not support 8 bpp on the portrait display.

◆ *Note:* The MDU in the Macintosh IIci allocates memory for the screen buffer in increments of 32 KB, so it takes 64 KB for 1 bit per pixel on a monochrome monitor, 320 KB for a color monitor with 8 bits per pixel.

Pseudo-slot video in the Macintosh IIci

Like the built-in video in the Macintosh SE/30, the video interface hardware in the Macintosh IIci simulates some features of a Macintosh II Video Card in a NuBus expansion slot. By simulating the features of an expansion card in a slot, the Macintosh IIci can share common system ROM with the other Macintosh models that use the MC68030 processor. This simulation of a video card in a NuBus slot is called *pseudo-slot video.*

The video screen buffer in the Macintosh IIci occupies memory starting at $0000 0000 in physical address space. Using the memory management unit in the MC68030, the Macintosh IIci maps the screen buffer to logical address space starting at $FB00 0000. That address space was chosen because it is the same as the address space used by expansion slot $B in the six-slot models of the Macintosh II family.

Built-in video components

The main components of the built-in video circuits in the Macintosh IIci are

- screen buffer in bank A
- the MDU, which generates video addresses
- data bus buffers, which separate bank A from the processor's data bus
- the RBV, which formats video data and provides synchronization signals
- the CLUT DAC, color look-up table and digital-to-analog converter
- a video connector for an external monitor

Because the operation of RAM bank A, the MDU, and the data-bus buffers is so interdependent, those three components are described together in the next section. Subsequent sections describe each of the other components.

Screen buffer in the Macintosh IIci

Three components work together to provide the video screen buffer in the Macintosh IIci: bank A of RAM, the MDU, and the data-bus buffers. In principle, the operation of the screen buffer is somewhat like that of the screen buffers in the Macintosh Plus and other models with built-in displays: The screen buffer occupies main memory and there is a bus buffer to disconnect that portion of memory from the main processor.

The screen buffer in the Macintosh IIci occupies 300 KB at the bottom of RAM bank A. The system software programs the memory management unit in the MC68030 to map the remainder of bank A as part of main memory.

◆ *Note:* The Macintosh IIci maps the portion of bank A used for main memory so that its logical address space appears above the memory in bank B. Even though the *physical* addresses of RAM bank B start at $0400 0000, the *logical* addresses start at $0000 0000, as required for software compatibility.

The MDU deals with addresses both for the main processor and for the video display circuits. Any time an address from the processor is in some portion of the address map other than bank A, the MDU can generate the multiplexed address signals for the processor's memory access and generate a video address in bank A at the same time. Whenever the MDU is about to make a video access to RAM, it sends a signal to the bus buffers causing them to disconnect the data bus for bank A from the processor so that both accesses can take place without interference.

If the main processor starts a memory access to RAM bank A while the MDU is making a video access, the main processor must wait. The probability of this happening depends on two components: the probability that a main-processor memory access is in bank A, and the probability that an access to the screen buffer is occurring at the same time.

The first probability—whether a main-processor memory access is in bank A—depends on the relative amounts of main memory in bank A and bank B. The more RAM there is in bank B, the greater the probability that the processor will be using bank B. The percentage of the time that the processor needs to access bank A is, on average, the same as the percentage of total main RAM that resides in bank A. The portion of bank A used for the video buffer does not count as main RAM; thus, in a machine with 1 MB in each bank, accesses to main RAM in bank A would be about 41 percent of the total.

The second probability—whether an access to the screen buffer is occurring—depends on the size of the monitor and on the number of bits per pixel selected for the display. The probability is larger for larger monitors and greater pixel depths, which require more video data per unit of time. Table 12-4 shows the percentage of the time required for video accesses in bank A for different monitor sizes and pixel depths.

■ **Table 12-4** Time spent making video RAM accesses in bank A

Pixel depth	640 × 480 display	640 × 870 display
1 bpp	6%	13%
2 bpp	13%	26%
4 bpp	26%	65%
8 bpp	64%	—*

*The Macintosh IIci does not support 8 bpp on the 640 × 870 display.

◆ *Note:* Only accesses to RAM bank A are affected by video. The processor has full access to RAM bank B at all times, as it has to ROM and I/O devices.

Video portion of the RBV

The video portion of the RBV contains the circuits that format the video data from RAM into pixel-sized pieces and the circuits that generate the horizontal and vertical video timing. The data-formatting circuits are described first.

The RBV's data-formatting circuits comprise a 16 × 32-bit FIFO buffer, logic to keep the FIFO filled with data from the RAM, and logic to arrange that data and shift it out in the appropriate format. The FIFO operates as two halves, each containing eight 32-bit longwords. While video data from one half of the FIFO is being arranged and shifted out, the other half of the FIFO is being loaded with data from the screen buffer.

Whenever data in one half of the FIFO is used up, the RBV asserts its data-request line to the MDU. That signal tells the MDU to disconnect the bank A data bus from the main processor and to begin a page-mode burst read of RAM data as soon as possible. As each longword of video data is read onto the bank A portion of the data bus, the MDU sends a data-load signal to the RBV. The data-load signal causes the RBV to read one 32-bit longword of data from the bus into the FIFO and to advance the input pointer to the next location in the FIFO. When the RBV has read seven longwords, it deasserts its data-request line, which causes the MDU to end the data burst after it has read the eighth longword and sent it to the RBV. That sequence of events fills the empty half of the FIFO.

Meanwhile, in the other half of the FIFO, eight longwords of data are being loaded, sixteen bits at a time, into a shift register. A dot clock causes the data to advance through the shift register one bit at a time. The shift register has output taps every two bits along its length. By using one, two, four, or all eight of these taps, the logic circuits in the RBV can make the data appear at the outputs in the required pixel size: one, two, four, or eight bits at a time. When all sixteen bits have been shifted out, the logic ciruits load the next sixteen bits from the FIFO into the shift register and advance the FIFO's output pointer. This process eventually empties the FIFO half, which must then be filled by another burst of eight longwords from the video RAM.

The RBV's video timing circuits generate the dot clock that advances the video data through the shift register and count out the appropriate number of dots per line. The video timing circuits also control the number of lines in the display and the timing of the synchronization pulses. The video timing circuits do all that based on the type of monitor connected to the computer, which the RBV determines by reading the sense lines from the video connector.

Tables 12-5 and 12-6 give the horizontal and vertical timing specifications for the video signals produced by the RBV in the Macintosh IIci. Figure 12-3 shows the horizontal and vertical video waveforms and identifies the parameters whose specifications are given in the tables.

■ **Table 12-5**   Horizontal video timing in the Macintosh IIci computer

Parameter	640 × 480 display	640 × 870 display
Dot clock	30.24 MHz	57.28 MHz
Dot time	33.07 ns	17.46 ns
Line rate	35.0 kHz	68.85 kHz
Line time	28.57 μs	14.52 μs
Full line	864 dots	832 dots
Visible line	640 dots	640 dots
Horizontal blanking	224 dots	192 dots
Front porch	64 dots	32 dots
Horizontal synchronization pulse	64 dots	80 dots
Back porch	96 dots	80 dots

■ **Table 12-6**   Vertical video timing in the Macintosh IIci computer

Parameter	640 × 480 display	640 × 870 display
Line rate	35.0 kHz	68.85 kHz
Line time	28.57 μs	14.52 μs
Frame rate	66.67 Hz	75.0 Hz
Frame time	15.00 ms	13.33 ms
Full frame	525 lines	918 lines
Visible frame	480 lines	870 lines
Vertical blanking	45 lines	48 lines
Front porch	3 lines	3 lines
Vertical synchronization pulse	3 lines	3 lines
Back porch	39 lines	42 lines

■ **Figure 12-3** Video timing parameters

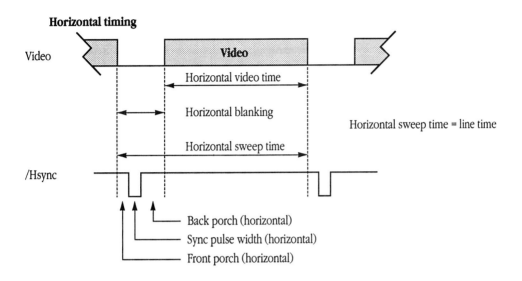

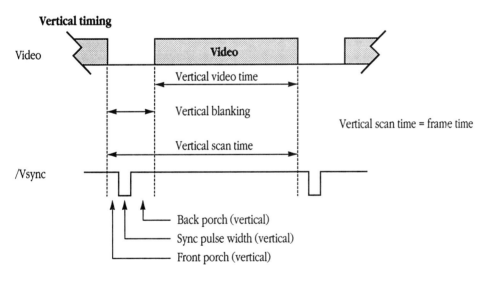

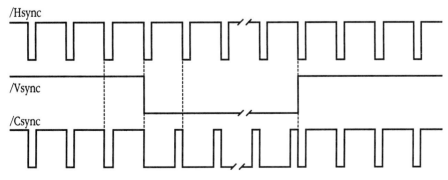

CLUT DAC in the Macintosh IIci

The CLUT (color look-up table) and the video DAC (digital-to-analog converter) are two parts of a single integrated circuit, the Brooktree Bt478. The CLUT converts each pixel value to three 8-bit color values; the DAC converts those digital values into voltage levels that are sent to the video monitor.

The CLUT DAC is the interface between the screen buffer and the video monitor. Digital video data is sent to the CLUT from the screen buffer in RAM bank A. The video RAM addresses are generated by the MDU under the control of the RBV.

The CLUT translates the digital data from the screen buffer to 24-bit color values by means of a table in its own RAM (hence the name *color look-up table*). Each color value comprises three 8-bit values, one each for red, green, and blue. The built-in digital-to-analog converters (DACs) convert the three 8-bit digital color values to three analog color signals. Each of the three DACs takes an 8-bit color value and produces the analog video signal for one of the three primary colors: red, green, or blue. The outputs of the DACs provide RS-343-A–compatible RGB video signals to the video connector at the rear of the computer.

As shown in Figure 12-4, the three color signals for the video monitor are produced by the Bt478, while the horizontal and vertical synchronization signals come directly from the RBV.

Video connector on the Macintosh IIci

The video connector on the Macintosh IIci is a 15-pin D-type connector like the one on the Macintosh II Video Card. It provides the red, blue, and green video output signals and the composite sync signal along with the three sense lines that the computer uses to determine the type of monitor that is connected. Table 12-7 shows the signals on the video connector. Table 12-8 shows the values of the sense lines corresponding to the different types of monitors supported by the Macintosh IIci.

♦ *Note:* The video connector on the Macintosh IIci is the same as the one on the Macintosh II Video Card and has the same signal assignments.

■ **Figure 12-4** Video interface circuit in the Macintosh IIci

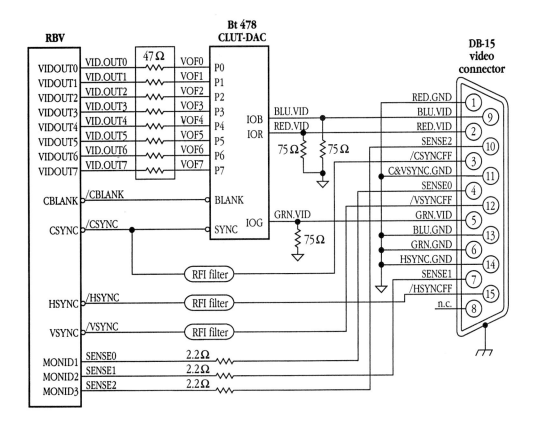

Note:

─(RFI filter)─ = ─\/\/\─•─||─
              R1   C

(R = 180 Ω, C = 33 pF)

■ **Table 12-7**   Signals on the video connector in the Macintosh IIci

Pin number	Signal name	Signal description
1	RED.GND	Red ground
2	RED.VID	Red video signal
3	/CSYNC	Composite synchronization signal
4	SENSE0	Monitor sense signal 0
5	GRN.VID	Green video signal
6	GRN.GND	Green ground
7	SENSE1	Monitor sense signal 1
8	n.c.	Not connected
9	BLU.VID	Blue video signal
10	SENSE2	Monitor sense signal 2
11	C&VSYNC.GND	Ground for CSYNC and VSYNC
12	/VSYNC	Vertical synchronization signal
13	BLU.GND	Blue ground
14	HSYNC.GND	HSYNC ground
15	/HSYNC	Horizontal synchronization signal

■ **Table 12-8**   Sense line values for video monitors on the Macintosh IIci computer

Sense line values	Monitor type
000	(not supported)
001	Portrait-size monitor (monochrome)
010	(reserved)
011	(not supported)
100	(not supported)
101	(reserved)
110	Standard-size monitor (monochrome or RGB)
111	(reserved)

If a type of monitor is connected that the built-in video circuits do not support, or if no external monitor is connected, the system software switches the built-in video circuits off. That is what happens in a Macintosh IIci using a monitor connected to a video card in a NuBus slot.

Displays on the Macintosh Portable

The primary display on the Macintosh Portable computer is a built-in flat-panel display. The Macintosh Portable can also drive an external video monitor with the appropriate adapter.

Flat-panel display

The flat-panel display on the Macintosh Portable gives a high-quality presentation of the screen of the Apple High-Resolution Monochrome Monitor. Display intensity, contrast ratio, and pixel turn-on and turn-off time are similar to the corresponding parameters of a video display using a CRT with P4 phosphor. The flat-panel display has the following features:

- display resolution of 640×400 pixels
- display area of 217 mm × 140 mm (8.5 inches × 5.5 inches)
- active matrix, reflective display
- driving method: 8-bit parallel
- 0.45 watts maximum power dissipation
- CMOS logic interface

The display buffer is a RAM array of 32,000 bytes (768 bytes are reserved by Apple for future use). The starting address of the buffer is in global variable ScrnBase; the last byte in the buffer is at address (ScrnBase) + 31,999. The interface from the MC68HC000 to the video controller IC is nominally 16 bits wide, but like main memory, the buffer is also byte addressable.

△ **Developer tip** For the sake of compatibility, you should never address the display buffer directly, but always use QuickDraw calls or other toolbox calls provided by the system software. △

The contents of the screen buffer are mapped onto the display as a linear array of pixels. The pixel displayed in the upper-left corner of the screen corresponds to the most significant bit of the first byte in the buffer; the pixel displayed in the lower-right corner of the screen is the least significant bit of the last byte. See Figure 12-5.

The display pixel map, Figure 12-5, shows the arrangement of the pixels on the flat-panel display, as viewed facing the display. Pixels are numbered from 1 to 640 in each row. The figure also shows the bit locations in the first and last bytes of the screen buffer; the other bytes in the buffer map to the display in the same fashion.

■ **Figure 12-5** Display pixel map

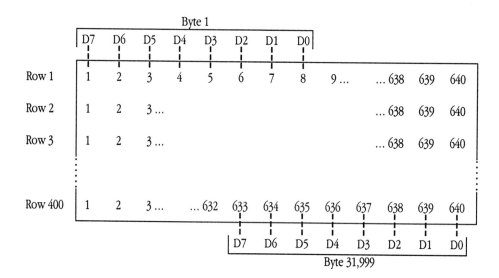

Contrast control

The contrast control output of the Macintosh Portable system is derived from the PWM (pulse-width-modulated) output pin of the Power Manager IC. The modulation has 256 steps, representing the range of screen contrast from low to high as displayed in the Control Panel and set by the user.

The PWM output is filtered to a DC level by an RC network before being sent to the display. The output of the filter has a voltage range from 0.5 to 5 V and less than 100 mV ripple.

Macintosh Portable external video

The Macintosh Portable computer produces signals for an external video display through an 8-bit interface that is similar to the internal interface for the flat-panel display. A video adapter (powered from the external video port) is required in order to convert the 8-bit data stream into a signal that will drive a conventional video monitor. Figure 12-6 shows the external video connector; Table 12-9 lists the signals.

Figure 12-7 shows the timing characteristics of the synchronization signals (M, FLM, CL1, CL2) and data signals (D0–D7) generated by the video controller in the Macintosh Portable. Table 12-10 lists the timing limits indicated in the figure.

The signal named FLM is the vertical synchronization signal; it marks the beginning of a new frame of video. A new frame starts every 16.32 ms, making the frame rate equal to 61.3 Hz. The signal named CL2 is the data byte clock; the video adapter uses the falling edge of CL2 to latch the data signals (D0–D7) into its shift register. The signals named M and CL1 are internal to the video controller; M is generated in the general logic IC by dividing the FLM frequency by two. CL1 is the horizontal synchronization signal; it marks the end of a 640-pixel line.

■ **Figure 12-6**   Pinout of the external video connector on the Macintosh Portable computer

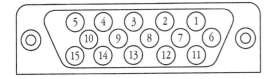

■ **Table 12-9** Signal assignments for the external video connector on the
Macintosh Portable computer

Pin number	Signal name	Description
1	D0	Video data bit 0*
2	D1	Video data bit 1*
3	+5/0V	Positive supply, 0 V in sleep state
4	D2	Video data bit 2*
5	D3	Video data bit 3*
6	D4	Video data bit 4*
7	GND	Ground
8	BATTERY VOLTAGE	Positive battery supply
9	GND	Ground
10	D5	Video data bit 5*
11	D6	Video data bit 6*
12	D7	Video data bit 7*
13	+5/0V	Positive supply, 0 V in sleep state
14	FLM	New frame
15	CL2	Video data clock

*See Figure 12-5 for the display pixel map.

◆ *Note:* The CL1 and M signals shown in Figure 12-7 are internal signals and not on the
external video connector.

■ **Figure 12-7** Timing diagram for external video in the Macintosh Portable computer

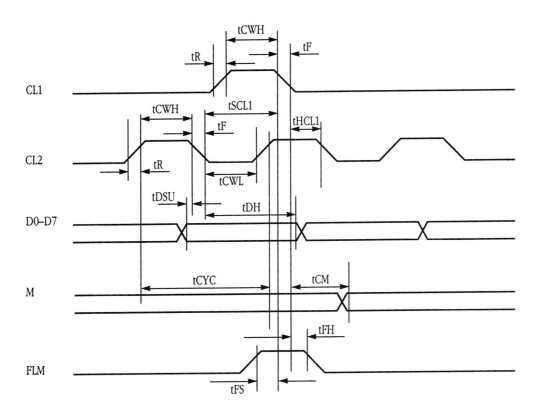

■ **Table 12-10** External video timing limits

Symbol	Description	Min	Max
tCYC	CL2 cycle time	—	190 ns
tCWH	CL2 pulse width (high)	95 ns	—
tCWL	CL2 pulse width (low)	95 ns	—
tR, tF	CL2 rise and fall times	—	30 ns
tDSU	Data setup time	60 ns	—
tDH	Data hold time	—	60 ns
tFS	FLM setup time	100 ns	—
tFH	FLM hold time	100 ns	—

Chapter 13 **Sound**

Different Macintosh models have different hardware for generating sound. All models support the basic sound features produced by the PWM (pulse-width-modulation) sound system on the original Macintosh computer. Recent models use an Apple custom integrated circuit called the *Apple Sound Chip* (ASC) to provide additional features.

The two types of sound hardware used on the different models are

- Macintosh PWM sound system: Macintosh Plus, Macintosh SE

- Macintosh ASC sound system: Macintosh SE/30, Macintosh Portable, Macintosh II, Macintosh IIx, Macintosh IIcx, Macintosh IIci, and Macintosh IIfx

All Macintosh computers produce sound from samples stored in RAM buffers. This chapter describes the sound systems and the use of the sound buffers. It also describes the sound circuits in the different models and discusses the functions of the ASC.

Sound

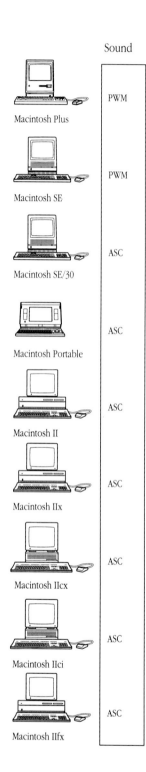

Macintosh Plus — PWM

Macintosh SE — PWM

Macintosh SE/30 — ASC

Macintosh Portable — ASC

Macintosh II — ASC

Macintosh IIx — ASC

Macintosh IIcx — ASC

Macintosh IIci — ASC

Macintosh IIfx — ASC

PWM sound system

The Macintosh models that use the PWM (pulse-width-modulation) sound system are

- Macintosh Plus
- Macintosh SE

The PWM sound stystem is also used on the earlier Macintosh models: Macintosh 128K, Macintosh 512K, and Macintosh 512K enhanced.

The Macintosh PWM sound system consists of these hardware components:

- sound buffers in system RAM
- sound circuitry in the general logic IC (PAL or BBU)
- an analog sound processing IC (the Sony sound chip)
- an internal speaker
- an external mini-phonejack

The PWM sound system takes a series of data values from the sound buffer in RAM and uses them to create a changing waveform in the output signal. That signal drives a small high-impedance speaker inside the computer and is also connected to the external sound jack on the back of the computer. Inserting a plug into the external sound jack disconnects the internal speaker. The external sound jack provides a low-impedance, high-level signal (8 volts peak-to-peak) that can drive a load impedance of 32 ohms or higher.

▲ **Warning**   The signal available at the external sound jack on the Macintosh Plus and Macintosh SE computers is capable of damaging some power amplifiers and can generate dangerous sound levels in headphones. You should use extreme caution when using this signal with amplifiers or headphones. ▲

Sound buffers

The Macintosh Plus and earlier Macintosh computers have two sound buffers; the Macintosh SE computer has only one. The starting addresses of the sound buffers depend on the amount of memory installed in the system. The address of the main sound buffer is stored in the global variable SoundBase and is also available as the constant soundLow. The address of the alternate sound buffer is SoundBase – $5C00.

◆ *Note:* The alternate sound buffer is not available in the Macintosh computers that use the ASC. See the section "ASC Sound System."

Each sound buffer contains 370 words of data. Sound information is stored in the high (even address) byte of each word, and disk-speed information is stored in the low (odd address) byte.

△ **Developer tip** The Macintosh SE, Macintosh Plus, and earlier Macintosh computers use the low-order byte of each word in the sound buffer for controlling the speed of the motor in single-sided floppy disk drives. Don't store any information in those bytes, or you'll interfere with disk control for single-sided drives. △

To use the alternate sound buffer, you have to specify that choice to the Segment Loader as described in *Inside Macintosh*. To switch to the alternate sound buffer, clear bit 3 of VIA Data register A to 0. To switch back to the main buffer, set the same bit to 1. The VIA is described in Chapter 4.

△ **Developer tip** The disk drivers in the Macintosh Plus and earlier Macintosh computers store disk-speed control information for single-sided floppy disk drives only in the main sound buffer. An application with its own sound driver software must switch back to the main sound buffer before accessing a single-sided drive, or the drive won't work properly. △

Generating sounds

By storing a range of values in the sound buffer, you can generate the corresponding waveform in the sound output line. The sound circuitry uses a form of pulse-width encoding to create sounds. The sound circuitry reads one word (16 bits) in the sound buffer during each horizontal blanking interval (including the virtual intervals during vertical blanking) and uses the high-order byte of the word to generate a pulse of electricity whose duration is proportional to the value in the byte. This pulse is sent to the Sony sound chip.

To make a sound access to RAM, the general logic IC (the PAL or the BBU) first disables the RAM data-bus buffers so that the CPU cannot read data from the RAM, and then generates a RAM address in the sound-buffer range. The RAM responds by putting the sound data on the data bus. The general logic IC then converts that data to a square wave. The square wave is a pulse-width-modulated (PWM) signal; that is, the width of each pulse is proportional to the value of a byte of data. The general logic IC sends this train of pulses to the Sony sound chip.

A circuit in the Sony sound chip integrates the train of pulses into a smoothly varying waveform, the amplitude of which is proportional to the pulse width. The amplitude of this signal is then attenuated according to a 3-bit volume-control value from the VIA. After attenuation, the sound signal is passed by the Sony sound chip to the audio output line.

To set the volume directly, store a 3-bit number in the low-order bits of VIA Data register A. You can turn the sound generator on or off by writing 1 (off) or 0 (on) to bit 7 of VIA Data register B. For more information, refer to the section "VIA Registers" in Chapter 4.

△ **Developer tip** The technique described in *Inside Macintosh* for generating square-wave sound by directly controlling a VIA timer can be used on the Macintosh SE, Macintosh Plus, and earlier Macintosh computers, but it does *not* work on the Macintosh SE/30, Macintosh Portable, or the Macintosh II–family computers, and it probably won't work on future Macintosh computers. You can use routines in the Sound Manager described in *Inside Macintosh* to achieve the same effect, with the added advantage that these routines will work on all Macintosh computers, present and future. △

Scanning the sound buffers

The sound circuitry in the Macintosh Plus and Macintosh SE scans the sound buffer at a fixed rate of 370 words per video frame, repeating the full cycle 60.147 times per second (the exact sample rate is 22.2545 kHz). Therefore, if you store one pattern in the sound buffer and do not change it, that pattern is repeated 60.147 times per second to generate the sound signal. To avoid creating an audible discontinuity or glitch each time the pattern is repeated, the pattern must correspond to one or more complete cycles; in other words, the frequency of the waveform must be an integer multiple of the scan rate.

Figure 13-1 illustrates a sine wave that has a frequency of exactly 2 times the scan rate (the period of the sine wave is exactly 1/2 the length of the sound buffer). You can scan such a wave repeatedly without producing glitches. To generate a glitch-free signal with a varying waveform or with a frequency that is not a multiple of the scan rate, you must store new data into the sound buffer between scans. Figure 13-2 illustrates a sine wave whose freqency is not an exact multiple of the scan rate.

■ **Figure 13-1** A sound waveform with a frequency of 2 times the scan rate

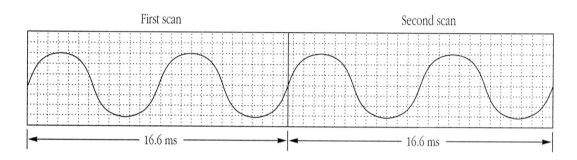

■ **Figure 13-2** A sound waveform with a frequency that is not a multiple of the scan rate

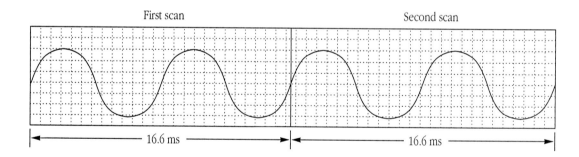

△ **Developer tip**   You can perform your own updates of the sound buffer using the vertical blanking interrupt from the VIA to synchronize your updates to the buffer scan. For the sake of compatibility with different models, Apple recommends that you use the routines in the Sound Driver and the Sound Manager to generate complex sounds. △

Circuit diagrams

Figures 13-3 and 13-4 show block diagrams for the PWM sound circuits used in the Macintosh Plus and Macintosh SE computers. Note that the Macintosh SE has only one sound buffer.

■ **Figure 13-3** Block diagram of the PWM sound circuit in the Macintosh Plus computer

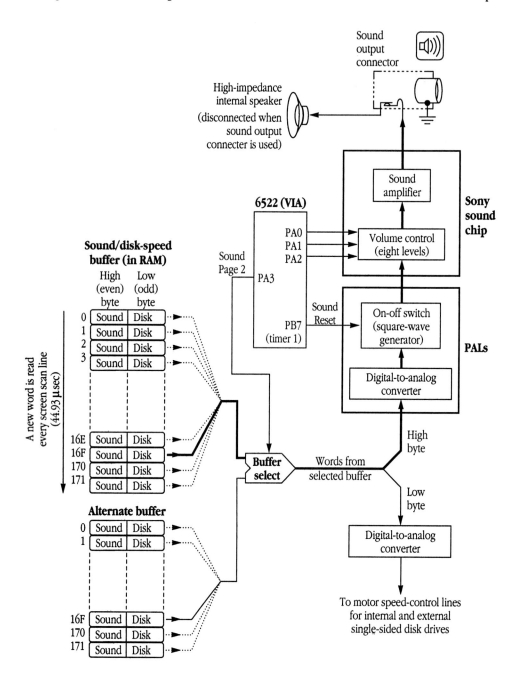

■ **Figure 13-4** Block diagram of the PWM sound circuit in the Macintosh SE computer

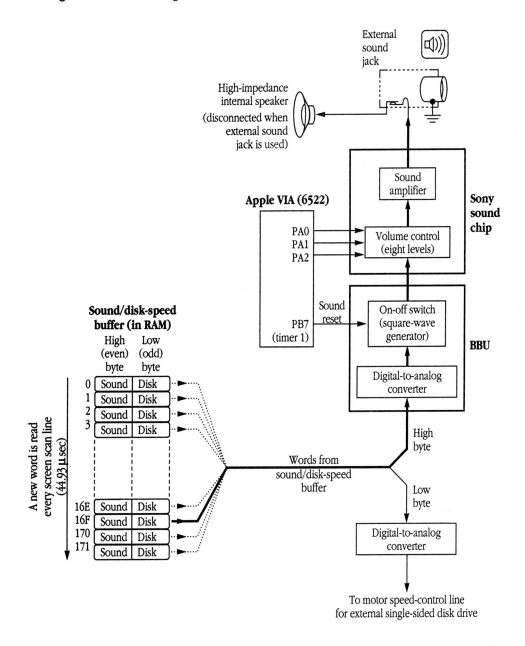

ASC sound system

The Macintosh ASC sound circuit uses an Apple custom IC called the **Apple Sound Chip** (ASC). The ASC is compatible with software written for Macintosh models that use the PWM sound circuit, and also offers stereo sound and other enhancements not available in those computers. The Macintosh models that use ASC sound are

- Macintosh SE/30
- Macintosh Portable
- Macintosh II
- Macintosh IIx
- Macintosh IIcx
- Macintosh IIci
- Macintosh IIfx

The hardware of the Macintosh ASC sound system consists of these hardware components:

- the digital Apple Sound Chip (ASC)
- two analog sound processing chips (the Sony sound chips)
- an internal speaker
- an external stereo mini-phonejack

The ASC has its own data buffers and implements in hardware many of the functions carried out by ROM code in the Macintosh Plus and Macintosh SE computers.

◆ *Note:* Unlike the Macintosh computers that use the PWM, Macintosh computers that use the ASC do not generate speed-control signals for single-sided floppy disk drives; therefore, those computers do not store disk-speed control information in their sound buffers.

ASC sound modes

The ASC contains 2 KB of RAM that can be configured as either two 1 KB sound buffers or as four 512-byte sound buffers. The ASC can operate in any of four functional modes:

- Monaural single-voice mode. The on-board RAM is configured as two 1 KB buffers. The output of the left-channel buffer is converted to a PWM signal and fed to both channels.

- Stereo single-voice mode. The on-board RAM is configured as two 1 KB buffers. The output of each buffer is converted into a PWM signal; one is sent to the left channel and the other is sent to the right channel.

- Monaural four-voice synthesis mode. The on-board RAM is configured as four independent 512-byte buffers. At each sample clock period, a sound value is taken from each of the four buffers, all four values are summed, and the result is converted to a PWM signal and output to both channels.

- Stereo four-voice synthesis mode. The on-board RAM is configured as four independent 512-byte buffers. At each sample clock period, a sound value is taken from each of the four buffers, the values are summed in pairs, and the result of each summed pair is converted to a PWM signal. One of the PWM signals is output to the right channel and the other is sent to the left channel.

Because the ASC uses its internal RAM and performs wavetable sound synthesis in hardware, it requires very little processor time. In addition, ASC sound does not have to be synchronized with the video blanking interval, unlike the PWM sound system used in the classic Macintosh and Macintosh SE computers.

Under control of the Sound Manager, the ASC can sample the values in its RAM at any increment to change the frequency of the output sound. Using every other sample (a sampling interval of 2.0) doubles the frequency of the signal (that is, raises the pitch by one octave). Using every sample twice (a sampling interval of 0.5) halves the frequency of the signal (that is, lowers the pitch by one octave). Through the Sound Manager, you can specify any fixed-point number for the sampling interval. The ASC picks the samples in the RAM locations that fall closest to the selected sampling interval. For example, if the interval is 1.4, the ASC picks samples in RAM locations 1, 3, 4, and 6 (rounding from 1.4, 2.8, 4.2, and 5.6). The increments used by the ASC are extremely precise, having a 24-bit resolution.

Generating sounds

The ASC generates a pulse-width-modulated square-wave output similar to that generated by the PWM system used in the Macintosh Plus and Macintosh SE. Every sample period, the ASC generates a pulse for each stereo channel, the width of which depends on the values read from the sound buffers. These trains of pulses are sent to the Sony sound chips, which filter them to produce smoothly varying waveforms. The Sony sound chips adjust the amplitudes of the waveforms according to a 3-bit value from the ASC and send the signals to the internal speaker or the external sound jack.

The useful bandwidth of the Macintosh ASC sound system is approximately 7.5 KHz. The sample rate can be either the compact-disc standard of 44.1 KHz, or 22.255 KHz (the sample rate used by the Macintosh PWM sound system described in the previous section).

△ **Developer tip** The Macintosh models that use the ASC do not provide the VIA timer signal (T1) to the sound circuit sometimes used in the classic Macintosh and Macintosh SE computers to generate square-wave sound. You can use routines in the Sound Manager to achieve the same effect, with the added advantage that these routines will work on all Macintosh computers, both present and future. The Sound Manager routines are described in *Inside Macintosh.* △

The internal 32-ohm, 2.25-inch speaker is driven by a 250 mW power amplifier in the Sony sound chip. Sound may be played through the internal speaker, or through the external sound jack. If a plug is inserted in the external sound jack, the internal speaker is disconnected. Mixing the two stereo channels together for the internal speaker is handled differently in different models.

In all ASC-equipped Macintosh models except the Macintosh SE/30, the internal speaker is connected to the left channel only. Whenever the internal speaker is in use, a logic signal goes to the Sound Manager causing it to send all sounds through the left channel. When a plug is inserted into the sound jack, the Sound Manager sets the ASC to stereo mode for the external headphones or amplifier. In the Macintosh SE/30, the two channels are added together for the internal speaker and the Sound Manager always operates in stereo mode.

The external sound jack is at standard line level (approximately 1.5 volts peak-to-peak) and its source impedance is approximately 47 ohms. The jack is capable of driving a headphone load of 8 to 600 ohms, or the input to almost any audio amplifier or amplified speakers. It will not adequately drive a directly connected external speaker. The external sound jack is short-circuit protected.

The Control Panel offers eight choices (0 through 7) for overall volume control. When the volume control setting is set to 0, the Sound Manager disables sound output and flashes the menu bar instead.

The ASC can emulate the behavior of the sound hardware of the classic Macintosh and Macintosh SE computers; however, the ASC also provides a variety of features not available in those Macintosh computers. For example, the ASC can generate stereo sound synthesized from two voices per channel, using on-board data buffers.

Circuit diagrams

Figure 13-5 shows a block diagram of the ASC sound circuit used in the Macintosh Portable, Macintosh II, Macintosh IIx, Macintosh IIcx, Macintosh IIci, and Macintosh IIfx computers. Notice that the internal speaker is connected to only one channel. When an external speaker or amplifier is plugged in, a signal indicating that both channels can be used goes to the VIA in the Macintosh Portable and to VIA2 in the Macintosh II, Macintosh IIx, and Macintosh IIcx. A similar signal goes to the RBV in the Macintosh IIci and to the OSS in the Macintosh IIfx.

The ASC sound circuit used in the Macintosh SE/30 is slightly different, as shown in Figure 13-6. That machine always operates in stereo and the sound circuitry mixes the channels together for the internal speaker.

△ **Developer tip** The information on the Apple Sound Chip presented in this chapter is specific to the Macintosh models that use that chip. The ASC is not used in all Macintosh computers, and future versions of the ASC are not guaranteed to be functionally identical to the present model. Furthermore, if your program addresses the ASC directly, it is likely to interfere with the operation of other programs that are running at the same time and that use the Sound Manager. The information in this chapter is provided for the sake of completeness only; Apple strongly recommends that you use the routines in the Sound Driver and Sound Manager to control sound in your applications. The Sound Manager and Sound Driver are described in *Inside Macintosh.* △

■ **Figure 13-5** Block diagram of the ASC sound circuit in the Macintosh Portable, Macintosh II, Macintosh IIx, Macintosh IIcx, Macintosh IIci, and Macintosh IIfx computers

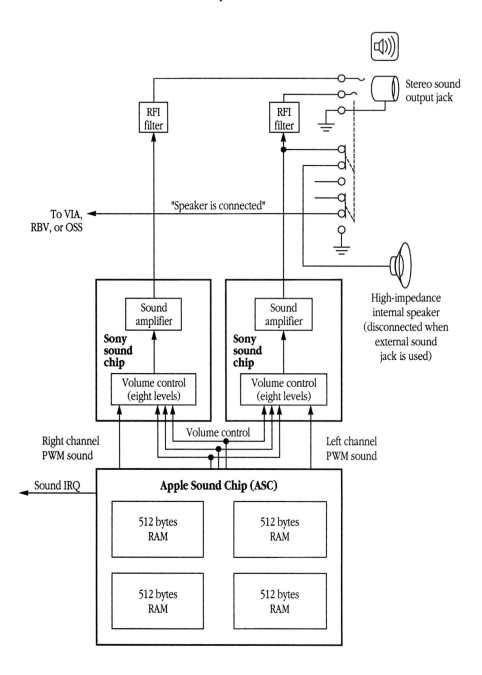

■ **Figure 13-6** Block diagram of the ASC sound circuit in the Macintosh SE/30 computer

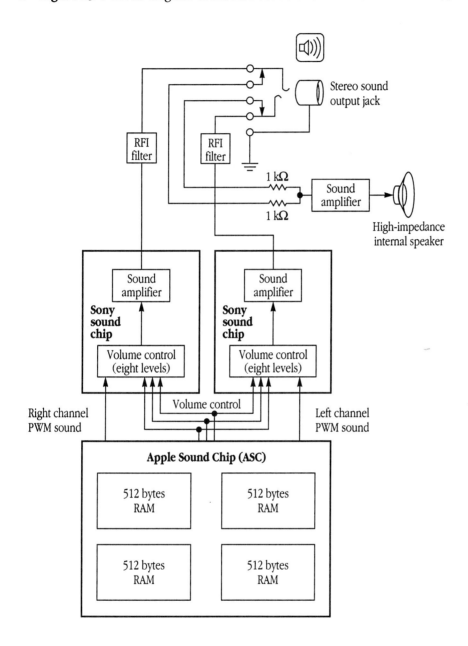

Chapter 14 **Expansion Interfaces**

Macintosh computers use two types of hardware expansion: a single processor-direct expansion slot (PDS), or several NuBus expansion slots:

- processor-direct slot: Macintosh SE, Macintosh SE/30, Macintosh Portable, and Macintosh IIfx computers

- NuBus slots: Macintosh II, Macintosh IIx, Macintosh IIcx, Macintosh IIci, and Macintosh IIfx computers

Note that the Macintosh IIfx computer has both kinds of expansion slots. The Macintosh Plus has no hardware expansion slot, although it does provide for internal memory expansion, as described in Chapter 5.

The **processor-direct slots** provide unbuffered access to their respective processor buses through a single expansion connector. The 68000 processor-direct slot in the Macintosh SE and Macintosh Portable computers uses a Euro-DIN 96-pin connector; the 68030 processor-direct slot in the Macintosh SE/30 and Macintosh IIfx computers uses a Euro-DIN 120-pin connector.

NuBus is a 32-bit-wide, processor-independent bus using Euro-DIN 96-pin connectors. The Macintosh II, Macintosh IIx, and Macintosh IIfx computers have six NuBus slots to support expansion cards. The Macintosh IIcx and Macintosh IIci have three NuBus slots.

◆ *Note:* For a description of memory expansion, including SIMMs for all models and the optional cache card for the Macintosh IIci, please refer to Chapter 5.

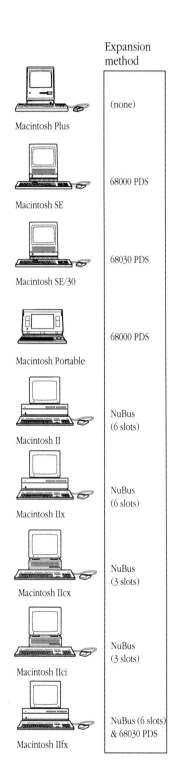

Expansion
method

(none)

Macintosh Plus

68000 PDS

Macintosh SE

68030 PDS

Macintosh SE/30

68000 PDS

Macintosh Portable

NuBus
(6 slots)

Macintosh II

NuBus
(6 slots)

Macintosh IIx

NuBus
(3 slots)

Macintosh IIcx

NuBus
(3 slots)

Macintosh IIci

NuBus (6 slots)
& 68030 PDS

Macintosh IIfx

The 68000 processor-direct slot (PDS)

The 68000 processor-direct slot (68000 PDS) provides unbuffered access to the MC68000 processor through a single Euro-DIN 96-pin expansion connector. There are two different versions of the 68000 PDS: one on the Macintosh SE computer and another on the Macintosh Portable. Although the two versions are mechanically the same, they are electrically different.

◆ *Note:* Some books, among them Apple's earlier manuals *Macintosh Family Hardware Reference* and *Designing Cards and Drivers for Macintosh II and Macintosh SE,* refer to the processor-direct slot in the Macintosh SE as the *Macintosh SE Bus.*

The 68000 processor-direct slot provides the same address and data lines used by the processor bus, several control lines, and power and grounding for expansion cards. A card in the 68000 PDS can access system RAM and ROM at the same rates as does the MC68000: RAM accesses are at an average rate of 3.22 MB per second, and ROM accesses are at 3.92 MB per second.

Each 68000 PDS has two clock signals: the CPU clock, which can be different on different models, and a 16 MHz clock that is the same on all models. The CPU clock on the Macintosh SE has a frequency of 8 MHz; the CPU clock on the Macintosh Portable runs at 16 MHz. The common 16 MHz clock makes it easier to design circuits that will work on more than one model.

Refer to Motorola's documentation for the MC68000 processor, the *MC68000 16-Bit Microprocessor User's Manual,* for more information on the MC68000 processor bus. Detailed guidelines for designing cards to operate in the 68000 PDS can be found in *Designing Cards and Drivers for the Macintosh Family,* second edition.

Examples of types of cards for the processor-direct slot include

- coprocessors
- memory expansion and RAM disks
- local area network (LAN) interfaces
- digital sound sampling and playback systems
- video image processors, frame grabbers, and additional displays

△ **Developer tip** Because the 68000 processor-direct slot is connected directly to the processor bus, any changes to the processor or processor bus in future Macintosh models (such as a change to a higher clock rate) could result in an expansion card's being incompatible with the new main logic board. △

Figure 14-1 shows the pinouts for the Euro-DIN 96-pin expansion connector used for the 68000 PDS on the Macintosh SE and the Macintosh Portable. Because the two versions of the 68000 PDS are electrically different, the signals are described in separate sections, following Figure 14-1.

■ **Figure 14-1** Pinout of the Euro-DIN 96-pin connector used for the 68000 PDS

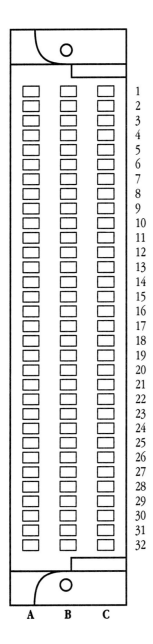

68000 PDS on the Macintosh SE computer

Table 14-1 shows the signal assignments and Table 14-2 describes the signals on the 68000 PDS in the Macintosh SE computer. For information about the 68000 PDS in the Macintosh Portable, please refer to the next section.

■ **Table 14-1**   Signal assignments for the 68000 PDS on the Macintosh SE computer

Pin	Row A	Row B	Row C
1	FC2	GND	/VPA
2	FC1	GND	/VMA
3	FC0	GND	/BR
4	A1	GND	/BGACK
5	A2	GND	/BG
6	A3	GND	/DTACK
7	A4	GND	R/W
8	A5	GND	/LDS
9	A6	GND	/UDS
10	A7	Reserved	/AS
11	A8	Reserved	/PMCYC
12	A9	/HALT	/RESET
13	A10	+5V	+5V
14	A11	+5V	D0
15	A12	+5V	D1
16	A13	+5V	D2
17	A14	+5V	D3
18	A15	/IPL0	D4
19	A16	/IPL1	D5
20	A17	/IPL2	D6
21	A18	/BERR	D7
22	A19	Spare	D8
23	A20	Reserved	D9
24	A21	Reserved	D10
25	A22	Reserved	D11
26	A23	Reserved	D12

(continued)

Pin	Row A	Row B	Row C
27	E	Reserved	D13
28	C8M	/EXT.DTK	D14
29	C16M	GND	D15
30	GND	+12V	GND
31	+12V	+12V	Spare
32	+12V	–5V	–12V

■ **Table 14-2**   Signal descriptions for the 68000 PDS in the Macintosh SE computer

Signal name	Usual source	Logic board destination	Signal description
FC2–FC0	MC68000	Euro-DIN 96-pin	MC68000 processor function codes.
A19–A1	MC68000	RAM, ROM, VIA, SCC, SWIM, SCSI	Memory and register addressing.
A23–20	MC68000	BBU	Decoded to select RAM, ROM, VIA, SCC, SWIM, and SCSI devices.
E	MC68000	VIA	783.36 KHz clock for VIA from CPU.
C8M	BBU	MC68000	7.8336 MHz clock for MC68000.
C16M	Oscillator	BBU, SWIM	15.6672 MHz master clock for BBU and SWIM.
/HALT	MC68000	/RES line	Halt signal; generated by CPU on double bus fault. Tied to MC68000 /RES line.
/IPL0	BBU	MC68000	Asserted on VIA or SCSI.IRQ interrupt; removed on SCC (/IPL1) interrupt.
/IPL1	SCC	MC68000	Interrupt from SCC.
/IPL2	NMI switch	MC68000	Programmer's interrupt switch.
/BERR	BBU	MC68000	In pseudo-DMA mode, indicates that the SCSI interface failed to complete a transaction in 265 ms.
/EXT.DTK	Euro-DIN	BBU	When an external device pulls this pin low, the 96-pin BBU makes its /DTACK output tri-state so that the external device can drive the /DTACK line.

(continued)

■ **Table 14-2**   Signal descriptions for the 68000 PDS in the Macintosh SE computer (continued)

Signal name	Usual source	Logic board destination	Signal description
/VPA	BBU	MC68000	Indicates that a 6800-type device (usually the VIA) is being addressed in the $E00000–$FFFFFF space, an access that needs to be synchronized with the MC68000's E clock.
/VMA	MC68000	VIA	Passes a /VPA access on to a 6800-type device, after proper synchronization to the MC68000's E-clock signal.
/BR	Euro-DIN 96-pin	MC68000	Bus request: asks the MC68000 to relinquish the bus (tri-state its lines and relinquish the address, data, and control buses).
/BG	MC68000	Euro-DIN 96-pin	Bus grant: tells the requesting device that the MC68000 will relinquish the bus at the end of the current bus cycle.
/BGACK	Euro-DIN 96-pin	MC68000	Indicates that the requesting device has taken over the bus.
/DTACK	BBU	MC68000	Indicates that valid data is on the data bus.
R/W	MC68000	BBU, VIA	When high, MC68000 is reading from the data bus; when low, MC68000 is writing to the data bus.
/LDS	MC68000	BBU	Selects the lower byte (D0–D7) of the data bus for reading or writing operations. This is the odd-address bit: A0 = 1.
/UDS	MC68000	BBU	Selects the upper byte (D8–D15) of the data bus for read or write operations. This is the even-address bit: A0 = 0.
/AS	MC68000	BBU	Indicates that a valid address is on the address bus. If this signal is low for more than 265 ms, the BBU generates /BERR.
/PMCYC	BBU	RAM address MUXs	Goes low when the MC68000 can access RAM; goes high when video is accessing RAM.

(continued)

Signal name	Usual source	Logic board destination	Signal description
/RESET	Sony chip	MC68000, VIA, SWIM SCC, SCSI, BBU	Master reset for entire board; tied to MC68000 /HALT line, Reset switch, and MC68000 /RES line.
D7–D0	MC68000, SWIM, ROM, RAM	MC68000, SWIM RAM	Lower (odd) byte of data bus.
D15–D8	MC68000, VIA, ROM, RAM, SCC, SCSI	MC68000, VIA, RAM, SCC, SCSI	Upper (even) byte of data bus.

68000 PDS on the Macintosh Portable

The processor-direct slot on the Macintosh Portable is similar to that of the Macintosh SE. The 68HC000 signals are brought out on a 96-pin Euro-DIN connector. Table 14-3 shows the signal assignments and Table 14-4 lists the functions of the signals on the 68000 PDS connector on the Macintosh Portable.

Pin number	Row A	Row B	Row C
1	GND	GND	GND
2	+5V	+5V	+5V
3	+5V	+5V	+5V
4	+5V	+5V	+5V
5	/DELAY.CS	SYS.PWR/	VPA/
6	/VMA	/BR	/BGACK
7	/BG	/DTACK	R/W
8	/LDS	/UDS	/AS
9	GND	+5/0 V*	A1
10	A2	A3	A4
11	A5	A6	A7
12	A8	A9	A10
13	A11	A12	A13
14	A14	A15	A16
15	A17	A18	Reserved
16	Reserved	Reserved	Reserved
17	Reserved	Reserved	Reserved
18	Reserved	Reserved	Reserved
19	Reserved	+12 V	D0
20	D1	D2	D3
21	D4	D5	D6
22	D7	D8	D9
23	D10	D11	D12
24	D13	D14	D15
25	+5/3.7 V	+5V	GND
26	A19	A20	A21
27	A22	A23	E
28	FC0	FC1	FC2
29	/IPL0	/IPL1	/IPL2
30	/BERR	/EXT.DTACK	/SYS.RST
31	GND	16M	GND
32	GND	GND	GND

*Switched by the Power Manager IC.

Signal name	Signal description
GND	Logic ground
D0–D15	68HC000 unbuffered data bus 0–15
A1–A23	68HC000 unbuffered address bus 1–23
16M	16 MHz clock
/EXT.DTACK	External DTACK, an input to the CPU logic glue that allows for external generation of /DTACK
E	68HC000 E clock
/BERR	68HC000 Bus Error
IPL2–IPL0	68HC000 Interrupt Priority Level 2–0
/SYS.RST	68HC000 Reset
/SYS.PWR	Power Manager IC signal that causes associated circuits to go into idle state; deasserted during sleep state
/AS	68HC000 Address Strobe
/UDS	68HC000 Upper Address Strobe
/LDS	68HC000 Lower Address Strobe
R/W	68HC000 Read/Write
/DTACK	68HC000 Data Transfer Acknowledge
/DELAY.CS	Signal indicating that the system is inserting wait states; can be used to strobe chip selects
/BG	68HC000 Bus Grant
/BGACK	68HC000 Bus Grant Acknowledge
/BR	68HC000 Bus Request
/VMA	68HC000 Valid Memory Address
/VPA	68HC000 Valid Peripheral Address
FC2–0	68HC000 Function Code 2 through 0
+5/0V	+5 volts when the system is active, 0 volts when the system is in sleep state
+5/3.7V	+5 volts when the system is active, 3.7 volts when the system is in sleep state

The 68030 processor-direct slot (PDS)

The 68030 processor-direct slot (PDS) provides unbuffered access to the MC68030 processor through a single Euro-DIN 120-pin expansion connector. The 68030 PDS is used in the Macintosh SE/30 and Macintosh IIfx computers.

In addition to the same 32-bit address and data lines used by the processor bus, the 68030 PDS provides DMA control signals, other CPU control signals, interrupt inputs, and status signals for expansion cards using protocols simulating those of the NuBus. The 68030 PDS also provides +5 volt, –5 volt, +12 volt, and –12 volt power and grounding for expansion cards.

In the Macintosh SE/30, a card in the 68030 PDS can access system RAM and ROM at the same rate as the main processor: 15.67 MB per second. In the Macintosh IIfx, the 68030 PDS can access system RAM and ROM at a rate of 20.0 MB per second. That is slower than the main processor's memory access rate, which averages about 60 MB per second, because the PDS cannot use burst-mode access to the cache.

△ **Developer tip** Whereas most of the signals on the 68030 processor-direct slot connector are the same on all models that use this expansion connector, a few signals are machine-specific. Please refer to Table 14-7 for machine-specific signals. △

In the Macintosh SE/30, two clock signals are available for use by cards plugged into the 68030 PDS: the CPU clock signal used by the MC68030 and a general-purpose clock signal. In the Macintosh SE/30, these two clock signals have the same frequency (15.6672 MHz) and phase. In the Macintosh IIfx, the general-purpose clock is divided down to a frequency of 20 MHz from the 40 MHz clock signal used by the main processor. The CPU clock signal is not available on the PDS.

△ **Developer tip** PDS expansion cards for the Macintosh SE/30 should use the general-purpose clock for on-board devices that are speed sensitive and use the CPU clock for synchronization with the MC68030. △

Refer to Motorola's documentation for the MC68030 processor, *MC68030 Enhanced 32-Bit Microprocessor User's Manual,* for more information on the MC68030 processor bus. Detailed information about the 68030 processor-direct slot and advice for developers designing PDS cards can be found in *Designing Cards and Drivers for the Macintosh Family,* second edition.

Figure 14-2 shows the pinouts for the Euro-DIN 120-pin expansion connector used for the 68030 PDS. Table 14-5 shows the signal assignments for the 68030 PDS.

The 68030 processor-direct slot has a set of address, data, and control signals that are common to all Macintosh computers that use the MC68030 processor—including the ones that have NuBus expansion slots. Table 14-6 lists the signals on the 68030 processor-direct slot that are common to all those machines.

Other signals on the 68030 processor-direct slot are not the same on different machines. Specifically, machines that also have NuBus slots are different from machines that don't. Table 14-7 lists the signals on the 68030 processor-direct slot that are different on different machines.

■ **Figure 14-2**   Pinout of the Euro-DIN 120-pin connector used for the 68030 PDS

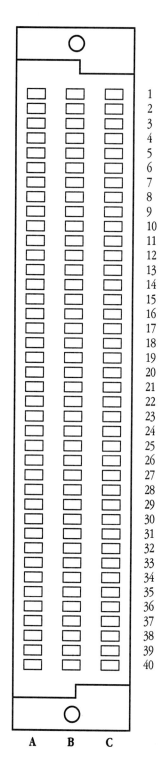

Pin	Row A	Row B	Row C
1	Reserved or GND*	Reserved or ECS*	PWROFF or /PFW*
2	Reserved or /PDS.MASTER*	GND or n.c.*	/NUBUS or n.c.*
3	/BUSLOCK or reserved*	/TM1A or /PDS.BG*	/TM0A or /PDS.BR*
4	/IRQ3 or n.c.*	/IRQ2 or /IRQ15*	/IRQ1 or /IRQ6*
5	/IPL2	/IPL1	/IPL0
6	/CIOUT	/DS	/RMC
7	/STERM	/CBACK	/CBREQ
8	/DSACK1	/DSACK0	R/W
9	SIZ1	SIZ0	/AS
10	/BGACK	/BG	/BR
11	FC2	FC1	FC0
12	/RESET	/BERR	/HALT
13	D0	+5V	D1
14	D2	D3	D4
15	D5	D6	D7
16	D8	GND	D9
17	D10	D11	D12
18	D13	D14	D15
19	D16	+5V	D17
20	D18	D19	D20
21	D21	D22	D23
22	D24	GND	D25
23	D26	D27	D28
24	D29	D30	D31
25	A31	+5V	A30
26	A29	A28	A27
27	A26	A25	A24
28	A23	GND	A22
29	A21	A20	A19

*Signals with two names are different on different models; signal names on the Macintosh SE/30 are given first. Refer to Table 14-7 for details of the machine-specific signals.

(continued)

Pin	Row A	Row B	Row C
30	A18	A17	A16
31	A15	+5V	A14
32	A13	A12	A11
33	A10	A9	A8
34	A7	GND	A6
35	A5	A4	A3
36	A2	A1	A0
37	+5V	+5V	+5V
38	CPUCLOCK or n.c.*	ECLK or n.c.*	C16M or CPUCLK*
39	GND	GND or /SLOT.E	GND
40	–12V	–5V	+12V

*Signals with two names are different on different models; signal names on the Macintosh SE/30 are given first. Refer to Table 14-7 for details of the machine-specific signals.

■ **Table 14-6**   Signal descriptions for the 68030 PDS: common signals

Signal name	Signal description
A(31–0)	Address lines
FC(2–0)	Function code; identifies the address space of the current bus cycle
D(31–0)	Data lines
/IPL(2–1)*	Interrupt priority level lines
/CIOUT†	Inhibits operation of an external cache
/CBREQ†	Identifies a burst request for the instruction or data cache
/CBACK	Indicates that the device can operate in burst mode
/STERM	A bus response signal indicating that the port size is 32 bits and that data can be latched on the next falling clock edge for a read cycle
/DSACK(1–0)	Indicates the completion of a data transfer operation
SIZ(1–0)	Indicates the number of bytes remaining to be transferred in the current cycle
/BR	Signal from an external device requesting to become bus master
/BG	Bus grant; indicates that an external device may become bus master following completion of the current processor bus cycle
/BGACK	Indicates that an external device has become bus master
/RESET	Initiates a system reset
/BERR	Bus error; signals an invalid bus operation
/RMC	Identifies the current bus cycle as part of an indivisible read-modify-write operation
R/W	Defines whether a bus transfer is a read or a write
/AS	Address strobe; indicates a valid address
/HALT	Directs the processor to suspend bus activity
/DS	Data strobe; during a read operation, directs a device to place data on the bus; during a write operation, indicates that data is valid

*Do not use interrupt priority lines on the Macintosh IIfx; instead, use /IRQ6, which is part of that machine's interrupt scheme.

†Do not use /CIOUT in conjunction with /CBREQ; in other words, do not inhibit the cache during burst-mode cycles.

■ **Table 14-7**   Signal descriptions for the 68030 PDS: machine-specific signals

Signal name on Macintosh SE/30	Signal name on Macintosh IIfx	Signal description
Reserved	/ECS	Early-cycle start signal from the MC68030.
PWROFF	/PFW	Status signal indicating that power is about to be removed (Shut Down has been chosen from the Special menu).
/NUBUS	n.c.	In the Macintosh SE/30, indicates address in the memory range $6000 0000 to $FFFF FFFF. This signal is active when the CPU addresses the built-in video display. (Expansion cards can use this signal and further decode the slot address ranges to avoid conflict with the video logic.)
/BUSLOCK	n.c.	In the Macintosh SE/30, the /BUSLOCK signal is not used.
n.c.	/PDS.MASTER	In the Macintosh IIfx, this signal indicates that the PDS card replaces the MC68030 as the bus master; used with /PDS.BG and /PDS.BR.
/TM1A	/PDS.BG	In the Macintosh SE/30, an input to VIA2; current system software does not use it. See the section "Data Register B in VIA2" in Chapter 4. In the Macintosh IIfx, indicates that an external device may become bus master following completion of the current PDS-card bus cycle when /PDS.MASTER is asserted.
/TM0A	/PDS.BR	In the Macintosh SE/30, an input to VIA2; current system software does not use it. See the section "Data Register B in VIA2" in Chapter 4. In the Macintosh IIfx, the signal from an external device requesting to become bus master when /PDS.MASTER is asserted.
/IRQ3–/IRQ2	/IRQ15	In the Macintosh SE/30, the /IRQ1, /IRQ2, and /IRQ3 signals are general-purpose interrupts that correspond to the pseudo-slot addresses (slots $9-$B). In the Macintosh IIfx, /IRQ15 is an additional interrupt (not pseudo-slot) for the address range $6000 0000–$7FFF FFFF.
/IRQ1	/IRQ6	In the Macintosh SE/30, an interrupt line like /IRQ2 and /IRQ3. In the Macintosh IIfx, the interrupt line that corresponds to the pseudo-slot address used in the Macintosh IIfx (slot $E).
CPUCLOCK	n.c.	Clock signal used for timing and synchronization on the Macintosh SE/30. Its frequency is 16.67 MHz.

(continued)

Signal name on Macintosh SE/30	Signal name on Macintosh IIfx	Signal description
ECLK	n.c.	Clock signal for the VIA chips on the main circuit board of the Macintosh SE/30.
C16M	CPUCLK	In the Macintosh SE/30, a general-purpose clock with a frequency of 15.6672 MHz. In the Macintosh IIfx, the clock signal for synchronizing to the main processor, but at a frequency of 20 MHz, half that of the processor.
GND	/SLOT.E	When this signal is low, the PDS replaces NuBus slot $E in the address map.

△ **Developer tip** Because many signals on the Macintosh IIfx are high-speed signals, you should have Apple's technical support group review any card you develop for the PDS in the Macintosh IIfx. △

For more information about developing cards for the 68030 PDS, you should read the companion book to this one, *Designing Cards and Drivers for the Macintosh Family*, second edition.

The NuBus expansion interface

NuBus is a 32-bit-wide, processor-independent bus using Euro-DIN 96-pin connectors. The expansion slots on the Macintosh II–family computers use Apple's implementation of the NuBus interface. The Macintosh II, Macintosh IIx, and Macintosh IIfx have six NuBus slots; the Macintosh IIcx and Macintosh IIci have three NuBus slots. Detailed information on this implementation of NuBus can be found in *Designing Cards and Drivers for the Macintosh Family*, second edition.

The Institute of Electrical and Electronics Engineers (IEEE) has established a standard for NuBus, described in IEEE 1196, *NuBus—A Simple 32-Bit Backplane Bus*.

△ **Important**   Texas Instruments, Inc. owns patents on NuBus. If you wish to make a
device that works with NuBus, you must obtain a license from Texas
Instruments. Write to the following address:

Texas Instruments, Inc.
12501 Research Boulevard
Austin, TX 78759
Attn: NuBus Licensing
M/S 2151 △

The Macintosh II Video Card and other video cards go in a NuBus expansion slot. Other
examples of uses for NuBus cards include

- coprocessors

- memory expansion and RAM disks

- local area network (LAN) interfaces

- additional SCSI ports

- digital sound sampling and playback systems

Figure 14-3 shows the pinouts of the 96-pin NuBus expansion connector on the main logic board.

Table 14-8 lists the signal assignments for the NuBus expansion connector. Table 14-9 lists
the use of each signal. NuBus data communications are described in *Designing Cards and
Drivers for the Macintosh Family,* second edition.

■ **Figure 14-3**   Pinout of the Euro-DIN 96-pin connector used for the NuBus

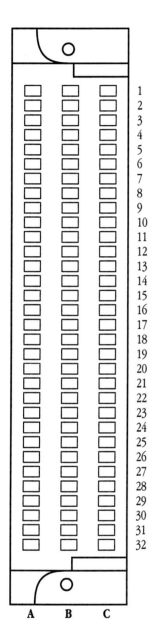

■ **Table 14-8**   Signal assignments for the NuBus expansion connector

Pin	Row A	Row B	Row C
1	−12	−12	/RESET
2	GND*	GND	GND*
3	/SPV	GND	+5
4	/SP	+5	+5
5	/TM1	+5	/TM0
6	/AD1	+5	/AD0
7	/AD3	+5	/AD2
8	/AD5	†	/AD4
9	/AD7	†	/AD6
10	/AD9	†	/AD8
11	/AD11	†	/AD10
12	/AD13	GND	/AD12
13	/AD15	GND	/AD14
14	/AD17	GND	/AD16
15	/AD19	GND	/AD18
16	/AD21	GND	/AD20
17	/AD23	GND	/AD22
18	/AD25	GND	/AD24
19	/AD27	GND	/AD26
20	/AD29	GND	/AD28
21	/AD31	GND	/AD30
22	GND	GND	GND
23	GND	GND	/PFW
24	/ARB1	†	/ARB0
25	/ARB3	†	/ARB2
26	/ID1	†	/ID0
27	/ID3	†	/ID2
28	/ACK	+5	/START
29	+5	+5	+5
30	/RQST	GND	+5
31	/NMRQ	GND	GND
32	+12	+12	/CLK

*These pins are reserved in the IEEE NuBus specification; in the Macintosh II, they are grounded.

†These pins are connected together, but not supplied with the −5.2 V described in the IEEE NuBus specification. This voltage could be supplied by a card, in which case −5.2 V would be available to all cards.

■ **Table 14-9** Signal descriptions for the NuBus expansion connector

Signal name	Signal description
/SPV	System Parity Valid
/SP	System Parity
TM1–TM0	Transfer mode lines
/AD30–/AD0	Address/data lines
/PFW	Power Fail Warning
/ARB3–/ARB0	Arbitration
/ID3–/ID0	Slot identification lines
/ACK	Acknowledge
/START	Start
/RQST	Request
/NMRQ	Non-Master Request
/CLK	Clock

Figure 14-4 shows a block diagram of the NuBus interface. The NuBus is a synchronous bus running on a 10 MHz clock; the processor bus is asynchronous and uses a clock with a rate of 15.67 MHz or higher, depending on the model. The blocks at the bottom of the figure are finite-state machines that implement the handshaking and synchronize transfers between the two buses. The state machines are part of the logic inside the NuBus controller IC (NuChip, NuChip30, or BIU30).

The NuBus uses a multiplexed address/data bus, whereas the main logic board uses separate address and data buses. The NuBus transceivers buffer, multiplex, and demultiplex the NuBus address/data bus signals. The /AD1, /AD0, /TM1, and /TM0 lines on the NuBus side of the interface, and the SIZ1 and SIZ0 lines on the processor side of the interface, control the size of a data transfer. Because of this dual use of the /AD1 and /AD0 lines, the encoder/decoder shown in Figure 14-4 translates the two low-order address bits between the processor-bus values and the values used on NuBus.

■ **Figure 14-4** NuBus block diagram

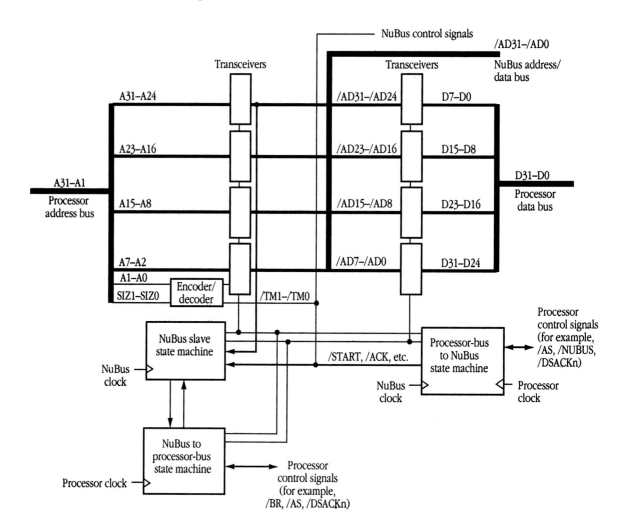

Appendix A **Macintosh Family Hardware Specifications**

This appendix gives the specifications for nine Macintosh models:

- Macintosh Plus
- Macintosh SE
- Macintosh SE/30
- Macintosh Portable
- Macintosh II
- Macintosh IIx
- Macintosh IIcx
- Macintosh IIci
- Macintosh IIfx

Macintosh Plus

Processor	MC68000, 32-bit internal architecture, 16-bit external data bus, 24-bit external address bus
Processor clock	7.8336 MHz
RAM	1 MB of system RAM (expandable to 4 MB); 256 bytes of parameter RAM in RTC
ROM	128 KB ROM (expandable to 256 KB)
Floppy disk drive	One internal 800 KB double-sided 3.5-inch disk drive; one external disk-drive connector
Hard disk drive	External DB-19 connector accepts an Apple Hard Disk 20; external SCSI connector accepts a SCSI hard disk
Video display	Built-in 9-inch (diagonal), 512-pixel by 342-pixel bit-mapped video display screen
I/O	Synchronous serial keyboard bus; two RS-422 serial ports; mouse interface; IWM port with one internal connector and one external connector; mono sound port for external amplifier
Sound generator	Four-voice mono sound with digital-to-analog conversion using 22.255 KHz sample rate
Keyboard	Macintosh Plus keyboard with built-in keypad
Mouse	Mechanical/optical mechanism generating 90 pulses per inch on each axis of travel
Real-time clock	CMOS custom chip containing 256 bytes of parameter RAM; rechargeable 4.5-volt (Eveready No. 523 or equivalent) user-replaceable battery backup
Power requirements	Line voltage: 85 to 135 or 170 to 270 V (rms) Frequency: 47 to 63 Hz Power: 80 W maximum for peak load
Power output	46.8 W at maximum sustainable load

■ **Table A-1** Size and weight of the Macintosh Plus computer

	Weight	Height	Width	Depth
Main unit	7.5 kg (16 lbs. 8 oz.)	344 mm (13.5 in.)	246 mm (9.7 in.)	276 mm (10.9 in.)
Keyboard	1.2 kg (2 lbs. 10 oz.)	65 mm (2.6 in.)	395 mm (15.6 in.)	146 mm (5.8 in.)
Mouse	0.2 kg (7 oz.)	37 mm (1.45 in.)	60 mm (2.4 in.)	109 mm (4.3 in.)

Environment

Operating temperature	10° C to 40° C (50° F to 104° F) No component inside the machine should get hotter than 80% of the manufacturer's maximum when operating at the maximum temperature.
Storage temperature	–40° C to 50° C (–40° F to 122° F)
Relative humidity	20% to 95% (noncondensing) at 25° C (77° F) to 40° C (104° F)
Altitude	0 to 4572 m (0 to 15,000 ft.)

Macintosh SE

Processor	MC68000, 32-bit internal architecture, 16-bit external data bus, 24-bit external address bus
Processor clock	7.8336 MHz
RAM	1 MB of system RAM (expandable to 4 MB); 256 bytes of parameter RAM in RTC
ROM	256 KB ROM
Floppy disk drive	One internal 1440 KB Macintosh FDHD disk drive; one optional second internal 1440 KB Macintosh FDHD drive; one external DB-19 connector
Hard disk drive	One optional internal 20 MB SCSI hard disk; external DB-19 connector accepts an Apple Hard Disk 20; external SCSI connector accepts a SCSI hard disk
Video display	Built-in 9-inch (diagonal), 512-pixel by 342-pixel bit-mapped video display screen
I/O	Apple Desktop Bus with two connectors for communication with keyboard, mouse, and other devices over low-speed, synchronous serial bus; two RS-422 serial ports with synchronous modem support on port A; SWIM port with one internal connector and one external connector; SCSI port with one internal connector and one external connector; mono sound port for external amplifier
Expansion slot	68000 processor-direct slot for expansion card
Sound generator	Four-voice mono sound with digital-to-analog conversion using 22.255 KHz sample rate
Keyboards	Apple Standard Keyboard or Apple Extended Keyboard (Apple Desktop Bus)
Mouse	Apple Standard Mouse (Apple Desktop Bus); mechanical/optical mechanism generating either 100 counts or 200 counts per inch on each axis of travel
Real-time clock	CMOS custom chip containing 256 bytes of parameter RAM; long-life lithium battery backup
Power requirements	Line voltage: 85 to 270 V (rms) Frequency: 47 to 63 Hz Power: 142 W maximum for peak load
Power output	76 W at maximum sustainable load

■ **Table A-2**   Size and weight of the Macintosh SE computer

	Weight	Height	Width	Depth
Main unit	7.7–10 kg* (17–22 lbs.*)	344 mm (13.55 in.)	246 mm (9.69 in.)	276 mm (10.87 in.)
Apple Standard Keyboard	1.0 kg (2 lbs. 4 oz.)	44.5 mm (1.8 in.)	418.3 mm (16.5 in.)	140.0 mm (5.5 in.)
Apple Extended Keyboard	1.6 kg (3 lbs. 10 oz.)	56.4 mm (2.22 in.)	486 mm (19.15 in.)	188 mm (7.4 in.)
Apple Standard Mouse	0.17 kg (6 oz.)	27.9 mm (1.1 in.)	53.3 mm (2.1 in.)	96.5 mm (3.8 in.)

*Weight varies depending on installation of optional hard disk drive or second 3.5-inch floppy disk drive.

Environment

Operating temperature	10° C to 40° C (50° F to 104° F) No component inside the machine should get hotter than 80% of the manufacturer's maximum when operating at the maximum temperature.
Storage temperature	–40° C to 47° C (–40° F to 116.6° F)
Relative humidity	20% to 95% (noncondensing) at 25° C (77° F) to 40° C (104° F)
Altitude	0 to 4572 m (0 to 15,000 ft.)

Macintosh SE/30

Processor	MC68030, 32-bit internal architecture, 32-bit external data bus, 32-bit external address bus
Processor clock	15.6672 MHz
Coprocessor	MC68882 floating-point unit
RAM	1 MB of system RAM, expandable to 64 MB; 256 bytes of parameter RAM in RTC; 2 KB of sound RAM in ASC;
ROM	256 KB, expandable to 2 MB
Floppy disk drive	One internal 1440 KB Macintosh FDHD disk drive; one optional second internal 1440 KB Macintosh FDHD drive; one external DB-19 connector
Hard disk drive	One optional internal 40 or 80 MB SCSI hard disk; external SCSI connector accepts a SCSI hard disk
Video display	Built-in 9-inch (diagonal), 512-pixel by 342-pixel bit-mapped video display screen; interface emulates expansion-bus architecture with 8 KB declaration ROM and 64 KB display buffer
I/O	Apple Desktop Bus with two connectors for communication with keyboard, mouse, and other devices over low-speed, synchronous serial bus; two RS-422 serial ports with synchronous modem support on port A; SWIM port with one internal connector and one external connector; SCSI port with one internal connector and one external connector; stereo sound port for external amplifier
Expansion slot	68030 processor-direct slot for expansion card
Sound generator	Four-voice stereo or mono sound with digital-to-analog conversion using either 22.255 KHz or 44.1 KHz sample rate
Keyboards	Apple Standard Keyboard or Apple Extended Keyboard (Apple Desktop Bus)
Mouse	Apple Standard Mouse (Apple Desktop Bus); mechanical/optical mechanism generating either 100 counts or 200 counts per inch on each axis of travel
Real-time clock	CMOS custom chip containing 256 bytes of parameter RAM; long-life lithium battery backup
Power requirements	Line voltage: 85 to 270 V (rms) Frequency: 47 to 63 Hz Power: 142 W maximum for peak load
Power output	76 W at maximum sustainable load

	Weight	Height	Width	Depth
Main unit	7.7–10 kg* (17–22 lbs.*)	344 mm (13.55 in.)	246 mm (9.69 in.)	276 mm (10.87 in.)
Apple Standard Keyboard	1.0 kg (2 lbs. 4 oz.)	44.5 mm (1.8 in.)	418.3 mm (16.5 in.)	140.0 mm (5.5 in.)
Apple Extended Keyboard	1.6 kg (3 lbs. 10 oz.)	56.4 mm (2.22 in.)	486 mm (19.15 in.)	188 mm (7.4 in.)
Apple Standard Mouse	0.17 kg (6 oz.)	27.9 mm (1.1 in.)	53.3 mm (2.1 in.)	96.5 mm (3.8 in.)

* Weight varies depending on installation of optional hard disk drive or second FDHD drive.

Environment

Operating temperature	10° C to 40° C (50° F to 104° F) No component inside the machine should get hotter than 80% of the manufacturer's maximum when operating at the maximum temperature.
Storage temperature	–40° C to 47° C (–40° F to 116.6° F)
Relative humidity	20% to 95% (noncondensing) at 25° C (77° F) to 40° C (104° F)
Altitude	0 to 4572 m (0 to 15,000 ft.)

Macintosh Portable

Processor	MC68000, 32-bit internal architecture, 16-bit external data bus, 24-bit external address bus
Processor clock	15.6672 MHz
RAM	1 MB of system RAM (expandable to 4 MB); 256 bytes of parameter RAM in RTC
ROM	256 KB ROM
Floppy disk drive	One internal 1440 KB Macintosh FDHD disk drive; one optional second internal FDHD disk drive
Hard disk drive	One optional internal 40 or 80 MB SCSI hard disk External SCSI connector accepts a SCSI hard disk
Flat-panel display	Built-in 9.8-inch diagonal, 512-pixel by 342-pixel flat-panel display screen; connector for external video monitor (adapter needed)
I/O	Apple Desktop Bus with one connector for communication with low-power keyboard, mouse, and other low-power devices over low-speed, synchronous serial bus; two RS-422 serial ports with synchronous modem support on one port; connector for internal modem (uses modem serial port); IWM port with two internal connectors and one external connector; SCSI port with one internal connector and one external connector; mono sound port for external amplifier
Sound generator	Four-voice stereo or mono sound with digital-to-analog conversion using either 22.255 KHz or 44.1 KHz sample rate
Keyboards	Built-in low-power version of Apple Standard Keyboard; accepts external low-power keyboard (Apple Desktop Bus)
Trackball	Stationary pointing device
Mouse	Accepts low-power version of Apple Standard Mouse (Apple Desktop Bus)
Real-time clock	CMOS custom chip containing 256 bytes of parameter RAM; long-life lithium battery backup
Power requirements*	Line voltage: 85 to 270 V (rms) Frequency: 48 to 62 Hz Power: 15 W maximum for peak load
Power output	Battery power for 8 hours of normal use 76 W at maximum sustainable load

* Wall-mounted battery recharger, AC input

■ **Table A-4** Size and weight of the Macintosh Portable computer

	Weight	Height	Width	Depth
Main unit	6.4–7.7 kg* (14–17 lbs.*)	51–102 mm† (2.0–4.0 in.†)	386 mm (15.2 in.)	349 mm (13.75 in.)
Apple Standard Mouse	0.17 kg (6 oz.)	27.9 mm (1.1 in.)	53.3 mm (2.1 in.)	96.5 mm (3.8 in.)

*Weight varies depending on installation of optional hard disk drive or second FDHD drive.

†Unit is wedge shaped, thicker toward the back.

Environment

Operating temperature	10° C to 40° C (50° F to 104° F) No component inside the machine should get hotter than 80% of the manufacturer's maximum when operating at the maximum temperature.
Storage temperature	–40° C to 47° C (–40° F to 116.6° F)
Relative humidity	20% to 95% (noncondensing) at 25° C (77° F) to 40° C (104° F)
Altitude	0 to 4572 m (0 to 15,000 ft.)

Macintosh II

Processor	MC68020, 32-bit internal architecture, 32-bit external data bus, 32-bit external address bus
Processor clock	15.6672 MHz
RAM	1 MB of system RAM, expandable to 128 MB, expandable to 2 GB in NuBus cards; 256 bytes of parameter RAM in RTC; 2 KB of sound RAM in ASC; video RAM and other special-purpose RAM in NuBus cards
ROM	256 KB, expandable to 512 KB
Coprocessor	MC68881 floating-point unit
Memory management	Apple custom Address Management Unit (AMU); replaceable by optional MC68851 Paged Memory Management Unit (PMMU)
Floppy disk drive	One internal 800 KB double-sided 3.5-inch disk drive; one optional second internal 800 KB double-sided 3.5-inch disk drive
Hard disk drive	One optional internal SCSI hard disk; external SCSI connector accepts a SCSI hard disk
Video display	Separate video display monitor connected to a NuBus card. Apple options include a 12-inch 640-by-480 pixel monochrome monitor, 13-inch 640-by-480 pixel RGB monitor, and 15-inch 640-by-870 pixel portrait monitor.
I/O	Apple Desktop Bus with two connectors for communication with keyboard, mouse, and other devices over low-speed, synchronous serial bus; two RS-422 serial ports with synchronous modem support on one port; IWM port with two internal connectors; SCSI port with one internal connector and one external connector; stereo sound port for external audio amplifier or earphones
Expansion slots	Six internal NuBus slots for expansion cards
Sound generator	Four-voice stereo or mono sound with digital-to-analog conversion using either 22.255 KHz or 44.1 KHz sample rate
Keyboards	Apple Standard Keyboard or Apple Extended Keyboard (Apple Desktop Bus)
Mouse	Apple Standard Mouse (Apple Desktop Bus); mechanical/optical mechanism generating either 100 counts or 200 counts per inch on each axis of travel

	Real-time clock	CMOS custom chip containing 256 bytes of parameter RAM; long-life lithium battery backup

Real-time clock   CMOS custom chip containing 256 bytes of parameter RAM; long-life lithium battery backup

Power requirements   Line voltage: 90 to 140 and 170 to 270 V (rms)
Frequency: 47 to 63 Hz
Power: 230 W maximum for peak load, not including power for monitor or other external peripheral devices

Power output   132 W at maximum sustainable load

■ **Table A-5** Size and weight of the Macintosh II computer

	Weight	Height	Width	Depth
Main unit	10.9 to 11.8 kg* (24 to 26 lbs.)	140 mm (5.51 in.)	474 mm (18.66 in.)	365 mm (14.37 in.)
Apple Standard Keyboard	1.0 kg (2 lbs. 4 oz.)	44.5 mm (1.8 in.)	418.3 mm (16.5 in.)	140.0 mm (5.5 in.)
Apple Extended Keyboard	1.6 kg (3 lbs. 10 oz.)	56.4 mm (2.22 in.)	486 mm (19.15 in.)	188 mm (7.4 in.)
Apple Standard Mouse	0.17 kg (6 oz.)	27.9 mm (1.1 in.)	53.3 mm (2.1 in.)	96.5 mm (3.8 in.)
Apple high-resolution monochrome monitor	7.7 kg (17 lbs.)	255 mm (10.04 in.)	310 mm (12.2 in.)	373 mm (14.68 in.)
Apple high-resolution RGB monitor	15.45 kg (34 lbs.)	281 mm (11.06 in.)	344 mm (13.54 in.)	402 mm (15.83 in.)

* Weight varies depending on installation of optional hard disk drive or second 3.5-inch floppy disk drive.

Environment

Operating temperature	10° C to 35° C (50° F to 95° F) No component inside the machine should get hotter than 80% of the manufacturer's maximum when operating at the maximum temperature.
Storage temperature	–40° C to 47° C (–40° F to 116.6° F)
Relative humidity	20% to 95% (noncondensing) at 25° C (77° F) to 40° C (104° F)
Altitude	0 to 3048 m (0 to 10,000 ft.)

Macintosh IIx

Processor	MC68030, 32-bit internal architecture, 32-bit external data bus, 32-bit external address bus
Processor clock	15.6672 MHz
RAM	1 MB of system RAM, expandable to 128 MB, expandable to 2 GB in NuBus cards; 256 bytes of parameter RAM in RTC; 2 KB of sound RAM in ASC; video RAM and other special-purpose RAM in NuBus cards
ROM	256 KB, expandable to 8 MB
Coprocessor	MC68882 floating-point unit
Memory management	Built into MC68030 processor
Floppy disk drive	One internal 1440 KB Macintosh FDHD disk drive; one optional second internal FDHD disk drive
Hard disk drive	One optional internal 40 or 80 MB SCSI hard disk; external SCSI connector accepts a SCSI hard disk
Video display	Separate video display monitor connected to a NuBus card. Apple options include a 12-inch 640-by-480 pixel monochrome monitor, 13-inch 640-by-480 pixel RGB monitor, and 15-inch 640-by-870 pixel portrait monitor.
I/O	Apple Desktop Bus with two connectors for communication with keyboard, mouse, and other devices over low-speed, synchronous serial bus; two RS-422 serial ports with synchronous modem support on one port; SWIM port with two internal connectors; SCSI port with one internal connector and one external connector; stereo sound port for external audio amplifier or earphones
Expansion slots	Six internal NuBus slots for expansion cards
Sound generator	Four-voice stereo or mono sound with digital-to-analog conversion using either 22.255 KHz or 44.1 KHz sample rate
Keyboards	Apple Standard Keyboard or Apple Extended Keyboard (Apple Desktop Bus)
Mouse	Apple Standard Mouse (Apple Desktop Bus); mechanical/optical mechanism generating either 100 counts or 200 counts per inch on each axis of travel
Real-time clock	CMOS custom chip containing 256 bytes of parameter RAM; long-life lithium battery backup

	Power requirements	Line voltage: 90 to 140 and 170 to 270 V (rms)
		Frequency: 47 to 63 Hz
		Power: 230 W maximum for peak load, not including power for
		monitor or other external peripheral devices
	Power output	132 W at maximum sustainable load

■ **Table A-6**   Size and weight of the Macintosh IIx computer

	Weight	Height	Width	Depth
Main unit	10.9 to 11.8 kg* (24 to 26 lbs.)	140 mm (5.51 in.)	474 mm (18.66 in.)	365 mm (14.37 in.)
Apple Standard Keyboard	1.0 kg (2 lbs. 4 oz.)	44.5 mm (1.8 in.)	418.3 mm (16.5 in.)	140.0 mm (5.5 in.)
Apple Extended Keyboard	1.6 kg (3 lbs. 10 oz.)	56.4 mm (2.22 in.)	486 mm (19.15 in.)	188 mm (7.4 in.)
Apple Standard Mouse	0.17 kg (6 oz.)	27.9 mm (1.1 in.)	53.3 mm (2.1 in.)	96.5 mm (3.8 in.)
Apple high- resolution monochrome monitor	7.7 kg (17 lbs.)	255 mm (10.04 in.)	310 mm (12.2 in.)	373 mm (14.68 in.)
Apple high- resolution RGB monitor	15.45 kg (34 lbs.)	281 mm (11.06 in.)	344 mm (13.54 in.)	402 mm (15.83 in.)

* Weight varies depending on installation of optional hard disk drive or second FDHD drive.

Environment

Operating temperature	10° C to 35° C
	(50° F to 95° F)
	No component inside the machine should get hotter than
	80% of the manufacturer's maximum when operating at the
	maximum temperature.
Storage temperature	–40° C to 47° C
	(–40° F to 116.6° F)
Relative humidity	20% to 95% (noncondensing) at 25° C (77° F) to
	40° C (104° F)
Altitude	0 to 3048 m (0 to 10,000 ft.)

Macintosh IIcx

Processor	MC68030, 32-bit internal architecture, 32-bit external data bus, 32-bit external address bus
Processor clock	15.6672 MHz
RAM	1 MB of system RAM, expandable to 128 MB, expandable to 2 GB in NuBus cards; 256 bytes of parameter RAM in RTC; 2 KB of sound RAM in ASC; video RAM and other special-purpose RAM in NuBus cards
ROM	256 KB, expandable to 8 MB
Coprocessor	MC68882 floating-point unit
Memory management	Built into MC68030 processor
Floppy disk drive	One internal 1440 KB Macintosh FDHD disk drive; one optional external FDHD disk drive
Hard disk drive	One optional internal 40 or 80 MB SCSI hard disk; external SCSI connector accepts a SCSI hard disk
Video display	Separate video display monitor connected to a NuBus card. Apple options include a 12-inch 640-by-480 pixel monochrome monitor, 13-inch 640-by-480 pixel RGB monitor, and 15-inch 640-by-870 pixel portrait monitor.
I/O	Apple Desktop Bus with two connectors for communication with keyboard, mouse, and other devices over low-speed, synchronous serial bus; two RS-422 serial ports with synchronous modem support on one port; SWIM port with one internal connector and one external connector; SCSI port with one internal connector and one external connector; stereo sound port for external audio amplifier or earphones
Expansion slots	Three internal NuBus slots for expansion cards
Sound generator	Four-voice stereo or mono sound with digital-to-analog conversion using either 22.255 KHz or 44.1 KHz sample rate
Keyboards	Apple Standard Keyboard or Apple Extended Keyboard (Apple Desktop Bus)
Mouse	Apple Standard Mouse (Apple Desktop Bus); mechanical/optical mechanism generating either 100 counts or 200 counts per inch on each axis of travel
Real-time clock	CMOS custom chip containing 256 bytes of parameter RAM; long-life lithium battery backup

Power requirements	Line voltage: 90 to 140 and 170 to 270 V (rms)
	Frequency: 47 to 63 Hz
	Power: 130 W maximum for peak load, not including power for monitor or other external peripheral devices
Power output	90 W at maximum sustainable load

■ **Table A-7**   Size and weight of the Macintosh IIcx computer

	Weight	Height	Width	Depth
Main unit	6.2 kg* (13 lbs. 10 oz.)	140 mm (5.51 in.)	302 mm (11.9 in.)	365 mm (14.4 in.)
Apple Standard Keyboard	1.0 kg (2 lbs. 4 oz.)	44.5 mm (1.8 in.)	418.3 mm (16.5 in.)	140.0 mm (5.5 in.)
Apple Extended Keyboard	1.6 kg (3 lbs. 10 oz.)	56.4 mm (2.22 in.)	486 mm (19.15 in.)	188 mm (7.4 in.)
Apple Standard Mouse	0.17 kg (6 oz.)	27.9 mm (1.1 in.)	53.3 mm (2.1 in.)	96.5 mm (3.8 in.)
Apple high-resolution monochrome monitor	7.7 kg (17 lbs.)	255 mm (10.04 in.)	310 mm (12.2 in.)	373 mm (14.68 in.)
Apple high-resolution RGB monitor	15.45 kg (34 lbs.)	281 mm (11.06 in.)	344 mm (13.54 in.)	402 mm (15.83 in.)

* Weight varies depending on installation of optional hard disk drive.

Environment

Operating temperature	10° C to 35° C
	(50° F to 95° F)
	No component inside the machine should get hotter than 80% of the manufacturer's maximum when operating at the maximum temperature.
Storage temperature	–40° C to 47° C
	(–40° F to 116.6° F)
Relative humidity	20% to 95% (noncondensing) at 25° C (77° F) to 40° C (104° F)
Altitude	0 to 3048 m (0 to 10,000 ft.)

Macintosh IIci

Processor	MC68030, 32-bit internal architecture, 32-bit external data bus, 32-bit external address bus
Processor clock	25.00 MHz
RAM	1 MB of system RAM, expandable to 128 MB, expandable to 2 GB in NuBus cards; slot for optional high-speed RAM cache card; 256 bytes of parameter RAM in RTC; 2 KB of sound RAM in ASC; video RAM and other special-purpose RAM in NuBus cards
ROM	512 KB, expandable to 8 MB
Coprocessor	MC68882 floating-point unit
Memory management	Built into MC68030 processor
Floppy disk drive	One internal 1440 KB Macintosh FDHD disk drive; one optional external FDHD disk drive
Hard disk drive	One optional internal 40 or 80 MB SCSI hard disk; external SCSI connector accepts a SCSI hard disk
Video display	Built-in video circuits for connecting a separate video display monitor; Apple options include a 12-inch 640-by-480 pixel monochrome monitor, 13-inch 640-by-480 pixel RGB monitor, and 15-inch 640-by-870 pixel portrait monitor. Can also use a video monitor connected to a NuBus card.
I/O	Apple Desktop Bus with two connectors for communication with keyboard, mouse, and other devices over low-speed, synchronous serial bus; two RS-422 serial ports with synchronous modem support on one port; SWIM port with one internal connector and one external connector; SCSI port with one internal connector and one external connector; stereo sound port for external audio amplifier or earphones
Expansion slots	Three internal NuBus slots for expansion cards
Sound generator	Four-voice stereo or mono sound with digital-to-analog conversion using either 22.255 KHz or 44.1 KHz sample rate
Keyboards	Apple Standard Keyboard or Apple Extended Keyboard (Apple Desktop Bus)
Mouse	Apple Standard Mouse (Apple Desktop Bus); mechanical/optical mechanism generating either 100 counts or 200 counts per inch on each axis of travel

Real-time clock	CMOS custom chip containing 256 bytes of parameter RAM; long-life lithium battery backup		
Power requirements	Line voltage: 90 to 140 and 170 to 270 V (rms) Frequency: 47 to 63 Hz Power: 130 W maximum for peak load, not including power for monitor or other external peripheral devices		
Power output	90 W at maximum sustainable load		

■ **Table A-8**   Size and weight of the Macintosh IIci computer

	Weight	Height	Width	Depth
Main unit	6.2 kg* (13 lbs. 10 oz.)	140 mm (5.51 in.)	302 mm (11.9 in.)	365 mm (14.4 in.)
Apple Standard Keyboard	1.0 kg (2 lbs. 4 oz.)	44.5 mm (1.8 in.)	418.3 mm (16.5 in.)	140.0 mm (5.5 in.)
Apple Extended Keyboard	1.6 kg (3 lbs. 10 oz.)	56.4 mm (2.22 in.)	486 mm (19.15 in.)	188 mm (7.4 in.)
Apple Standard Mouse	0.17 kg (6 oz.)	27.9 mm (1.1 in.)	53.3 mm (2.1 in.)	96.5 mm (3.8 in.)
Apple high-resolution monochrome monitor	7.7 kg (17 lbs.)	255 mm (10.04 in.)	310 mm (12.2 in.)	373 mm (14.68 in.)
Apple high-resolution RGB monitor	15.45 kg (34 lbs.)	281 mm (11.06 in.)	344 mm (13.54 in.)	402 mm (15.83 in.)

*Weight varies depending on installation of optional hard disk drive.

Environment

Operating temperature	10° C to 35° C
	(50° F to 95° F)
	No component inside the machine should get hotter than 80% of the manufacturer's maximum when operating at the maximum temperature.
Storage temperature	–40° C to 47° C
	(–40° F to 116.6° F)
Relative humidity	20% to 95% (noncondensing) at 25° C (77° F) to 40° C (104° F)
Altitude	0 to 3048 m (0 to 10,000 ft.)

Macintosh IIfx

Processor	MC68030, 32-bit internal architecture, 32-bit external data bus, 32-bit external address bus
Processor clock	40.00 MHz
RAM	4 MB of system RAM, expandable to 128 MB, expandable to 2 GB in NuBus cards; 32 KB of fast RAM cache; 256 bytes of parameter RAM in RTC; 2 KB of sound RAM in ASC; video RAM and other special-purpose RAM in NuBus cards
ROM	512 KB, expandable to 8 MB
Coprocessor	MC68882 floating-point unit, clock speed of 40.00 MHz
Memory management	Built into the MC68030 processor
Floppy disk drive	One internal 1440 KB Macintosh FDHD disk drive; one optional second internal FDHD disk drive
Hard disk drive	One optional internal 80 or 160 MB SCSI hard disk; external SCSI connector accepts a SCSI hard disk
Video display	Separate video display monitor connected to a NuBus card. Apple options include a 12-inch 640-by-480 pixel monochrome monitor, 13-inch 640-by-480 pixel RGB monitor, and 15-inch 640-by-870 pixel portrait monitor.
I/O	Apple Desktop Bus with two connectors for communication with keyboard, mouse, and other devices over low-speed, synchronous serial bus; I/O processor controlling two RS-422 serial ports with synchronous modem support on one port; I/O processor controlling SWIM port with two internal connectors; SCSI port with one internal connector and one external connector; stereo sound port for external audio amplifier or earphones
Expansion slots	Six internal NuBus slots for expansion cards; 68030 processor-direct slot for expansion card
Sound generator	Four-voice stereo or mono sound with digital-to-analog conversion using either 22.255 KHz or 44.1 KHz sample rate
Keyboards	Apple Standard Keyboard or Apple Extended Keyboard (Apple Desktop Bus)
Mouse	Apple Standard Mouse (Apple Desktop Bus); mechanical/optical mechanism generating either 100 counts or 200 counts per inch on each axis of travel

	Real-time clock	CMOS custom chip containing 256 bytes of parameter RAM; long-life lithium battery backup

Real-time clock   CMOS custom chip containing 256 bytes of parameter RAM; long-life lithium battery backup

Power requirements   Line voltage: 100 to 240 V (rms)
Frequency: 48 to 62 Hz
Power: 230 W maximum for peak load, not including power for monitor or other external peripheral devices

Power output   90 W at maximum sustainable load

■ **Table A-9**   Size and weight of the Macintosh IIfx computer

	Weight	Height	Width	Depth
Main unit	10.9 to 11.8 kg* (24 to 26 lbs.)	140 mm (5.51 in.)	474 mm (18.66 in.)	365 mm (14.37 in.)
Apple Standard Keyboard	1.0 kg (2 lbs. 4 oz.)	44.5 mm (1.8 in.)	418.3 mm (16.5 in.)	140.0 mm (5.5 in.)
Apple Extended Keyboard	1.6 kg (3 lbs. 10 oz.)	56.4 mm (2.22 in.)	486 mm (19.15 in.)	188 mm (7.4 in.)
Apple Standard Mouse	0.17 kg (6.0 oz.)	27.9 mm (1.1 in.)	53.3 mm (2.1 in.)	96.5 mm (3.8 in.)
Apple high-resolution monochrome monitor	7.7 kg (17 lbs.)	255 mm (10.04 in.)	310 mm (12.2 in.)	373 mm (14.68 in.)
Apple high-resolution RGB monitor	15.45 kg (34 lbs.)	281 mm (11.06 in.)	344 mm (13.54 in.)	402 mm (15.83 in.)

*Weight varies depending on installation of optional hard disk drive or second FDHD drive.

Environment

Operating temperature	10° C to 40° C
	(50° F to 95° F)
	No component inside the machine should get hotter than 80% of the manufacturer's maximum when operating at the maximum temperature.
Storage temperature	–40° C to 47° C
	(–40° F to 116.6° F)
Relative humidity	5% to 95% (noncondensing) at 25° C (77° F) to 40° C (104° F)
Altitude	0 to 3048 m (0 to 10,000 ft.)

Appendix B **Hardware-Related Global Variables**

Table B-1 lists the system global variables that relate to hardware components. For a complete list of system global variables, see the *Inside Macintosh X-Ref*. System global variables are included as equate (EQU) statements in Macintosh Programmer's Workshop (MPW) Assembly Language files named HardwareEqu.a and SysEqu.a. These files are located in a folder named AIncludes.

The MPW development system, which includes the MPW Assembler and the AIncludes folder, is available from APDA. The AIncludes folder is also available as a separate product from APDA. The address of APDA is given in the section "How to Get More Information," in the Preface.

■ **Table B-1**   Hardware-related global variables

Name	Contents
HWCfgFlags	Hardware components connected
IWM	IWM base address
KbdLast	ADB address of the keyboard last used (byte)
KbdType	Keyboard type of the keyboard last used (byte)
MemTop	Address of end of RAM
PortBUse	Current availability of serial port B (byte)
RAMBase	Trap dispatch table's base address for routines in RAM
ROMBase	Base address of ROM
ROM85	Version number of ROM (word)
SCCRd	SCC read base address
SCCWr	SCC write base address
ScrHRes	Pixels per inch horizontally (word)
ScrnBase	Address of main screen buffer
ScrVRes	Pixels per inch vertically (word)
SdVolume	Current speaker volume (byte: low-order 3 bits only)
SoundBase	Pointer to free-form synthesizer buffer
SoundLevel	Amplitude in 740-byte buffer (byte)
SoundPtr	Pointer to four-voice sound definition table
SPPortA	Modem port configuration (word)
SPPortB	Printer port configuration (word)
SPVolCtl	Speaker volume setting in parameter RAM (byte)
SysParam	Low-memory copy of parameter RAM (20 bytes)
TimeSCCDB	Number of times the SCC can be accessed per millisecond (word)
TimeSCSIDB	Number of times the SCSI can be accessed per millisecond (word)
VIA	VIA base address

Glossary

active: See **asserted.** See also **active high, active low.**

active high: Said of a signal that is True when the voltage on that line goes high. Compare **active low.**

active low: Said of a signal that is True when the voltage on that line goes low. Compare **active high.**

ADB: See **Apple Desktop Bus.**

ADB transceiver: A 4-bit microprocessor that, in conjunction with the main processor, controls the ADB network. In the Macintosh Portable, the Power Manager IC also functions as the ADB transceiver.

address: A number that specifies the location of a byte in memory.

address bus: The set of electrical wires along which addresses are transmitted. The width of the address bus (number of wires) determines how many addresses can be addressed directly by the main processor. For example, the Macintosh SE computer has a 24-bit address bus and so has a 16 MB (2^{24}) address space. The Macintosh II has a 32-bit address bus and so has a 16 MB (2^{24}) address space. The Macintosh II has a 32-bit address bus and so has a 4 GB (2^{32}) address space. Compare **control lines, data bus.**

Address Management Unit (AMU): The Apple custom integrated circuit in the Macintosh II that performs 24-to-32 bit address mapping. Also

called *Hochsprung Memory Management Unit* (HMMU). It can be replaced by the optional Paged Memory Management Unit (PMMU), the Motorola MC68851.

address map: The assignment of portions of the address space of the computer to specific devices. See also **memory-mapped device selection.**

address mapping: See **address translation.**

address space: A range of accessible memory. See also **address map.**

address translation: The conversion of one set of addresses into another, corresponding set. For example, software designed for the classic Macintosh uses only 24 bits for addresses whereas the Macintosh II has a 32-bit address bus; therefore, the Macintosh II converts (maps) the 24-bit addresses coming from the software into 32-bit addresses for use by the hardware. Same as address mapping. See also **address map, memory-mapped device selection.**

AMU: See **Address Management Unit.**

analog board: In Macintosh models that have a built-in video monitor, the printed circuit board that contains the power supply and the video circuitry. Compare **logic board.**

Apple Desktop Bus (ADB): A low-speed serial bus that connects the keyboard, mouse, and optional input devices to the Macintosh SE, Macintosh Portable, and Macintosh II–family computers.

Apple Sound Chip (ASC): The Apple custom sound IC in all Macintosh models except the classic Macintosh and the Macintosh SE. It generates a stereo audio signal that, in conjunction with other sound circuitry, drives the internal speaker or an external sound jack.

ASC: See **Apple Sound Chip.**

asserted: Indicates that a signal is True, independent of whether that logical condition is represented by a high or low voltage. Same as active. Opposite of deasserted.

asynchronous: Not synchronized by a mutual timing signal or clock. Compare **synchronous.**

automatic vectoring: A mode of operation in which the interrupt vector is based on the level of the interrupt, so that the main processor automatically jumps to an interrupt handler that corresponds to the priority of an interrupt.

auxiliary processor: A processor that communicates with the main processor at the level of a device. An example is the Power Manager IC in the Macintosh Portable. See also **coprocessor, main processor.**

BBU: The Apple custom IC in the Macintosh SE that handles RAM, video, and sound; selects devices; and performs other control functions. BBU stands for *Bob Bailey Unit.*

BIU2: The custom IC that contains the NuBus transceivers in the Macintosh IIfx computer. See also **BIU30, NuBus controller.**

BIU30: The custom IC that controls the NuBus interface in the Macintosh IIfx computer. See also **BIU2, NuBus controller.**

blanking interval: See **horizontal blanking interval, vertical blanking interval.**

block: A group regarded as a unit; usually refers to data or memory in which data is stored.

block device: A device that reads and writes blocks of bytes at a time. It can read or write any accessible block on demand. A disk drive is an example of a block device. Compare **character device.**

board: A printed circuit board that is a built-in part of the computer. Compare **card.**

Bob Bailey Unit: See **BBU.**

cache RAM: A small amount of high-speed RAM used as a buffer to make data and instructions available to the main processor more quickly than they can be read from normal RAM.

cache slot: A slot in the Macintosh IIci for installing an optional cache card.

card: A removable printed circuit board that plugs into a connector inside the computer. Cards are used to expand the capabilities of the computer, and are sometimes referred to as *expansion cards.* Compare **board.**

character device: A device that reads or writes a stream of characters, one at a time. It can neither skip characters nor go back to a previous character. A printer is an example of a character device. Compare **block device.**

classic Macintosh: A term encompassing the original Macintosh computer (128K and 512K models), the Macintosh 512K enhanced, and the Macintosh Plus.

clock chip: See **real-time clock.**

CLUT DAC: An IC in an expansion video card or in the Macintosh IIci that converts digital video data into analog signals for an external video monitor. See also **RBV.**

control lines: Wires that carry status or control signals.

coprocessor: A processor that communicates directly with the main processor, sharing its data and address buses. An example is the MC68882 floating-point unit. See also **main processor, auxiliary processor.**

CPU: Central processing unit. See **main processor.**

CPU GLU: An Apple custom IC in the Macintosh Portable computer that selects devices and performs other control functions. See also **general logic unit.**

data bus: The wires along which general information (all information except for memory addresses and control signals) is transmitted within the computer. The wider the data bus, the more information can be transmitted at once. The Macintosh computers that use the MC68000 have 16-bit data buses. The Macintosh computers that use the MC68020 and MC68030 have 32-bit data buses. Compare **address bus, control lines.**

deasserted: Indicates that a signal is False, independent of whether that logical condition is represented by a high or low voltage. Same as inactive. Opposite of asserted.

debounce: To condition the signal from a mechanical switch (such as a pushbutton) so as to remove the multiple connections or disconnections commonly produced by such switches.

declaration ROM: A ROM on a NuBus expansion card that contains information about the card and may also contain code or other data.

delta guide: A book that describes only changes in a hardware device or software program. A delta guide is written to supplement a book that completely describes an earlier version of a product.

device: (1) A component on the Macintosh logic board that can exchange information with the CPU. The Serial Communications Chip is an example of a device. (2) A **peripheral device.** A printer is an example of a peripheral device.

device address space: A portion of address space used for addressing internal devices. See also **address map, memory-mapped device selection.**

digital board: Same as **logic board.**

DMA: Direct memory access. A technique for transferring data in or out of memory without using the CPU.

DRAM: Pronounced "dee-ram." See **dynamic random-access memory.**

dynamic bus sizing: A procedure by which the MC68020 or MC68030 processor determines the bus size of a device and automatically performs as many bus cycles as necessary to transfer data. For example, to read a longword (32 bits) from the SCSI chip—which has an 8-bit data bus—the processor runs four successive 8-bit read cycles.

dynamic random-access memory (DRAM): Random-access memory that must be periodically refreshed to prevent it from losing the information it contains. See also **random-access memory, static random-access memory.**

exception: An error or abnormal condition detected by the processor in the course of program execution. Exceptions include resets, bus errors, interrupts, and traps.

exception event: See **exception.**

exception vector: A location in memory containing the starting address of the routine that takes control in the event of a particular exception.

expansion card: See **card.**

expansion slot: See **slot.**

5380: See **SCSI chip.**

finite-state machine: A block of logic, implemented in hardware or software, that can assume a finite number of values or states, and that makes a transition from one state to another in a set sequence in response to specific inputs. For each state, a state machine generates a specific output, or asserts or deasserts a specific signal.

floating-point unit (FPU): An IC that provides high-speed support for extended-precision arithmetic. The Motorola MC68881 is used in the Macintosh II computer; the MC68882 is used in the Macintosh SE/30, Macintosh IIx, Macintosh IIcx, Macintosh IIci, and Macintosh IIfx.

FPU: See **floating-point unit.**

GB: Abbreviation for gigabyte. A gigabyte is 1,024 megabytes, or 1,073,741,824 bytes.

GCR: See **group code recording.**

general logic unit (GLU): A generic term for an Apple custom IC used to perform several control functions. See also **BBU, CPU GLU, GLUE, MDU, Miscellaneous GLU, RBV.**

genlock: In a device that produces a video display signal, the process of synchronizing its output with a video signal produced by some other device.

GLU: See **general logic unit.**

GLUE: The Apple custom IC in the Macintosh SE/30, Macintosh II, Macintosh IIx, and Macintosh IIcx computers that selects devices and performs other control functions. See also **general logic unit.**

group-code recording (GCR): A method of formatting data in which each 3 bytes are written as four 8-bit patterns constructed so that no pattern contains more than two consecutive 0's. Group-code recording is used in conjunction with NRZI encoding to write data on Apple 3.5-inch floppy disks and Hard Disk 20 hard disks. Compare **modified frequency modulation.**

hard disk interleave: To place consecutive sectors in noncontiguous locations on the disk, alternating with other sectors. For example, a 2:1 interleave might include sectors in the sequence 1, 5, 2, 6, 3,...; whereas a 3:1 interleave might include sectors in the sequence 1, 4, 7, 2, 5, 8, 3,...

heap: The area of memory in which space is dynamically allocated and released as needed by applications and the operating system.

high address: The ending address of a block of code or data in memory. Compare **low address.**

HMMU: See **Address Management Unit.**

Hochsprung Memory Management Unit (HMMU): See **Address Management Unit.**

horizontal blanking interval: The time between the display of the rightmost pixel on one line and the leftmost pixel on the next line. Same as horizontal retrace time. Compare **vertical blanking interval.**

horizontal retrace time: See **horizontal blanking interval.**

inactive: Same as **deasserted.**

initialize: To bring to some known state, usually when a system is started up or reset.

Integrated Woz Machine (IWM): The custom IC that controls the floppy disk drives in the Macintosh Plus and Macintosh II computers and in Macintosh SE computers manufactured before September 1989.

interleave: To alternate between two or more distinct events or entities. See also **hard disk interleave, video interleave.**

interrupt: An exception that is signaled to the processor by a device to notify the processor of a change in condition of the device, such as the completion of an I/O request.

interrupt handler: The routine that gets control in the event of an interrupt.

interrupt priority level: A number that indicates the importance of an interrupt. If the priority level of an interrupt is higher than the current processor priority, the exception processing sequence is started.

interrupt vector: An exception vector for an interrupt.

IOP: See **I/O Processor.**

I/O Processor (IOP): An Apple custom IC. In the Macintosh IIfx, one IOP controls the SCC and another controls the SWIM and the ADB interface.

IWM: See **Integrated Woz Machine.**

KB: Abbreviation for kilobyte; 1024 bytes.

Kbit: Abbreviation for kilobit; 1024 bits.

logical address: An address used by software. The logical address may be translated into a physical address by the memory management unit.

logic board: A circuit board that holds the CPU, RAM, ROM, and other integrated circuits that perform the built-in logic functions of the computer. Compare **analog board, card.**

longword: In MC68000 terminology (including the MC68020 and MC68030), a longword comprises two 16-bit words.

low address: The starting address of a block of code or data in memory. Compare **high address.**

main logic board: Same as **logic board.**

main processor: The microprocessor that executes program code; the central processing unit. See **MC68000, MC68HC000, MC68020, MC68030.**

main system unit: In a modular computer such as the Macintosh II, the module that contains the logic board, the expansion slots, the power supply, and the built-in disk drives.

manager: A type of routine found in the Macintosh Operating System or Toolbox. Some managers—such as the SCSI Manager and the ADB Manager—control the exchange of information between a Macintosh and peripheral devices.

MB: Abbreviation for megabyte; 1,024 kilobytes, or 1,048,576 bytes.

Mbit: Abbreviation for megabit; 1,024 kilobits, or 1,048,576 bits.

MC68000: The integrated circuit used as the main processor in the Macintosh SE, Macintosh Plus, and earlier Macintosh computers.

MC68000 PDS: The processor-direct slot in the Macintosh SE and Macintosh Portable computers. See also **processor-direct slot.**

MC68HC000: The integrated circuit used as the main processor in the Macintosh Portable computer.

MC68020: The integrated circuit used as the main processor in the Macintosh II computer.

MC68030: The integrated circuit used as the main processor in the Macintosh SE/30, Macintosh IIx, Macintosh IIcx, Macintosh IIci, and Macintosh IIfx computers.

MC68030 PDS: The processor-direct slot in the Macintosh SE/30 and the Macintosh IIfx. See also **processor-direct slot.**

MC68851: The integrated circuit used as the optional Paged Memory Management Unit (PMMU) in the Macintosh II computer.

MC68881: The integrated circuit used as the floating-point unit (FPU) in the Macintosh II computer.

MC68882: The integrated circuit used as the floating-point unit (FPU) in the Macintosh IIx, Macintosh IIcx, Macintosh IIci, and Macintosh IIfx computers.

MDU (Memory Decode Unit): An Apple custom IC in the Macintosh IIci that selects devices and performs other control functions. See also **general logic unit.**

Memory Decode Unit: See **MDU.**

memory management unit (MMU): A generic term for the component that performs address mapping in a Macintosh computer. In the Macintosh II, it is either the Address Management Unit (AMU) or the Paged Memory Management Unit (PMMU). The MMU function is built into the MC68030, the main processor in many Macintosh models.

memory map: See **address map.**

memory-mapped device selection: The selection of devices and expansion cards by addressing specific locations in the computer's address space. Portions of the computer's address space are assigned to RAM and ROM and the rest of the address space is divided among various devices such as I/O interfaces and expansion slots. When the CPU puts an address on the address bus, logic circuits in the computer decode that address to determine which device to activate and what function that device is to perform. The logic circuits then assert select and control signals to that device as appropriate. See also **slot space.**

MFM: See **modified frequency modulation.**

Michael Dhuey Unit: See **MDU.**

Miscellaneous GLU: An Apple custom IC in the Macintosh Portable computer that selects devices and performs other control functions. See also **general logic unit.**

modified frequency modulation (MFM): A method of recording data onto magnetic media such as floppy disks. MFM encoding can be used to write data on high-density disks. Compare **group-code recording.**

motherboard: Same as **logic board.**

mouse scaling: An operating-system option that increases the screen pointer movement as the mouse is moved faster.

multiplex: To encode information so that a single set of wires can carry different sets of information or different kinds of information.

NCR 5380: The integrated circuit chip used to implement the Small Computer System Interface (SCSI) in Macintosh computers. See also **Small Computer System Interface.**

NRZI encoding: A method of encoding data in which a 1 is written as a transition and a 0 is written as no transition. NRZI stands for *nonreturn to zero, inverted.* See also **group-code recording.**

NuBus: The 32-bit wide synchronous bus used for expansion cards in the Macintosh II family of computers. See also **NuBus controller, NuBus expansion slot.**

NuBus controller: An IC that controls the NuBus interface. See also **NuChip, NuChip30, BIU30.**

NuBus expansion slot: A connector attached to the NuBus in the Macintosh II family, into which an expansion card can be installed.

NuChip: The custom IC that controls the NuBus interface in the Macintosh II, Macintosh IIx, and Macintosh IIcx computers. See also **NuBus controller.**

NuChip30: The custom IC that controls the NuBus interface in the Macintosh IIci computer. See also **NuBus controller.**

open-collector signal: A signal driven by an output device that can drive the line low (about zero volts), but cannot drive the line high (about +5 volts). When the device stops driving the line low, the device goes into a high-impedance state and a resistor, connected between +5 volts and the line, pulls the line up to a high level (near +5 volts). This arrangement allows more than one device to drive the same signal line, because the inactive devices are essentially disconnected from the line.

operating system: The lowest-level software in the Macintosh. It does basic tasks such as I/O, memory management, and interrupt handling.

OR operation: A logical operation in which an output signal is asserted if one or more of the input signals are asserted.

overlay: See **ROM overlay, video overlay.**

overlay bit: A bit in Data register A in the VIA (or VIA1 in machines with two VIAs) that, when set to 1, causes a signal that invokes the ROM overlay.

Paged Memory Management Unit (PMMU): The Motorola MC68851 chip, used in the Macintosh II computer to perform logical-to-physical address translation and paged memory management for virtual-memory operating systems such as A/UX. The PMMU can be installed as an option, replacing the AMU. The PMMU can also perform 24-to-32 bit address mapping to emulate the AMU. See also **page table, virtual memory.**

page table: A table used by the PMMU that relates logical addresses to the actual physical locations of blocks of data to support virtual-memory operating systems.

PAL: An integrated circuit implementing programmable array logic.

parameter RAM: A small random-access memory in which certain system parameters and Control Panel settings are stored. Parameter RAM is powered by a battery when the system is off, thus preserving the information.

parity: A process of error detection using an extra bit for each byte stored in RAM (or sent through a serial port) in such as way as to detect whenever the value read (or received) is not the same as the value stored (or sent).

parity bit: An extra bit appended to a byte of memory and used for error detection. See **parity.**

PDS: See **processor-direct slot.**

peripheral device: A piece of external equipment that can transfer information into or out of the computer. A disk drive is an example of a peripheral device. Compare **device.**

physical address: An address represented by bits on a physical address bus, such as the MC68020 processor bus. The physical address may be different from the logical address used by software, in which case the memory management unit translates the logical address into a physical address.

port: (1) A connector on the back panel of the computer where you can plug in a cable to connect a peripheral device, another computer, or a network. (2) An interface through which data enters or exits an internal device or a peripheral device.

Power Manager: A set of routines in the ROM of the Macintosh Portable computer that controls the Power Manager IC and that determines when to put the Macintosh Portable into the sleep state.

Power Manager IC: A single-chip microprocessor (Mitsubishi 50753) in the Macintosh Portable computer that directs the power-control circuits and serves as the real-time clock (RTC) and ADB transceiver. Compare **Power Manager.**

power supply: A circuit that draws electrical power from a power outlet and converts it to the kind of power the computer can use.

processor-direct slot: A type of expansion slot that provides unbuffered access to the main processor. See **MC68000 PDS, MC68030 PDS.**

program counter: A register in the CPU that contains a pointer to the memory location of the next instruction to be executed.

programmer's switch: An optional pair of buttons that can be installed on a Macintosh computer. One button asserts a nonmaskable interrupt to the CPU and one button asserts a Reset signal to the CPU and other chips.

pseudo-slot video: The technique used in the Macintosh SE/30 and Macintosh IIci to enable software to address built-in video circuitry the same way it addresses a video expansion card in a slot.

pulse-width-modulated signal: A rectangular-wave signal in which the width of each pulse is proportional to the value of a byte of data.

PWM: See **pulse-width-modulated signal.**

RAM: See **random-access memory.**

RAM-Based Video controller: See **RBV.**

random-access memory (RAM): Memory whose contents can be changed; read-write memory. The RAM in a Macintosh computer is used for exception vectors, buffers used by hardware devices, the system and application heaps, the stack, and other information used by applications. See also **dynamic random-access memory, static random-access memory.**

RBV (RAM-Based Video controller): An Apple custom IC in the Macintosh IIci that reads and formats video data and controls the video CLUT DAC. See also **CLUT DAC.**

RC network: A resistor and a capacitor connected so as to function as a frequency-dependent filter.

read-only memory (ROM): Memory whose contents are permanent. The Macintosh computer's ROM contains routines for the toolbox and operating system; the ROM also contains the various system traps.

real-time clock (RTC): A chip that keeps track of the current time and date and that contains parameter RAM. The real-time clock is powered by a battery when the system is off, thus preserving the information.

reset: In the Macintosh, a reset is the highest level of exception. The system generates a reset by asserting the /RESET signal to the CPU. The /RESET signal is asserted whenever the machine is turned on or reset by pressing the reset button on the programmer's switch. See also **Reset handler, Reset vector.**

Reset handler: The ROM routine executed by the CPU after a reset. See also **Reset vector.**

Reset vector: An exception vector pointing to the Reset handler.

retrace time: See **horizontal blanking interval, vertical blanking interval.**

rms: Abbreviation for *root mean square*. The square root of the mean of the squares of a set of values. The rms value of a sinusoidal alternating-current voltage equals 0.707 times the maximum value of the voltage.

Robert Bailey Video: See **RBV.**

ROM: See **read-only memory.**

ROM overlay: Address remapping, used at system startup, that creates an address map with ROM at the lowest addresses in the computer's address space. After system startup, ROM is remapped to addresses above those used for RAM.

RTC: See **real-time clock.**

SCC: See **Serial Communications Controller.**

SCC port A: The modem port. See also **Serial Communications Controller.**

SCC port B: The printer port. See also **Serial Communications Controller.**

screen buffer: An area of memory from which the video circuitry reads information to create a screen display.

SCSI: Pronounced "skuzzy." See **Small Computer System Interface.**

SCSI chip: The NCR 53C80 or NCR 5380 chip used in Macintosh computers to implement the Small Computer System Interface (SCSI).

SCSI devices: Devices, such as hard disks and tape backup units, that use the Small Computer System Interface.

sector: A unit of disk space composed of 512 consecutive bytes of standard information and 12 bytes of file tags.

Serial Communications Controller (SCC): The integrated circuit (Zilog Z8530) that handles serial I/O through the modem and printer ports.

SIMM: See **Single In-line Memory Module.**

Single In-line Memory Module (SIMM): A small printed circuit board that can be plugged into a socket on the logic board to expand the size of RAM or ROM. Many Macintosh models use SIMMs for RAM expansion; the Macintosh IIx, Macintosh IIcx, Macintosh IIci, and Macintosh IIfx also use SIMMs for ROM expansion.

60.15 Hz interrupt: In the Macintosh II–family computers, a periodic interrupt that simulates the **vertical blanking interrupt** found in the Macintosh SE and earlier models. It is used for general-purpose timing but is not realted to the **SLOT interrupt** generated in the Macintosh IIci or on an expansion video card.

6522: See **Versatile Interface Adapter.**

sleep state: In the Macintosh Portable computer, a non-operational state that uses negligible power, corresponding to the power-off state in other machines.

slot: A connector into which a card can be installed to expand the capabilities of a computer. See **cache slot, NuBus expansion slot, processor-direct slot.**

SLOT interrupt: An interrupt generated at the beginning of the vertical blanking interval by the built-in video circuits in the Macintosh IIci or by a Macintosh II Video Card. See also **60.15 Hz interrupt, vertical blanking interrupt.**

slot space: The address space assigned to NuBus slots in Macintosh II–family computers and to expansion cards that emulate NuBus cards in the Macintosh SE/30 and Macintosh IIfx computers. See also **memory-mapped device selection, standard slot space, super slot space.**

Small Computer System Interface (SCSI): An industry standard high-speed parallel bus that provides a method of connecting small computers with intelligent peripherals such as hard disks, printers, and optical disks. See also **NCR 5380.**

Sony sound chip: The chip that drives the internal speaker or external sound jack in Macintosh computers. The Sony sound chip accepts PWM and volume-control signals from the sound circuitry in the computer and converts them to analog sound at the specified volume.

sound buffer: An area of memory from which the sound circuitry reads data to create a sound signal.

SRAM: Pronounced "ess-ram." See **static random-access memory.**

standard slot space: The address space from $F100 0000 through $FFFF FFFF in the Macintosh SE/30 computer and in Macintosh II–family computers. In Macintosh II–family computers, 16 MB of address space within this range is assigned to each NuBus slot. In the Macintosh SE/30 and Macintosh IIfx computers, a PDS card that emulates a NuBus card responds to an address in this range. See also **super slot space.**

state machine: See **finite-state machine.**

static random-access memory (SRAM): A type of random-access memory that retains data as long as power is on without the necessity for refreshing. See **dynamic random-access memory, random-access memory.**

super slot space: The address space from $6000 0000 through $EFFF FFFF in the Macintosh SE/30 computer and in Macintosh II–family computers. In Macintosh II–family computers, 256 MB of address space within this range is assigned to each NuBus slot. In the Macintosh SE/30 and Macintosh IIfx computers, a PDS card that emulates a NuBus card responds to an address in this range. See also **standard slot space.**

supervisor stack pointer: A register in the CPU that indicates the next byte on the system stack when the processor is in supervisor mode.

Super Woz Integrated Machine (SWIM): The custom IC that controls the FDHD drives. It can read and write 400 KB and 800 KB GCR-format disks and 1.4 MB MFM-format disks.

SWIM: See **Super Woz Integrated Machine.**
synchronous: Operations or data transmission synchronized by a mutual timing signal or clock. In a synchronous system, a constant time interval exists between successive events executed by different devices. Compare **asynchronous.**

synchronous modem: A modem that provides two clocks for synchronous communication with its host computer—one clock for sending data from the host computer to the modem, and a second clock for sending data from the modem to the host computer.

system startup information: Configurable system parameters that are stored in the first two logical blocks of a volume and are read in at system startup.

timing out: The condition that occurs when a process, such as a data transfer over the SCSI bus, takes longer than a preset limit. When a process times out, it is normally terminated and a bus error or other error condition may result.

trap: An exception caused by recognition of abnormal conditions during instruction execution (such as an attempt to execute an unimplemented instruction) or from use of an instruction that normally causes an exception.

trap dispatcher: The part of the Macintosh Operating System that examines the instruction that caused a trap in order to determine what operation it stands for, looks up the address of the corresponding routine in the trap dispatch table, and jumps to that routine.

trap dispatch table: A table in RAM containing the addresses of all Macintosh Toolbox and Operating System routines in encoded form.

unimplemented instruction: An instruction word that doesn't correspond to any valid machine-language instruction. The attempt to execute an unimplemented instruction causes a trap.

VBL: See **vertical blanking interrupt, vertical blanking interval.**

Versatile Interface Adapter (VIA): The IC (6522) that handles most of the Macintosh computer's I/O and interrupts. The Macintosh SE/30, Macintosh II, Macintosh IIx, and Macintosh IIcx have two VIAs. Some VIA functions are performed by the RBV in the Macintosh IIci and by the OSS in the Macintosh IIfx.

vertical blanking interrupt: In the Macintosh SE and earlier models, an interrupt generated by the VIA at the beginning of the vertical blanking interval. In the Macintosh II family, the equivalent interrupt is the **60.15 Hz interrupt** generated by the VIA1. The built-in video circuits in the Macintosh IIci and on an expansion video operate independently of this interrupt. See also **SLOT interrupt.**

vertical blanking interval: The time between the display of the rightmost pixel on the last line of the screen and the leftmost pixel on the first line of the screen. Same as vertical retrace time. See also **vertical blanking interrupt.** Compare **horizontal blanking interval.**

vertical retrace time: See **vertical blanking interval.**

VIA: See **Versatile Interface Adapter.**

video interleave: In Macintosh computers with built-in video, the alternation of the CPU's RAM access cycles with video circuitry's RAM access cycles.

video overlay: The ability of a device that produces a video display signal to accept the video signal from some other device and combine the signals so as to superimpose additional images onto the display.

video RAM (VRAM): A type of dual-ported RAM that supports conventional reading and writing as well as having built-in shift registers that provide rapid bit-stream output; used in most video expansion cards.

virtual memory: A memory management scheme in which the full range of address space used for memory is not necessarily implemented in RAM. The logical address used by software is translated by a memory management chip (such as the PMMU) into a physical address; if the block of data referred to by the logical address is not currently in RAM, the operating system reads the block of data into RAM before accessing the data. See also **Paged Memory Management Unit, page table.**

VRAM: Pronounced "vee-ram." See **video RAM.**

word: (1) For the MC68000 family of microprocessors (including the MC68020 and MC68030), 2 bytes (16 bits). (2) For the NuBus, 4 bytes (32 bits).

Z8530: See **Serial Communications Controller.**

Index

THE APPLE PUBLISHING SYSTEM

This Apple manual was written, edited, and
composed on a desktop publishing system using
Apple Macintosh® computers and
Microsoft® Word software. Proof pages were
created on Apple LaserWriter® printers. Final pages
were created on the Varityper VT600 imagesetter.
Line art was created using Adobe Illustrator™.
PostScript®, the page-description language for the
LaserWriter, was developed by Adobe Systems
Incorporated.

Text type and display type are Apple's corporate
font, a condensed version of ITC Garamond. Bullets
are ITC Zapf Dingbats®.

Lead Writer: Allen Watson III
Writer: Paul Black
Book Design: Lisa Mirski
Developmental Editors: Laurel Rezeau and Anne Szabla
Art Direction: Barbara Smyth
Illustrators: Pat Coleman, Mil Madamba, and
              George Vrana
Production Supervisor: J. Renee Ekleberry
Production: Janet M. Anders

Special thanks to Mark Baumwell, Rich Collyer,
Mary Fitzsimmons, Denis Hescox, Ron Hochsprung,
Brian Howard, Todd Kessler, Brian Kliment, Jon
Krakower, Ann Nunziata, Noah Price, and Jim Stockdale.